MUSEUM OF WORDS

MUSEUM
OF
WORDS

*The Poetics
of Ekphrasis
from Homer
to Ashbery*

JAMES A. W. HEFFERNAN

THE UNIVERSITY OF CHICAGO PRESS
Chicago and London

JAMES A. W. HEFFERNAN is professor of English at
Dartmouth College.

The University of Chicago Press, Chicago 60637
The University of Chicago Press, Ltd., London
© 1993 by The University of Chicago
All rights reserved. Published 1993
Printed in the United States of America

02 01 00 99 98 97 96 95 94 93   1 2 3 4 5

ISBN: 0-226-32313-7 (cloth)

Library of Congress Cataloging-in-Publication Data
Heffernan, James A. W.
Museum of words : the poetics of ekphrasis from Homer
to Ashbery /
James A. W. Heffernan.
p.   cm.
Includes bibliographical references and index.
1. Literature—History and criticism.   2. Ekphrasis.
I. Title.
PN56.E45H44   1993
809—dc20   93-4509
                                                CIP

For Virginia and Andrew

Contents

Illustrations

Acknowledgments

My first debt is to the National Endowment for the Humanities, which awarded me the fellowship that enabled me to write nearly all of this book in 1991. But the book actually began—though I did not realize it at the time—when Michael Riffaterre invited me to give a paper on ekphrasis at the 1986 Columbia Colloquium on Poetics. With the benefit of comments from participants in the colloquium and—later on—from Stuart Curran and George T. Wright—that paper appeared as "Ekphrasis and Representation" in the spring 1991 issue of *New Literary History,* and I thank Ralph Cohen, the editor, for allowing me to use material from it here. In the spring of 1992, Kaisa Kurikka and Pertti Karkama invited me to a conference on literature and art at the University of Turku, Finland, where I gave a paper based on the Shakespearean section of chapter 2. I am grateful to them and to many others for various kinds of stimulation, advice, and support: to the Dartmouth undergraduates who have taken my Comparative Literature course on English romantic literature and the visual arts; to the participants in my 1987 and 1989 NEH Summer Seminars on this topic; to James Tatum for his expert advice on classical ekphrasis; to Jonathan Crewe and Martha Swanson for provocative comments on chapter 2; to Grant Scott for his thoughtful remarks on chapter 3; and to Thomas Sleigh for reading chapter 4.

More thanks to Dartmouth College, which arranged my teaching duties in 1991–92 so that I could take full advantage of my NEH Fellowship; to the ever-helpful staffs of Dartmouth's Baker Library and Sherman Art Library; and to David Lea, Uli Rainer, and Anatolia Prinz, who graciously helped me to procure several of the reproductions.

I owe further debts to those who guided this book into print, beginning with Alan Thomas, who proved to be a singularly supportive editor. I appreciate all the suggestions made by the two anonymous scholars who read the entire book for the University of Chicago Press, and I owe particular thanks to W. J. T. Mitchell, who not only read the whole book and generously wrote the Press on its behalf, but also helped me to solve the vexing problem of what to call it. In addition, I am happy to thank Randy Petilos at the Press and to salute the special contributions made by two others: Kathryn Krug, who copyedited this book, and Michael Brehm, who designed it.

Once again I thank my wife, Nancy Coffey Heffernan, who has given me all the wisdom, patience, and kindness that anyone writing a book could want.

I take great pleasure in dedicating this book on poetry and the visual arts to my daughter Virginia, who has already published some of her poems, and my son Andrew, whose many talents include a remarkable ability to draw.

Introduction

In recent years, the study of the relation between literature and the visual arts has become a major intellectual industry. Much of this industry is comparative. Empirically minded critics compare specific texts with specific works of visual art; theoretically oriented critics aim to show that we can read a work of literature spatially, as a we view a painting, or decode a painting semiotically as if it were a text, a web of verbal signs. Critics who do comparative work in one of these senses typically aim to breach the theoretical barriers that Lessing erected between poetry and the visual arts: between poetry as an art of conventional signs marching along in time and painting as an art of would-be "natural" signs deployed in space. But I suspect we are nearing the end of what we can learn about the sister arts by simply comparing them, by observing similarities that help us to read—more accurately to construct—the signature of a "period" or to formulate a master theory of signification. In my judgment, the most promising line of inquiry in the field of sister arts studies is the one drawn by W. J. T. Mitchell's *Iconology,* which treats the relation between literature and the visual arts as essentially *paragonal,* a struggle for dominance between the image and the word.[1]

The present book seeks to elucidate this struggle by investigating ekphrasis, the literary representation of visual art.[2] Ekphrasis fascinates me for several reasons. First, because it evokes the power of the silent image even as it subjects that power to the rival authority of language, it is intensely paragonal. Second, the contest it stages is often powerfully gendered: the expression of a duel between male and female gazes, the voice of male speech striving to control a female image that is both alluring and threatening, of male narrative striving to overcome the fixating impact of beauty poised in space. Third, the relation between the arts in an ekphrastic work of literature is not impressionistic—not something conjured up by an act of juxtaposition and founded on a nebulous "sense" of affinity. On the contrary, it is tangible and manifest, demonstrably declared by the very nature of ekphrastic representation. And finally, though we have scarcely begun to investigate the history and poetics of this mode, it is extraordinarily enduring: as ancient as the description of the shield of Achilles in Homer's *Iliad,* as recent as John Ashbery's "Self-Portrait in a Convex Mirror" (1974), his poetic meditation on a painting by Parmigianino. To see how painting and sculpture have been represented by poets ranging from Homer's time to

1

our own is to see that the history of literature can be written as a history of its perennially conflicted response to visual art.

Why should the word *ekphrasis* be used to write such a history? If critics such as Helen Vendler can meticulously explicate poems about works of visual art without ever using the word, why do we need it at all? Why not leave it with the ancient Greek rhetoricians who invented it? My answer to these questions is that we have no other word for the mode of literature that *ekphrasis* designates: for a mode of literature whose complexity and vitality—not to mention its astonishing longevity—entitle it to full and widespread recognition.

It is already enjoying some recognition. A quarter century ago, Murray Krieger published what has since become the single most influential attempt to formulate a theory of ekphrasis: an essay called "*Ekphrasis* and the Still Movement of Poetry; or, *Laokoon* Revisited."[3] Krieger's essay might also have been called "Joseph Frank Revisited" or "W. J. T. Mitchell Anticipated," for in the face of Lessing what it seeks to demonstrate is the "generic spatiality of literary form."[4] To this end, Krieger elevates ekphrasis from a particular mode of literature—"a classic genre," he calls it (265)—to a literary principle. The plastic, spatial object of poetic imitation, he says, symbolizes "the frozen, stilled world of plastic relationships which must be superimposed upon literature's turning world to 'still' it" (265–66). Almost inevitably, Keats's "Ode on a Grecian Urn" serves as Krieger's prime example, but he also finds ekphrasis in rather different poems, such as in Marvell's "Coy Mistress," where the ball, he says, is a "physical, spatial . . . emblem of [the speaker's] mastery over time" (282). In Krieger's essay, then, ekphrasis becomes "a general principle of poetics, asserted by every poem in the assertion of its integrity" (284).

While Krieger's theory of ekphrasis seems to give this moribund term a new lease on life, it actually stretches ekphrasis to the breaking point: to the point where it no longer serves to contain any particular body of literature and merely becomes a new name for formalism.[5] So it has appeared, in any case, to critics of Heideggerian persuasion, to those who believe that only a hermeneutics of contingency, historicity, and existential temporality can explain literature to us. In the eyes of such critics, as Michael Davidson has recently observed, Krieger's theory of ekphrasis would hermetically seal literature within the well-wrought urn of pure, self-enclosed spatiality, where the ashes of New Criticism (still glowing, as ashes will) now repose. So Krieger's ekphrastic principle has been shaken. According to Davidson, it has been undermined even by certain kinds of poems about paintings—specifically by the "contemporary painterly poem." This Davidson contrasts with "the classical painter poem," a poem written "about" a painting or work of sculpture and designed to imitate the self-sufficiency of the object. A "painterly" poem, says Davidson, "activates strategies of composition equivalent to but not dependent on the painting itself. Instead of pausing at a reflective distance from the work of art, the poet reads the painting as a text, rather than as a static object, or else reads the larger painterly aesthetic generated by the painting" (72).

Davidson's formulation helps him to explain such postmodern poems as Ashbery's "Self-Portrait," which is based on Parmigianino's painting but which questions the ideas of stability, self-sufficiency, and authentic self-representation that the painting is said to convey. Yet Davidson hardly formulates a new theory of ekphrasis. Having replaced Krieger's ekphrastic principle with a diachronic polarity between classical and contemporary ekphrasis, he leaves us with no coherent sense of the synchronic mode that might contain them both, as well as with an oversimplified view of classical ekphrasis, which typically treats the work of art as considerably *more* than a static object.

The weaknesses of these two theories of ekphrasis—the one too broad, the other too polarized—help us to see what we need. If ekphrasis is to be defined as a mode, the definition must be sharp enough to identify a distinguishable body of literature and yet also elastic enough to reach from classicism to post-modernism, from Homer to Ashbery. As the point of departure for my own theory of ekphrasis, I propose a definition simple in form but complex in its implications: *ekphrasis is the verbal representation of visual representation.*

This definition excludes a good deal of what some critics would have *ekphrasis* include—namely literature about texts.[6] It also allows us to distinguish ekphrasis from two other ways of mingling literature and the visual arts: pictorialism and iconicity. What distinguishes those two things from ekphrasis is that both of them aim chiefly to represent natural objects and artifacts rather than works of representational art. Of course pictorialism and iconicity may each *remind* us of graphic representation. Pictorialism generates in language effects similar to those created by pictures, so that in Spenser's *Faerie Queene,* for instance, John M. Bender has found instances of focusing, framing, and scanning (40–80, 105–48). But in such cases Spenser is representing the world *with the aid of* pictorial techniques; he is not representing pictures themselves. The distinction holds even when a pictorial poem can be linked to the style of particular painter. We know, for example, that the austere clarity of William Carlos Williams's "The Red Wheelbarrow" owes something to the photographs of Alfred Stieglitz and to the precisionist style of Charles Sheeler, the American photographer-painter whom Williams met shortly before he wrote the poem. But Williams's poem makes no reference to Sheeler or Stieglitz and does not represent any one of their pictures. Unlike Williams's *Pictures from Breughel,* which explicitly represent specific paintings, "The Red Wheelbarrow" uses the verbal equivalent of pictorial precision in order to represent a set of objects.[7]

Iconicity is more complicated than pictorialism because it embraces sounds and sets of relations as well as visual properties.[8] But the visual iconicity of the pattern poem, which is what concerns me here, is a visible resemblance between the arrangement of words or letters on a page and what they signify, as in Herbert's "Easter Wings." Like pictorialism, visual iconicity usually entails an implicit reference to graphic representation. The wavy shape of an iconically printed line about a stream, for instance, will look much more like Hogarth's line of beauty than like any wave one might actually see from a shore.[9] But once again, iconic poetry does not aim to *represent* pictures; it apes the shapes of pictures in order to represent natural objects.

These three terms—*ekphrasis, pictorialism,* and *iconicity*—are not mutually exclusive. An ekphrastic poem may use pictorial techniques to represent a picture and may be printed in a shape that resembles the painting it verbally represents. But ekphrasis differs from both iconicity and pictorialism because it explicitly represents representation itself. What ekphrasis represents in words, therefore, must itself be *representational.* The Brooklyn Bridge may be considered a work of art and construed as a symbol of many things, but since it was not created to represent anything, a poem such as Hart Crane's *The Bridge* is no more ekphrastic than Williams's "The Red Wheelbarrow."[10]

When we understand that ekphrasis uses one medium of representation to represent another, we can begin to see what makes ekphrasis a distinguishable mode and what binds together all ekphrastic literature from the age of Homer to our own. Comparing such apparently disparate phenomena as classic and postmodern ekphrasis, some critics see only differences between the two. While classic ekphrasis, they say, salutes the skill of the artist and the miraculous verisimilitude of the forms that he—it is always he—creates, postmodern ekphrasis undermines the concept of verisimilitude itself. Thus Ashbery's "Self-Portrait" has been called "a radical criticism of the illusions and deceptions inherent in forms of traditional representation that insist on the ideal, essential, and totalized nature of the copied images they portray" (Stamelman 608). Nothing so nakedly deconstructive can be found in Homer's account of Achilles' shield, but if Ashbery's poem is a "meditation on difference" rather than on likeness, as Stamelman says (608), Homer's account of Achilles' shield is a meditation on both, a verbal tribute to visual verisimilitude and a sustained commentary on the difference between representation and reality. Describing the ploughmen depicted on the shield, Homer writes (in Lattimore's translation), "The earth darkened behind them and looked like earth that has been ploughed / *though it was gold*" (18.548–49, emphasis mine).[11] By explicitly noting the difference between the medium of visual representation (gold) and its referent (earth), Homer implicitly draws our attention to the *friction* between the fixed forms of visual art and the narrative thrust of his words. Shortly after describing the earth made of gold, in fact, Homer tells us that the cattle sculpted elsewhere on the shield were "wrought of gold and of tin, and thronged in speed and with lowing / out of the dung of the farmyard to a pasturing place by a sounding / river, and beside the moving field of a reed bed" (18.574–76).

Homer does two things in this passage. First, he reminds us again of the difference between the media of representation (gold and tin) and the referent (cattle); second and more importantly, he animates the fixed figures of visual art, turning the picture of a single moment into a narrative of successive actions: the cattle move out of the farmyard and make their way to a pasture. From Homer's time to our own, ekphrastic literature reveals again and again this narrative response to pictorial stasis, this storytelling impulse that language by its very nature seems to release and stimulate. Virgil turns the shield of Aeneas into a history of Rome; Dante turns a set of sculpted figures into the story of Trajan and the widow; Byron turns the statue of a dying man into a taut narrative of his dying; Ashbery begins "Self-Portrait" by recalling Vasari's story of how Parmigianino painted his picture. Given the pervasiveness of narrative in the history of ekphrasis, I must disagree with Krieger when he treats ekphrasis as a way of freezing time in space, and also with Wendy Steiner when she defines ekphrasis as the verbal equivalent of the "pregnant moment" in art—the literary mode "in which a poem aspires to the atemporal 'eternity' of the stopped-action painting" (*Pictures of Romance* 13–14). The "pregnant moment" of an action is the arrested point which most clearly implies what came before the moment and what is to follow it.[12] But as we will see in this book, ekphrasis is dynamic and obstetric; it typically delivers *from* the pregnant moment of visual art its embryonically narrative impulse, and thus makes explicit the story that visual art tells only by implication.[13]

In spite of the narrative energy that repeatedly drives ekphrasis, it often looks like a form of description. If Gerard Genette is right to define *narration* as the depiction of objects or people in movement and *description* as the depiction of objects or people in stasis (*Figures II* 57), ekphrasis would seem bound to the category of description, for it does indeed represent fixed forms. And as description, it would rank decisively below narrative in Genette's rigorously stratified scheme, where narration delivers the "pure processes" of dramatic temporality while description suspends time, spreads the narrative "in space," and thus serves as "a mere auxiliary of narrative," as "the ever-necessary, ever-submissive, never emancipated slave" (*Figures* 136, 134).[14] But Genette's metaphor should give us pause. If ekphrasis "frustrates narrative movement," as C. S. Baldwin long ago asserted (19), it is anything but submissive. It is the unruly antagonist of narrative, the ornamental digression that refuses to be merely ornamental. If we say, as is commonly said, that ekphrasis first appears as a descriptive detour from the high road of epic narrative, or that it is simply a detachable fragment which can be moved from one work to another,[15] then we must explain why and how it challenges both the movement and the meaning of the narratives in which it appears.

Part of the answer is that the categorical barrier between narration and description simply cannot keep them apart, or—in terms of Genette's metaphor—forestall miscegenation between master and slave. Genette himself admits that the boundaries between narration and description "are very uncertain, since obviously pure description (purified of any narration) and pure narration (purified of any description) do not exist, and since the counting of 'descriptive passages' necessarily omits thousands of sentences, portions of sentences, or descriptive words set among scenes where narrative is dominant" (*Narrative Discourse* 99n). We can say, as Genette here implies, that narration *or* description predominates in a particular passage, and it may even be possible to discriminate—as one critic recently has—between "narratized description" and "descriptized narration" (Mosher 426–27). But the instability of the boundaries between description and narration makes it implausible to identify ekphrasis with anything like pure description, or to define it simply as a brake on narrative progression. In epic narratives, ekphrasis is just as likely to constitute a rival or supervening narrative, like the history of Rome embedded in Book 8 of the *Aeneid.* Ekphrasis, writes Page Dubois, "is a narrative *poetic* discourse that purports often to be a model, or icon, literally, of past *and future* structures in the interest of explaining what they were, what they will be, by representing them *in relation to an enlightening narrative discourse,* the progress of the hero" (4). Synecdochically standing for the whole poem "made visible in the [verbalized] object," it is spatio-temporal, revealing "as a coherent synchronic model, the shape of time for its audience" (7–8).

But this definition of ekphrasis applies only to the way it works in the epics of Homer and Virgil. Dubois herself argues that the fortunes of ekphrasis follow the fortunes of epic: as the Homeric sense of community and the Virgilian ideal of national destiny give way to uncertainty and the vagaries of individuality, "the individual hero finally loses his ability to stand for the community as a whole, or for all the men within it," and correspondingly, ekphrasis loses its capacity to manifest the shape of time (8). Dubois's theory of ekphrasis, then, is really a theory about its role in ancient epics. To understand it as an enduring literary mode, we need to understand what has kept it alive from Homer's time to our own: its paragonal energy. Because it verbally represents visual art, ekphrasis stages a contest between rival modes of representation: between the driving force of the narrating word and the stubborn resistance of the fixed image.

As I have already suggested, this struggle for mastery between word and image is repeatedly gendered. In the *Aeneid,* the fixating power of the image that threatens the forward progress of the hero is decisively linked to *pulcherrima Dido,* queen of picture-perfect beauty and—like Cleopatra later—threat to male authority.[16] In Keats's "Ode on a Grecian Urn," the figures sculpted on the womblike urn that is called an unravished bride of quietness refuse to cooperate with a male narrative of desire and consummation. In Ashbery's "Self-Portrait," the painter's explicitly feminized image—enclosed by the "shield" of his elongated hand—balks the poet's struggle to penetrate it with his words. And in the Ovidian myth of Philomela, which begets a remarkable series of variations culminating in Shakespeare's *Rape of Lucrece,* a picture of rape woven by a mutilated woman unweaves the story told by a man. Philomela's power to speak is woven into and hence bound up with the power of pictures to speak— to break through the silence in which they, like women, are traditionally bound. We do well to remember the root meaning of ekphrasis: "speaking out" or "telling in full." To recall this root meaning is to recognize that besides representational friction and the turning of fixed forms into narrative, ekphrasis entails prosopopeia, or the rhetorical technique of envoicing a silent object.[17]

Ekphrasis speaks not only *about* works of art but also *to* and *for* them. In so doing, it stages—within the theater of language itself—a revolution of the image against the word, and particularly the word of Lessing, who decreed that the duty of pictures was to be silent and beautiful (like a woman), leaving expression to poetry.[18] In talking back to and looking back at the male viewer, the images envoiced by ekphrasis challenge at once the controlling authority of the male gaze and the power of the male word.[19]

Ekphrasis, then, is a literary mode that turns on the antagonism—the commonly gendered antagonism—between verbal and visual representation.[20] Since this contest is fought on the field of language itself, it would be grossly unequal but for one thing: ekphrasis commonly reveals a profound ambivalence toward visual art, a fusion of iconophilia and iconophobia, of veneration and anxiety. To represent a painting or sculpted figure in words is to evoke its power—the power to fix, excite, amaze, entrance, disturb, or intimidate the viewer—even as language strives to keep that power under control.

Since ekphrasis has been with us for nearly three thousand years, this book is two things: a continuing meditation on the poetics of ekphrasis as a synchronic literary mode, and a selectively diachronic study of its development from ancient times to our own. Much as I affirm the continuity of its distinguishing features, I recognize the considerable differences between, let us say, Homer's account of the shield of Achilles in the *Iliad* and W. H. Auden's response to a painting by Breughel in "Musée des Beaux Arts." Besides playing a subordinate role in the epic that contains and surrounds it, Homer's passage exemplifies what John Hollander has usefully called "notional ekphrasis"—the representation of an imaginary work of art ("Poetics" 209).[21] By contrast, Auden's "Musée" is a self-contained poem about an actual painting that anyone can see on the walls of the Brussels museum or in a book of reproductions. In one sense, the *availability* of a painting represented by a poem should make no difference to our experience of the poem, which—like any specimen of notional ekphrasis—is made wholly of words. But the availability of the painting allows us to see how the poem reconstructs it, how the poet's word seeks to gain its mastery over the painter's image. To see the difference between a passage about an imaginary work of art and a poem about a real one is to learn something of what has happened to ekphrasis in our time—especially as poetry enters what I call the museum of words.

The road to that museum is laid out here in four roughly chronological chapters. In chapter 1, I consider what I call the canonical specimens of ekphrasis to be found in the epics of Homer, Virgil, and Dante. In the ekphrastic passages of these works, which are genealogically linked by a succession of influences, the image is largely dominated by the authority of the male word. By contrast, chapter 2 treats an ekphrastic tradition that begins with the Ovidian story of how the tongueless Philomela depicted Tereus's rape and mutilation of her and thus overturned his verbal report of her death. Variations on this theme permeate literature from Ovid to Shakespeare. In the Greek novels of

Longus and Achilles Tatius, in Chaucer's "Knight's Tale," in Marlowe's *Hero and Leander,* in Spenser's *Faerie Queen,* and most especially in *The Rape of Lucrece,* verbalized depictions of rape are repeatedly used to prefigure or represent the violence men do to women under the "color" of their words. Turning from Shakespeare to the English romantic poets, chapter 3 shows how romantic ekphrasis brings a combination of iconoclasm and iconophilia to painting and sculpture: to works of art which begin to seem transcendently beautiful in the protective enclosure of the newly born public museum, but which nonetheless provoke the ravishment of interrogating words and the abrasive skepticism of minds tempered by contingency and change. Finally, chapter 4 shows how modern and postmodern ekphrasis enters the museum of art.

In one sense, the whole collection of ekphrastic poetry treated in this book can be seen as a museum of words—a gallery of art constructed by language alone. But the metaphor gains a special resonance in this century, when ekphrastic poems typically evoke actual museums of art along with the words they offer us: the whole complex of titles, curatorial notes, and art historical commentary that surround the works of art we now see on museum walls. Starting with Browning's "My Last Duchess," where the curatorial Duke strives to control by his rhetoric the meaning of a painting that declines to obey his word, I turn to a succession of twentieth-century poems about paintings that come to the viewer framed in commentary. In Auden's "Musée," in the Breughel poems of William Carlos Williams, and in Ashbery's "Self-Portrait," we will find a gradually intensifying struggle for mastery between the language of interpretation and the impenetrable silence of what Ashbery calls "the strict / Otherness of the painter in his / Other room."

This book does not pretend to be either comprehensive or definitive. Aside from its pages on Dante, it has nothing to say about ekphrastic poetry written on the Continent in modern languages, and except for its discussion of the ancient Greek novel, it has nothing to say about ekphrasis in fiction.[22] In addition, it almost wholly skirts the formidable body of writing about works of art that begins with the third-century A.D. *Imagines* of Philostratus the Elder, sometimes called the father of art criticism. A truly comprehensive survey of ekphrasis would have to examine the work of major art critics from Philostratus onward: of figures such as Vasari, Diderot, Hazlitt, Baudelaire, Ruskin, and Robert Hughes.[23] This body of work may become the subject of a future book. In the meantime, I have treated art criticism only insofar as it invades and inflects the ekphrastic poetry of the modern and postmodern poets treated in chapter 4.

Chapter One

HOMER, VIRGIL, DANTE
A Genealogy of Ekphrasis

The earliest known example of ekphrasis in western literature is the lengthy description of the shield that Hephaestus makes for Achilles in the eighteenth book of Homer's *Iliad*. Since Homer's epics are generally dated to the eighth century B.C., about the time that writing originates in Greece, it is hardly an exaggeration to say that ekphrasis is as old as writing itself in the western world. In writing at length about visual art, Homer—or whoever first transcribed the words we credit him with—frankly invites us to measure the newborn powers of writing itself against those of a much older mode of representation, and this is the invitation latently or manifestly made by all ekphrastic writing from Homer's time right up to our own. For Homer's re-creation of the scenes sculpted on the shield is not simply the earliest example of ekphrasis we know in western literature; it is paradigmatic, establishing conventions, contentions, and strategies that would inform ekphrastic poetry for centuries to come, however distant Homer's way of representing visual art may seem from what John Ashbery does with Parmigianino's *Self Portrait* or W. H. Auden does with the shield of Achilles itself. To set such specimens of twentieth-century ekphrasis beside Homer's re-creation of the shield is of course to see enormous differences, beginning with the fact that Homer's lines do not constitute a self-contained poem but rather play a part in the epic that contains them. Yet they can be read against the background of the epic—not in isolation, but in relief, like the figures on the shield itself. In this capacity they set an example that successively leads to two other remarkable passages of ekphrasis set within epics: Virgil's account of the shield of Aeneas in the *Aeneid* and Dante's description of the sculptures on the terrace of the proud in the *Purgatorio*. Homer's lines, therefore, are the logical as well as chronological point of departure for this study.

I begin with these passages from Homer, Virgil, and Dante because they allow us to construct what I call a canonical genealogy of ekphrasis: not the only story that might be told of its early development, and certainly not the full story, but a deliberately selective story of how three great epics bound by ties of

9

something like filial succession have represented visual art. Though other poets (such as Hesiod and Catullus, as we will see) play subordinate roles in this story, it largely emerges from within the epic tradition. As Homer's account of the shield of Achilles begets Virgil's account of the shield of Aeneas, the scenes on Aeneas's shield lead—with the help of Scripture and other sources—to the sculpted figures represented by Dante, who explicitly salutes Virgil as his *maestro* and *autore* (*Inferno* 1.85). In this genealogy of epic fathers and sons, we shall see how the word comes to master the painted or sculpted image it represents, and at the same time how the power of this image-mastering word serves to reinforce an authority that is essentially male.

I

HOMER: A SHIELD SCULPTED IN WORDS

At first sight, the long passage on the shield of Achilles (18.478–608) seems wholly detachable from the rest of the *Iliad* because few of the scenes described have any obvious connection to the poem that surrounds them. In this respect—as in many others—the passage on the shield differs sharply from previous examples of ekphrasis in the poem, such as the brief description of the red robe in which Helen weaves unspecified pictures of the "numerous struggles" endured by the Trojans and the Greeks on her behalf (3.126–28). Unlike those pictures, the scenes wrought in metal on the shield do not seem—or do not immediately seem—to mirror the action of the poem. Nor do they open a window on the past of the major characters, as the *Odyssey* does when it interrupts the story of Odysseus's homecoming to explain how the disguised wanderer acquired the scar that is suddenly recognized by Eurykleia. Nevertheless, the making of the shield completes a turning point in the poem—the point at which Achilles has finally decided to bury his anger at Agamemnon and join the war against Troy to avenge Hector's slaying of Patroclus. Since Hector has stripped Patroclus of the armor that Achilles gave him, Thetis asks Hephaestus to make a new set of armor, and it is the creation and delivery of this armor that actually sends Achilles into battle.[1]

The fact that the making of the shield plays a crucial part in developing the action of the poem does not by itself explain what the scenes on the shield contribute to our understanding of the poem. But Kenneth Atchity argues that the shield microcosmically reflects the whole "thematic expanse" of the *Iliad* (Atchity 241), and some of its scenes actually do mirror the world of the poem. The city besieged by armed forces (509–16), for instance, evokes the plight of Troy, and the scene of the lions attacking the bull (579–84) symbolically recalls the death of Patroclus, who—when Hector's spear fatally penetrates his belly—is compared to a boar overpowered by a lion.[2] In the scenes of war and peace we can also see represented what Lattimore calls "the life of [Homer's] day" (43), or more precisely the civilization of twelfth-century B.C. Mycenae, which had faded by Homer's time but which left behind (for Schliemann to find) actual pictures remarkably close to Homer's scenes, such as a picture of warriors fighting outside a city on whose walls sit women and children with uplifted hands (Monro 340).

Yet even if the shield symbolizes the Mycenean civilization that Achilles sets out to defend, even if Hephaestus's masterpiece is metaphorically interchangeable with Achilles himself, who becomes—as recently suggested—the shield for the whole Greek world (Thibaud 306), the shield's capacity to represent and thus perpetuate that world is compromised by the depth of its very involvement in mortal vicissitudes—in human contingency. The shield is no more immortal or indestructible than the short-lived Achilles for whom it is made. Magnificently wrought though it is by the divine god of fire and forge, it is nonetheless made not to be sealed in a museum cabinet but to be borne into battle and to bear the shocks of fighting: in the course of combat, it is halfway penetrated by Aeneas's spear (20.269–72) as well as struck by Hector's (22.290).[3]

The shield seems to transcend war because it represents so many other kinds of human experience: marriage, litigation, ploughing, sheep-herding, cattle-driving, grape-harvesting, festivals, dancing, singing, and acrobatics. Hence the shield has been read as the embodiment of an "idealized temporality" and a "respite . . . from the pressures of reality."[4] As Oliver Taplin persuasively argues, it works like many of Homer's similes, which touchingly open up windows "through the war to the peace that lies behind it, to the peace that the warriors have abandoned and which many of them will never know again" (15). But even as the scenes on the shield evoke peace and offer a respite from the reality of war, what emerges from Hephaestus's forge is a real instrument of combat and a subject of fierce contention. It is not only used and damaged on the battlefield; it also provokes a dispute between Odysseus and Ajax that leads Ajax to kill himself in rage and frustration.[5]

What does it mean, then, that the shield is prodigally ornamented with scenes of human life—that the shield represents precisely the life it is ostensibly designed to protect? What does it mean that every one of the figures in the designs of the shield is unshielded, unprotected, fully exposed to the spears of the enemy?[6] It suggests, at the very least, that this meticulously wrought piece of armor is a radically ambiguous symbol of protection. If Achilles is himself the shield of Mycenean civilization, he is nonetheless shielding himself behind something that symbolically offers that civilization to the enemy, and that will eventually prove unable to protect his own life. Even before he gets the shield, Achilles learns that he must die soon after killing Hector (18.90–99), and when Thetis goes to Hephaestus, she begs him to make the shield for *huei emoi okumoroi* (18.458)—"my short-lived son." Indeed, at the very moment when Hephaestus agrees to make the shield for Achilles, he can do no more than wish that he "could hide him away from death and its sorrow / at that time when his hard fate comes upon him" (18.466–67).

The ambiguity of the shield as a symbol of protection is accentuated by the indeterminacy of the language used to describe its materials and construction.

Made of tin, gold, bronze, and perhaps silver (474–75) cut into five layers or plates (*ptuches,* 481) generally thought to be stacked in concentric rings, it offers a series of scenes that—we are commonly told—Homer describes in centrifugal order, moving from the innermost circle to the rim, where the Ocean River encircles everything (607–8). But the poem gives conflicting accounts of how the metals are used,[7] and we must reckon with drastic disparities of scale in the scenes described. Under what scheme of proportion could the two gold talents (coins) of line 507 be visually signified in a relief that also represented— among many other things—the earth, the sun and moon, the constellations, and two cities? Different scenes, of course, may be rendered in different scales, but can a single scene include both a multitude of spectators and a close-up view of silver sword-belts, which is what we find in the passage on the dancing scene (590–606)? The "realism" that critics regularly ascribe to this passage applies to the figures and actions said to be represented on the shield—to dancing, ploughing, disputing, and the like—not to the *manner* in which they are said to be represented.

The question of just what Hephaestus puts on the shield—the verb *etithei* (641, 550, 561, 607) repeatedly stresses the act of fixing various scenes in place—arises with special force when we consider the narrative energy that drives the poet's re-creation of these scenes. Curiously, Lessing recognized only a tiny fraction of this energy. Anxious to exculpate Homer from the charge that he had turned the temporal art of poetry into mere verbal painting of figures fixed in space, Lessing declared:

> Homer does not paint the shield as finished and complete, but as a shield that is being made. Thus [he transforms] . . . what is coexistent in his subject into what is consecutive and thereby [makes] the living picture of an action out of the tedious painting of an object. We do not see the shield, but the divine master as he is making it. . . . We do not lose sight of him until all is finished. (95)

The fact that Homer narrates the making of the shield of Achilles is one of several things that distinguish it from the shields of Ajax and Agamemnon, which are represented as already made (7.219–23; 11.32–37). To see the passage on the shield simply as description is to miss the narrative force of its principal verbs. Consistently past in tense, varying between imperfect and aorist (*eteuxe* [483], *poiese* [490, 573, 587], *etithei* [541, 550, 561, 607], *poikille* [590]), they satisfy the elementary requirements of narrative by telling the story of how Hephaestus forged, fashioned, and placed the figures on the shield.[8] Yet narrative does not stop at the frame of each scene Hephaestus creates. It penetrates that frame, animating the figures within it, and thus subverting any effort to visualize just where in space the figures are deployed, just what sort of pattern or configuration they assume.[9]

Even to speak of a "frame" for any one of the scenes described is to say more than the text authorizes. For all that has been written about the presumed circularity of the shield and its pattern of concentric circles, nowhere in the 130 lines on its making does Homer call it circular; and though he mentions "the circles of the dance" in the wedding scene (494) and the "sacred circle" of elders in the disputation scene (504), he says nothing like what he earlier said about the *overall* design of Agamemnon's shield: "there were ten circles of bronze upon it" [11.33]). There are enclosures on Achilles' shield, such as the rampart surrounding the besieged city (514), the tin fence set around the vineyard (565), and the outer rim around which the Ocean River flows (607–8). But we are not told the shapes of these enclosures; for all we know they could be triangular, rectangular, or elliptical. Dynamic and mobile, the figures and elements in these scenes elude fixed geometrical definition. In the dancing scene, for instance, the figures shift from one kind of dance to another (599–602). They momentarily suggest a circle when their feet touch the ground as lightly as a potter touches his wheel "to see if it will run smooth" (601), but the point of contact in this simile is not so much circularity as tactile sensitivity: the dancers' feet are as "understanding" (*epistamenoisi* [599]) as the potter's fingers. The only shape the dancers are explicitly said to form is "rows" (602), but since they run in rows "crossing each other," the picture is explicitly moving; they are nowhere fixed in space.

The structure of narrative is still more evident in scenes that clearly meet all three of what Wendy Steiner calls the most important conditions of narrative: "more than one temporal moment," a subject "repeated from one moment to another," and "a minimally realistic setting" (Steiner, *Pictures* 2). The disputation passage, for instance, provides at least three distinct and temporally successive phases of action: (1) a quarrel arises in the marketplace (497–500); (2) "then" (if Lattimore's rendering of the *d'* in line 501 is accurate) the disputants go to an arbitrator (501–2); and (3) they make their arguments before the elders (503–8). Some of these phases contain further sequences: in the first phase, the promise of restitution for the murdered man is followed by the refusal to accept it; in the third, the disputants take turns speaking. It would be possible, of course, for a metal sculptor to forge this whole sequence—or set of sequences—in a series of reliefs, but for the most part the text reports speech acts directly (promised, refused, spoke) rather than representing the gestures which could visually signify them, as we will see in Dante's *Purgatorio*. Except for the circle of seated elders who constitute an audience for the disputants and who would logically belong in the background of any picture of them, the characters in this passage never assume a picturable pose. The picture or pictures said to be wrought on the shield at this point have been turned so thoroughly into narrative that we can hardly see a picture through Homer's words.

This is why Homer's words subvert the distinctions that Lessing formulates to explain them. According to Lessing, Homer wanted to draw just "one picture" (99) in the disputation passage—by which Lessing can only mean that Homer sought to *represent* one picture, for according to Lessing, "the artist who executes this subject cannot make use of more than one single moment at one time: either the moment of judgment, or the examination of witnesses, or the passing of judgment, or any other moment before, after, or between these points which he deems most suitable" (99). Yet the history of art hardly supports the would-be universal law enunciated here, for it dates only from the Renaissance; before Alberti's theory of perspective led artists to paint only what could be seen from one point of view at one moment of time, graphic artists felt free to tell stories in paint, sometimes representing several temporally distinct episodes within a single picture, as Benozzo Gozzoli does in his *Dance of Salome* (1461–62).[10] Hence Lessing's notion that "the artist" can depict only one moment in a picture or cannot use more than one picture to represent an action is an utterly arbitrary imposition of post-Renaissance conventions on Mycenean or simply ancient Greek art.

Furthermore, even if Lessing were right about the universal unitemporality of art, not even he knows how to infer from Homer's language what "one picture" Homer represents. Before commenting specifically on the disputation passage, Lessing observes generally: "I find that Homer represents nothing but progressive actions" (79). How then does he represent a single picture? By converting it into a narrative, exercising the poet's liberty of extending "his description over that which preceded and that which followed the single moment represented in the work of art; and the power of showing not only what the artist shows, but also that which the artist must leave to the imagination" (99). This is useful and highly applicable, as we will see, to later specimens of ekphrasis, but it hardly explains the disputation passage, where Homer makes no distinction between what the artist actually puts on the shield and what can be inferred about the narrative context surrounding the moment putatively depicted. So when Lessing says that just "one picture" is represented in the disputation passage, he radically equivocates.

The work of poetic conversion here—the turning of spatial composition into verbal narrative—is impossible to discern or define because we have no inferential access to the composition itself. As a whole, in fact, the shield is shielded by the very language that purports to reveal it to us. In spite of diagrams and even works of sculpture such as Flaxman's *Shield of Achilles* (figure 1), the basic design of the shield—let alone the disposition of its multifarious details—is nowhere unequivocally disclosed to us.[11] Exactly what Hephaestus wrought on the shield is ultimately impossible to visualize. Consequently, as I have already noted, Homer's account of the shield is an extreme specimen of "notional ekphrasis"—the representation of an imaginary work of art.[12] All we can see—all that really exists in this passage—is Homer's language, which not only rivals but actually displaces the work of art it ostensibly describes and salutes.

The theme of rivalry is in fact embedded in the whole story of the shield-making here. As the god of fire, Hephaestus is superior to any mortal craftsman—even to Tychios, "the best of all workers in leather" (7.221). Yet as soon as he begins to forge the shield by *daidallon,* elaborating designs on it

1. Abraham Flaxman. *The Shield of Achilles.* Gilt silver cast in bas-relief, 1821.
Henry E. Huntington Library and Art Gallery, San Marino, California.

(479), Hephaestus becomes the rival of Daedalus, the mortal albeit legendary
maker of the Cretan labyrinth.[13] Himself homocidally competitive, Daedalus
was expelled from Athens for killing his nephew Perdix, who surpassed him in
skill (*OCD*). He is much better known, of course, for constructing the wings
with which he and his son Icarus escaped from the labyrinth, but lurking behind the story of Icarus's fall—which we will meet again in this book—may be
a further punishment for unbridled artistic ambition: like Arachne, turned
into a spider for presuming to surpass Pallas Athene in the art of weaving,
Daedalus is forced to witness the catastrophic consequences of his supreme
achievement. Yet in Homer's language, it is the art and craft of the mortal
Daedalus that the divine Hephaestus seeks to recreate in *daidallon*—in the
Daedalian elaborating—of *daidala* (482), cunningly wrought works. The rivalry implied by the repeated—almost redundant—invocation of Daedalus in

these words for what Hephaestus does and makes becomes explicit when we are told of the *koron* or dancing floor that he represents in the dancing scene: "a dancing floor, like that which once in the wide spaces of Knossos / Daedalus built for Ariadne of the lovely tresses" (591–92).

Homer could be referring to a dancing floor in white marble relief that Daedalus reportedly created at Knossos and that could still be seen there in the time of Pausanias (Monro 353). If so, Hephaestus is taking the *representational* art of Daedalus as the precedent he seeks to rival. But even if—as is more probable—Homer is referring to or thinking of an actual dancing floor built at Knossos, he draws us into a labyrinth of representation. The Greek word for what Hephaestus does at this point is *poikille* (line 590), "fashioned"—a verb used only here instead of *etithei* (placed) or *poiese* (made), which are used to denote the construction of other scenes. The rarity of the verb accentuates the distinctiveness of the line in which it appears—*En de koron poikille periklutos amphigueeis,* literally "and a dancing floor was made by the renowned double-cripple."[14] The re-creation of the dancing floor is a triumph over disfigurement for the smith who cannot dance himself but who can represent both the floor and the young figures on it: the figures whose "understanding feet" run lightly in a way that not only resembles the potter making trial of his wheel but also— as Monro notes (353)—mimics the windings of the labyrinth through which Ariadne guided Theseus. All the movements and footsteps of the running dance in this scene run back to the artist: the potter, the crippled sculptor modeling his art on that of Daedalus, and beyond him to Homer himself, the blind poet who—like the blind Demodocus of the *Odyssey*—so vividly sees.

But if Homer is deliberately asking us to measure his verbal craftsmanship against the graphic art of Hephaestus, if he is aiming to rival the very art he ostensibly salutes, we must scrutinize more closely the kind of narratives he constructs about that art. According to Lessing, the poet is free to reproduce every phase of an action. While the painter is confined to a single moment, the poet "may, if he so chooses, take up each action at its origin and pursue it through all possible variations to its end" (23–24). But besides ignoring the possibility of multi-temporal depiction, as we have seen, this polarizing formulation ignores the indeterminacy of narrative—the gaps it inevitably leaves. As Roman Ingarden observes,

> time-filling events are never represented in *all their phases,* regardless of whether it is a single event, constituting a whole, or a plurality of successive events. . . . It is always only *isolated* longer or shorter phases, or simply, only momentary occurrences, that are represented, and what takes place between these phases or occurrences remains *indeterminate.* It is always—to echo Bergson—only *isolated* 'segments' of 'reality' that are represented, a reality which is being represented but which is never representable in its flowing continuity. (237)

Represented time is therefore analogous to represented space, which can never be more than a segment—or set of segments—of real space. The gaps between the segments correspond to portions of space or time that are merely "corepresented," furnished or "taken as existing" by the imagination of the reader.[15]

Homer's ekphrastic narratives about the scenes on the shield accentuate the fragmentation and indeterminacy that Ingarden finds in all narrative. As Michael Lynn-George notes (180), the stories Homer tells are inconclusive. We never learn who won the dispute about recompense for the murdered man (506–8), nor do we learn the outcome of the battle between the defenders and attackers of the besieged city (539–40). "Both cities of mortal men," Lynn-George observes, "are left in the unresolved dispute of death" (186). Real death is said to occur three times (529, 535–37, 582–83) in passages I will consider below. But the inconclusive shape of the stories about the disputation and the siege—the two most extended stories in the whole passage on the shield—mirrors the narrative structure of the epic as a whole. The story of the dispute begins *in medias res,* when one man refuses to take money as recompense for the killing of another, and the refusal clearly implies a desire for vengeance.[16] The *Iliad* as a whole is a narrative of disputation, recompense, and violent retaliation, beginning with Agamemnon's refusal of ransom for the daughter of Chryses, priest of Apollo. When Apollo retaliates by shooting his murderous arrows at the Greeks and thereby forces Agamemnon to give up his consort, he takes Achilles' consort in recompense, antagonizing Achilles so much that nothing Agamemnon later does—even offering to return the consort, untouched (he swears) with other gifts—can recompense Achilles for the insult done to him. The only thing that overcomes Achilles' resentment is Hector's killing of Patroclus, which turns that resentment into a yearning for revenge. Finally, though Achilles kills Hector, the price that Achilles must pay for doing so is merely intimated—not narrated—at the end of the poem, and the fate of the besieged city remains untold.[17]

To read the *Iliad* in light of the passage on the shield, then, is to see how the stories of the dispute and the besieged city recapitulate the larger story of the poem. In an epic where recompense finally comes to mean only vengeance, the shield stands out because Hephaestus makes it "to give recompense to lovely-haired Thetis" (18.407), who saved his life when Hera cast him out of heaven for being lame. But if the shield signifies a generosity of recompense unmet elsewhere in the poem, the stories told about its graphic features epitomize the indeterminacy and incompleteness of the narrative as a whole. Paradoxically, while Homer's account of the pictures on the shield largely converts them into narratives of movement without pause or pose, the structure of the epic narrative itself reveals the suspensive effect of depiction. As Lynn-George says, both sides in the disputation passage urgently seek a *pierar* (18. 501), "an end, a limit, a determination, a decision." But in the epic as in the scenes on the shield, the desire for finality "is indefinitely deferred" (Lynn-George 183).

To withhold finality, of course, is to admit vicissitude. Just as Homer's way of turning pictures into stories complicates any simple opposition between the spatiality of graphic art and the temporality of verbal art, it likewise precludes any formulation that would equate sculpted stasis with a timeless, transcendent peace securely distanced from all the shocks of contingency. When Hephaestus begins his work by putting "the tireless sun" (*eelion t'akamanta*) on the shield along with the earth, the sky, the sea, the full moon, and all the constellations (483–85), he seems to place his work beyond time and change. Yet as Lynn-George points out (176), the tireless sun has already been made to "sink in the depth of the Ocean" after the day of fighting "and the doubtful collision of battle" (18.239–42). The battle is interrupted for the night, but not resolved, and when we are told of the constellation known as the Bear or Wagon that "she *alone* is never plunged in the wash of the Ocean" (489, emphasis added), we are reminded that this is what happens every day to nearly all the other stars— including the sun.

Besides the note of contingency sounded even in the description of seemingly timeless constellations, violent deaths are reported no less than three times in Homer's account of what is represented on the shield. The shepherds outside the besieged city are killed by the soldiers who come from the city to ambush them (520–29); the ensuing battle with the besieging army takes more lives (535–41);[18] and in the pasturing scene, the great ox is seized by two lions who tear open its hide, gulp its black blood, and devour its guts (579–83). Here as elsewhere in Homer's account of the shield, we have no direct access to the series of reliefs it putatively signifies and no way of knowing from Homer's language just how they represent the deaths, which are not inferred as the probable consequence of a sculpturally arrested action but simply narrated in the past tense: the soldiers killed (*kteinon*) the shepherds, the lions devoured (*laphusseton*) the ox. Each of these killings is a treacherous, unprovoked assault on peaceful figures in a tranquil setting; the shepherds "playing happily on pipes" (526) have no more idea of what is coming than the pasturing ox does. But we can hardly construe the deaths as simply the products of time and verbal narrative arbitrarily invading the inviolate space of visual art and timeless pastoral peace. If we read these passages as ekphrastic, we must imagine that the deaths are at least implied by what is actually on the shield, which—as Michael Lynn-George suggests (188)—could well be something like the poses caught on the pin of Odysseus's mantle: a hound holds a fawn in his forepaws while the fawn struggles to escape (*Odyssey* 19.225–31). The *stasis* traditionally identified with visual art, in fact, is evoked at precisely the point where the soldiers who ambushed the shepherds are suddenly confronted by the other army and set their ranks against them, taking their stand or literally "placing [*stesamenoi*] the battle" (533). Since the participle here derives from a verb that can also be used of erecting statues (*istanai tina kalkoun,* for instance, means "to set up a person in brass"), the soldiers are implicitly assuming a graphic pose even as they plunge into deadly combat.[19]

The lines on the battle epitomize the way in which the energy of narrative permeates and animates the whole passage on the sculptural art of the shield. Yet the battle section also includes the only clear signal that the figures represented in words before us are wrought of metal, not made of flesh. While everywhere else in the passage the figures could be characters in a more-or-less realistic narrative, here the fighting soldiers are explicitly said to engage each other *hos te zooi brotoi*—"like living mortals" (539). This phrase echoes the one used earlier of the golden robots who attend Hephaestus and look "like living young women" (418). But unlike those gynekoids, who actually have intelligence and speech and who learned from the gods how to act (419–20), the figures in the battle scene do not function as human beings; they *represent* living men in the act of fighting to the death and dragging away the corpses of their fallen comrades (540).

These subtle allusions to sculptural stasis and to the inorganic condition of the figures on the shield exemplify what might be called *representational friction,* which occurs whenever the dynamic pressure of verbal narrative meets the fixed forms of visual representation and acknowledges them as such. But as I have already noted, this sort of friction also occurs when the poet's language registers the difference between the medium of visual representation and its referent. In the ploughing sequence, we are told that "the earth darkened behind [the ploughmen] and looked like earth that has been ploughed / *though it was gold.* Such was the wonder of the shield's forging" (548–49, emphasis mine). Homer thus reminds us that he is representing representation. His tribute to the wonder (*thauma*) of graphic verisimilitude—the forging and forgery of art—springs precisely from the recognition that what appears on the shield is not the ploughed earth itself, but gold that has been somehow made dark enough to resemble it.[20]

Representational friction becomes still more complex and subtle when the metal of the signifier approximates or even matches the substance of the signified. In the course of this long ekphrastic passage, we see an astonishing range of representational relations. At one extreme, gold is made to look like ploughed earth. At the other, the gold talents said to be lying on the ground in the disputation passage (507) are undoubtedly represented by disks of gold that are distinguishable from actual talents—if at all—only in size. Between these extremes are fine degrees of difference and ambiguity. In the vineyard passage, the "field ditch of dark metal" (564) is an achievement of verisimilitude comparable to the golden earth, but the metals used in the "poles of silver" supporting the vines and the "fence of tin" surrounding the whole vineyard (563–65) could conceivably be used to make the poles and fence they represent. This convergence of the referent and the medium of representation becomes highly ambiguous in the dancing passage, where the young men "carried golden knives that hung from sword-belts of silver" (598). Here we have no way of knowing whether gold and silver are used to represent some other materials, or are simply representing themselves in a display of extraordinarily rich costuming that includes, in any case, finespun tunics (596). Earlier, Ares and Pallas Athene emerge from the besieged city wearing "golden raiment" (517) that can hardly represent anything but itself, and the same passage then offers a specimen of supreme ambiguity: waiting to ambush the cattle and the herdsmen at the waterhole, the soldiers from the city "sat down in place shrouding themselves in the fiery bronze [*aithopi kalko*]" (522), which may of course refer to represented shields, to the metal used to represent them on *this* shield, or to both.

Permeating as they do the whole fabric of the passage, these variously subtle and ambiguous instances of representational friction suggest that the mind of Homer—or at any rate the mind of the text[21]—is continuously engaged in meditating, sometimes playfully, on the complexities of representation itself: on the startling oppositions and equally startling convergences between the media of visual representation and their referents. The differences between the two and the friction generated by the difference becomes still more evident when figures that are said to be made of metal are also said to move. The passage on the oxen begins with a narrative statement about their construction as metal objects fixed on the shield: "He made upon it a herd of horn-straight oxen. The cattle / were wrought of gold and of tin" (573–74). But no sooner were they thus constructed than they "thronged in speed and with lowing / out of the dung of the farmyard to a pasturing place by a sounding / river, and beside the moving field of a reed bed" (574–76). The medium of representation is metal, but the cattle represented by it are animated by the poet's narrative, which likewise animates the herdsmen who marched them along in ranks (*estichooonto* [577]).

What makes this passage on the oxen distinctively ekphrastic, however, is not just its conversion of fixed metal objects into moving figures, but the subtlety of its return to fixity at the end. In the middle lines, the poet seems to forget that he is representing graphic art; he suppresses all reference to metal as he tells the gruesome story of the lions and the ox. But in the last four lines, the engine of narrative slowly grinds to a halt. Goaded and urged by the herdsmen to attack the lions, the dogs balk: "they, before they could get their teeth in, turned back from the lions, / but would come and take their stand very close, and bayed, and kept clear" (585–86). Once again, a passage of insistent movement and violent action concludes on a note of intensely charged *stasis*. Like the soldiers earlier, the dogs take their stand (*istamenoi*), but this time it is not a battle stand. It is a stand-off, a moment of violence indefinitely suspended as the dogs hover between charging and fleeing, rigid with apprehension.

Recalling as it does the violent conclusion of the passage on the city at war, this stasis of taut confrontation at the end of the cattle-driving passage becomes especially striking when we realize that it ends the second major movement of the whole account of the shield. The first major movement—following the prelude on the depiction of the universe (483–89)—is the sequence of passages about the two cities. The second is the sequence of passages about life in the country—a sequence that, as often noted, evokes the seasons of the year. Ploughing (541–49) signals spring, reaping (550–60) summer, grape-harvesting (561–66) autumn, and by process of elimination, cattle-driving presumably signifies winter. The narrative of this seasonal sequence bears witness to almost unceasing activity. The only manifestation of what might be called perfectly sculptural stasis comes in the reaping passage, where the figure of the king stands happily in silence holding his staff (556–67)—a double stillness that occurs nowhere else. Ironically, the scene on which the king smiles so benignly includes a freshly slaughtered ox (559) whose condition anticipates what the lions will shortly do to another of his kind. But in any case, each of the first three seasonal passages ends on a note of sustained activity: the ploughmen hastening to reach the flagon of wine at the edge of the field (546–47), the women scattering barley for the reapers' feast (560), and the grape-harvesters dancing along with the singing youth (571–72). Only at the end of the last of the four—the end of the whole seasonal sequence—is the narrative movement suspended and the narration made to approximate a description of sculptured stasis even as it rises to a pitch of dramatic intensity.

The sudden shift from the violence and tension of this ending to the scene of pastoral tranquillity (587–89) typifies the narrative structure of the shield passage as a whole. Each of the separate narratives about the figures and objects on the shield is embedded in a framing narrative about its making—a narrative that proceeds, as already noted, by repeating verbs of making and placing such as *poiese* and *etithei*. Except for the final placing of the Ocean River around the rim of the shield (606–7), the framing is verbal, not spatial; rather than fixing the position or linear boundaries of any one episode, the key verbs simply mark the shift from one to another, with no causal link between the two. The making of the shield, therefore, is a continuous cycle of beginnings, endings, and new beginnings—a process best exemplified, as Michael Lynn-George suggests (190), by the turn from fighting and corpses at the end of the urban sequence to the springtime ploughing that initiates the seasonal sequence (538–43).[22] Appropriately, then, the last major segment of the passage on the shield represents a depiction of festive dancing and song, with just a hint of literal framing in the placement of the dancers on a *koron* or dancing ground (590–606).

We can now see the kind of narrative Homeric ekphrasis entails. Besides leading to indeterminacy rather than resolution, it is *framed* narrative—by which I mean verbally framed, delimited by an abruptness of opening and closing that occludes both explanatory causes and decisive consequences. The suppression of a surrounding context goes hand in hand with the nearly complete suppression of names and their attendant histories. In the larger narrative of the *Iliad*, we learn the full story behind Achilles' quarrel with Agamemnon; in the disputation passage, we learn only that a dispute between unnamed parties was provoked by the murder of an unnamed man, and we never learn who is besieging the unnamed city or—aside from the attractions of plunder—why.

Besides framed narrative and representational friction, Homer's protracted account of Achilles' shield includes one other element that will become increasingly conspicuous in the ekphrastic literature to come: *prosopopoeia,* the dramatic personification or more precisely the *envoicing* of a mute, inanimate object. No speeches are actually quoted in Homer's passage, as they will be later in the ekphrastic prose of Philostratus the Elder's third-century A.D. *Imagines* and much later in Dante's *Purgatorio.* But the poet mentions a variety of sounds emanating from the figures on the shield, beginning with the nuptial song of the wedding party in the first city (493) and ending with the song led by the acrobats and—in a disputed line—by an inspired minstrel playing the lyre.[23] In between, we are told the gist of what the disputants in the first city say (499– 500); we learn that the young man with the lyre in the grape-harvesting passage is singing a dirge for Linos (570), the Adonis-like youth who died young; and in the pasturing scene, we read, the bull bellows (580) and the dogs bay at the lions (586). Significantly, every one of these sounds is reported as if the poet had actually heard it. None is presented in the way later ekphrastic literature presents sound and speech: as the product of inference from the appearance of a figure.

The reporting of speech and song without reference to the postures or visible expressions that might signify such things to the eye reinforces the momentum of a passage which, as we have already seen, repeatedly turns sculpted scenes into narratives, absorbing the fixed poses of visual art in the moving flow of language. Yet Homer never forgets that he is representing representation itself: that he is describing both the act of sculpting and a work of sculpture as well as all the things it represents. He starts each narrative by referring to the making and placing of the scene he narrates; he concludes his most dramatic narratives on a note of charged suspension that evokes the stasis of sculpture; and he fully exploits the representational friction between the sculptor's medium—the various metals of the sheild—and its referents. He thus bears continual witness to the Daedalian power, complexity, and verisimilitude of visual art even as he aspires to rival that art in language that both imagines and represents it.

II
VIRGIL: RE-IMAGINING THE SHIELD

After Homer, the closest Greek parallel to the passage we have just examined appears in the pseudo-Hesiodic *Shield of Hercules,* a poetic fragment about Hercules' fight with Cycnus that includes a 181-line description of the shield itself.[24] Unlike the shield of Achilles, the shield of Hercules is designed to be terrifying. Though it recalls Achilles' shield in representing such peaceful activities as a marriage festival, ploughing, reaping, and grape-harvesting, it also includes—among other grotesqueries—a fiery-eyed dragon, twelve serpents with gnashing teeth, a host of personified horrors (Strife, Tumult, Fear, Carnage, and so on), the head of the Gorgon in a silver knapsack with bright gold tassels worn by Perseus, and more Gorgons chasing Perseus with gnashing teeth. To compare these two shields is chiefly to see, as Oliver Taplin suggests (1–2), how curiously unthreatening as well as how human and ordinary are the scenes on Achilles' shield. The horrifying face of the Gorgon stares from the center of Agamemnon's shield (*Iliad* 11.36–37), but is nowhere to be found on the shield of Achilles, which offers just one glimpse of deities (Ares and Athene coming from the besieged city) amid its multitudes of mortals.

Yet in spite of the many peaceful human figures on Achilles' shield and of its generally benign appearance, the total effect of all the armor that Hephaestus makes for Achilles is apotropaic. When Thetis delivers the armor to him, his men (the Myrmidons) tremble: "None had the courage / to look straight at it. They were afraid of it" (19.14–15). Achilles alone beholds it—with a combination of anger (presumably at Hector) and admiration for the intricacy of Hephaestus's handiwork. Aside from these two reactions, Achilles makes no effort to read the scenes on the shield, nor does the text make any connection between his emotional response to the armor (anger) and what the shield represents.

To grasp this fact is to begin to understand how the shield is re-imagined in Virgil's *Aeneid*.[25] According to Lessing, the chief difference between the shield of Achilles and the shield of Aeneas is that while Homer narrates the making of a shield, Virgil simply describes a finished object, and "the action comes to a standstill during this time" (Lessing 95–96). But besides converting the scenes on the shield into narratives, as Homer did, Virgil represents Aeneas's response to the scenes—even though he cannot understand what they signify. This set of sculpted scenes is in fact just one of several works of visual art that affect Aeneas in the course of the poem. As he successively views and absorbs them, these works not only reveal the origin and final goal of his mission but gradually reconstruct his gender, turning womanly compassion for suffering into the violent aggression manifested by his very last act, which is provoked by a work of visual art.

The passage on the shield of Aeneas at the end of book 8, then, is best read in light of the ekphrastic passages that precede and follow it, including those that antedate the *Aeneid* itself in Virgil's work. Virgilian ekphrasis actually begins in his third eclogue, where two herdsmen take turns describing the beechwood cups newly carved by the divine Alcimedon—"caelatum divini opus Alcimedontis" (line 37)—that each stakes as a prize in the singing contest held between them. The beauty and order of the natural world represented on these cups, which display two astronomers in the midst of ivy clusters and Orpheus charming the woods with his song, has been read as an implied critique of the rancor and animosity permeating the conversation between the two rustic singers.[26] But just as significant as the scenes on the cups is the scene of contention in which the cups play their part. After Homer, all ekphrasis becomes doubly paragonal: a contest staged not just between the word and the image but also between one poet and another.[27] In describing a set of decorated cups for which two singers compete, Virgil emulates the first idyll of Theocritus, where the goatherd describes the scenes of fishing, petty thievery, and unrequited love freshly carved on the pristine cup that he offers to a shepherd named Thyrsis for singing a song. But while Thyrsis wins both the cup and six pails of goat's milk, Virgil's singers are judged to be equally deserving only of a heifer—and no cups at all.[28] Thus the critique of their contentiousness implied by the description of the scenes on the cups is reinforced by the ending, which leaves their quarrel unsettled. Virgil here thematizes his own singing contest with Theocritus, his own rewriting of Theocritan ekphrasis as well as Theocritan pastoral. In so doing, he points the way to his reconstruction of Homeric ekphrasis in the *Aeneid.*

The difference between Homeric and Virgilian ekphrasis begins to emerge in book 1 of the *Aeneid,* where the sea-battered Aeneas and his men land exhausted on the shores of a Carthage then under construction and find their way to a temple being built for Juno in the midst of an urban grove. On the temple walls Aeneas sees paintings depicting just what he has recently survived: the Trojan War.[29] Unlike the scenes on the shield of Achilles, these pictures represent world-renowned events—battles "fama totum vulgata per orbem" (457). Virgil also tells us something about the arrangement of the pictures. Whereas Homer locates only the picture of the Ocean River, Virgil writes that Aeneas sees the Trojan battles pictured in succession ("ex ordine" [456]), and also indicates that each scene is pictured separately, with the ill-fated tents of Rhesus not far ("nec procul") from the picture of Achilles chasing Trojans (468–69) and on another part of the wall ("parte alia" [474]) the picture of Troilus (474–78). But just as important as the arrangement of these paintings and their subject matter is Aeneas's response to them. While the scenes on the shield of Achilles are unmediated by the viewpoint or feelings of any character in the poem, we repeatedly see the temple paintings of the Trojan War through the tear-filled eyes of Virgil's hero.[30]

Remarkably enough, the poignantly lacrimal tone of this first ekphrastic passage in the *Aeneid* echoes the tone of what is nearly the final scene in the *Iliad,* wherein Priam tearfully begs Achilles for the body of Hector and both men break down weeping for their dead (24.509–12). The Virgilian line describing the picture of Priam stretching out his unarmed hands to Achilles ("tendentemque manus . . . inermis" [487]) actually evokes the Homeric scene. But the temple paintings give no sign of Achilles' capacity for commiseration. They represent him simply as a ruthless predator, chasing down Trojans in his chariot (468), terrifying the unarmed Troilus (474–78), dragging Hector's body three times around the walls of Troy, and mercenarily giving up the body only for gold (483–84). Equally heartless is the bloodthirsty ("cruentus") Diomedes, who is shown widely slaughtering men ("multa vastabat caede") in their first sleep ("primo . . . somno") [469–71]. As R. D. Williams observes (149), the pictures plainly reveal the *perfidia* and *crudelitas* of the Greeks—the very qualities that reappear in Aeneas's story of the Trojan War in book 2. For the ruthlessness of the Greeks is something constructed by Virgil and by Aeneas himself as the foil to his own sensitivity. Before the picture of a raging Achilles furious at both sides in the war ("saevum ambobus" [458]), Aeneas stands and weeps. He reads the pictures not only as evidence that the Trojans are already known to the Carthaginians—"what country on earth," he says to Achates, "is not fully aware of our ordeal?" (460)—but also as a sign that he and his men will find pity in Carthage.[31] In the eyes of Aeneas the pictures themselves express pity for all the Trojans represented as suffering in them, beginning with Priam, whose pathetic image (later described in line 487) moves Aeneas to utter what is perhaps the most celebrated line in the whole poem: "sunt lacrimae rerum et mentem mortalia tangunt" (462).

The gist of this stubbornly untranslatable line is surely something like "These pictures weep for us and our mortality." To say "sunt [hic] lacrimae"— literally "[here] there are tears"—is to project onto the pictures the sorrow Aeneas feels within himself.[32] Michael Baxendall notes that ekphrasis tends to represent not so much a picture as "thought after seeing a picture" (4). Yet this passage plainly expresses what Aeneas feels *while* seeing the pictures. As soon as he sees them, he stops and tearfully questions Achates ("constitit et lacrimans . . . inquit" [459]). He views them with frequent sighs ("multa gemens") and with a face rivered by tears ("largoque umectat flumine vultum" [465]). "He recognizes tearfully" ("agnoscit lacrimans" [470]) the snowy canvas tents of the doomed Rhesus, King of Thrace and ally of Priam, who with twelve of his men was killed in ambush as he slept. And from the depths of his heart he gives a mighty sigh ("ingentum gemitum dat pectore ab imo," [485]) when he sees Priam supplicating for the body of Hector.

Aeneas's response to these pictures is so intense that he can scarcely distinguish what he sees from what he imagines himself seeing. We can make this distinction because, as R. D. Williams notes (151), the tenses of the verbs used to describe the pictures indicate which actions are depicted and which are added by the narrative about the pictures. Thus the picture of the Rhesus episode shows Diomedes while he "was devastating" ("vastabat," imperfect tense) the tented sleepers and before he "turned away" ("avertit," perfect tense) the king's horses. Troilus is shown after he has lost or set aside his arms ("amissis . . . armis") and found himself unequally matched ("impar congressus") with Achilles; in the picture he is *being* carried away ("fertur," present tense) by the horses. Likewise, the picture of Achilles shows him while he "was selling" ("vendebat") Hector's corpse *after* he "had dragged" ("raptaverat," pluperfect) Hector's body three times around Troy. This kind of distinction, which Homer does not make in his ekphrastic narratives, helps to reveal what Aeneas experiences when he sees the picture of Achilles selling Hector's body.

Aeneas, we are told, gave a mighty sigh "ut spolia, ut currus, utque ipsum corpus amici / tendentemque manus Priamum conspexit inermis" (486–87)—"as he caught sight of the spoils, the chariot, and even the very body of his friend, and Priam holding out his weaponless hands." Aeneas sees more here than is likely to be shown in a painting of Achilles selling Hector's corpse. Such a painting *might* include—in the background, presumably—Achilles' chariot and the spoils (armor) he took from Hector, but it is more probable that Aeneas draws them into the picture from his memory or from the other pictures he has just seen. These include a painting of Achilles riding down Trojans in his chariot (468) and a vivid picture of an unarmed Troilus in his own chariot fleeing Achilles, thrown backwards ("resupinus") still holding the reins, and dragged along with his neck and hair in the dirt (474–78). Virgil's account of this picture closely resembles Homer's description of Hector's body tied by his feet to Achilles' chariot "so as to let the head drag" (*Iliad* 22.398) when Achilles drives his horses from the battlefield to the Greek ships (464–65), taking Hector's "glorious armour" (399) with him. The spoils and chariot that Aeneas sees in the painting of Achilles and Priam, therefore, might well be something Aeneas brought to the painting from the pictures he has already seen and from his own experience. In any case, he would scarcely be able to look at a painting of Achilles selling Hector's spiritless corpse ("exanimum . . . corpus" [484]) without remembering and even seeing again what Achilles had done to it.

Such memories generate groans, sighs, and tears—the language of sorrow, which is chiefly expressed here by women. I do not mean that the paintings represent militancy as exclusively male or as something alien to a wholly feminized Aeneas. The last picture described shows a raging Penthesilea leading her Amazon troops into battle with one breast aggressively bared,[33] and just before seeing this final picture, Aeneas recognizes himself in a painting that shows him locked in combat with leading Greeks ("se quoque principibus permixtum . . . Achivis" [488]). But the only true mirror of Aeneas's weeping face in this temple gallery is the painting of the Trojan women.[34] They, we read, were shown going to the temple of Pallas Athena "with their hair unbound, and were carrying the *peplum* [robe of offering] in supplication, mournful and beating their breasts with their palms" (479–81). The goddess is "non aequa"—partial to the enemy and unyielding to them: "looking away, she was holding her eyes fixed on the ground" (482). She thus embodies the inexorability of fate itself, which—as R. D. Williams notes (149)—has already made Troy vulnerable by allowing Rhesus's horses to be taken and Troilus to die young.[35] But while Pallas's eyes are fixed on the ground, Aeneas's eyes are fastened to the paintings. As the doomed Troilus clings to his empty chariot ("curruque haeret . . . inani" [476]), Aeneas feeds his soul with an empty painting ("animum pictura pascit inani" [464]) and sticks (again "haeret") to his place, stupefied and transfixed in a single act of beholding ("stupet obtutuque . . . defixus in uno" [495]).

This entrancement shows more than a trace of narcissism. The paintings captivate him because they weep for him *and* because they assure him that he is already a celebrity on these foreign shores even though he has just washed up on them. Immediately before he speaks the line about tears ("sunt lacrimae rerum . . ."), the sight of Priam's picture—which we later learn is one of the most pathetic of all—prompts Aeneas to say that "here too are the rewards of fame" ("sunt hic etiam sua praemia laudi" [461]). Tears then *are* the reward, the tribute paid by lachrymogenic pictures that signify not just sympathy for these wave-worn refugees—the original boat people—but also fame. Though the pictures represent what for Aeneas was a catastrophe, they also perpetuate and disseminate his name, which now becomes a marketable commodity. No sooner has he spoken the line about tears than he tells the faithful Achates: "Don't worry; this notoriety will pay your way here."[36] Aeneas feeds his soul with the pictures, and they almost literally become the meal ticket for his body, for it is during Dido's sumptuous feast that he repays her hospitality by telling her the story of what the pictures represent.[37]

Dido competes with the pictures. Though Aeneas is so entranced by them that he does not even see at first the living beauty of her picture-perfect figure (she is "forma pulcherrima" [496], most beautiful in form) when she enters the temple, this full-blooded woman will of course supplant the empty images— the "pictura[s] . . . inan[es]" (464)—that for a time transfix him.[38] But the pictures themselves have a potency generated by the very language which at once reveals and hides them. Beyond what he suggests about the arrangement of the paintings, Virgil says nothing about the composition of individual works, and except for the snowy ("niveis") tents of Rhesus he mentions no colors. Nor does he refer (as Homer does) to the medium of representation, so there is no representational friction between medium and referent. Yet in spite of this apparent suppression of pictorial features, he creates pictures in words. As we have seen already, he distinguishes what *has* happened from what *is* happening in each picture described. Rather than turning every painting into a narrative that virtually erases graphic poses, as Homer does, he catches a series of figures in specific actions, gestures, and positions: Greeks in flight (467), Priam with outstretched hands (487), women beating their breasts (481), and Troilus dragged along with his neck and hair in the dirt (478).

Paradoxically, this last item—the most graphic description of all—is also the most conspicuously verbal. To grasp its full impact, we must understand the events that lead up to it: events that Virgil briefly narrates before representing the picture itself. Like the ambushed shepherds in the description of the shield of Achilles, and like Rhesus in the picture described just before this one, Troilus is caught unawares and unarmed, "amissis . . . armis," yet another victim of Greek treachery.[39] His spear does not count as a weapon because before he meets Achilles, as R. D. Williams notes, he has evidently been using the butt end of it to goad his horses, just as the Rutulians are later said to use the reversed spear ("versaque . . . hasta" [9.609–10]) to prod their cattle (Williams 148). Holding the spear in one hand and the reins in the other, he is thrown backwards so that the point of the spear—which has all along been behind him— trails in the dust. But what Virgil says is "versa pulvis inscribitur hasta": literally, "the dust *is inscribed* with the [point of the] reversed spear." No longer a weapon or goad, the spear becomes a writing implement, a sign that all war and all pictures of war are being turned into language by this poem. The ekphrastic effect of the entire passage is epitomized by the picture of Troilus writing— helplessly leaving his own epitaph in the dust. "Here," writes Françoise Meltzer, "is truly the image of an image: for the scribble of the spearhead at once mirrors the tragedy of Troy and the trace left by the tragedy—a trace the frescoes reiterate. This trace—inscription that is not writing per se, but rather recording— insists upon memory and therefore makes the slaughter of Troy an event with meaning" (55). Yet it is Virgil's language that represents the undulating line in the dust *as* a trace of historical meaning; it is Virgil's metaphor that turns the line into a kind of inscription. Exposing the scriptive force of a sub-verbal sign—of a spear-turned-stylus that scribbles over and all but effaces the border between image and word—Virgil's language nonetheless demonstrates its own mastery of the image it creates.[40]

The paintings in the temple of Juno, then, are supplanted by the very language that represents them and their impact on Aeneas. Repeatedly moved to tears, mourning like the women of Troy, he is stupefied and transfixed by empty images. In spite of the masculine ferocity of what most of them portray, they are silent and seductive; they offer themselves to be consumed by the gaze of a man who is thereby threatened with emasculation.[41] That their entrancing power soon gives way to the beauty of Dido suggests that she is herself a work of art, the most beautiful picture—*pulcherrima forma*—to be seen in all Carthage.[42] But Aeneas cannot remain transfixed by her; the imperatives of his mission—the inexorability of the narrative that drives him onward—compel him to forsake her and at the same time to suppress the desire and the pity she excites. So when Dido tearfully begs him to stay, Virgil tells us: "His mind remains unmoved; [her] tears roll in vain" ("Mens immota manet; lacrimae volvuntur inanes" [4.449]). This line shows us what Aeneas has become. The man moved to rivers of tears and to incomparably poignant utterance ("sunt lacrimae rerum . . .") by the empty pictures in Juno's temple is now utterly unmoved by the tears of a living, three-dimensional woman. Her tears are "inanes," empty and powerless to move him.

We are not explicitly told just how Aeneas is affected by the next major work of art he sees: the set of scenes in the temple of Apollo that Daedalus built at Cumae after escaping from Crete.[43] But among several other things represented here is Pasiphae's inhuman lust for the bull when she furtively took the place of a cow ("supposta . . . furto") and begot the "biformis" Minotaur— half-human, half-beast (6.24–26). As Putnam suggestively observes, Pasiphae's cow-disguise recalls the wooden horse that Aeneas has earlier described to Dido, for both of these artifacts are instruments of deceit (Putnam 184). To Aeneas, who *reads* the paintings along with his companions,[44] this one would surely express the danger of a woman's desire and its deceitful effects. But since the cow-disguise was furnished by Daedalus, the deceitfulness of women goes hand in hand with the deceitfulness of art. The painting next described, in fact, shows the "inextricabilis error"—the inextricable winding of the labyrinth Daedalus wrought at Crete. "Error"—literally "wandering" from his predestined path—is precisely what Dido signified to an Aeneas bent on reaching Italy and founding a new nation.

Yet Daedalus is an undeceiver as well as a deceiver. According to Virgil, he himself—not Ariadne—undid the twistings and illusions of the labyrinth by furnishing the thread ("filo") that guided Theseus out of the labyrinth after he had slain the Minotaur.[45] This is an act of compensation. Having used deceit to help Queen Pasiphae gratify her brutish lust and beget a monstrosity, Daedalus unraveled the tangles of his labyrinth because he sympathized with Princess Ariadne's great love for Theseus ("magnum reginae . . . miseratus amorem" [28]). Since the sculptural art or artisanship of Daedalus has led to deception and monstrosity and "inextricabilis error," he must undo its tangles to gratify a legitimate desire. In effect, he must renounce his art and break his spells.

To be sure, this Daedalus is no Prospero. So far from leaving his art behind in leaving Crete, he built the Cumaean temple in which the sculptures of his own disguises and artifacts appear and is also the artist responsible for those paintings. Yet he significantly differs from the Daedalus of Homer, the artist whose very name became a verb for "elaborate." Virgil's Daedalus must recognize both the deceptiveness of his art and his incapacity to represent all that he wishes to sculpt. To dramatize this incapacity, Virgil injects a surprising apostrophe. Addressing neither Daedalus nor any other character in his paintings, he speaks rather to the missing Icarus:

> tu quoque magnam
> partem opere in tanto, sineret dolor, Icare, haberes.
> bis conatus erat casus effingere in auro,
> bis patriae cecidere manus.
>
> (6.30–33)

You also, Icarus, would have had a great share in such a work, if sorrow had permitted. Twice he tried to catch the fall in gold, twice the father's hand fell.

Art doubles life, but here the representational doubling of a fall gives way to the repetition of it: to a double fall, a double failure quadruply underscored by the repetition of *bis* and the doubling of *casus* and *cecidere*, both derived from *cadere*, "to fall." The art of Daedalus failed to keep Icarus aloft when he flew too close to the sun, and the sculptor's own hand fell twice when he tried to catch the fall in gold—to save for art the son he could not save for life. Just as importantly, the pathos of this double failure in the sculptor's art is something represented here by language alone. So while the Carthaginian paintings wring rivers of tears from Aeneas, the sculptures of Daedalus are eclipsed by the superior poignancy of words.

Yet the story of Daedalus told in this ekphrastic passage is more than a story of artistic failure. The central image described here is Daedalus's sculpture of his own labyrinth, the maze of "inextricabilis error." Into this maze was put Pasiphae's misbegotten Minotaur. To this maze and its monstrous inmate were sent each year the seven Athenian sons: the recompense Minos demanded for

the killing in Athens of his own son Androgeus—an event depicted in the entrance way ("in foribus") of the temple (20). In furnishing Theseus with the
thread that leads him out of the maze, Daedalus extricates him from the tangles
of art itself, and thus provides a model for the epic poet, who leads us first into
and then out of the windings of narrative.

To fully understand how Virgil uses the verbal representation of visual art to
guide us along this sinuous trail, we must finally consider the description of the
shield in book 8—the most elaborate ekphrastic passage in the whole poem.
Lessing saw this passage as purely interruptive. Besides describing a finished
shield rather than telling the story of its making, as Homer did, Virgil—says
Lessing—brings "the action . . . to a standstill" with "an insertion, intended
solely to flatter the national pride of the Romans" (96–97).

It is not hard to find justification for this complaint. The scenes on the shield
are said to represent "res Italas Romanorumque triumphos" (625)—Italian
history and Roman conquests. Since more than half the ninety-eight lines of
Virgil's ekphrastic commentary (630–728) concern the victory of Augustus in
the battle of Actium and his triumphal return to Rome, we can safely infer that
Virgil fully intended to celebrate him as the savior of Rome and as its new god
of peace. This propagandistic aim is apparently reinforced by the divine source
and Homeric structure of the shield's commissioning. When Vulcan makes a
shield for Aeneas at the request of his divine mother Venus, he is reenacting
what Hephaestus—the Greek Vulcan—did for Achilles at the request of his
divine mother Thetis.[46] But the circumstances of these two commissions are
suggestively different. Hephaestus does the bidding of Thetis because he is profoundly grateful to her for saving his life when he was thrown out of heaven
(*Iliad* 18.395–408). Vulcan gratifies Venus's request for a shield because he is
sexually captivated by her when, ironically enough, she does to him in the name
of desire something very like what he once did to her as punishment for adultery. From the song of Demodocus in the *Odyssey*, we learn what Hephaestus
did when he discovered an affair between Aphrodite (his wife in the *Odyssey* as
in the *Aeneid*, though not in the *Iliad*) and Mars: he wove a web of superfine
bonds around his marriage bed and caught the lovers in it (*Odyssey* 266–99). In
the *Aeneid*, Venus captures Vulcan with the net of desire. He is "devinctus
amore"—fettered by love—when he agrees to make the shield for her son
(8.394) even though that son was conceived by another of her lovers.[47]

The shield of Aeneas, then, is wrought by and out of the entanglements of
desire. As such, it offers more than either Roman propaganda or recycled
Homer. When we read Virgil's account of the shield in light of the ekphrastic
passages that come before it, we can see how it serves to guide both Aeneas and
us through the net or labyrinth of Virgil's narrative. Already disentangled from
his (technically) adulterous affair with Dido and destined to marry the Latin
princess Lavinia, he learns from the shield that the only way to establish the
Roman nation in peace—"Romanam condere gentem" (1.30)—is to follow
the winding passages of war.

War is the essential link between the Carthaginian paintings of book 1 and the shield of book 8. But while the paintings represent for Aeneas the memory of catastrophic loss and therefore elicit rivers of tears for the past, the shield signifies the promise of future triumph for his descendants. Taking the shield on his shoulder ("atollens umero") in the very last line of book 8 (731), he reminds us that he carried his father on his shoulders out of Troy (2.721–23), literally bearing the burden of the past. But the shield signifies the glory and destiny of his descendants—the "famam . . . et fata nepotum" (8.731). Consequently, he cannot read the shield as he earlier read the paintings and the Cumaean sculptures of Daedalus; he cannot recognize Augustus and Antony and Cleopatra as he recognized Priam and Achilles and Pasiphae. Not knowing the meaning of the scenes on the shield—"ignarus rerum"—he can only wonder at it ("miratur"), take pleasure in the beauty of its figures ("imagine gaudet"), and shoulder it in the faith that in signifying what is ultimately to come, it justifies the war he is about to fight.

The reading of the shield, then, is the task of the narrator, who mediates between the twelfth-century B.C. world of Aeneas and the Augustan age. The narrator often speaks directly to his contemporaries. On the shield, he says, "you could have observed" ("aspiceres") Porsenna in a rage (649–50); "you could have seen" ("videres") all Leucata seething with war (676–77); "you might believe" ("credas") the mass of ships in the battle of Actium were floating islands (691–92). Thus the reader is repeatedly invited to visualize the scenes on the shield even as the narrator's language converts those scenes into a kind of history. Yet remarkably enough, Virgil introduces his ekphrastic commentary by referring to "clipei non enarrabile textum" (625). While this could be safely translated as "the indescribable fabric (or handiwork) of the shield," the earlier emphasis on the reading of sculpted works could well justify our construing it as "the non-narratable text of the shield."[48] Daedalus's labyrinth was a construct of "inextricabilis error." The shield is a fabric of interwoven images that cannot be turned into a single continuous thread of narrative but is nonetheless reconstructed in words that give us a fragmentary history of Rome.

In treating the scenes on the shield as fragments of a history, Virgil reconstructs Homeric ekphrasis with the aid of something written in his own tongue and century: Catullus's poem 64. Produced only about thirty years before Virgil started work on the *Aeneid,* this miniature epic includes a long description of a coverlet depicting—in a series of tableaux—the story of Ariadne. Since I will return to Catullus's poem below, I will note here only how much this passage differs from Homer's account of the shield. Homer gives us a series of thematically linked but sequentially discontinuous segments; whether description, narration, or both, each is discrete and self-contained. By contrast, Catullus turns a series of four tableaux into a continuous story that begins with Ariadne waking on the island of Dia (Naxos) to find herself abandoned, cuts back to her falling in love with Theseus when he comes to Crete, then takes us up to his bitter return to Athens, where the gods exact the revenge Ariadne demands.

Similarly, Virgil's account of the shield of Aeneas represents—with a number of *lacunae*—a sequence of actions culminating in the triumph of Augustus over Cleopatra. But unlike Catullus, Virgil never allows narrative sequence to thwart the recognition of visual representation as such. He is surely indebted to textual narratives, including—along with Catullus 64—the *Annales* of Ennius, which may well have influenced him more than any actual work of graphic art or sculpture he ever saw (Eden 164–65). But like Homer, he knows how to make notional ekphrasis sound actual. He not only locates on the shield several of the scenes he identifies; he periodically registers the friction between the medium of representation and what it signifies.

First of all, crucial events and figures in the history of Rome are assigned to specific places on the shield. The figure of Manlius defending the Capitol against the Gallic invasion is represented "in summo" (652), at the top, a location that iconically signifies his position as "custos Tarpeiae"—guardian of the high Tarpeian Rock. Far removed ("hinc procul") from the scene of chaste matrons on cushioned carriages bearing sacred images through Rome (665–66) is Tartarus, where Cataline pays the penalty for his crimes by hanging from a threatening cliff and quaking at the Furies' glare (668–69); and separate ("secretosque") from these are the righteous, with Cato giving them laws (670). Most conspicuously of all, the battle of Actium and the triumphant return of Augustus are represented "haec inter"—amid all the other scenes, with the image of the sea ("maris . . . imago") around them and in the very center ("in medio") the ships fighting the battle.[49]

Just as notable as the placing of specific scenes on the shield is the frequency and complexity of references to the metals that represent them. Before the description of the shield begins, we learn that the Cyclops working for Vulcan melted down for it brass, gold, and steel (445–46). In the passage on the shield itself, these three metals—along with silver—play various parts—sometimes (as in Homer) with ambiguous effects. The figure of Mars raging in the battle of Actium is wrought in iron ("caelatus ferro" [701]). The goose that warns Manlius of the approaching Gauls is "argenteus" (silver) and flies through "auratis . . . porticibus"—the gilded porticos of the Capitoline temple (655–56). The goose on the shield has evidently been sculpted in silver, but "argenteus" may also refer to the silver used in the statue of the goose on the Capitol, just as "auratis" may refer either to the sculptor's medium or to the metal used on the Capitol itself, which (says Eden) was actually gilded—though not until after the Gallic invasion (Eden 173). The Gauls themselves, we are told, had come through brambles and were shown holding the citadel "defensi tenebris et dono noctis opacae" (658)—"protected by darkness and by the gift of a shadowy night," a night whose tenebrous texture is verbally signified by the doubling of references to it (*tenebris* and *opacae*). Yet through this Rembrandtian shadow that has been somehow wrought in metal shines gold: "golden [*aurea*] their hair and golden [*aurea*] their clothing; they glowed in striped cloaks, and their milky necks [*lactea cola*] were hung with gold [*auro*]" (659–61). The same word—*aurea*—describes both the hair and the clothing of the Gauls, and a kindred word—*auro*—identifies their necklaces. The three different uses of a word for gold denote three different kinds of relation between sculpted sign and thing signified: the necklaces represented by Vulcan's gold may have been gold in fact, but actual hair can be gold only in color, and the actual substance of clothing represented by gold is indeterminate.

When we come to the sea in the middle of the shield, Virgil's words further complicate the friction between metallic signs and what they signify. The "imago" (image or likeness) of the sea was "aurea," but was foaming dark blue in the white wave ("sed fluctu spumabat caerula cano" [671–72]). This can only mean that a sea sculptured in gold has been somehow made to appear both white and blue, just as Hephaestus makes gold look like dark, freshly ploughed earth. Also in the midst of this sculpted sea is "classis aeratas" (675)—a "bronzed fleet" representing an actual fleet that must have been chiefly made of something else.[50] On the other hand, when the narrator says that "you could see the waves glowing with gold" ("auro . . . effulgere fluctus" [677]), he may well refer both to the sculptor's metal and the sunlit color of what it here represents.

These occasional hints at *con*vergence between the sculptor's medium and its referent only heighten the sense of *di*vergence conveyed elsewhere. As Andrew Becker observes of ancient Greek ekphrasis generally ("Reading" 7), Virgil's ekphrasis here entails a double movement of illusion-making and illusion-breaking. The poet's tribute to the sculptor's illusionistic skill in duplicating the visible world, in making his art a transparent window on it, is repeatedly complicated by illusion-breaking references to the artist's medium. When the poet thus exposes the difference—the representational friction—between the visual medium and its referent, he reminds us of the corresponding difference between the visual medium and the verbal one: between visual art and the words that represent it. In so doing, he reactivates the struggle for mastery between the image and the word. A golden likeness ("imago aurea") of the sea resists conversion into the kind of sea that words signify when they describe it as blue foaming white—dynamic and fluid. So even as Virgil locates specific scenes on the shield, names particular colors, and identifies the metallic media of representation, even as he highlights the distinctively visual features that were suppressed in the passage on the Carthaginian frescoes, he mobilizes all the powers of language and narrative to overcome the fixity of the sculpted pose.

We have seen how the pose recurs in Virgil's account of the frescoes, which take possession of Aeneas's gaze precisely because they represent objects and figures caught in crucially significant positions: the snowy tents of the doomed Rhesus, Troilus flung backwards with his spearpoint trailing in the dust, Priam stretching out his hands for the body of Hector. Aeneas is stupefied by the fixating power of these poses, which are supplanted, as we have seen, by the superlatively beautiful form of Dido. Yet by the time he gets the shield, he has put behind him both her picture-perfect beauty and the pictures she has commissioned for her new temple: pictures that threaten to fix him in what the text would have us see as impotent, effeminate mourning for an immutable past, just as Dido herself threatens to fix him in Carthage.

Unlike the frescoes, the shield represents not only the future but a sequence of actions culminating in the triumph of Augustus, who demonstrates his masculine power and authority precisely by defeating the barbarous alliance of Antony and Cleopatra, the Egyptian "conjunx" who shamefully follows him into battle ["sequiturque (nefas)"] (688). If Aeneas could recognize his past self in the Carthaginian frescoes, the shield shows him what he might have become in a marriage to Dido: party to a conjunction that would seem to Roman eyes just about as nefarious as the "mixtum genus" of the Minotaur, monument to the shameful lust ("Veneris monumenta nefandae") of Pasiphae that Aeneas saw sculpted at Cumae (6.26). In the shield's sculptured display of what lies *beyond* Aeneas, Cleopatra actually evokes two pictured women he has seen before: Pasiphae and the "bellatrix" Penthesilea, whose bare-breasted figure raging and burning amidst her soldiers ("furens mediisque in milibus ardet") is the very last picture that captivates Aeneas's eye at Carthage (1.490–93). Likewise "in mediis" (8.696), Cleopatra is shown on the shield calling her fleet with the ancestral rattle and never looking back ("a tergo") at the twin snakes ("geminos . . . anguis") behind her (696–97). The twin snakes link her to the Medusa-like figure of Allecto, whose writhing hair sprouts "geminos . . . anguis" as she makes the eyes of Turnus stiffen with terror (7.446–50).[51] But unlike Allecto, and unlike the face of Medusa herself on the shield of Agamemnon (*Iliad* 11.36–37), Cleopatra has no apotropaic power. She who would not look back is forced to *go* back, to retreat with all her forces ("omnes vertebant terga" [706]), and as she is shown borne along by waves and the northwest wind ("undis et Iapyge ferri" [710]), she is caught in a moment of blank terror for what the immediate future will bring—just as Dido was earlier. Preparing her own immolation, Dido was "pallida morte futura" (4.644), pale at the prospect of imminent death. The last image of Cleopatra that Vulcan wrought on the shield was likewise a figure shown amid the slaughter "pallentem morte futura" (8.709), terrified of time itself even as it passes "now, this instant" ("iam iamque" [708]). Neither Cleopatra nor Dido can face the future, can endure the passage of time; both are vanquished by men who move inexorably forward, like the narrative Virgil makes from the scenes on the shield.

At some level, then, the man who recognized his past self in the Carthaginian frescoes might see his future self in the figure of Augustus, who epitomizes both decisive action and decisive conquest of a shamefully bellicose woman. Envoiced by the poet, the scenes fixed on the center of the shield are made to tell a story that moves in every sense. While Aeneas is grief-stricken and fixated by the Carthaginian frescoes, he is mobilized by the shield, which he takes upon his shoulder ("atollens umero" [731]) in preparation for battle even as he admires it. Yet for all its claims to temporal progression, for all its apparent overcoming of both the sculpted pose and the apotropaic figure of the raging female, the passage on the shield cannot simply be read as a story in which the fixed and fixating image is mastered by the moving narrative word. The Romans are indeed represented as fighting against barbarous Egyptian idols—the "omnigenumque deum monstra et latrator Anubis" (698), monstrous effigies of gods of every kind (recalling Pasiphae's "mixtum genus") and the barking dog Anubis. But Augustus is no iconoclast. He enters the battle with household gods and great gods—"penatibus et magnis dis" (679)—and against the Egyptian icons the Romans hold up images of their own: Neptune, Venus, Minerva (699).[52] Furthermore, Augustus himself is iconized, successively cast in two magisterial poses.[53] Leading the way into battle, he is first shown standing on the high stern of his ship ("stans celsa in puppi") sprouting twin flames ("geminas . . . flammas" [680]) from his temples—the celestial antithesis to the twin snakes of Cleopatra and Allecto. Next, he appears in the midst of his triumphant return to Rome reviewing the procession of conquered races while sitting at the snow-white threshold of shining Phoebus ("sedens niveo candentis limine Phoebi" [720])—that is, at the entrance to the brand-new temple built with solid blocks of Luna marble on Palatine hill and dedicated to Apollo.[54] In occupying the very spot where the statue of Apollo would stand— the *limen* of the new temple—Augustus becomes at once a god and an icon.

The narrative generated from the scenes on the shield, then, culminates in an image—the relief of Augustus apotheosized and enthroned. The iconoclasm implied by the Roman conquest of Cleopatra and her barbarous foreign idols is negated by what Virgil makes of Augustus himself, who is represented as something very like a sculpted white marble figure. Yet the embossed figure of Augustus differs from any other work of visual art described so far. Against the Dionysian fury of Cleopatra and her raging precursors, his figure embodies an Apollonian serenity, and in its assurance and repose, it is the antithesis of the Trojan figures in the Carthaginian frescoes. While their poses of desperation and vulnerability provoke tears of impotent regret for the past, his seated figure excites confidence in the future, which may help to explain why Aeneas rejoices in the scenes on the shield ("imagine gaudet" [730]) even though he does not know what they mean.[55] Thus for all its narrativity, the passage on the shield bears renewed witness to the power of visual art, and specifically to its *political* power—its capacity to represent and perpetuate political authority.[56] While virtually all the graphic works described earlier in this poem suggest narratives that move beyond the moment depicted, the relief of Augustus divinely enthroned is the chronological *terminus ad quem* of Virgil's entire narrative—the ultimate destination of his epic about the founding of Rome.

But the epic narrative of Aeneas's exploits stops, of course, far short of this destination. It ends not with a picture of authority in repose but with a killing precipitated by a work of graphic art: the studded swordbelt that Turnus took from Pallas, son of Aeneas's ally Evander, after mortally wounding him. Having himself now wounded Turnus, Aeneas recognizes the belt just as Turnus has nearly convinced him to spare his life. Enraged by this reminder of what Turnus has done to the boy that Evander entrusted to Aeneas's care, Aeneas plunges his blade into Turnus's chest.

Since Virgil makes no reference here to the scene on the belt, we cannot know for certain just what Aeneas saw at this crucial moment. But we do know that "oculis . . . saevi monimenta doloris / exuviasque hausit" (12.945–46)— "with his eyes he devoured the reminders and spoils of a bitter sorrow." The word "hausit"—devoured or drank in—recalls the metaphor used for Aeneas's response to the Carthaginian frescoes: "pascit"—he fed his soul with depiction (1.464). So it seems more than likely that Aeneas's recognition of the belt was prompted partly by the scene sculpted on it, which is described at precisely the point where Turnus takes the belt from Pallas (10.495–500). Here we learn that the belt is embossed ("impressum") with a scene of filthy slaughter and bloody marriage beds ("caesa . . . foede thalamique cruenti"): the sons of Ae- gyptus murdered on their wedding night ("una sub nocte iugali") by their brides, the daughters of Danaus, who had been driven out of Egypt by the sons and then forced to marry them. Like Aeneas's killing of Turnus, the killing de- picted on the swordbelt was an act of revenge, and since one daughter of Danaus begot the royal line that ruled the Danaans (i.e., the Greeks), there may be a further parallel; in both cases, a vengeful murder precedes the founding of a nation.[57] But in any case, the very last thing Aeneas sees in this poem is a pic- ture of murder. Prompting neither the sorrow he drew from the Carthaginian frescoes nor the joy he drew from the scenes on the shield, the swordbelt infuri- ates him. Insofar as its visual art affects him, it no longer usurps his gaze, reduc- ing him to impotent mourning. Ironically, it drives him instead to reenact the behavior of the murderous women.

The final act recorded in the poem, then, ambiguously testifies to the power of visual art. On the one hand, since Aeneas takes no explicit notice of the scene on the shield, we can read the final act as evidence that he has broken the mes- meric grip of the visual arts to enter a world of action. On the other hand, since he visually devours the belt, we can infer that he fully experiences the scene depicted, so that the swordbelt gives him at once the motive and the cue for immediate action. No longer fixated by pictures of an irrecoverable past or sub- tly mobilized by grand prefigurations of a scarcely intelligible future, Aeneas sees in the swordbelt what he must do: strike a blow for Pallas, in whose name he kills Turnus (12.948–49). The work of art has entered so deeply into the rhythm and texture of the narrative—has been so fully converted from the fix- ity of its poses to the dynamism of its kinetic effect—that it ceases to be inter- ruptive, ornamental, or even antithetical to the poetic word. Language itself has devoured depiction.

III

VISIBLE SPEECH: THE ENVOICING OF SCULPTURE
IN DANTE'S *PURGATORIO*

So far we have seen that a recurrent feature of ekphrasis is contention. To represent the technique as well as the content of a work of graphic art, the poet must reckon with representational friction, with the conflict between the signifier or material medium of representation and the signified—the objects or figures represented. On the shield of Achilles, how is gold made to look like earth that has been ploughed? On the shield of Aeneas, how is the golden image ("imago / aurea") of the sea made to resemble or even signify deep-blue waves foaming in whitecaps? We might answer these questions by some fancy hypotheses about enameling or by simply invoking the superhuman virtuosity of the sculptor (Hephaestus / Vulcan). But no matter how the questions are answered, and no matter how lifelike the craftsmanship is said to be, the poet's language continually acknowledges the fact that it *is* craftsmanship, that it is visual representation: we are asked to imagine not real earth or real waves but rather gold that has been made to resemble these things. To experience visual representation as such, or to even to imagine this experience, we must be conscious of difference permeating and complicating likeness. The consciousness of difference—the sense of friction between the medium and the subject matter of a work of art—is precisely what makes the difference between a copy and an imitation, or between delusion and aesthetic illusion.[58]

At the very beginning of Dante's account of the sculptures seen by Virgil and himself on the terrace of the proud in canto 10 of the *Purgatorio,* this difference between reality and graphic verisimilitude is explicitly defined as a rivalry. The wall of the cliff beside the path encircling the mountain, Dante tells us, "was adorned with such carvings that not only Polycletus but Nature herself would there be put to shame" (10.32–33). These sculptures not only surpass the work of the late fifth-century B.C. Greek sculptor who "was supposed to be unsurpassed in carving images of men" (Singleton 2:202); they surpass "la natura." Here Dante's lines prompt the first of many questions: in what sense can sculpture surpass nature?

Traditionally, the virtuosity of a representational work of art is measured by its fidelity to nature. When Arachne challenges Minerva to a weaving contest in the *Metamorphoses,* Arachne wins (a Pyrrhic victory, of course) because her pictures of such figures as Europa and the bull are so lifelike: "verum taurum, freta vera putares" (6.104)—"a real bull and real waves you would think them." Dante himself salutes in this way the verisimilitude of the figures carved in the pavement trod by Virgil and himself: "Morti li morti e i vivi parean vivi" (12.67)—"Dead the dead, and the living seemed alive." In fact when Dante goes on to say "whoever saw the truth saw no better than I" ("non vide mei di mi chi vide il vero" [12.68]), he claims to have experienced just as much as—

but not necessarily any more than—eyewitnesses to the reality of what the pavement sculptures represent.[59] Yet the wall sculptures are said to surpass nature, for they are made by God, the omnipotent *fabbro*. We can begin to understand this claim, perhaps, if we think of Nature itself as a *fabbro*—that is, a reproducer of living creatures.[60] Sculptures made directly by God surpass any natural being or object for the same reason that the prelapsarian Adam and Eve—made directly by God—surpass in their physical perfection anyone created by natural reproduction.

With singular aptness, then, the very first of the wall sculptures described in canto 10 of the *Purgatorio* represents the moment at which Mary learns that she is to be the vessel of supernatural reproduction—directly inseminated by God. The "Ave" silently spoken by the gentle appearance ("atto soave" [40]) of the sculpted angel reverses the name of "Eva," which we have heard as recently as canto 8 (line 99) and which is subtly echoed in the main verb of the sentence introducing the angel figure: "pareva" (10.37), "appeared." Mary evokes the prelapsarian perfection of Eve, but her child will reverse the consequences of Eve's sin even as her exemplary humility reverses the pride that—as we are shortly reminded—Eve has bequeathed to her children (12.70–72). But an equally important reversal here involves the characteristically ekphrastic translation of icon into word. Traditionally, the moment at which Mary conceived Christ—here signified by the angel's "Ave"—is the moment at which, in the words of John, the Word became Flesh, the *logos* became *sarx*. In the sculpture that represents this moment, the flesh of the living Mary has been turned into white marble. To this extent she recalls Niobe, sculpted on the pavement (12.37–39), who was actually turned to stone for boasting of a fecundity surpassing Latona's. But unlike Niobe, whose petrified form can now do no more than weep for her slain children, the sculpted Mary can speak with her "atto" (10.43): with a pose or gesture so eloquent that speech is stamped ("impressa") upon it just as a figure ("figura") is stamped on wax (10.43–45). Dante's ekphrasis brings the incarnation full circle. The Word is made flesh, which in turn is made stone, which in turn is made to speak, to become Word again: *Ecce ancilla Dei,* behold the handmaid of God. Word and figure are interchangeable. For us if not for Dante himself, the very word "impressa," which here denotes the graphic stamping of a figure on wax, adumbrates the meaning it would come to have as soon as printing made possible the stamping of words on paper.

As much as anything else, it is their uncanny eloquence—their capacity for what Dante calls "visible speech" ("visible parlare" [10.95])—that makes these God-created sculptures surpass all human handiwork and even nature herself. Natural figures—more precisely the shades of living persons that Dante sees here—can say a little with posture alone; at the end of the canto, one of the many shades bent double under the weight of the stones they must carry to expiate the sin of pride seems to say in his looks ("ne li atti") "I can no more" ("Piu non posso" [139]). But since these suffering stone-bearers are themselves compared to the figures sometimes sculpted as corbels, holding up a roof or ceiling with their knees doubled up to their chests (10.130–32), the shades' ability to speak with posture alone is mediated through sculpture, and even their sculpturesque poses "can [say] no more," essentially, than the tears of the petrified Niobe. The little they can say with their burdened bodies cannot match the visible speech of the actual sculptures beside them.

The sense of competition and rivalry that permeates Dante's whole treatment of sculpture in the *Purgatorio* springs at once from the ekphrastic tradition that stands behind him and from his own ambition to remake it. Homer and Virgil have shown us that ekphrasis activates various kinds of contention— friction between the visual medium and what it represents, conflict between graphic or sculptural stasis and narrative momentum, the struggle for power between word and image as rival modes of representation and rival instruments of political power. In the *Purgatorio,* the conflicts traditionally stirred by ekphrasis are intensified by Dante's determination to contend with his predecessors—ultimately and implicitly with Homer, directly and explicitly with Virgil.

Dante heightens the sense of contention by reminding us of what Virgil did with ekphrasis. Consider first the story of Dante's flight to the gateway of Purgatory proper. When he tells us that he dreamed of being snatched up into the sky like Ganymede by a gold-feathered eagle (9.19–24), he recalls the design woven into the gold cloak awarded to the captain of the winning boat in the rowing races that Aeneas conducts at Sicily: there, says Virgil, was depicted the boy "whom Jove's quick weapon-carrier took up high in his talons from Mount Ida" ("quem praepes ab Ida / sublimem pedibus rapuit Iovis armiger uncis" [*Aeneid* 5.254–55]). Since Ganymede figures so prominently in Virgil's ekphrastic account of a cloak offered as the prize in a competition, Dante's comparison of himself with Ganymede at the very moment when he is wafted to the gate of Purgatory subtly hints that an ekphrastic competition with Virgil himself is about to begin. The hint is confirmed at the beginning of canto 10, when Dante and Virgil both stand just "within the threshold [*soglia*] of the gate" of purgatory, where they find the incomparable bas-reliefs carved from pure white marble ("di marmo candido" [10.31]). The reference to white marble reliefs carved just within the threshold of the purgatorial gate plainly links this whole ekphrastic passage to Virgil's account of the shield of Aeneas, for Virgil's account culminates with the spectacle of Augustus sitting "niveo candentis limine Phoebi" (*Aeneid* 8.720)—on the snowy threshold of the shining new white marble temple of Apollo, where the statue of the god would shortly stand. With this sculpted icon of a conquering emperor virtually deified by his power and glory Dante asks us to compare a set of sculpted figures distinguished for their humility—including a Roman emperor who postpones the glory of conquest in order to help a widow.

The sense of competition implied by these two allusions to Virgil's ekphrastic art is intensified in canto 12, where the litany of once-proud figures sculpted in the pavement concludes with Troy in ruins, "basso e vile" [12.62]—cast

down and vile. Here is Dante's version of the frescoes that made Aeneas weep—
the Carthaginian pictures of the desperate Troilus, the doomed Rhesus, the pathetic Priam. These pictures of "mortalia" designed to touch and move the
mind and heart of the viewer become in Dante's poem the sculpted sign ("il
segno" [12.63]) of pride brought down to contemptible ruin. The pictures are
effaced by the pavement design just as—in another pavement—the tapestry
woven by Arachne in the *Metamorphoses* gives way in the *Purgatorio* to the
sculpted figure of Arachne hanging on the shreds ("li stracci") of her
handiwork.

Arachne's humiliation is particularly striking here because the weaving con-
test she has with Minerva in Ovid's poem can be read as a poetry contest. As
Teodolinda Barolini notes (51), each tapestry is woven ("texitur" [6.62]) to represent an ancient story ("vetus . . . argumentum" [69]), and in describing what
Minerva does, Ovid alternates between "pingit" (71) and "inscribit" (74),
which—as we have seen already—may mean either "mark" or "write."
Arachne's challenge to Minerva is implicitly textual and explicitly subversive.
While Minerva shows twelve gods symmetrically seated on either side of Jupiter
and—in each corner of her web—a cautionary scene of what happens to those
who dare to defy or challenge the gods, Arachne weaves pictures of Jupiter and
other gods disguising themselves to deceive, seduce, or rape mortal women. As
Eleanor Leach suggests, Arachne's irreverent portrayal of the gods in libidinous
heat corrects and balances the authoritarian picture of divine power and justice
that we get from Minerva (Leach 103–4). But when Dante juxtaposes the
sculpted scene of a contemptibly ruined Troy with the sculpted figure of a
woman punished for striving to outdo a goddess in textile (proto-textual) representation, he reconstructs the meaning of Arachne's flawless tapestry. Standing,
I believe, for every masterpiece of visual art represented in classical literature
and surviving now only in shreds ("li stracci" [44]), Arachne's tapestry suggests
that nothing wrought by any human or divine artist of the classical world—
whether Polycletus, Daedalus, or even Hephaestus / Vulcan—can match the
sculptures of *Purgatorio*. And by implication, nothing woven in words to represent any classical work of visual art can match what Dante says about those
sculptures.

Dante also comes close to making this claim in canto 11, where Oderisi
modestly dismisses the fame he has earned as an illuminator and observes how
the glory of each great painter—and then each great poet—is eclipsed by a
successor: "Cimabue thought to hold the field in painting, and now Giotto has
the cry, so that the other's fame is dim; so has the one Guido taken from the
other the glory of our tongue—and he perchance is born that shall chase the
one and the other from the nest" (11.94–99). As Cimabue gives way to Giotto
in graphic art, the verbal art of Guido Guinizelli and Guido Cavalcanti may be
surpassed by what Dante is now writing. Even though Oderisi condemns his
own pride in what is just one of three cantos devoted to the purgation of this
sin, Dante does not hesitate to imply the superiority of his art, and at the same

time to imply the superiority of word to image, of "la gloria de la lingua" (98) to "la pittura" (94). "His pride," writes Barolini, "exists for good reason: if anyone's fame will endure, it will be his; if anyone's mimesis can rival God's, it is his" (56). Yet Dante does not presume to rival God's mimesis, as he would if he himself were sculpting the Annunciation or simply describing his own independent vision of it. Instead, he is the translator or interpreter of God's art, turning the image back into the word from which it emanates.

The presence of Dante as interpreter and articulator of God's art is crucial to this process of conversion, and one of many things that distinguish Dantean ekphrasis from its precursors. In the *Iliad* and the *Aeneid*, interpretation is subordinate to exhibition, and virtually all inferences about the meaning of the graphic work described must be made by the reader. Every narrative about a work of visual art, of course, is implicitly interpretive; when Virgil says that Vulcan had made on the shield the mother wolf nursing the legendary twins and fondling each in turn ("mulcere alternos" [8.634]), the poet is inferring motion from the sculpted pose, just as Homer does regularly when he tells us what the scenes on the shield of Achilles represent. But Homer never explains how the meaning of the scenes is made, and no character *in* the poem has anything to say about what they mean; Achilles himself simply looks at the shield with a paradoxical combination of rage and joy (19.15–18). Visual art in the *Aeneid* is likewise uninterpreted. Aeneas reacts to the Carthaginian frescoes only with tears, and though he and his companions "would have read through" ("perlegerent") the sculptures in the Cumaean temple of Apollo (*Aeneid* 6.34), Aeneas never offers a read*ing* of any picture he sees. He has no idea what the scenes on the shield signify, and Virgil himself offers no more than a minimally interpretive word about them now and then, as when he says of the sculpted fleets, "you would believe [*credas*] the Cyclades were floating on the sea" (8.691–92).[61]

While there is virtually no explicit interpretation of the visual art represented in the *Iliad* and the *Aeneid*, interpretation is implied by occasional passages of prosopopeia—passages in which the silent work of art is given the power to speak. In Homer's account of the shield of Achilles, we learn the gist of what is said by the two disputants in the first city scene (18.497–500) and the two factions of the besieging army in the second one (510–12), and we are also told that the youth with the lyre in the vineyard scene sings the song of Linos (570). Between Homer and Virgil, the first *Idyll* of Theocritus (third century B.C.) contains a description of a decorated cup which shows, among other things, a beautiful woman with two men contending for her "from either side in alternate speech" (35–36).[62] The *Aeneid* offers just one notable instance of prosopopeia: the poet's apostrophe to Icarus in the passage describing the sculpted temple walls at Cumae (6.30–31). But Icarus is called upon precisely because he is *not* sculpted on the walls, and the only sound Virgil draws from the scenes on the shield is that of Cleopatra calling her fleet with a sistrum—a sort of rattle (8.696).

In the *Purgatorio,* prosopopeia permeates the description of the sculptures because Dante is continually representing not just the sculptures themselves, but his response to them. Commentators have often noted that the set of twelve tercets on the pavement sculptures (12.25–60)—the tercets anaphorically starting with "Vedea" ("I saw"), "O," and "Monstrava" ("It showed")—may be read as an acrostic spelling of UOM, man, and hence a way of vividly inscribing the name of man into the verbal versions of sculptures representing his most characteristic sin—pride. But the "man" most conspicuously present in these stanzas is not just a generic construct. It is Dante himself, who admits his own pride at the end of the very next canto (13.136–38) and who emphatically represents himself as both viewer and interviewer of the sculptures he describes. In the progress of the acrostic, what each pavement showed (third-person "Monstrava") depends on what the eye of the first-person "I" saw ("Vedea"), and the apostrophic "O" addressed to four of the sculpted figures implicitly gives them the power to speak. It is surely no accident that Dante recapitulates his acrostic in a final tercet on the pavement sculpture of the fallen Troy ("*V*edeva . . . / *O* Ilion . . . / *M*onstrava . . ." [61–63]), for in personalizing the ekphrastic mode, in making his own visual reading and invocation of the sculptures central to his account of them, he is walking over and past the precedent set by Virgilian ekphrasis.

In fact he has already passed this precedent by the time he reaches canto 12, for in canto 10 he has represented the wall sculptures as visible speech. To understand the kind of prosopopeia offered in canto 10, we must realize that for Dante at this point—as later for Keats in the "Ode on a Grecian Urn"—the complex effect of visual art makes it transcend the purely auditory art of song. Earlier in the *Purgatorio,* Dante and Virgil are both momentarily enraptured by familiar notes: the opening words from one of Dante's own *canzoni* sung to him by Casella. But from this seductive entrancement with the music of his own song he and Virgil are harshly awakened by Cato, who bids them shake off their langor and get moving (2.112–23). As James Chiampi suggests (103), Dante writes here in the spirit of Augustine, who recalls in the *Confessions* his struggle to break free of musical enchantment: "The delights of the ear had more firmly entangled and subdued me, but you broke them and set me free. I confess that when melodies that your words bring to life are sung by a sweet and well-trained voice, I now find therein a little rest, not such that I cling to them, but such that I may rise up when I wish" (10.33). In moving literally upward from the shore where he hears the music to the terrace where he sees the sculptures, Dante makes a double ascent: from sound to vision, and from his own art to the art of God. Yet he scarcely leaves sound behind. He is ushered onto the terrace of the sculptures by the "dolce suono"—the "sweet sound"—of the *Te Deum laudamus* (9. 139–40), and to represent the supreme and visionary art of God for us, he must translate it into the words of the song he is even now singing. He must make it speak.

To make it speak is in one sense to presume to rival God's art, to replace the divinely made image with the poet's own word. But as I have already suggested, Dante does not aim to rival the images he represents; he turns them back into the words from which they originated—the words of Scripture and sacred legend. He represents the sculptures as the very embodiment of those words, just as Christ himself embodied the word of God.[63] Thus Dante dramatically heightens the ekphrastic techniques we have seen in the work of his ancient predecessors: prosopopeia, representational friction, and narrative. While Homer and Theocritus refer to speeches represented by visual art but never quote them, Dante tells us exactly what the sculpted figures say.[64] Secondly, by showing how a silent art generates audible meaning, he sharpens the friction between the visible image and the spoken words it signifies, between the graphic medium and its quite literal message. Finally, he uses spoken words to construct or evoke a series of complete dramatic narratives concluding with the "story" ("istoria" [71]) of Trajan that is "storied" ("storiata" [73]) in marble—a redundancy clearly calculated to underline the narrative force of the sculptures.[65]

"Visible speech"—"visible parlare" (10.95)—is Dante's phrase for the silent eloquence of the sculptures. There is of course nothing inherently oxymoronic about the phrase. It can be used to designate not just all sign language and all gesture but also all writing, and in spite of the ancient Simonidean assumption that visual art must be silent or dumb, there is nothing in the nature of painting or sculpture that makes either one fundamentally incompatible with the visible speech of inscription. Long before Dante, statues, tombs, and funerary columns were customarily inscribed with words that gave them a voice, such as "I am the tomb of famous Glauca" (third century B.C.).[66] About a hundred years after the composition of the *Purgatorio,* an unknown Florentine painter produced a fresco in which a kneeling Mary cups one naked breast to a kneeling adult Christ, gestures to a group of miniature penitents gathered at her knees, and says—in an inscription stretching from her head to Christ's—"Dearest son, because of the milk I gave you, have mercy on them" (Miles 193, 195). Nevertheless, the sculptures Dante describes in canto 10 are unaccompanied by inscriptions of any kind. What makes their speech unprecedented on earth— "novello a noi perche qui non si trova" (10.96)—is the fact that it emanates from marble walls unmarked by any words.

To be sure, the sculpted figures have been cut into the marble *like* words; scene after scene is called *intagliato* (38, 55), "engraved." But Dante repeatedly insists on the physical silence of the sculptures so as to heighten our sense of representational friction, so as to show how the expressiveness of poses alone— beginning with the "atto soave" ("gentle pose") of the angel (38)—makes the viewer feel the silence overcome. In the first sculpture, Dante says, the angel of the annunciation "appeared to us so truly graven in a gentle pose that it seemed not a silent image: one would have sworn that he was saying '*Ave!*'" (10.37– 40). The second sculpture intensifies the friction between the medium and what it represents. In front of the holy ark on the ox-drawn cart "appeared people, and all the company, divided into seven choirs, made two of my senses say, the one 'No,' the other 'Yes, they are singing'" (10.58–60). Out of the contradiction between one sense and another rises the sense—both cognitive and sensory—of silent speech. The poet's ears cannot hear the music, but his eyes ("li occhi" [54]) see it, just as they see in sculpted smoke the incense that his nose cannot smell (61–63).

This emphasis on what his senses say—or said—about the sculpted choir reinforces what Dante clearly implies throughout his account of the sculptures: their speech—their overcoming of silence—requires the full cooperation of the viewer as interpreter of what is seen. Dante's experience of speech in the viewing of the sculptures actually results from three things: the expressiveness of the engraved figure itself mimicking the visible language of gesture ("atto"), Dante's inference ("one would have sworn") about the meaning of the way the figure appeared ("pareva"), and—most of the time—his prior knowledge of the story represented. Without such knowledge he could presumably see that the sculptures represented a winged figure with a young woman bowing to him, a crowd of open-mouthed people, a man dancing, and a man on horseback confronted by an old woman. But all of the words and sounds he attributes to the sculpted figures could be plausibly inferred only by a viewer familiar with the stories behind them, and especially with Scripture. Only a viewer who knows the story of the Annunciation in the Latin of Saint Jerome's Vulgate, for instance, could see or hear the words "Ecce ancilla Dei" emanating from the "atto" of a sculpted young woman.

The envoicing of the sculpted figures, therefore, inevitably returns them to the Word that begot them: the Word that made not only the figures but the creatures they represent, and that also initiated the first of the stories they visually reenact. Even as he turns or returns figures to words, the poet turns their poses into dramatized narrative, *storia:* the angel's salutation prompts Mary's humble answer; David's dancing before the ark provokes Michal's scorn; and in the fullest story of all, a grieving widow gradually persuades the emperor Trajan to delay his expedition so as to take vengeance for the killing of her son. But these three narratives do not form a simple chain. Though the sculptures representing them follow one another in space—David is beyond Mary ("di retro da Maria" [50]) and Trajan is beyond Michal (72)—the narratives do not follow each other in time; instead, starting with the originating moment of the New Testament, they move back to the Old Testament and then forward again to the period after Christ's death. The effect is palimpsestic or pentimental, as if one scene were superimposed on another. Seen from the vantage point of the annunciation, David prefigures Mary, especially if we know the full text of his marbled *istoria:* when Michal scorned David for dancing girt up "in the sight of the maidservants of his retainers," he replied: "Blessed be the Lord, who chose me . . . as a leader over the people of the Lord, over Israel. Therefore I will disport myself before the Lord and . . . I will be vile in your eyes. But with the maidservants . . . I shall indeed be held in honor" (2 Samuel 6:20–22). David's humility, then, explicitly anticipates that of the *ancilla Dei*. Likewise, Trajan and the grieving widow replay—in more earthly fashion—the drama enacted by the angel and Mary: the widow hails Trajan, and he humbly offers to serve her.

Nancy Vickers has shown that the text describing the sculpted figures of Trajan and the widow has been woven of strands both verbal and visual.[67] According to Vickers, the passage on Trajan verbally reconstructs an actual piece of sculpture—a scene from Trajan's column in Rome—by means of a story first written down in the early eighth century and overlaid with allusions to scripture: to the words of God urging justice for widows (Isaiah 1:17–18) and to Christ's story of the widow who persuades an unjust judge to take vengeance on her behalf (Luke 18:1–8). In the actual relief on Trajan's column, the seated emperor gazes down on a kneeling man who symbolizes a conquered nation (Vickers, "Seeing" 76). But if this is the sculpted scene that moved Gregory to pray for Trajan's salvation, its imperial meaning has been radically revised. The conquered man who kneels to the emperor in submission becomes a woman who masters him with her eloquence. Turning from the imperial project of conquest signified by the golden eagles on the banners fluttering above his troops, Trajan becomes the very model of humility. In this case, then, ekphrasis not only envoices sculpted figures and thus elicits a story from them; it also doubly demonstrates the power of the word over the image. Even as the widow's words boldly penetrate the intimidating spectacle of Roman military might, Dante's text remakes the meaning of a sculpted work originally designed to say essentially what Shelley's Ozymandias declares: "Look on my works, ye mighty, and despair." In Dante, as in Homer and Virgil, the image is finally mastered by the word.

Chapter Two

WEAVING RAPE
Ekphrastic Metamorphoses of the Philomela Myth from Ovid to Shakespeare

Above the antique mantel was displayed
As though a window gave upon the sylvan scene
The change of Philomel, by the barbarous king
So rudely forced; . . .
T. S. Eliot, *The Waste Land*

To this point we have traced a genealogy of ekphrasis that is predominantly male. The shield of Achilles, made by the male Hephaestus for a warrior whose ferocious masculinity seems calculated to suppress all memory of the transvestism thrust upon him in childhood by his overprotective mother, is decorated with scenes that chiefly represent the doings of men. The temple frescoes described in the first book of the *Aeneid* likewise give us almost exclusively men at war, and the shield of Aeneas, made by the male Vulcan for a man who has already sacrificed the needs of a woman to the imperatives of his mission, represents the succession of men who would establish the Roman empire, culminating in the victory of Augustus over a barbarous queen. Women appear in all of the sculptures on Dante's terrace of pride, but their figures are wrought by an explicitly male craftsman, *lo fabbro* (*Purgatorio* 10.99), and they play subordinate roles: the paradigmatically submissive *ancilla Dei,* the scornful wife doomed to be punished for her haughtiness, and the grieving supplicant. The supplicant gets her way with Trajan, of course, just as Homer's Thetis and Virgil's Venus talk—or body-talk—their men into making shields, but in all these cases visual art is represented as largely a medium made by, for, and about men, who—even when they supposedly embody humility—can appear as emperors and kings.

I

PHILOMELA'S GRAPHIC TALE

Against this formidable tradition of what might be called masculine ekphrasis, it is striking to consider an alternative genealogy of the mode that begins with Ovid's account of how Philomela wove for her sister's eye the story of her own rape. The verbal version of the story appears in the sixth book of the *Metamorphoses,* where we are told that Philomela was violated by Tereus, king of Thrace and husband of her sister Procne, when—at Procne's own request—he had gone to fetch Philomela from her native Athens to visit her sister's new home. The rape is doubly heinous because it subtly reeks of incest. In Athens, after the very first sight of Philomela's beauty has ignited Tereus's desire for her, the sight of her kissing and embracing her father Pandion to gain his consent for her departure fuels his desire to be in the father's place—"esse parens vellet" (6.482); and in entrusting Philomela to him, Pandion unwittingly sanctions this incestuous wish by voicing the prayer that he guard her with a father's love—"patrio ut tuearis amore" (6.499). Tereus guards her as a captor ("raptor") guards its prey, as the ravenous bird of Jupiter—"predator . . . / . . . Iovis ales" clutches a hare in its talons (6.516–18). He drags her to a lonely stone hut hidden deep in a forest, locks her in, and rapes her. Then, when she threatens to proclaim what he has done, he seizes her tongue with pincers, cuts it off with his sword even as it struggles to speak ("luctantemque loqui" [556]), and repeatedly rapes her again.

Held under guard in the stone hut, mutilated and mute, her "os mutum" (574) powerless to contradict what Tereus tells Procne of her death, Philomela nonetheless manages to reveal the truth by weaving the story of the rape into a web that she gives to her sole attendant for delivery to Procne. Ovid says little about this weaving; he writes only that Philomela wrought the sign of the crime—"indicium sceleris"—when she wove purple marks through white threads ("purpureasque notas filis intexuit albis" [577]). The "notas" could be either graphic signs or letters, just as "intexuit" suggestively hovers between the literal meaning of "wove" and the figurative meaning of "compose" with which writers such as Cicero had already been using *texuit.* The suggestion of words here seems reinforced by what Procne does when she gets the cloth and unrolls it: there she reads—"legit"—the wretched fate of her sister (582). But as we have already seen in the *Aeneid* (6.34), "legere" can denote the scanning of a picture as well as the construing of a text, and in Ovid's own text, early on in the very book of the *Metamorphoses* that includes the Philomela story, Arachne and Minerva both use purple thread ("purpura . . . / texitur" [6.61–62] to weave what are unequivocally pictures ("Pallas scopulum Mavortis in arce / *pingit*" [70–71], "Maeonis elusam *designat* imagine tauri / Europam" [103–4]). Furthermore, even if the purple marks woven by Philomela are letters, the stark contrast between purple and white graphically expresses the bloody violation of her innocence. Her body itself has been recently described as "the original page on which a tale was written in blood" (Joplin 54). If we instead imagine what she wove as a picture of her mutilated body, then the whole story of the rape might be construed as ekphrastic, the verbal version of a tale first told by Philomela herself for the eyes alone.[1]

As Joplin has shown, this literally graphic tale—a tale told by a picture—

profoundly threatens the political order of Greece, and more precisely of Athens. Before her tongue is amputated, Philomela herself tells Tereus that he has destroyed all legitimate kinship structures:

> omnia turbasti; paelex ego facta sororis
> tu geminus coniunx, hostis mihi debita Procne!
>
> (6.537–38)

> You have confused everything; I have been made my sister's concubine, you a double husband, and Procne is bound to me only as an enemy!
>
> (translation mine)

Commonly lost in translation, the extraordinary compression of Ovid's syntax here underscores the wholesale confusion of marriage and adultery, legitimate conjunction and sexual transgression. Instead of calling herself Tereus's concubine, Philomela calls herself her *sister's* concubine ("paelex . . . sororis"), leaving us to puzzle out what she means. She means, I think, that Tereus's act has made her a substitute for his wife, her counterfeit, her meretricious understudy, her illicit double—as confirmed by the word "geminus" in the very next line. Yet for Philomela, the very notion of a "geminus coniunx"—a twin marriage yoking one man to two women—is even more nefarious than the union of Antony with his "Aegyptia coniunx" depicted on the shield of Aeneas. This is a union of incompatibles, as Philomela hastens to say: her sister Procne, she instinctively feels, is now "hostis mihi debita"—bound to her only in enmity.

Nothing could more vividly illustrate the point Joplin develops (40–41) about the political significance of the rape. Procne was given to Tereus by her father in exchange for the peace and security of Athens. When Tereus repelled the barbarian hordes ("barbara . . . agmina") that threatened to breach the walls of Athens (423), Pandion bound ("iunxit") this powerful man to himself ("sibi") by "connubio Procnes"—Procne's marriage to him (426–28). Ovid's "junxit" is appropriative; by giving up his daughter, Pandion gains an ally, binds to himself a powerful man who has protected and will protect the walls of Athens from barbarous invaders. But as king of Thrace, Tereus is himself a barbarian,[2] and proves it when he rapes Philomela, who promptly calls him barbarous for doing so: "o diris barbare factis" (533). By raping her, he has breached the wall that not only defines and contains virginity but also signifies the border between political order and barbarous upheaval. "The exchange of women," Joplin observes, "articulates the culture's boundaries, the woman's hymen serving as the physical or sexual sign for the limen or wall defining the city's limits" (43). In asking Tereus to guard Philomela with a father's love, Pandion presumes that he will defend her virginity against barbarous assault just as if she were Athens itself and he its paternal king manning the walls against the barbarians. Instead, Tereus himself has symbolically breached the inmost limits of the city by violently penetrating the virgin daughter of its king.

Joplin develops this point very well—though without reference to Ovid's own words. She does equally well to show how the impact of Philomela's depiction of the brutality of rape is blunted by the ending of the tale, wherein she and her sister become even more savage than Tereus: vengefully murdering his son, they cut him up and cook his flesh, serve it to the unwitting father, gleefully tell and show him what they have done, and thus goad him into an eternal pursuit that turns them all into birds—with Philomela herself, as we learn from other sources, becoming a nightingale.[3] As a result, Joplin observes, "the end of the story overtakes all that preceded it; the women are remembered as *more* violent than the man."[4] The true meaning of the tale, she contends, lies not in its gruesome ending but in its middle, where we hear what Sophocles called "the voice of the shuttle."[5]

For Joplin, this is the voice of the woman artist as weaver struggling to make herself heard and to release "the power of the text to teach the man to know himself" (53). Yet the most telling thing about Philomela's voice is that it is literally graphic: not textu*al* but textilic, not verbal but visual.[6] Philomela's power to speak in this story is woven into and hence bound up with the power of pictures to speak—to break through the silence in which they, like women, are traditionally bound.[7] In the Western world, the oldest recorded comment about the difference between painting and poetry is the one Plutarch attributes to Simonides of Ceos (ca. 556–467 B.C.)—that "painting is mute poetry and poetry a speaking picture."[8] It is not at all surprising to learn that Simonides was a poet, for as Wendy Steiner notes, this superficially balanced formulation actually loads the scales in favor of poetry. "Next to the 'speaking picture,'" she writes, "the mute poem seems a blighted thing; painting is poetry minus voice" (*Colors* 6). Poets, orators, and teachers of rhetoric have often acknowledged the expressive power of pictures, but "speaking picture" is a metaphor that harnesses this power to the chariot of the word, as when Sidney says that philosophic precepts must be "illuminated or figured forth by the speaking picture of Poesie."[9]

While thus exploiting pictorial vividness for rhetorical and poetic ends, guardians of the word have traditionally feared and resisted the possibility that pictures might assume an independent eloquence of their own. The link between this pictorial threat to the supremacy of the word and the female challenge to male authority is suggested by the story of Phryne, the famous Athenian courtesan of the fourth century B.C. who inspired a statue by Praxiteles as well as modeling for pictures of Venus painted by Apelles and other ancient artists.[10] Put on trial for unrecorded offenses, Phryne was reportedly saved not by the eloquence of Hyperides, the orator who defended her, but by the sight of her own naked beauty, which she displayed to the jurors by discarding her clothes.[11] In the *Institutio Oratoria,* written at the end of the first cen-

tury A.D. (about ninety years after the *Metamorphoses*), Quintilian cites this
story to show that "even some sight unsupported by language" may be persuasive (*Inst.* 2.15.6–9 in Quintilian 1:305). But he goes on to say that a picture
should never be allowed to take the place of a speech. "I would not . . . go so far
as to approve," he writes, "a practice of which I have read, and which indeed I
have occasionally witnessed, of bringing onto court a picture of the crime
painted on wood or canvas, that the judge might be stirred to fury by the horror
of the sight. For the pleader who prefers a voiceless picture to speak for him in
place of his own eloquence must be singularly incompetent."[12]

Quintilian's iconophobia is clear. It was all right for Phryne to display her
exquisite figure to an undoubtedly all-male audience of jurors, for in doing so
she was simply reenacting what is customarily done by the picture of a beautiful
woman when it silently offers itself to be consumed by the male gaze.[13] But
when a "voiceless picture" presumes to represent a crime, when it uses ugly
forms to incite rage and horror rather than lovely forms to excite pleasure, it
threatens to displace the orator, just as the tongueless Philomela's woven picture
of what Tereus did to her supplants the speech he gave to Procne about her
would-be death.

Because weaving can generate either a plain cloth or a figured one, it can
serve either the socially respectable purposes of covering and warmth or the
potentially dangerous ends of representation. Plain weaving threatens no one.
In a passage of speculation that he himself admits may seem "fantastic," Freud
suggests that women invented weaving at the prompting of "Nature," which
furnishes the pubic hair that grows to cover the vagina and thus shows women
how to mingle threads (22:132). Whatever the truth of this notion, weaving
(along with spinning) is a traditional sign of female virtue: a means of ensuring
that women control their sexual appetites and lead lives of dutiful quiet. Spinning plays just such a role in all early versions of the story of Lucretia. When
Collatine and his fellow soldiers at the siege of Ardea gallop off to Rome one
night to check up on their wives, they see Collatine's account of Lucretia's chastity fully justified when they find her not drinking and carousing, like the king's
daughters, but rather spinning wool with her maids.[14] In Euripides' *Bacchae*, as
Joplin notes (50), the loom signifies silent submission to male authority as an
alternative to raucous, orgiastic rites. "Driven from shuttle and loom / possessed by Dionysius" (Euripides 118–19), the women of Thebes are ordered
back to their weaving by Pentheus, who says, "I shall have them sold as slaves or
put to work / at my looms. That will silence their drums" (513–14). In the
Odyssey, it is precisely by weaving and unweaving a shroud for her father-in-law
that Penelope keeps her insistent suitors at bay, preserving her chastity for her
absent husband. And here too weaving signifies silent submission. When Penelope ventures to say that she cannot bear to hear Phemios singing about the
bitter homecoming of the Greeks who fought at Troy, Telemachos tells her to go
back to "the loom and the distaff," and she silently obeys (1.337–59).[15]

But if plain weaving keeps women chaste, submissive, and silent, figured weaving—a way of painting—gives them a voice capable of seriously challenging the authority of the male word. Philomela is just one of the women in the *Metamorphoses* who show what a picture can silently say. In the opening section of book 6—the very book that ends with the story of Philomela—Arachne not only challenges Minerva (Athena Pallas) to a weaving contest but dares to depict the sexual rapacity of the gods. In doing so, she effectively unweaves what Athena creates. Athena's tapestry shows twelve gods seated on lofty thrones to judge whether the new Greek city should be named for Neptune or for Athena, who wins the dispute by making an olive tree spring from the ground (6.70–84). Also, to show Arachne where her mad daring will lead, Athena weaves into the corners of her web various pictures of the punishments visited on those who presumed to rival or question the gods' supremacy (84–100). In place of this "completely symmetrical" display of authoritarian order and judgment (Leach 102), Arachne weaves a baroque panoply of gods who turn themselves into beasts and birds in order to rape or seduce a variety of women. Beginning with Jupiter's taurine rape of Europa, Arachne depicts twenty-one acts of sexual assault or sexual duplicity in all—nine committed by Jupiter, six by Neptune, four by Apollo, and one each by Liber and Saturn.[16] Ovid's tone in this brief, nimble passage is generally exuberant. The sheer variety and plenitude of guises assumed by the randy gods—a bull, an eagle, a swan, a snake, a horse, and so on—animates and drives his ekphrasis, which turns Arachne's graphic collage into something like cinematic montage. But in the giddy stream of images we catch telling glimpses of anguish and pain: Europa looking back on the receding shores ("terras . . . relictas") of her homeland and calling on her companions ("comites clamare suas") (105–6), Asteria clutched by Jupiter in the guise of a struggling eagle ("aquila luctante") (108).

The images Ovid evokes in describing the pictures of these two abductions (the first he enumerates) prefigure what we later find in the Philomela story, where at times the very words used earlier are echoed in a darker key. Once Tereus has Philomela on his ship, he gloats over his prize like an eagle—the predatory bird of Jupiter ("Iovis ales")—clutching a hare (516–18). At the moment of the rape, the terrified girl calls vainly and repeatedly on her father ("clamato saepe parente" [525]), her sister, and above all on the great gods ("magnis super omnia divis" [526]): the gods who have already shown themselves to be the greatest rapists of all. And just as Asteria struggles in the claws of Arachne's aquiline Jupiter, whose own struggling ("aquila luctante") is obviously prompted by hers, the tongue of Philomela struggles to speak ("luctantemque loqui") even as Tereus grips it with pincers (556).

But if Tereus's abuse of Philomela brings out the violence and brutality latent in Arachne's pictures of abduction, Philomela's fate is prefigured only too vividly by what happens to Arachne's tapestry and to Arachne herself at the hands of Minerva. As the unmothered daughter of Jupiter, Minerva is every inch her father's child, the ruthless champion of male gods and their prerogatives. By the time we reach the story of Arachne in Ovid's poem, we have already learned what happened to the once beautiful Medusa when Neptune raped her in Minerva's temple: punishing the victim, Minerva turned Medusa's locks into snakes and put her snaky image on her own shield to frighten her enemies (4.794–803).[17] So even if Arachne had not surpassed her in weaving, Minerva was ready to punish any woman who would thrust before her so many images of rape, so much graphic evidence of bestial lust in all the gods, above all in her own father. Outraged just as much by the content of these pictures as by the virtuosity that created them, Minerva "tore the figured tapestry, the heaven-descended crimes" ("et rupit, caelestia crimina, vestes" [4.131]). Significantly, the word for "tore"—*rupit,* from *rumpere,* to rend, break in pieces, or tear asunder—comes from the same etymological family as the word for *rape,* whose Latin ancestor is *rapire,* to sieze or take by force: Tereus himself is called a *raptor* (6.518). Minerva rapes Arachne's pictures of rape. She rends the garment (*vestes*) of Arachne's art, beats her into suicidal despair, and turns her into a spider who can speak no more with her weaving, who can weave, as Joplin says, "only literal webs . . . incomprehensible designs" (52).

Arachne's art, then, is violated just as savagely as Philomela's body is, and each woman is finally silenced by a metamorphosis that leaves her powerless to speak or weave any more graphic stories of rape. If Philomela is remembered as much for her vengefulness as for her sufferings, Arachne has come to signify almost nothing but the fate of the hubristic artist—a fate clearly signified by the sculpted figure Dante invokes in the long ekphrastic passage of *Purgatorio* 12: "O mad Arachne, so did I see you already half spider, wretched on the shreds of the work that you so catastrophically wrought" (43–45). Ironically, the last line of this tercet—"de l'opera che mal per te si fe"—literally means "of the work that was badly wrought by you."[18] Arachne's tapestry was hubristically "bad" precisely because it was artistically superb, and though it survives only in Ovid's ekphrastic words, it remains profoundly provocative—especially in what it suggests about the first of the sculptures Dante represents in the *Purgatorio:* the figure of Mary with the angel.

To read Dante's lines on this sculpture in light of Ovid's lines on Arachne's tapestry—lines written, incidentally, just about the time of Christ's birth—is to see that Mary's encounter with a winged figure subtly reenacts the third of the sights Arachne depicts: Leda lying under the wings ("sub alis") of a swan (6.109). Ovid's swan is Jupiter, of course, and in Dante the winged figure who salutes the virgin with his *Ave* is the emissary of a God who will come to her winged—the Holy Spirit in the form of a dove—to impregnate her.[19]

If it is hard to imagine the virgin Mary as the victim of divine rape, to cross the line between a wanton episode from Greek myth and the originating moment of Christianity, it is nonetheless clear that the story of Philomela—reinforced by the graphic stories of Arachne—blurs the line between rape and marriage.[20] In raping Philomela, Tereus becomes a "geminus coniunx" (6.538)—a double husband; conversely, his marriage to Procne resembles a rape. Made with no reference to her wishes or consent, it is supervised by the furies, lit with torches stolen from a funeral, and consummated to the music of a screech owl (6.430–32). Though Pandion gives his daughter to a powerful man in return for security against future threats of barbarous invasion, this exchange requires that the daughter be sent away from the father and sister she loves—in a sense, that she be abducted by a barbarous king. As Joplin argues, marriages of this kind always entail the sacrifice of a daughter, and sacrifice typically requires the shedding of blood.[21]

II
VERBALIZED DESCRIPTIONS OF RAPE
IN THE ANCIENT NOVEL

The blurring of the line between marriage and rape suggested by the story of Philomela becomes even more evident in two ancient Greek novels that I wish to examine now: Longus's *Daphnis and Chloe* and Achilles Tatius's *Leucippe and Clitophon*. Probably written in the second century A.D., some hundred years or more after the *Metamorphoses,* they are both conspicuously ekphrastic, and though neither one represents marriage as a politically motivated sacrifice, both use paintings that signify rape to prefigure the violence that men too often do—or imagine they do—in taking a bride's virginity.[22]

Before I get to the novels, however, I must clarify that sentence with a brief excursus. I do not mean to say that the sexual initiation of a virgin is always a violent act. Nor do I take the line of Catharine MacKinnon (see note 20), who strongly implies that because the law permits a married man to take his wife against her will, that is what he frequently or even typically does—with all the aggressive force at his command. To speak of marriage as little or nothing more than an institution which legalizes rape is not just demonstrably false, as a generalization; it also reinforces—rather than challenges—the characteristically male conception of sexual intercourse as an inherently violent or coercive act. Because a virgin usually bleeds when her hymen is first penetrated, and because men like to think of themselves as hunters and conquerors, most of our metaphors for sexual intercourse—especially for intercourse with a virgin—are figures of violent penetration: poking, wounding, piercing, stabbing, screwing, ramming, cutting. While these metaphors may be used (by feminist critics) to expose the brutality of what men do in the marriage bed under the sign of the law, such metaphors can also gratify the ego of any man who *wants* to measure his sexual potency by the quantity of pain he inflicts or of force he deploys in order to enter a woman's body. Metaphors of violence exalt male power quite as much as they expose male brutality.

But these metaphors of violence are also figures of fantasy. When a man entering a virgin imagines that his phallic sword is the first to make her vagina bleed, he forgets that it has been bleeding every month since she began to menstruate—usually for several years before her first sexual experience. When we shift the focus from male fantasies of bloody conquest to the rhythms of the woman's body and the pressure of her own desires, male metaphors of violent penetration give way to female metaphors of reception and enclosure. The best poetic treatment I know of the difference between these two sets of metaphors appears in William Blake's *Visions of the Daughters of Albion* (1793), a short "prophecy" about the sexual initiation of a virgin named Oothoon. Plucking the flower of her own virginity, impetuously running across the waves "in wing'd exulting swift delight" to meet her lover, she is raped or more precisely "rent"—split, torn violently asunder—by a figure named Bromion, a champion of the "law" who hypocritically condemns her for harlotry (*Visions*, plate 1, lines 11–18). Bromion thus turns Oothoon's desire for her lover into a justification for sexual violence, and his violence is repeated by the punishment she is made to undergo. With bitter irony, she herself calls upon the eagles of the jealous Thetormon to purify her by reenacting the rape, to "rend away" her defiled bosom and "rend their bleeding prey" (plate 2, lines 15–17). But these metaphors simply express the male view of sexual intercourse as violent, bloody penetration. Her own view, which vigorously survives the rape, is that sexual intercourse is an act of joyous welcoming, of sensual receiving, of hospitable opening: in her own words, she is "open to joy and to delight where ever beauty appears" (plate 6, line 22).[23] To the male eye and the male ego, this kind of openness appears as harlotry and promiscuity because it refuses to co-operate with male metaphors of conquest and violent penetration. Paradoxically, it unmans the battering ram by treating it as a guest.

I say all this to underscore a crucial point about the discussion that follows. When literary works use paintings of rape to prefigure the brutality and violence of sexual initiation, they are not exposing what actually happens *every* time the mystical substantive called "virginity" is "lost." Nor are they revealing the bedrock "truth" of sexual violence that invariably or even typically subverts the would-be harmony and legitimacy of the marriage bed. Rather than showing what actually or inevitably happens in sexual intercourse, they show where male metaphors for sexual intercourse lead, what sort of violence these metaphors implicitly authorize. And in so doing, they invite the reader to imagine alternative metaphors—as well as alternatives to sexual violence itself.

With this caveat firmly in mind, let us see how verbalized depictions of rape inflect the meaning of the sexual activity represented in the novels of Longus and Achilles Tatius. What these two novelists do with ekphrasis in the second century A.D. is in part anticipated by what Catullus does two centuries earlier in his poem 64. As already noted, this miniature epic about the wedding of Peleus and Thetis includes a long description of a marriage bed coverlet depicting—in a series of tableaux—the story of Ariadne, who fell in love with Theseus when he came to Crete, helped him kill the Minotaur and find his way out of the labyrinth, left with him for Dia (Naxos), and then awoke one day to find he had abandoned her while she slept. Though certainly not a victim of rape, she sounds very much like one in the prosopopeial description of the first tableau.

Desperately denouncing the faithless man who tore her away from her ancestral altars ("me patriis avectam, perfide, ab aris" [132]) and left her on a deserted shore, she predicts she will become the prey ("praeda" [153]) of birds and wild beasts when she dies, and in the final tableau she does in fact become the prey of a drunken Iacchus (Dionysius) "burning with desire" ("incensus amore" [253]). In light of the violence and rapacity that the painted Ariadne is said to expect or actually to endure, it is startling to learn—when the poem returns from the tableaux on the coverlet to the wedding of Thetis and Peleus—what will come of their nuptial union. According to the Parcae, who chant the future as they spin their threads at the wedding feast, Peleus and Thetis will beget the ferocious Achilles, whose tomb when he dies will be soaked with the blood of a sacrificed virgin: the blood of Polyxena beheaded with an axe (362–70). Iron-ically, the prospect of this final bloody necrophilic marriage is precisely what the Parcae hold out to Thetis and Peleus while urging them to join their pas-sions in nuptial bliss: "coniungite amores" (372).

The part played by verbalized depictions of rape in narratives about the sac-rifice of virginity is still more conspicuous in the two Greek novels mentioned above, both of which begin by describing pictures of rape. In the proem to *Daphnis and Chloe*, Longus introduces the novel as a narrative specifically prompted by a painting:

> While hunting game on Lesbos I saw in a grove of Nymphs the most beautiful vision I ever saw—an image inscribed, a narrative of desire.
>
> The grove indeed was very pleasant, thickset with trees and starred with flowers everywhere, and watered all from one fountain with divers meanders and rills. But that picture, as having in it not an excellent and wonderful piece of art but also a tale of ancient love, was far more amiable.
>
> In the painting there were women giving birth and others wrapping the infants in swaddling clothes, babies exposed, herd animals nursing them, shepherds raking them up, youngsters coming together, an incur-sion of brigands, an attack of enemies, many other things and all to do with *eros*.
>
> As I watched and wondered a yearning seized me to counterscribe the painting [*antigrapsai tei graphei*—i.e., duplicate or rival]; I searched out an exegete of the icon and I carefully crafted four books. . . . [24]

The urge excited by the painting here described is quintessentially ekphras-tic. Using a word (*antigrapsai*) that may mean either "make an exact transcrip-tion" or "rival with answering version" (Winkler, "Education" 32n), the narrator tells us that he yearns to "counterscribe" the painting, to represent it in a medium that will at once mirror and transform it—even as very word *anti-grapsai* mirrors and transforms *tei graphei,* the painting. The complexity of this mirroring is underscored by the fact that in ancient Greek, *graphei* can mean either painting or writing, just as in modern English we use *graph* to denote a kind of picture and bio*graphy* to denote a kind of text. In this passage, the narrator tells us that he saw in a grove of nymphs *eikona graptein, istorian erotos:* an "image inscribed [or painted], a narrative of desire." Though it is clearly a painting, the language introducing it nearly erases the line between drawing and writing, depicting and narrating, image and word. The story we read, then, is both transcription and counterscription, the verbal record of a story already inscribed in paint and a paragonal re-writing of that story, a re-vision of what the painting shows.[25]

The painting plainly demands interpretation. Discovered in a leafy, floriferous, lavishly watered grove, it stands both in and out of its setting, a little like the picture displayed in Magritte's *La Condition Humaine,* where a canvas depicting a tree in a meadow under a cloudy sky is itself depicted standing against window open to clouds and a meadow. In Longus's proem, the line between picture and setting—or art and "nature"—is less equivocally drawn; while the setting is all vegetation, the account of the painting mentions only figures—humans and animals. Yet merely to imagine the painting, we must visualize these figures in some sort of space: "babies exposed" near a fountain, perhaps, "youngsters coming together" under the trees, and so on. The "real" grove here—the most readily available space—furnishes the elements of landscape with which we begin to fill out the painting for ourselves.

In doing so, we begin the work of interpreting the picture, or more precisely of interpreting the narrator's description of it. And just as we must infer a spatial context for the figures in the painting in order to visualize it, we must infer a temporal context for them in order to understand it.[26] Readers familiar with Greek storytelling, as John J. Winkler has shown, would readily recognize the narrative implied by a picture of infants exposed and nursed by animals: they are typically the product of rape or seduction ("Education" 28–29). Along with the brigands and the enemy attack, the juxtaposition of young lovers meeting ("youngsters coming together") with childbirth and infant exposure implies and in this instance prefigures a story in which—for all its apparent sweetness—sexual union is repeatedly infected with the violence characteristic of rape. As Winkler shows, Chloe is not just threatened with rape by figures like the enemy soldiers who appear in book 2; she is actually made to learn— significantly as a "mute pupil"—that sex is a socially constructed system requiring violence, so that even her beloved Daphnis must act like a rapist on their wedding night (17–18, 29).

The strongest point Winkler makes in support of this provocative thesis is that Daphnis literally does not know how to consummate his love for Chloe until he is taught by a woman named Lykainion, who tells him that in taking Chloe's virginity, he must make her scream and cry and bleed (3.19). Though Daphnis does not wish to make her do any of these things, we are plainly told at the end of the poem that on his wedding night he "did some of what Lykainion had taught him" (4.40, Winkler 27). We are also told that the music played to escort the couple to their bedroom on this occasion was "not a hymenation" but a cacophony—something like the voice of the screech owl who sat on the roof of the chamber of the newly wedded Procne and Tereus:

> Some [played] on syrinxes, some on flutes. . . . And when they were near the doors, they were singing in a harsh and unpleasant voice, as if breaking up the earth with tridents, not singing a hymenation. (4.40, Winkler 28)

Two things are notable here. First, the harshness of the voice is specifically linked to an image of sowing as violent penetration—a phallic invasion of the earth. Secondly, the first instrument mentioned is the syrinx, the reed named for the maiden chased by the goat-god Pan, who sought to rape her. Fleeing from him to the river Radon, she begged its nymphs to help her, and was changed into a reed. Joined with other reeds of different length, this became known as the syrinx: the pipes of Pan, the rapist's consolation prize (*Metamorphoses* 1.698–713).

The mention of the syrinx in the final passage above should remind us that Pan is not only a dedicatee of the poem—it is "an offering to Eros and Nymphs and Pan," the proem says—but also plays a leading part in one of its episodes. Appearing in a dream to the general of a small army that has abducted Chloe, he frightens the man into releasing her (2.27–28). But at the celebration that follows, the story of Pan's attempt to rape Syrinx is told and then reenacted in a dance by Daphnis and Chloe, with Chloe in flight and Daphnis running after her on tiptoes, mimicking the goat-footed god (2.34–37). Though Chloe is not raped and does not even know yet what rape is, she is caught up in a festival of rape. Saved *from* rape by Pan, she unwittingly helps to commemorate him *as* a rapist. Thus the whole festival recalls the irony of Philomela's desperate appeal to the "great gods" at the moment she is being raped (6.526): the great gods are the great rapists of Arachne's tapestry.

In *Leucippe and Clitophon* as in *Daphnis and Chloe*, the story of a passionate quest originates in response to a painting. But if the rape signified by the painting described at the outset of *Daphnis and Chloe* can be discovered only by inference, the subject of the painting described at the beginning of *Leucippe and Clitophon* is immediately clear: it is the rape of Europa, the first of the rapes that Ovid's Arachne weaves into her tapestry. According to the narrator, the painting shows a flowery, tree-shaded meadow on one side and the Phoenician Ocean on the other. As a group of girls gaze out from the water's edge with a mixture of joy and fear in their looks, the bull swims far away with Europa sitting sideways on his back and Eros leading him on (*L&C* 1.1.6–13). Unlike Arachne's figure, the Europa of this painting shows no signs of fear or dismay. As Shadi Bartsch observes, the calm control with which she "steers" the bull through the waves (holding his horn as a charioteer holds reins [1.1.10]) suggests that she acquiesces to her abduction, and once we get into the novel, her acquiescence seems reenacted by its heroine, who agrees to yield her virginity to Clitophon and even urges him to take her away from her mother (Bartsch 54).

But in the course of her travels (with and without Clitophon), Leucippe is repeatedly threatened with sexual assault—right up to the end of the novel, when
she and Clitophon finally consummate their love. If the painting of Europa
turns rape into a pleasurable escapade, the story of Leucippe and Clitophon
returns us to the brutality of rape—by representing sexual initiation and marriage itself as an ordeal of violence.

The story is told by Clitophon himself in front of the painting. When the
painting prompts the narrator to say aloud how it shows Eros ruling sky and
earth and sea, a young man beside him mentions his own sufferings for love
(*L&C* 1.2.1). When asked to tell his story, the young man—Clitophon—
complies with a story that is not just precipitated by the painting of Europa but
periodically advanced by other paintings representing rape and mutilation, including a painting of Philomela.

Analyzing these paintings in context, Bartsch argues that they excite expectations which the narrative seems at first to confirm and then to subvert; just
when we think that Leucippe has been victimized in a way foreshadowed by the
paintings, we learn that she is alive and well (59). But Bartsch underestimates, I
believe, the final impact of the paintings on our perception of what actually
happens to Leucippe. That she lives to marry Clitophon at the end of the novel
does not mean that she escapes the violence which the paintings have so vividly
connected to sexual initiation. Just as the notes of the syrinx and the final reference to the teachings of Lykainion drop echoes of rape right into the wedding-
night chamber of Daphnis and Chloe, the paintings described in *Leucippe and
Clitophon* forge links between rape and marriage that the plot never wholly
dissolves.

The first two paintings described after the one showing the rape of Europa
are seen by Clitophon and Leucippe just after they are shipwrecked on the
Egyptian coast. First they find a statue of Zeus holding out a pomegranate of
"mystical signification" (*L&C* 3.6.1), which can be read as a covert sign of
rape.[27] Then, after asking Zeus for an omen about their shipwrecked friends,
they go to the temple and find a pair of pictures. One shows Prometheus bound
to a rock and forced to watch himself being disemboweled by an eagle (3.8.7)—
something very like what Leucippe *seems* to undergo later, as Bartsch observes
(58). But the other painting has far more to say about what will later happen to
Leucippe in fact.

Ostensibly, this second picture represents a rescue. Exposed to a sea-monster
by her father Cepheus as a sacrificial offering to Neptune (here called by his
Greek name Poseidon), Andromeda is said to appear chained to a rock as the
winged Perseus descends to attack the monster, which has just put its head
above the waves (*L&C* 3.7.1–2, 7). But the circumstances surrounding this rescue recall the equivocal conditions under which Chloe is rescued by Pan.[28]
Himself a child of rape (when Zeus came to Danae in a shower of gold), Perseus
has already proved himself no champion of its victims. Before this adventure
with Andromeda, he decapitated Medusa after she was raped by Neptune (*Met.*

4.772–801), the same god to whom Andromeda is offered as sacrifice, and in the painting he is shown carrying Medusa's head in his left hand like a shield (*L&C* 3.7.7). In Ovid's account, moreover, he descends on the monster like "the speedster of Jupiter" ("Iovis praepes") when it spies a serpent in an open field (*Met.* 4.714–15): a simile anticipating the aquiline form in which Jupiter rapes Asteria, as depicted by Arachne (6.108), as well as the passage in which Tereus the "raptor" is compared to the predatory "Iovis ales"—"bird of Jupiter" (6.516–18). Equally striking here is the fact that Andromeda, originally offered as a sacrifice to Neptune, has now been offered to Perseus in exchange for killing the monster (4.697–705)—an arrangement which suggests, once again, that marriage and sacrifice may be interchangeable.

That suggestion is powerfully made by the painting of Andromeda described in *Leucippe and Clitophon.* In this painting, we are told, Andromeda lies chained in a hollow of rock that looks like an improvised grave and awaits her fate "decked out for her marriage, like a bride adorned for Hades" wearing a silk tunic of spider-web thinness (3.7.5; Bartsch 56). Her tunic recalls the diaphanous clothing worn by Europa in the first painting described (1.1.10), and like Persephone—a figure already evoked by the pomegranate of Zeus (see note 27)—she is decked out for a marriage that is scarcely distinguishable from a fatal abduction.[29] Furthermore, Perseus is shown brandishing a complex weapon—"something between a sickle and a sword"—which can be used both to stab and to cut (3.7.8–9). That he comes to claim his bride with such a phallic weapon in his hand clearly strengthens the connection between marriage and bloodletting.

What the painting implies about marriage seems emphatically confirmed by what happens shortly after the couple sees it. Captured by a gang of Egyptian robbers, they are shut up in a little hut, where Clitophon tells Leucippe that the earth will be "your marriage bed, ropes and cords your necklaces and bracelets . . . A dirge is your marriage-hymn" (3.10.5). Significantly, she has nothing to say in reply because, she says, "my voice is dead, even before the departure of my soul" (3.11.2). Already silenced by despair, she is taken away to be sacrificed by the robbers so as to purify their camp (3.12.1–2), and before Clitophon's eyes, she is apparently disemboweled with a sword that first stabs her in the heart and then cuts open her belly (3.15.4–5). She is thus violated with just the kind of weapon Perseus wields in quest of his bride.

Shortly afterwards, the grief-stricken Clitophon learns that this apparently fearful sword was an actor's knife with a retractable blade, that the would-be disemboweling of Leucippe was a sham staged by two men who pretended to join the robber band so they could rescue her, and that she is actually alive and well. What now can be inferred about the predictive significance of the paintings of Andromeda and Prometheus? Bartsch suggests (60) that one meaning gives way to another. While the apparent sacrifice of Leucippe as bride of death leads us to think that this fulfills the grim promise made by the paintings, the rescue of Leucippe reminds us that both paintings represent figures being res-

cued: in the painting of the agonized Prometheus, Hercules is shown just about
to shoot an arrow at his torturer (3.8.5). But if Leucippe is rescued *for* marriage,
can her future be wholly detached from the things with which the painting of
Andromeda links marriage—from violation, mutilation, and sacrifice? A negative answer to this question is strongly implied by the very next work of art the
lovers see: a painting of the Philomela story.

They find it in an artist's studio in Alexandria, shortly after Leucippe has
been rescued from a drug-induced insanity by the intervention of a fisherman
named Chaereas, who has invited them to a birthday dinner at his home on the
island of Pharos. One more indication of just how ambiguous rescue can be in
this novel—as in *Daphnis and Chloe*—is the fact that the invitation is a mere
pretext: Chaereas has developed a lust for Leucippe and has hired a band of
pirates to abduct her when she and Clitophon come to his house. But before the
lovers accept his treacherous invitation, they examine and discuss the painting.

The painting includes Philomela's tapestry, which is held up by a serving-
maid as Philomela points to its subjects and Procne bows her head in furious
acknowledgment. The tapestry itself shows Tereus clutching Philomela to him
and Philomela fighting back: hair disheveled, tunic torn, girdle undone and
one breast exposed, she aims her right hand at Tereus's eyes and tries to cover
her breasts. Besides depicting in this way the moment of the rape and Philomela's graphic way of reporting it to her sister, the painting also represents the
penultimate phase of her story: with expressions mingling ridicule and fear, the
women show to a feasting Tereus the head and hands of his son in a basket while
he leaps up with his sword drawn against them and his leg pressing against the
table, which appears about to fall (5.3.4–8). The final phase—the metamorphoses of the three—is not mentioned in the description but is apparently
part of the painting, as the comments on it reveal.

There are three sets of comments. First, a friend of the lovers named
Menelaus takes the painting as an omen of disaster and a warning that they
should decline Chaereas's invitation (5.4.1–2). Then Leucippe asks Clitophon
to explain the painting, including an element she is the first to mention: "What
are these birds? Who are those women and that vile man?" (5.5.1). Finally, in
answer to her questions, Clitophon furnishes the only exegesis of a painting we
find in the whole novel (Bartsch 65)—something that gives this painting special importance.

Clitophon's exegesis is a narrative, a characteristically ekphrastic conversion
of the picture elements into a story that connects them not only with each other
but with the newly mentioned birds. Besides explaining the birds, Clitophon
stresses three things: the barbarousness of the rape as a second marriage, the use
of the tapestry as a silent voice, and the hideousness of the vengeance taken,
which leads to a generalization about the single-minded vengefulness of all
women wronged by their husbands (5.5.7). Since Clitophon will later forget his
love for Leucippe long enough to have intercourse with a lovely Ephesian
woman named Melite (5.27.3), his comment on the vengefulness of women is

ironic, as is also his way of defining the rape. Like Ovid's Philomela, who sees Tereus after the rape as a "geminus conjunx," a double husband, Clitophon comments that "one wife at a time, it seems, is not enough for a barbarian's love" (5.5.2). Tereus, he adds, made Philomela "a second Procne," and his would-be wedding present to her was tonguelessness (5.5.4).

Since Clitophon explains at length just how much Philomela manages to say with the "silent voice" (*sioposan phonein*) of her weaving (5.5.4), we may well ask what the painting of her story says about the outcome of the novel in which it appears. As Bartsch shows (69–70), the painting does not simply prefigure what happens after the lovers see it.[30] Though Leucippe is abducted by Chaereas's pirates and later bought from them by the servant of another man who attacks her (like Tereus) in a remote hut, she is never actually raped, nor does she take vengeance on Clitophon for his infidelity to her—or even learn of it. At the end she is tested for virginity by being sent into a grotto containing the pipes of Pan, and when its harmonious notes announce that she has passed the test (8.13–14), she comes out and marries Clitophon at last. But Pan is a curious arbiter of virginity—"a god too fond of virgins," as Clitophon himself ruefully observes when Leucippe enters the grotto (8.13.3). Even when she emerges in triumph, the music of a rapist's pipes launches her marriage on the same note of ambiguity we heard from the Syrinx that was played for the wedding night of Daphnis and Chloe. Initiated by a verbalized painting of the rape of Europa and signposted by verbalized paintings of sacrifice, ambiguous rescue, and further rape, the story of Leucippe and Clitophon ends with a marriage that covertly makes of Clitophon what Tereus became for Philomela—a "geminus conjunx." The final passage of the novel speaks of the sacrifices made for the wedding of Clitophon's sister, which takes place shortly after his own (8.19.3). Thus, the marriage of Leucippe is linked to sacrifice as well as rape, and the silent voice of Philomela's weaving—so powerfully evoked by the commentary on the painting of her—remains audible to the end.

III
EKPHRASIS AND RAPE FROM CHAUCER TO SPENSER

In the late fourteenth century, John Gower and Geoffrey Chaucer each retold the Philomela story in poems largely based on Ovid's version of it.[31] Inconveniently enough for my purposes, neither poem has much to say about the weaving of pictures representing the rape. Gower tells us that the violated woman—whom he and Chaucer call Philome*n*a—wove a white silk cloth "with lettres and ymagerie, / In which was al the felonie, / Which Tereus to hire hath do."[32] In Chaucer's version of the story, which appears in his *Legend of Good Women,* this composite embroidery of words and pictures becomes purely verbal: by weaving "letters . . . to and fro" Philomena "wrot the storye" of what Tereus did (*Legend* 2358–63).

Yet if Chaucer's version of the Philomela story offers no ekphrasis at all, the rest of his poetry includes plenty of it. Besides the prolonged account of the personified vices painted on the garden wall in his translation of the *Roman de la Rose* (132–474), ekphrastic passages appear in four of his works: in *The Knight's Tale,* where the statues and paintings in the temples of Venus, Mars, and Diana are described at length (1918–2088); in *The Book of the Duchess,* where the narrator dreams that the walls of his room are painted with the Romance of the Rose and the windows filled with stained glass depicting the story of Troy (321–34); in the dream vision of *The Parliament of Fowles,* where the narrator tells of the paintings he found on the walls of the temple of Venus (284–94); and in book 1 of *The House of Fame,* where the description of a painting based on the *Aeneid* runs to over three hundred lines (151–467).[33]

For all its prolixity, however, Chaucerian ekphrasis can be oddly nonpictorial: not just inattentive to features such as composition or to the representational friction between medium and referent, but sometimes less imagistic than descriptions of what his narrators see in the would-be "real" world. Francis Beaumont once singled out Chaucer above all other authors for "the excellencie of his descriptions to possesse his Readers with a stronger imagination of seeing that done before their eyes, which they reade, than any other that euer writ in any tongue."[34] Yet this singular talent for verbal depiction is nowhere evident in the passage on the paintings that adorn the temple of Venus in *The Parliament of Fowles,* where the narrator simply lists the names of the figures painted: Semiramis, Candace, Hercules, and so on (288–92). As Margaret Bridges observes (153), his account of the paintings is considerably less pictorial than his description of Venus *in propria persona* (265–73).

This complaint will not stick to the long ekphrastic passage in *The Knight's Tale.* Here, the narrator *does* gratify the reader's inner eye, vividly recreating the appearance of a statue of Venus (1955–66) as well of the paintings on the wall of her temple and the temple of Mars. But thematically, it is the least pictorial section of the whole passage on the temples that reveals the most. While the knight's "descripsioun" of the wall paintings in the temple of Diana says nothing about their colors or the shapes of their figures, it casts a powerfully illuminating light on what finally happens to Emelye.

This beautiful young woman has been brought to Athens by Duke Theseus, who married the Amazon Queen Ypolita, her older sister, after conquering "al the regne of Femenye" (866). Both women are spoils of war and subjects of male authority. As such, they have only the power to supplicate that authority, never the power to initiate action or—except incidentally—to gratify their own desires. In the first part of the tale, the only thing we learn of Emelye's desires is that she wants to make a garland of flowers for her long golden hair. In the act of realizing this incidental wish, she becomes an object of male desire. Palamon and Arcite, the two young Theban knights whom Theseus has recently captured, are each successively smitten with longing for Emelye when, early one May morning, they see her from their prison chamber high in the great tower overlooking the duke's garden.

The plot of this elaborate romance turns on what these two men want. Once they see her, the only important question to be answered by the plot is which man will have her. The question is answered when Arcite beats Palamon in a tournament held to resolve it but is then mortally wounded by a fury: Arcite dies, and Emelye marries Palamon. Authorized and justified by the duke in a grandiloquently Boethian speech on "the faire cheyne of love" (2988), this marriage seems the perfect resolution to the passionate conflicts generated by the romance plot, especially since we are told at the end how "tendrely" Emelye loved her new husband (3103). But this apparently perfect match looks a little less than blissful when we read it in light of the paintings Emelye finds in the temple of Diana when she goes there to pray before the tournament.

Three of the four paintings represent metamorphoses: Callisto changed to a bear, Daphne into a laurel, and Actaeon into a hart (2056–66). "All this," writes V. A. Kolve in his widely acclaimed study of Chaucer's imagery, "demonstrates Diana's power, the power of virginity" (*Chaucer* 121). Yet only one of these metamorphoses was wrought by Diana, who transformed Actaeon "for vengeance that he saugh [her] al naked" (2066) bathing with her nymphs. What Kolve curiously fails to note is that the other two paintings of metamorphoses in the temple of Diana represent the consequences of rape.

Consider first what the knight says of these paintings:

> Ther saugh I how woful Calistopee,
> Whan that Diane agreved was with here,
> Was turned from a womman til a bere,
> And after she was maad the loode-sterre;
> Thus was it paynted, I kan sey yow no ferre.
> Her sone is eek a sterre, as men may see.
> There saugh I Dane, yturned til a tree,—
> I mene nat the goddesse Diane,
> But Penneus doghter, which that highte Dane.
>   (2056–64)

The Arcadian nymph Calistopee, better known as Callisto, was devoted to Diana and a favorite of hers until she was raped by Jupiter, who—in Ovid's version of the story—came to her disguised as Diana while she was resting in a forest. Though she soon realized who he was and fought against him with all her might ("illa quidem contra, quantum modo femina posset / . . . / illa quidem pugnat" [*Met.* 2.434–36]), he overpowered and impregnated her. As a result, she was banished from Diana's company, turned into a bear by Jupiter's angry wife Juno, and finally set among the stars with her son Arcas.

Daphne—Chaucer's Dane—fared no better than Callisto. Daughter of the river-god Penneus, she was desired by many but resolutely resisted them all. When her father exhorted her to marry and bear him grandchildren, she begged him to grant her the perpetual virginity that Diana had already obtained from *her* father. But Apollo burned for Daphne ("deus in flammis abiit"

[*Met.* 1.495]) as soon as Cupid struck him with a golden dart. Even while assuring her that he was not her enemy, that she did not need to flee him as the lamb flees the predatory wolf ("sic agna lupum" [1.505]), he pursued her as relentlessly as a hound chasing a hare (1.533–34). Frightened and exhausted, she begged her father to transform her, and was turned into a laurel: the tree whose leaves, by Apollo's order, would henceforth adorn the temples of triumphant Roman generals (1.560–61). It is perhaps significant that when Theseus returns from his victory in Thebes, he too is "with laurer crowned as a conquerour" (1027).

The knight's description suggests that the paintings of these two women depict in each case the moment of metamorphosis—perhaps something like Bernini's sculpture of Apollo and Daphne in Rome's Villa Borghese. But the brief account of the paintings presupposes at least some knowledge of the stories leading up to the moment depicted. Callisto and Daphne appear on the walls of Diana's temple because each was wholly devoted to the virginity Diana personifies. The knight's little disquisition on the near-homonyms *Dane* and *Diane* should in fact remind us how close to Diana both women were: Callisto welcomed the treacherous Apollo because she thought he was Diana, and Daphne took Diana as her model. But neither she nor Callisto could follow that model because each was overpowered by a sexually rapacious god.

To know the full stories signified by the paintings of Callisto and Daphne is to begin to understand what Emelye asks of Diana when she goes to her temple. Since this is the first and only passage in which she expresses her deepest wishes, her prayer deserves to be quoted at length. "Chaste goddesse," she says,

> wel wostow that I
> Desire to ben a mayden al my lyf,
> Ne nevere wol I be no love ne wyf.
> I am, thow woost, yet of thy compaignye,
> A mayde, and love huntynge and venerye,
> And for to walken in the wodes wilde,
> And noght to ben a wyf and be with childe
> Nor wol I knowe compaignye of man.
> Now help me, lady, sith ye may and kan,
> For tho thre formes that thou hast in me,
> And Palamon, that hath swich love to me,
> And eek Arcite, that loveth me so soore,
> (This grace I preye thee withoute moore)
> As sende love and pees betwixe hem two,
> And fro me turne awey hir hertes so
> That al hire hoote love and hir desir,
> And al hir bisy torment, and hir fir
> Be queynt, or turned in another place.
> And if so be thou wolt nat do me grace,

Or if my destynee be shapen so
That I shal nedes have oon of hem two,
As sende me hym that moost desireth me.
Bihoold, goddesse of clene chastitee,
The bittre teeris that on my chekes falle.
Syn thou art mayde and kepere of us alle,
My maydenhede thou kepe and wel conserve,
And whil I lyve, a mayde I wol thee serve.
(2304–30)

Essentially, this is what Daphne prayed to Peneus. Like Daphne and Callisto too, Emelye longs to remain a virgin, to be neither wife nor mother, to enjoy the company of Diana rather than the company of man. She wants neither of the two men who love her so desperately that they are going fight for her, and she prays with "bittre teeris" because she fears she might be forced to marry one of them. But significantly, her prayer is not wholly for herself. Even as she earlier joined Ypolita in begging Theseus to spare the lives of the cousins when he caught them fighting in a grove over her (1748–57), she now asks the goddess to "send love and peace betwixe" them, and if she must marry, she asks for "hym that moost desireth me." She is tearfully prepared to sacrifice her own desires for the sake of a man's desire.

Diana's response to this prayer comes immediately. One of the two sacrificial fires that Emelye has lit at the altar fades and revives; the other shrivels up with a hissing sound like that of wet branches burning, and "at the brondes ende out ran anon / As it were blody dropes many oon" (2340). What does this signify? Not until later can we know that it prefigures the defeat of Palamon, who nonetheless survives to marry Emelye, and the sudden fatal wounding of Arcite. But Emelye knows at once what this display of fire and blood means for her. Though the knight says that "she ne wiste what it signyfied" (2343), she knows—or instinctively feels—that it portends the end of her virginity. Remembering what Lykanion told Daphnis about the need to make a virgin scream and cry and bleed in order to take her virginity, and remembering too the paintings of raped women that surround this scene of fire and blood, we can hardly fail to understand the "feere" with which Emelye "crie[s] / And weep[s] that it was pitee for to heere" (2344–45).

The resolution of the plot demands the silencing of her cries. Even as she weeps, Diana appears and coolly announces what the gods and the "eterne word" have decreed: she must marry one of the men (2349–52). When Diana then disappears, the astonished Emelye asks herself how the goddess of virginity—the goddess whose "proteccioun" from men and marriage she so earnestly sought—could thus dispose of her (2362–64).[35] And those are the very last words Emelye speaks in the tale.

Kolve suggests that "Emelye worships Diana not as a dedicated virgin or a nun bound to chastity but as a young girl not yet awakened to love, who will consent to marry in the fulness of time" (*Chaucer* 122). This reading of Emelye makes her the beneficiary of mature male wisdom: when the philosophic duke asks this unawakened virgin to take her place in the "faire cheyne of love" which the "Firste Moevere" (2987–88) made to regulate the universe, she wisely accepts "the bond / That highte matrimoigne or mariage" (3095–96). But careful scrutiny of Emelye's prayer to Diana reveals nothing immature about her original dedication to virginity. Nor does Emelye ever explicitly "consent" to marry Palamon. Echoing Diana's nonnegotiable announcement in the temple, Theseus simply informs Emelye that he and his parliament have decided that she will take Palamon "for housbonde and for lord" (3081). She has nothing whatever to say in reply, and in spite of the "blisse and melodye" (3097) that are said to mark her wedding to Palamon, we are left to wonder what her silence means.[36]

I believe it signifies a painfully coerced surrender subtly prefigured by the paintings of Callisto and Daphne in the temple of Diana. The ending of the tale suppresses Emelye's pain because the tale as a whole essentially turns on the conflict between the two men. Once that conflict has been resolved, once the gods have determined that Palamon will have Emelye after Arcite has been killed and duly mourned, Emelye's consent can be taken for granted, or readily elicited by a philosophic speech. Thus the male word triumphs at once over virginity and the image of virginity assaulted. Together with the knight's concluding words on the "blisse" of Emelye's marriage to Palamon (3102), the final words of Theseus preempt anything she might say and all but obliterate the memory of what she has seen: the painted images of sexual violation.

Like Emelye, the heroine of Marlowe's *Hero and Leander* takes a vow of chastity in a temple decorated with images of rape. In Marlowe's poem, an erotic mythological verse narrative left unfinished at his death in 1593, the exquisitely handsome Leander crosses the Hellespont from Abydos to attend the feast of Adonis at Sestos, where—in the temple of Venus—he first sees the beautiful Hero and falls instantly in love with her. After courting her with speeches that rouse her affection but do not quite vanquish her chastity, he returns to Abydos, swims back to Sestos, talks his way into her bed, and consummates his love. Like the marriages of Daphnis and Chloe and of Leucippe and Clitophon, the mating of Hero and Leander seems at first sight far removed from rape— especially since, after Leander has taken her "inestimable gemme" (2.78), she can hardly bear to think that sunrise should break in upon their pleasure (2.301–4). But once again, a verbalized depiction of rape leads us to see the signs of violence, sacrifice, and coercion that mark and darken what Douglas Bush has called "an almost unclouded celebration of youthful passion" (122).

The picture of rape described in this poem appears in the floor of the temple of Venus at Sestos. Set in a pavement of shining crystal,[37] the picture represents

> the gods in sundrie shapes,
> Committing headdie ryots, incest, rapes:

For know, that underneath this radiant floure,
Was *Danaes* statue in a brazen tower,
Jove, slylie stealing from his sisters bed
To dallie with *Idalian Ganymed:*
And for his love *Europa,* bellowing loud,
And tumbling with the Rainbow in a cloud:
Blood-quaffing *Mars,* heaving the yron net,
Which limping *Vulcan* and his *Cyclops* set:
Love kindling fire, to burne such townes as *Troy,*
Sylvanus weeping for the lovely boy
That now is turn'd into a *Cypres* tree,
Under whose shade the Wood-gods love to bee.

(1.143–56)

The profusion of rapes and violent acts of love depicted in the pavement recalls the way Arachne represents the gods in her tapestry. Here is Jove descending on Danae in a golden shower, abducting Ganymede, "bellowing loud" as he rapes Europa, and evidently "tumbling" with Iris, goddess of the rainbow.[38] Here is the bloodthirsty god of war caught in adulterous intercourse with Venus and struggling in the iron net cast over them both by her husband Vulcan. Here is the incendiary force of desire, which can lead from the abduction of a woman to the burning of a city. And here is the wood-god Silvanus, weeping for the lovely boy who was dendrified after what may have been a vain attempt to seduce him.[39]

At a silver altar in the very midst of these pictures of rape and violent sexuality, Hero is sacrificing the blood of turtle doves when she is first seen by Leander, who gazes on her until "her gentle heart was strooke" (165) by the fire blazing from his face. Since Hero feels immediately drawn to Leander and actually approaches his kneeling form (1.180), we may well ask what the pictures of rape portend. Do they signify that both partners will be equally raped or victimized by a love that overpowers the ungendered "will," as the narrator at once suggests (1.167–68)? Or do they prefigure, more specifically, yet another sacrifice of a virgin?

To answer these questions fairly, we must first determine just what kind of virgin Hero is. Her situation and appearance in the opening scene have prompted some readers to question her devotion to chastity. In Marlowe's source, a fifth-century A.D. epyllion by Musaeus of Alexandria, the heroine is *kupridos iereia*—priestess of the Cyprian Aphrodite, goddess of earthly love, to whom she has ironically sworn a vow of chastity (Keach 88–89). Having likewise sworn such a vow, Marlowe's Hero is "*Venus* Nun" (1.44). But since Elizabethan writers used this phrase to mean a prostitute, Keach argues that Marlowe seizes every opportunity to exploit the irony of its implications, to reveal "the superficiality and falseness of [Hero's] pose as chaste nun of Venus" (90, 93). In the very opening lines of the poem, for instance, we learn that the sleeves of her linen dress are bordered with a scene showing how Venus "in her naked glory strove" to catch the eyes of the disdainful Adonis (1.11–14). Venus's erotic behavior in this verbalized depiction, Keach suggests, resurfaces later in Hero herself when she "trembling strove" in Leander's arms (2.291) and then stood "all naked to [Leander's] sight displayd" as he lay in bed watching her (2.324).[40]

Crucial differences, however, separate Hero's behavior from the seductive exhibitionism of Venus. When Hero's naked body is displayed to Leander, she is not striving to catch his eye. She has rather been *caught by* Leander—quite literally seized as she tried to slip out of bed secretly before dawn came; and after slithering through his arms to the floor and gaining her feet, she blushes to find her body "betrayed" (the rhyme for "displayd") to his sight (310–24). Still more revealing—conceptually speaking, that is—is the difference between the ways in which Venus and Hero "strove." While Venus strove to catch Adonis's eye, Hero strove to slip from Leander's grip. Having admitted him to the "fort" of her bed on condition of a "truce" in their war of desire and resistance, she soon finds

> that the truce was broke, and she alas
> (Poore sillie maiden) at his mercie was.
> Love is not ful of pittie (as men say)
> But deaffe and cruell, where he meanes to pray.
> Even as a bird, which in our hands we wring,
> Foorth plungeth, and oft flutters with her wing,
> She trembling strove, this strife of hers (like that
> Which made the world) another world begat,
> Of unknowne joy.
>
> (2.285–93)

Scrupulously resisting the temptation to stop at "strove," I quote the whole passage. But its apparently blissful resolution cannot erase the meaning of the struggle it represents.[41] With the brilliant pun on "pray," the narrator turns Leander from votary to predator, from pitiful, shivering, wave-worn supplicant to merciless *raptor*. He grips Hero as "we" (meaning of course *we men*) wring a bird in our hands, as Ovid's aquiline Jupiter gripped the struggling Asterie, as his eagle-like Tereus gripped the terrified Philomela, and as Marlowe's own Mercury in the present poem gripped the country maid who checked his efforts to rape her only after she had "striv'ne in vaine" (1.413).[42] Like all these other women, Hero "trembling strove" against the grip of male desire—without hope of breaking it by speech. From the beginning, Leander was drawn to Hero not by anything she said, but by the mute beauty on which he rapturously "gazed" (1.163). He who has spoken to her at far greater length than she has replied is now "deaffe" to her entreaties. She is caught in Leander's silencing embrace.

The metaphors of predator and prey used to represent the moment of consummation are reinforced by the imagery of sacrifice used elsewhere in the poem. When Leander comes to Hero's turret for the first time after they meet, she throws herself "Upon his bosome, where with yeelding eyes, / She offers up her selfe a sacrifice / To slake his anger, if he were displeas'd" (47–49). Sacrifice—even loving sacrifice—all too easily leads to bloodshed. In the ekphrastic account of the pavement picture, the description of the adulterously heaving Mars as "blood-quaffing" not only reminds us of his status as the god of war but also suggests—since his partner is Venus—the intensity of the intercourse between war and love, the bloodthirsty violence of lust. The very first line of the poem speaks of "*Hellespont* guiltie of True-loves blood," and when first seen by Leander, Hero is "sacrificing turtles [i.e., turtle-doves'] blood" (1.158). Keach reads the second line as an almost comic rewriting of the passage in which Hero's blue kirtle is said to be stained with the blood of "wretched Lovers slaine" (1.15–16)—presumably in suicidal frustration. "The initial impression of human sacrifice," writes Keach, "followed by the discovery of what the bloodstains are [from slain doves, not slain men], makes us uncomfortably aware of the rather silly way in which Hero worships her goddess" (97). But "sacrificing turtles blood" plainly echoes "guilty of True-loves blood," and the doves she sacrifices in the fateful moment when Leander first sees her prefigure the bird of prey she will later become in his rapacious grip. At the end of the story that Marlowe did not live to finish, the woman who "offers up her selfe a sacrifice" to the living Leander throws herself into the ocean after he is drowned there.

To say that his passionate seizing of Hero amounts to rape is of course to overlook her own desire for Leander and the spirit of self-sacrifice that drives her to join him even in death. But in *Hero and Leander,* as in the novels of Longus and Achilles Tatius, the verbalized depiction of rape gives us a way of perceiving what is silently experienced—covertly endured—by a woman who may seem all too willing to accept her lover's demands. Hero, as David Lee Miller observes, never assumes the masculine position "of the desiring subject, which is also that of the speaking subject"—the position shared by Leander and the narrator (Miller 770). From the moment Leander first sees her, she is at once the object and victim of male desire. While Leander grows "enamoured" of her when he gazes on her, she is simply "strooke" in the heart by the fire of *his* longing, and when she takes a vow of chastity to Venus, Cupid rejects her vow "and shot a shaft that burning from him went, / Wherewith she strooken, look'd so dolefully, / As made Love sigh, to see his tirannie" (1.372–74). Cupid's would-be pitying sigh at her weeping thinly veils what Miller calls "a predatory delight in her humiliation" (764). The burning shaft that strikes Hero after her heart has already been "strooke" by Leander's gaze prefigures only too clearly what she must undergo. To experience the world "of unknowne joy," she must be seized and penetrated even as she tremblingly strives against it.

A verbalized depiction that serves as an interpretive signpost for the reader works quite differently from the kind of ekphrasis we find in Sidney's *New Ar-*

cadia (published 1590), where pictures of women are early on presented as objects of consumption by the male gaze. When the shipwrecked Musidorus finds his way to the house of Kalander in Arcadia, he finds there—among other things—a painting of Diana and her nymphs seen bathing by Actaeon, and a painting of an extraordinarily beautiful young woman standing between an attractive middle-aged woman and a handsome old man (Sidney 15). When Musidorus's friend Pyrocles sees the pictures and learns that the young beauty is a princess named Philoclea who has been forbidden by her father to marry, he sets out to pursue her by disguising himself as a woman—in which guise he voyeuristically watches her bathing and then, inspired by a "divine fury," writes a song celebrating the beauty of every part of her body (Sidney 188–95).[43] Paintings serving in this way as models of voyeuristic gazing or as simple provocations to a passionate quest do not guide us to see what pictures of rape prefigure beneath the surface of an erotic narrative. Verbalized depictions of beauty excite desire by prompting the reader to identify with a male gaze.[44] Verbalized depictions of rape prompt the reader to scrutinize the narrative with the eyes of a woman, and thus to hear a voice that might otherwise be silenced by suppression.

Spenserian ekphrasis does not fit wholly into either of these two categories. By turns erotic, admonitory, or both, it focuses at least as much on the seductive power of women as on the sexually predatory violence of men, and in the emasculating worlds of sensuality that Spenser represents, rape is sometimes strangely transmuted. In book 3 of *The Faerie Queene,* for instance, the walls of the Castle Joyeous are adorned with tapestries depicting the story of Venus and Adonis. While Spenser's woven Venus is less overtly erotic than the "naked beauty" embroidered on the sleeve of Marlowe's Hero, Spenser nonetheless turns the tapestries into a story of sexual enticement and fatal separation. With "slights and sweet allurements" Venus draws Adonis into a shady bower where she puts him to sleep and, reversing what Actaeon does with Diana, secretly spies on "each daintie lim" while he bathes, before vainly trying to dissuade him from hunting big game. The closest we get to rape in this ekphrastic story is the verbalized picture of Adonis himself "Deadly engored of a great wild Bore" and staining "his snowy skin with hatefull hew" until Venus turns him into a flower depicted so vividly on the tapestry that it seems to grow there (3.1.35–38).

Before this ekphrastic passage, Arthur and Guyon have already set off to rescue Florimell from a forester who is lustfully pursuing her with "a sharp bore speare" (3.1.17–18). But in the Castle Joyeous itself, the counterparts of Venus and Adonis are Malecasta ("badly chaste") and the heroically chaste Britomart, armed as a male and taken for one by all she meets.[45] Like Venus with Adonis, Malecasta tries to seduce Britomart, entreating "her to disarme, and with delightfull sport / To loose her warlike limbs and strong effort" (3.1.52). Unlike Venus, Malecasta fails in her effort at seduction, but the outcome of her effort subtly evokes both rape and the fatal goring of Adonis. When the sleeping Britomart awakens to find that Malecasta has crept into her bed, she runs for her sword "to gride / The loathed leachour" (3.1.62): to stab what she takes to be a male predator. Malecasta's shriek of terror then awakens her six knights, one of whom shoots an arrow at Britomart that "was seene / To gore her side"—not deeply, but enough to draw out drops of blood "Which did her lilly smock with staines of vermeil steppe" (3.1.65). The vivid goring of both Adonis and Britomart links them to the intended victim of the forester's phallic bore spear, and suggests that for Spenser, rape becomes a kind of sexual violence that is equally destructive to both men and women.[46]

A similar suggestion is made by the description of the carvings on the gate of the Bower of Bliss in book 2:

> Yt framéd was of precious yvory,
>   That seemd a worke of admirable wit;
>   And therein all the famous history
>   Of Jason and Medaea was ywrit
>   Her mighty charmes, her furious loving fit,
>   His goodly conquest of the golden fleece,
>   His falséd faith, and love too lightly flit,
>   The wondred Argo, which in venturous peece
> First through the Euxine seas bore all the flowr of Greece.
>
> Ye might have seene the frothy billowes fry
>   Under the ship, as thorough them she went,
>   That seemd the waves were into yvory,
>   Or yvory into the waves were sent;
>   And other where the snowy substaunce sprent
>   With vermell, like the boyes bloud therein shed,
>   A piteous spectacle did represent,
>   And otherwhiles with gold besprinkeléd;
> Yt seemd th'enchaunted flame, which did Creüsa wed.
>   (2.12.44–45)

This passage plainly exemplifies two familiar components of ekphrasis. First, as we have seen so often in ancient ekphrasis, a strong narrative impulse turns graphic scenes into a story: here a "history" of Medea's passion for Jason, his conquest of the Golden Fleece with the aid of the "mighty charmes" she furnished to drug the dragon guarding it, their flight across the sea together in the *Argo*, their killing of Medea's brother Apsyrtus and scattering of his limbs on the sea to delay their pursuers, Jason's "falsed faith" in abandoning Medea for Creusa, and Medea's treacherous gift of the poisoned robe that burst into flames when Creusa donned it. The forward momentum of this ekphrastic narrative, however, is reversed (after the reference to Jason's "falséd faith") and suspended by a fixed focus on the carving of the voyage. The lines on this carving richly display a second familiar feature of ekphrasis: representational friction. Ivory masquerades as foam, and vermilion (vermell) as blood. The subject matter and the medium of representation become virtually interchangeable, with waves turning into ivory, and ivory turning into waves. Exemplifying the triumph of artificiality, the ivory gate fittingly introduces us to the realm of Acrasia, whose power to seduce young noblemen is bound up with the cunning artistry exemplified by her "vele of silk and silver thin, / That hid no whit her alabaster skin, / But rather shewd more white, if more might be" (2.12.77).[47]

In this case, then, representational friction becomes representational indeterminacy, an almost lubricous sliding back and forth between art and nature, medium and referent. Embedded in this play of indeterminacy and never quite elided by it are the signs—the graphic traces—of violence. If the foamy waves can turn into ivory, the enchanted flame might be read as gold and the blood of the boy might be seen as a purely decorative vermilion (vermell).[48] But the passage makes us see "piteous spectacle[s]": vermilion signifying the blood of the boy sprinkled on the foam, gold signifying the flame that devoured Creusa. The verbalized depiction of the story of Medea and Jason exemplifies what permeates Spenser's treatment of love: the violence wrought by unbridled desire.

In book 3, the generalized character of this violence seems reaffirmed by the tapestries we find in the house of Busirane. Representing the "cruell batels" Cupid fought against gods, kings, and emperors to establish his power, the woven scenes display a succession of divine and human males struck by Cupid's "hart-percing dart" (3.11.30) as well as the females—such as Europa and Semele—whom they victimized in turn.[49] It is clear, however, that the violence wrought by passion in these tapestries falls unequally on the two sexes. Semele dies when Jove comes to her in thunder and lightning (3.11.33); Apollo kills Coronis in a jealous rage (3.11.37), and Daphne eludes him only by turning into a laurel so that Cupid can punish Apollo for exposing his mother's affair with Mars: "yet was thy love her death," says the poet, apostrophizing Apollo, "and her death was thy smart" (3.11.36). The lust-smitten gods depicted here do not die. They make women die, and except for Ganymede it is women who are repeatedly seized and abducted.[50] To this extent, the Busirane tapestries reflect the precedent set by the mythical weaver of multiple rapes: Arachne.

Spenser generally treats Arachne no better than Dante does. In the Bower of Bliss, her art is compared with that of Acrasia (2.12.77), who knows at once how to weave a seductively diaphanous veil and to entrap men.[51] In *Muiopotmos: or the Fate of the Butterfly,* a mock-epic "complaint" published in 1591, Arachne becomes a second-rate weaver. To explain why a spider named Aragnoll—who turns out to be Arachne's son—set out to trap a butterfly, Spenser drastically revises Ovid's story of the weaving contest. This time Minerva (Dame Pallas) adds a splendidly lifelike butterfly to her portrayal of the gods in council and thereby wins the contest, leaving Arachne to fret and burn in a rage that turns her into a spider—with a grudge against butterflies that her son inherits (329–52).[52] For all his disparagement of Arachne, however, Spenser gives full weight to her depiction of rape. The many rapes depicted in the Arachnean tapestry Ovid describes contract to just one—the rape of Europa—but this one episode is represented in what appears to be a succession of two verbalized pictures:

> She seemed still backe unto the land to looke,
> And her play-fellowes aide to call, and feare
> The dashing of the waves, that up she tooke
> Her daintie feete, and garments gathered neare:
> But (Lord) how she in everie member shooke,
> When as the land she saw no more appeare,
> But a wide wildernes of waters deepe:
> Then gan she greatly to lament and weepe.
>
> (281–88)

The first half of the stanza translates Ovid almost word for word. But while Ovid reports on just one picture of Europa looking back, calling on her companions, and drawing up her feet from the leaping waves (*Met* 6.105–7), Spenser transcribes two pictures of her mounting anguish. Both pictures present Europa not as an object to be consumed by our gaze but as a viewing subject in her own right: first looking back longingly at the receding shore, then looking out desolately at the wilderness of open sea.

The passage on the Busirane tapestries includes nothing so poignant as this account—written not long after the Busirane passage—of what Arachne wove.[53] In the seventeen stanzas (29–46) on the Busirane tapestries, Europa herself gets just one line: Jove is reportedly depicted "Now like a Bull, Europa to withdraw" (3.11.30). But in describing at length a set of tapestries that chiefly depict rapes committed by gods in animal form, Spenser is clearly recalling Ovid's description of Arachne's handiwork. More importantly, he is using the manifold depiction of rape in the Busirane tapestries to prefigure what comes at the end of book 3: the spectacle of Amoret tortured by the lustful Busirane.

Amoret, a virgin beloved by Scudamour, has been captured by Busirane the "Enchaunter," who tortures her because she will not renounce Scudamour for him. She first appears in the middle room of Busirane's house, which Britomart enters after viewing the tapestries in the outer room. In the middle room, decorated with "monstrous formes" of false loves in gold relief (3.11.51–52), Britomart sees the "maske" of Cupid: a phantasmal procession of allegorical figures dominated by the god himself riding on a ravenous lion. Marching before him is "a most faire Dame" led by Despight and Cruelty, who have cut open her naked breast, drawn out her trembling heart, transfixed it with a "deadly dart," and laid its blood-soaked mass in a silver basin (3.12.19–21). After all these figures return to the inner room from which they came, the door is locked behind them, and Britomart, who has resolved to rescue Amoret, waits two days for them to reappear. When the door to the inner room suddenly opens, she enters to find the "same woeful Ladie"—Amoret—bound fast by her hands to a brass pillar, where Busirane sits "figuring"—i.e., drawing— "straunge characters" with blood "dripping from her dying hart, / Seeming transfixed with a cruell dart / And all perforce to make her him to love" (3.12.31).

What to make of these ghastly pageants? Harry Berger reads them as manifestations of Scudamour's jealous desire to dominate Amoret, of his tendency "to see his relation to Amoret as one of assault and conquest rather than one of persuasion, protection, and companionship" (189). Alternatively, since Amoret (as we learn in 4.1.3) was abducted into Busirane's masque during the feast held to celebrate her wedding to Scudamour, Theresa Krier suggests that her torments may signify what she suffers when her interior life is publicly exposed—and thus violated—during her boisterous wedding day" (Krier 190).[54] But whatever the tortures may tell us about Amoret's feelings or Scudamour's possessiveness, the dart that transfixes Amoret's heart in this scene has a tangible counterpart in the ekphrastic passage on the tapestries, wherein "was writ," we learn, "how often thundering Jove / Had felt the point of [Cupid's] hart-percing dart" (3.11.30). Transfixed by Cupid's dart, Jove feels compelled to fix his own phallic dart in a succession of women from Helle to Proserpine, and in the narrative of book 3 as a whole, women are repeatedly threatened by or subjected to violent penetration.[55] Florimell is menaced by the bore-spear of the lustful forester; Britomart is gored by the arrow of Gardante (3.1.65); Amoret is stuck with a dart; and Britomart again is stuck in the "snowie chest" with a knife as soon as Busirane sees her (3.12.32–33).

In drawing "straunge characters of his art" with the blood he has drawn from Amoret's own heart, Busirane recalls the "purpureas notas" with which Philomela depicted Tereus's violation of her. But now the woman's tormenter is advertising the brutality of his lust rather than ruthlessly silencing its object.[56] As the collector (and probably the commissioner) of tapestries depicting rape, Busirane knows only too well how to represent it himself, and he does so not only in the characters of his art but in the bloody picture he draws with his knife as soon as he sees Britomart: "it strooke into her snowie chest, / That little drops empurpled her faire brest" (3.12.33). The wound is shallow enough so that Britomart can strike back at Busirane, break the torturing power of his charms, and thus liberate Amoret, but the picture he draws in blood takes its place with the pictures drawn in colored threads on the walls of his outer room. In the other works we have examined in this chapter, ekphrastically represented pictures of rape prefigure acts of sexual violence. Here an attempt at sexual violence generates a new kind of depiction. In place of the purple "notas" that Philomela weaves into her tapestry, the assaulted woman's own purple blood now tells a graphic tale.

IV

THE PAINTED RAPE OF TROY IN SHAKESPEARE'S *LUCRECE*

Though English poetry repeatedly invokes or echoes the story of Philomela, the verbalized painting in Eliot's *Waste Land* suggestively recalls what most references to her omit or suppress: the picture of rape woven by Philomela herself. In Renaissance versions of the Philomela story, the closest we get to its ekphrastic center is in Shakespeare's *Titus Andronicus* (circa 1594), where Titus's daughter Lavinia suffers a fate even worse than Philomela's: raped by Chiron and Demetrius, sons of the Gothic Queen Tamora, she loses not only her tongue but her hands. When her uncle Marcus finds her in this condition, he says at first, "Be sure some Tereus has deflow'red thee, / And lest thou shouldst detect him, cut thy tongue" (2.4.26–27). But Marcus then realizes that a handless Lavinia cannot even speak with her threads:

> Fair Philomel, why she but lost her tongue,
> And in a tedious sampler sewed her mind:
> But, lovely niece, that mean is cut from thee;
> A craftier Tereus, cousin, hast thou met,
> And he hath cut those pretty fingers off
> That could have better sewed than Philomel.
> (2.4.38–43)

Lavinia nonetheless finds a way of speaking. To explain what has happened to her, she literally returns to Ovid's text, using her stumps to rummage in a pile of books until she finds the *Metamorphoses,* then turning its leaves so that her father can see "the tragic tale of Philomel" and realize what has happened to her (4.1.29–49). But since Ovid cannot name *her* rapists, she must "give signs" of their identities (4.1.61), and Marcus shows her how to do so by putting his staff in his mouth and using his feet to guide it as he writes his name in the sand. Following his example, she simply inscribes the crime and the names of the criminals: "Stuprum [rape]. Chiron. Demetrius" (4.1.78).[57]

The revenge taken for the rape and mutilation of Lavinia closely resembles the revenge taken by Philomela and Procne: Titus has Chiron and Demetrius ground up into a pie that is baked with their blood and served to their mother. But precisely because the story of Lavinia follows so closely that of Philomela, the differences stand out. While Ovid's Philomela weaves a picture of the rape, or at least weaves graphic words ("purple signs on white threads"), the Shakespearean heroine who best recalls her simply writes.[58]

To see what Shakespeare does with the ekphrastic heart of the Philomela myth, then, we must consider the painting described in his version of the story of Lucrece.[59] In *The Rape of Lucrece,* published in 1594, Shakespeare explicitly links his violated heroine both to the myth of Philomela and to a work of art: "a piece / Of skillful painting" representing the fall of Troy" (1366–67). The connection between the painting and Shakespeare's allusions to the Philomela myth emerges only after we have carefully studied them both. As Coppelia Kahn observes, the Philomela whom Shakespeare explicitly links to Lucrece is not the weaver of a tapestry depicting the barbarity of a rapist but simply the mournful nightingale Philomela became ("*Lucrece*" 152). Recounting her woes at length after the rape and resolving on suicide, Lucrece is called "lamenting

Philomele" protracting "the well-tuned warble of her nightly sorrow" (1079–80), and she herself shortly summons the bird as a kindred mourner: "Come, Philomele, that sing'st of ravishment, / Make thy sad grove in my disheveled hair" (1128–29). But having sung to herself her own sad song, Lucrece seeks a painting—a visual rather than auditory correlative for her suffering. "To see sad sights," the narrator observes

> moves more than hear them told,
> For then the eye interprets to the ear
> The heavy motion that it doth behold
> When every part a part of woe doth bear.
> (1324–27)

In this extraordinary tribute to the eloquence of what is traditionally considered a mute art, Shakespeare begins to suggest why a painting will play such a crucial role in this poem. Lucrece's only confidant is a painting of the fall of Troy. It is to this she turns for solace while waiting for her husband to come home in response to the letter she writes about her unspecified "grief" (1308).

The more than two hundred lines that Shakespeare gives us on this painting (1367–1568) display several of the formal features we have seen in ancient and Dantean ekphrasis. Representational friction surfaces when we are told that "many a dry drop seemed a weeping tear / Shed for the slaught'red husband by the wife" (1375–76). To show how "the eye interprets to the ear," the narrator prosopopeially elicits a visual speech from the painted faces of Ulysses and Ajax, which "most expressly told" their respective temperaments (1394–1400), and from the painted figure of Nestor, who stands "as 'twere encouraging the Greeks to fight" (1402). Nevertheless, in spite of its extraordinary length, this passage refuses to furnish one of the most important things that ekphrasis traditionally provides: a coherent narrative about the picture it describes.

Unlike his predecessors, Shakespeare does not simply turn the painting of a single action into a story, or represent the painting as a succession of chronologically ordered scenes. Instead he enumerates scenes in the chronologically random order with which a viewer might pick them up from a multitemporal canvas. Starting, for instance, with a few lines on the Greek army drawn up before the walls of Troy (1367–68), he turns to the Trojan women weeping for their slaughtered husbands (1375–76), then the "laboring pioner" [engineer] trying (presumably) to scale the towers from which Trojan eyes look out (1380–86), then an army on the march (1387–93), the faces of Ajax and Ulysses (1394–1400), Nestor urging a crowd of Greek soldiers to fight (1401–21), Trojan mothers rejoicing to see Hector and their sons marching out to meet the Greeks (1429), the red tide of battle blood running to the Simois river by the Trojan shore (1436–42), Hecuba looking at Priam bleeding under Pyrrhus's foot (1447–49), the bound and treacherously mild-looking Sinon brought to Troy by Phrygian shepherds (1501–5), and finally, Priam weeping in sympathy with Sinon's "borrowed tears" (1548–49). The scenes are clearly not simultaneous, and just as clearly not in chronological order.[60] They make coherent sense only to a viewer—more accurately a reader—who already knows the full story which they fragmentarily depict. To connect, for instance, the scene of the mortally wounded Priam with the Sinon scenes mentioned after it, we have to know that Sinon's deceitful story about the Trojan horse (curiously mentioned nowhere in this long account) led Priam to admit its bellyful of Greeks, including the bloodthirsty Pyrrhus.

What then does the painting mean in context? To answer this question, we must be able to say what it means to Lucrece, for like the passage on the painting of Philomela in Achilles Tatius's *Leucippe and Clitophon,* the stanzas on the painting of Troy in Shakespeare's poem combine extensive commentary by the narrator with further commentary by a major character, who in this case links the painting directly to herself. What then does it say to Lucrece? And what does it say to us about her? The variety and randomness of the scenes described here give these questions a special urgency, but the germ of an answer to them lies in a phrase with which the painting is introduced. It is, we are told, a painting of Troy attacked by Greeks in vengeance "for Helen's rape" (1369)—i.e., for the raping of Helen.[61]

The pointed reference to rape at the very beginning of this long ekphrastic passage is just one of many things that connects the painting to the Philomelan plight of Shakespeare's heroine. As the painting of an attack made in vengeance for rape, it seems essentially to represent what Lucrece has just said she wants her husband to take: "revenge on him that made me stop my breath" (1180), revenge on Tarquin, who has left her blood so "defiled" (1029) that she feels she must take her own life to purge her body of the stain. Yet to read the painting as a model for the revenge that Lucrece wants taken on her behalf is to overlook what she says about Helen, her would-be counterpart in the Trojan scenario. So far from seeing Helen as a fellow-victim of sexual violation or even of abduction, Lucrece holds her responsible for the disaster represented by the painting. "Show me," she says, "the strumpet that began this stir, / That with my nails her beauty I may tear" (1471–72).

Since Lucrece has already chastised herself for what she calls her "trespass" (1070) and her "fault" (1073) in failing to resist Tarquin effectively, this denunciation of Helen could be either a covert expression of self-hatred or a desperate attempt to project onto another the strumpet role that she herself has been made to play.[62] In either case, Helen is nowhere described as a figure in the painting. The central woman in it is Hecuba, whose ravaged form is the antithesis of Helen's:

> In her the painter had anatomized
> Time's ruin, beauty's rack, and grim care's reign. . . .
>
> On this sad shadow Lucrece spends her eyes
> And shapes her sorrow to the beldame's woes,
> Who nothing wants to answer her but cries

And bitter words to ban her cruel foes.
The painter was no god to lend her those;
And therefore Lucrece swears he did her wrong
To give her so much grief and not a tongue.
(1450–51, 1457–63)

In the ravaged figure of Hecuba, Lucrece sees both herself and the tongueless Philomela. Suppressing momentarily the cause of her own sorrow, she prosopopeially gives her voice to the painted figure who speaks only in graphic signs, in the "chops and wrinkles" of her careworn cheeks (1452). "Poor instrument . . . without a sound," says Lucrece to her; "I'll tune thy woes with my lamenting tongue" (1464–65). This is a dialogue of sound and painted sights in which Lucrece "lends them words, and she their looks doth borrow" (1498). Like the tapestry woven by the silenced Philomela, the painted Hecuba silently speaks of suffering which "the eye interprets to the ear"; in turn Lucrece speaks for her, answering one who has already "answer[ed]" her with her stricken look.

This way of looking differs radically from Tarquin's way of looking at Lucrece herself. In the first part of the poem, when the "lust-breathed" Tarquin rushes from the siege of Ardea to the wife of his fellow-soldier Collatine, Lucrece is chiefly a silent object of his devouring gaze. His lust for her is first aroused, to be sure, by Collatine's praise of her beauty and chastity in Tarquin's own tent—a praise reinforced by the narrator's elaborate blazoning of "Beauty's red and Virtue's white" in the heraldry of her shieldlike face.[63] But when Tarquin reaches Collatium, he finds Collatine's superlatives far surpassed by the beauty of Lucrece in person, which he consumes "in silent wonder of still-gazing eyes" (84). While she says next to nothing and does not know how to read his looks because she has "never coped with stranger eyes" (99), he praises Collatine to conceal his real intent (106–14), and after she has gone to bed, he steals into her chamber and draws the curtains of her bed to watch her while she sleeps: the helpless and supremely vulnerable object of his enraptured and piti-less gaze.[64] The ekphrastically elaborate description of what Tarquin sees—the lily-white hands, the rosy cheek, the golden hair, the blue-veined breasts, the coral lips, the dimpled chin—nearly turns Lucrece into a picture, but it is the kind of picture that presupposes a male viewer. "Within a 'heterosexual' optic where specialized functions are assigned to each sex," writes Norman Bryson, "pleasure in looking is broken between active (= male) and passive (= female)" (*Word* 96). For the active male viewer, gazing at the picture of a beau-tiful woman—more precisely a woman of picture-perfect beauty—is a com-plex activity in which the aesthetic can all too easily become the erotic, in which the image of static perfection that gratifies a disinterested love of beauty can readily activate the desire to possess and violate the body of that image.[65]

When the sexually violated Lucrece "spends her eyes" on the picture of the grief-stricken Hecuba, then, she is doing something wholly different from what

Tarquin initially did to her. Rather than simply gazing at Hecuba, she weeps for her and with her. Hecuba epitomizes the ruin of a city that was surprised in sleep, like Lucrece herself, after being deceived by Sinon—a man who seemed just as trustworthy as Tarquin did to her. Says Lucrece to herself:

> To me came Tarquin armed, to beguiled [i.e., beguile]
> With outward honesty, but yet defiled
> With inward vice. As Priam him [Sinon] did cherish,
> So did I Tarquin; so my Troy did perish.
>
> (1544–47)

Here is the most explicit point of contact between the rape and the painting of Troy: Lucrece sees her own body—"my Troy"—as a city invaded and despoiled. The metaphorical representation of rape as invasion is implicitly announced in the very first stanza of the poem: when Tarquin turns from the besieging of Ardea to gallop "all in post" (1) to Collatium, he aims to besiege Lucrece and fire the Troy of her chastity with the "embracing flames" of his lust.[66] I will shortly say more about just how and why Shakespeare represents the rape as a military invasion. But from the lines just quoted I must first unwind two other strands: the problematic relation between viewers *of* the painting and viewers *in* the painting, and the equally problematic relation between the deceptiveness of Sinon and the deceptiveness of painting itself.

First of all, the two viewers *of* the painting—the narrator and Lucrece herself—lead us to see the viewers *in* the painting precisely in terms of what Kahn calls the "scopic economy" (143) established in the first part of the poem. Before the rape, Tarquin gazes lustfully at his prey, who cannot see the meaning of his gaze when awake and of course has no power to return it when she sleeps. The Trojans represented in the painting reveal scarcely any more power to face down the Greeks. "From the tow'rs of Troy," writes the narrator, appeared "the very eyes of men through loopholes thrust, / Gazing upon the Greeks with little lust" (1382–84). If we can manage to overlook the comic-book effect of exophthalmic protrusion here, the second line of the couplet articulates a brilliant re-viewing of the gaze. Like Tarquin, the Trojan warriors gaze, but unlike him, they feel little lust because the men they see have come to rape their city; in this case, they can scarcely hope to dominate or master those they are gazing at. Conversely, when Lucrece sees the painted eyes of the Greeks through the eyes of Hecuba, whom she looks *with* rather than at, she perceives their look of conquering rage and yearns with her knife to "scratch out the angry eyes / Of all the Greeks that are thine enemies" (1470). Knowing only too well now how to read the meaning of their furious gaze, she desperately yearns to annihilate its power. Likewise, when she detects "signs of truth in [Sinon's] plain face" while gazing on him ("on him she gazed, and gazing still"), she first concludes that the picture cannot be trusted, and then—remembering Tarquin's shape—that she cannot trust the face (1531–40). Shedding false tears to gain Priam's pity,

the painted Sinon uses his eyes on the king just as pitilessly as the gazing
Tarquin used his eyes on Lucrece. In response, she does to Sinon's image what
she wanted to do to the painted eyes of the Greek soldiers and the painted
beauty of Helen: "she tears the senseless Sinon with her nails" (1564).

Superficially, this outraged rending of the painted image recalls what Athena
did to Arachne's woven pictures of rape. But Lucrece's attack on the painted
Sinon here is actually the counterpart of what Philomela and Procne do to the
living body of Tereus's son. This is as close as she gets to revenge for the rape.
Unable or unwilling to avenge it directly—she makes Collatine and his men
swear to do that after her death—Lucrece strikes Tarquin in a manner doubly
vicarious: she tears the painted image of his ancient Greek surrogate.

Thus attacked, the painted image of a deceiver inevitably calls to mind the
deceitfulness of painting itself and thus underscores the theme of pictorial illusion that permeates the whole ekphrastic passage. We can gauge the intensity of
Shakespeare's concentration on the complexities of pictorial illusion—on what
the picture shows and hides—when we compare this passage with another
lengthy piece of ekphrasis written slightly over a hundred years earlier and describing a painting, or set of paintings, based on the *Aeneid.*

In the first book of Chaucer's *House of Fame,* the narrator tells us that on one
December night he fell asleep and dreamed he was in a richly decorated temple
of Venus, which he identifies as such when he sees a painted figure:

> I saugh anoon-ryght hir figure
> Naked fletying in a see.
> And also on hir hed, pardee,
> Hir rose garlond whit and red,
> And hir comb to kembe hyr hed,
> Hir dowves, and daun Cupido,
> Hir blynde sone, and Vulcano,
> That in his face was ful broun.
>   (132–39)

The narrator quickly recognizes this figure because he knows how to read the
iconographic signs. A naked lady painted floating in the sea with a garland of
red and white roses, a set of doves, and a blind boy hovering about her—what
can all this mean if not Venus?[67] But when the narrator turns from this portrait
to the painted story of Aeneas, which he describes in a passage of over three
hundred lines (151–467), he makes virtually no effort to say how the pictures
tell the story. After first quoting what he saw "writen on a table of bras" (142),
which gives the opening lines of the *Aeneid,* he writes:

> First sawgh I the destruction
> Of Troye, thurgh the Grek Synon,
> [That] with his false forswerynge,
> And his chere and his lesynge,

Made the hors brought into Troye,
Thorgh which Troyens loste al her joye.
(151–56)

While the opening verb ("sawgh") denotes the act of seeing, these lines say
nothing specific about what is *depicted,* and they make no reference to the appearance of Sinon except for "his chere," which could mean either his "good
cheer"—his treacherously ingratiating manner—or just his "look," whatever it
was.[68] Unlike Shakespeare's Sinon, whose face is meticulously described (*Rape*
1506–12), this agent of "lesynge" (deceit) is virtually faceless. Chaucer's narrator is simply not concerned with or constrained by the distinctive features of
pictorial representation. As several commentators have noted, his ekphrastic
language is ambiguous and fluid.[69] When he speaks of what is "grave" (i.e.,
graven) on the wall (157), he could mean either drawn or written, and when he
tells us flatly that he *hears* what the ghost of Creusa says to Aeneas (189–92), he
does not even try to explain—as Dante does with the sculpted figure of
Mary—how her appearance signifies speech, or leads him to infer it. Though
the narrator ends the long ekphrastic passage by extolling the beauty of the pictures ("Yet sawgh I never such noblesse / Of ymages" [471–72]), he scarcely
allows us to see the pictures as such. Rather than describing them or explaining
how they make their meanings, he narrates the events they represent.

By contrast, Shakespeare's narrator carefully explains just what the painting
of Troy presents to the eye. He salutes the verisimilitude with which the painter
has rendered such things as the tears shed by wives for their slaughtered husbands (1375–76) and the trembling gait of pale cowards on the march (1391–
93). Furthermore, to prepare us for the painting of the consummately deceptive Sinon, the narrator carefully explains the "conceit deceitful" exemplified by
the painting of Greek soldiers gathered to hear Nestor speak:

> Some high, some low—the painter was so nice,
> The scalps of many, almost hid behind,
> To jump up higher seemed, to mock the mind.
>
> Here one man's hand leaned on another's head,
> His nose being shadowed by his neighbor's ear;
> . . . .
> For much imaginary work was there:
> Conceit deceitful, so compact, so kind,
> That for Achilles' image stood his spear,
> Griped in an armèd hand; himself behind
> Was left unseen, save to the eye of mind:
> A hand, a foot, a face, a leg, a head
> Stood for the whole to be imaginèd.
> (1412–16, 1422–28)

Wrought of overlapping figures and body parts representing whole bodies, the visual effects of this picture seem to epitomize the kind of thing that Plato attacked when he defined painting as an art of appearances designed to trick the eye rather than reveal to the mind the truth about the objects it represents.[70] Hulse, in fact, finds Shakespeare probably indebted here to Philostratus's explanation of how a painting of the siege of Thebes deceives the viewer: "Some [of the troops] are seen in full figure, others with the legs hidden, others from the waist up, then only the busts of some, heads only, helmets only, and finally just spear-points. This, my boy, is perspective; since the problem is to deceive the eyes as they travel back along with the proper receding planes of the picture."[71] Whether or not Shakespeare knew this passage, Hulse believes that he shared Philostratus's conception of pictorial—and rhetorical—representation. "The representation, either in word, paint, or marble, is not true to life, much less to an objective ideal. It is distorted to accommodate the process of perception, and those very distortions are Shakespeare's main interest" (*Metamorphic Verse* 183).

But this itself distorts the meaning of Shakespeare's passage, which says something fundamentally different from what Philostratus says about a particular painting and what Plato says about all painting. Besides the minor fact that Shakespeare's narrator is not discussing linear perspective, as Philostratus is, but simply the overlapping of forms, the narrator's account of pictorial representation is primarily semiotic rather than illusionistic. No mere optical illusion—not even the "mechanism of projection" by which a blurred or fragmented image may prompt us to imagine that we see a definite whole one—can explain how a spear gripped in an armed hand could signify Achilles.[72] This combination of visual synecdoche and visual metonymy is explicitly addressed "to the eye of the mind." To grasp the meaning of the image, we would have to know how to decode the images of a particular hand and a particular spear. Otherwise we could in no sense see Achilles.

The depiction of the crowd in this painting, then, exemplifies the kind of "deceitful" effect that requires the full and conscious cooperation of the beholder's mind. The way in which the painting makes its meaning can hardly be explained by any theory of pictorial illusion—especially since one of the most conspicuous figures in the painting is himself a master of deceit. Can a painting represent deceitfulness as such? Pliny thought that the ancient Greek Euphranor had done so, representing Ulysses "so that you could recognize his insanity was only feigned and not real."[73] But in depicting Sinon, the man who painted Troy

> labored with his skill
> To hide deceit, and give the harmless show
> An humble gait, calm looks, eyes wailing still,
> A brow unbent that seemed to welcome woe,
> Cheeks neither red nor pale, but mingled so

That blushing red no guilty instance gave
Nor ashy pale the fear that false hearts have.
(1506–12)

Ironically, the balance of red and white in Sinon's painted face is delicate enough to recall the decorous struggle of Beauty's red and Virtue's white in the real face of Lucrece at the beginning of the poem. If deceit walks like hypocrisy, "Invisible, except to God alone," as Milton says (*Paradise Lost* 3.683–84), no visual art can represent it. Unlike feelings such as "blunt rage," which is "expressly told" by the painted face of Ajax (1397–98), the true intentions of a truly effective deceiver cannot be visually disclosed. The painstaking verisimilitude with which the painter renders the appearance of Sinon's woeful figure serves only to hide Sinon's real aim. Hence Lucrece, while gazing on the figure, chides the painter precisely "for his wondrous skill" (1528).

But she would not and could not chide him for his wondrous skill if she did not already know who Sinon was. Just as the painting presupposes a viewer capable of recognizing the spear and hand of Achilles, it also presupposes a viewer familiar with the story of Troy and Sinon's role in its fall. Lucrece of course is such a viewer. But because she has not yet firmly grasped the insidious nature of duplicity, the "signs of truth" she sees in the "plain face" of the painted Sinon (1532) contradict rather than deepen her understanding of his character. She resolves the contradiction only by recalling how much "outward honesty" Tarquin displayed (1545), so that for her, plain signs of truth in a painted face now come to signify precisely the opposite of truth: "It cannot be, I find," she says to herself, "But such a face should bear a wicked mind" (1539–40).[74]

In tearing this painted face with her nails, Lucrece seeks not only to strike back vicariously at Tarquin; she also yearns to slash the face of duplicity itself, which at this moment she sees embodied in the art of painting. Picture-painting is always liable to this charge, in part because it can so easily be linked to cosmetics, the art of face-decorating. Donne neatly links them in his epigram on the famous courtesan who inspired (as noted earlier) a number of ancient paintings: "Thy flattering picture, Phryne, is like thee, / Onely in this, that you both painted be."[75] Shakespeare's plays treat both kinds of face-painting in terms of dissimulation. The painter who appears in the opening scene of *Timon of Athens* has prepared a flattering portrait of Timon—"a pretty mocking of the life," he calls it (1.1.35)—which is clearly less candid than the poet's allegorical exemplum on Timon's vulnerability to the fickleness of fortune. In *Hamlet,* painting means nothing but cosmetic artifice as an instrument of hypocrisy and self-delusion.[76] It is clearly this sense of "painting" that Lucrece invokes when she resolves to tell Collatine all about the rape. "My sable ground of sin," she says, "I will not paint / To hide the truth of this false night's abuses. / My tongue shall utter all . . ." (1074–76).

Yet for all this, painting in *The Rape of Lucrece* serves less to hide the truth than to reveal it with special force. Lucrece's very tearing of the painted Sinon is prompted in part by the contrast between this counterfeit simulacrum of misery ("a wretched image bound" [1501]) and the true face of suffering—the painted face of Hecuba, where "all distress is stelled [engraved]" (1444). Lucrece is moved by this painted face precisely because sights have already been credited with an emotive power that can surpass that of words. Early in the poem, chastising Collatine for boasting about the beauty of his wife, the narrator echoes Quintilian's rueful comment on Phryne when he says, "Beauty itself doth of itself persuade / The eyes of men without an orator" (29–30), and as already noted, Tarquin finds Collatine's praise far surpassed by Lucrece's appearance (78–81). After the rape, Lucrece decides to tell Collatine of it not in a letter but in person because, the narrator suggests, "to see sad sights moves more than hear them told / For then the eye interprets to the ear / The heavy motion that it doth behold" (1324–26). The same kind of reasoning also explains why Lucrece is so profoundly moved by the painting of sad sights.

At the same time, no sight represented in a poem can escape the mediation of language. When the war between word and image is fought on the field of language itself, it becomes essentially a war of words. Thus when Lucrece awakens to find Tarquin with his hand on her breast and with his "dumb demeanor" pantomiming lust (474), she begs to know "under what color he commits this ill" (476)—i.e., what pretext he could verbally formulate to justify it. In response, Tarquin uses the key term in her request to shift from word to image: "the color in thy face," he says

> That even for anger makes the lily pale,
> And the red rose blush at her own disgrace,
> Shall plead for me and tell my loving tale.
> (477–80)

These lines seem to affirm what the narrator has already said: that beauty is more eloquent than words. Red and white—the traditional colors of love typically found in a lady's face—plead more effectively than any sort of pretext that might be verbally expressed. Yet there is no visible color in this passage. It is all made of words, and the only thing pleading for Tarquin here is Tarquin's language. He makes his claim for the superior persuasiveness of visible "color" simply to score a rhetorical point.[77]

To reformulate my earlier question, then, we may ask what the *verbalized* painting in this poem tells us about the rape of Lucrece. In quest of an answer, we might compare Lucrece's response to the painting with Hamlet's response to something very similar: a vividly graphic narrative of Priam's end.[78] While preparing the play within the play, Hamlet asks one of the players to demonstrate his ability by reciting a speech on Pyrrhus's slaughter of Priam. In the speech begun by Hamlet himself and then continued by the player, the figure of Pyrrhus is richly pictorial. Dressed in the "heraldry" of red and black—in black armor smeared with the heat-impasted blood of those he has already slaughtered—he strikes at Priam with his sword, misses him in his rage, and—

with his sword once more descending—is momentarily transfixed by the crash of falling masonry, so that his sword "seemed i' th' air to stick" while "as a painted tyrant Prryhus stood / And like a neutral to his will and matter, / Did nothing" (2.451–53). This verbal picture of Pyrrhus suddenly mirrors Hamlet's incapacity to act. Just as Hamlet cannot bring himself to avenge the murder of his father by killing Claudius, Pyrrhus is balked in his determination to avenge the death of Achilles, his own father, who was slain by Priam's son. But Pyrrhus's paralysis is momentary. Newly energized after this pause by a "roused vengeance," he strikes Priam with absolute remorselessness. He thus rouses a "burst of clamor" from Hecuba, whose bare feet, tear-blinded eyes, and "mobled" (i.e., muffled) figure make her a living picture of desperation.

This graphic story of Priam's end, which recalls in many ways the painting of it described in *The Rape of Lucrece*, prompts us to ask—as with the painting—how the story may be linked to the central character of the work in which it appears. Part of the answer is that Hecuba's weeping leads us back to Hamlet. As Harry Levin has shown, her anguish at seeing Pyrrhus mince her husband's limbs initiates a chain of reactions: the gods weep (or ought to) at this pathetic sight, the actor's eyes fill with tears, and his enactment of passion rouses Hamlet to realize that the murder of King Hamlet has given him far greater cause to weep and rage.[79] Yet Hamlet cannot simply identify his feelings with Hecuba's mourning for Priam. The question he asks himself about the actor—"What would he do / Had he the motive and the cue for passion / That I have?" (2.2.526–28)—must inevitably remind Hamlet that his motive for action is just as strong as his motive for passion, and that his mourning for his father will never be adequate until he *does* what his father has commissioned him to do: take revenge. In so doing, he must take the avenging Pyrrhus as his model. He who now resembles Pyrrhus only insofar as Pyrrhus is fleetingly balked must be willing to do what Pyrrhus has done, must become the ruthless killer of a king. Though he never openly acknowledges the fact, Hamlet is thus drawn to identify with two radically antithetical figures in the bloody scenario of Priam's death: with the murderer and the mourner.

Lucrece's response to the painting of Troy is at once more explicit and more subtly conflicted. Exhausted with weeping and groaning for herself and impatient for Collatine's return, she turns to the painting of Troy in order to find "means to mourn some newer way" (1365). As she contemplates Hecuba's stricken face staring at the bleeding body of Priam under Pyrrhus's foot, she identifies at first only with Hecuba's despair. Weeping with and speaking for this voiceless figure with her own "lamenting tongue," she pledges to drop balm on Priam's painted wound and to rail on Pyrrhus (1465–67). She weeps for all "Troy's painted woes," and for anyone in the painting whom "she finds forlorn" (1492, 1500). But Lucrece soon learns that weeping eyes do not always signify suffering or sympathy. Sinon's "borrowed tears" mask his treacherous intent, and the weeping he provokes in Priam indicates not so much the king's sensitivity as his gullibility: "Priam," Lucrece apostrophizes,

why art thou old, and yet not wise?
For every tear he falls a Trojan bleeds.
His eye drops fire, no water thence proceeds.
Those round clear pearls of his that move thy pity
Are balls of quenchless fire to burn thy city.
(1550–54)

Priam is not just pitiable; he is also foolish. The "doting" king who failed to check his son's desire for Helen (1490) compounds his folly by trusting Sinon's tears. Precisely because Lucrece sees her former self in Priam's response to Sinon—"As Priam him did cherish, / So did I Tarquin" (1545–46)—her own response to the painted faces of sorrow turns from sympathetic mourning to rage, and "She tears the senseless Sinon with her nails" (1564).

This extraordinary act of violence by Lucrece—the only one she directs at anyone or anything but herself in the whole poem—results from a series of misidentifications. First, looking at the apparently truthful face used to represent Sinon, she recklessly identifies all such faces with deceit: "It cannot be, I find, / But such a face should bear a wicked mind" (1539–40). Second, she identifies her response to Tarquin with Priam's "cherish[ing]" of Sinon even though the two things differed sharply: while Priam trusted Sinon far enough to let the wooden horse enter the city, Lucrece fervently pleads against Tarquin's invasion of her body—her Troy, she later calls it (1547)—and clearly sees the disparity between his appearance and his intent: "In Tarquin's likeness I did entertain thee. / Hast thou put on his shape to do him shame?" (596–97). Third, besides momentarily identifying the art of painting itself with Sinon's duplicity, as I have already suggested, she identifies the painted Sinon with the real Tarquin, seeking to punish "that unhappy guest" (1565) by flaying the image of his Greek surrogate.

The violence of her act and the extravagance of the misidentifications that help to motivate it show just how fully she appropriates the painting of Troy as a graphic metaphor for what she has suffered. Though she soon enough realizes that her clawing of a painted figure hurts no one—"Fool, fool!" she says to herself, "his wounds will not be sore" (1568)—she reads the painting as a true representation of her own wound. She is herself a city invaded. To be sure, Shakespeare revivifies the imagery of predation that we have seen in Ovid and Marlowe, as when the newly awakened Lucrece lies before Tarquin "like a new-killed bird . . . trembling" (457).[80] But military metaphors permeate the poem from its very first stanza, where Tarquin leaves the siege of Ardea to besiege his kinsman's wife. Both characters define the rape in military terms. Having resolved "to make the breach and enter this sweet city" (469), Tarquin tells Lucrece that he has come "to scale / Thy never-conquered fort" (481–82). Just after the rape, Lucrece justifies her decision to commit suicide by calling herself a sacked house, a battered mansion, a temple profaned: "Then let it not be called impiety," she says, "If in this blemished fort I make some hole / Through which I may convey this troubled soul" (1174–76).

By the time Lucrece goes to the painting, then, she has already come to see the rape as a military invasion. And since the metaphor is reversible, she implicitly construes the painting of Troy as the representation of a rape.[81] When the image of Sinon as the insidious agent of invasion makes the rapist seem momentarily assailable, she strikes, and her gesture is resistive as well as vengeful. By clawing a Sinon who is depicted *in the act* of deceiving Priam, she not only takes vicarious revenge on the man "whose deed hath made herself herself detest" (1566); she also enacts the resistance that she hates herself for having failed to show when Tarquin took her.[82] A woman whose personal city is lost becomes for an instant a Troy not yet taken, a city fighting back.

In thus identifying herself with an invaded city, Lucrece once more recalls the rape of Philomela. This rape, as we have seen, reenacts the barbarian siege of Athens. Having obtained Procne in exchange for his services in protecting Athens *against* barbarous invaders, and having undertaken to escort Philomela on the understanding that he will "guard her with a father's love," Tereus shows his true barbarian colors by violating her, symbolically invading the very city he was pledged to guard. Tarquin does something quite similar when he turns from besieging Ardea to invading Lucrece. As capital of the Rutulians and home of Turnus, archenemy of Aeneas, Ardea would seem to epitomize barbarian resistance to the spread of the Roman empire. In leaving Ardea for Collatium, Tarquin abandons a war against the traditional enemies of Rome in order to assault what Kahn calls "a Vesta figure," guardian of a hearth that signifies "the sacredness and permanence of home and state."[83] Tarquin is therefore a traitor, as Lucrece herself calls him (1686) just before her suicide.

The suicide itself is the Lucretian equivalent of Philomela's graphic weaving. Both constitute a way of speaking the unspeakable, of revealing to the eye what cannot be articulated for the ear. Just as Philomela has been deprived of her tongue, Lucrece is silenced by the very act of rape. Cutting off her pleas in midsentence (666–67), Tarquin smothers her voice with the "white fleece" of her own nightgown and "entombs her outcry in her lips' sweet fold" (678–79).[84] After the rape, of course, Lucrece speaks at length, including the words she utters on behalf of the painted and tongueless Hecuba. But until Collatine arrives, she speaks almost entirely to herself, and she says nothing about the rape in her brief letter to Collatine because "she would not blot the letter / With words till action might become them better" (1322–23). The letter is a Philomelan tapestry *manqué;* unlike the white cloth on which Philomela weaves the *purpureas notas* of her bloody tale, it is unstained by any representation of rape. But like Philomela, Lucrece is determined to show what she cannot bring herself to tell, on the principle that "to see sad sights moves more than hear them told" (1324).

I have already noted that this line just precedes the passage on the painting of Troy and thus helps to explain why its depiction of misery should so poignantly speak to Lucrece. At once introducing the painting and prefiguring the final sight of Lucrece's suicide, this line firmly links the two under the heading of graphic representation. Lucrece cannot fully tell what has happened to her except by reenacting it in the most graphic way possible. Before doing so, she manages to tell much of what happened in words, to demand of Collatine and his men a vow of revenge, and to ask whether or not the purity of her mind clears her "from this compelled stain" (1707). But she can barely bring herself to utter the name of Tarquin (1716), and she can represent what he has done only by reenacting it. "'Tis he," she says, "that guides this hand to give this wound to me" (1722). Representing the wound of rape with a mortal wound, she "sheathe[s] in her harmless breast / A harmful knife" (1723–24). She has long been holding a knife at her heart expressly to imitate Philomela, who, while she descants on Tereus, "against a thorn . . . bear'st [her] part / To keep [her] sharp woes waking" (1134–38). Now this phallic knife finds its sheath (Latin *vagina*) in Lucrece's breast, thereby releasing a "purple fountain" of blood—the counterpart of Philomela's *purpureas notas*.

It may seem that Lucrece is simply completing the assault that Tarquin began, as Maus observes (72). But she intends something quite different. Aside from desperately seeking to purge her body of the blood "false Tarquin stained" (1742), she aims to represent the full brutality of his violent penetration. And for Collatine and his men, that is precisely what her suicide signifies. Having sworn to avenge her death, they decide—in the very last stanza of the poem—

> to bear dead Lucrece thence,
> To show her bleeding body thorough Rome,
> And so to publish Tarquin's foul offense. . . .
> (1850–52)

Earlier we saw that Spenser's Busirane uses the blood of two women—Amoret and Britomart—to draw "straunge characters of his art": pictures of sexual violence that take their place with his collection of tapestries depicting rape. Lucrece draws a picture of rape with her own blood. Her bleeding body is the final record—at once graphic and public—of Tarquin's foul offense. Silenced in and by sexual violation, Lucrece speaks through her body to all of Rome. She herself becomes a publicly exhibited painting of rape.

Shakespeare's Lucrece, then, is bound to Ovid's Philomela by considerably more than the songs of lament they sing together. In reading the painting of Troy and its tonguelessly grieving Hecuba as a graphic metaphor for the sexual violation she has undergone, Lucrece recalls the tongueless weaver of purple signs. Unlike Philomela, the raped Lucrece retains her tongue, and she uses it to speak prosopopeially for the painted Hecuba. But the power of her words cannot match the eloquence of the picture she finally constructs with her own blood. Starkly displacing the sleeping beauty on which Tarquin had covertly and lustfully gazed before the rape, Lucrece's bloody corpse publishes his infamy for all to see.

༈

The few examples treated in this chapter cannot support the claim that verbalized depictions of rape always speak for the victimized woman, that they invariably represent the violence of sexual intercourse from her point of view. But in at least the works I have discussed, verbalized depictions of rape prefigure or postfigure acts of sexual violence in the surrounding narratives. Philomela's tapestry is postfigurative, woven to represent what she has already experienced. By contrast, the pictures of rape described at the beginning of the novels by Longus and Achilles Tatius and near the beginning of Marlowe's *Hero and Leander* are prefigurative, adumbrating sexual violence or sexual coercion to come. In between these simple antitheses come descriptions of pictures that signify a continuing ordeal: the tapestries depicting rape at Busirane's house are displayed by a man bent on torturing Amoret into submission, and for the raped Lucrece, the painting of Troy signifies not just what she *has* suffered but also what she *is* suffering even as she contemplates it.

The Rape of Lucrece is unique among the works we have examined because of the way it integrates the heroine's ordeal with a picture she mentally reweaves, making its portrayal of invasion a graphic metaphor for rape. But all the depictions of rape we have considered share one important feature: they bring to the surface of the text the brutality of sexual violence, and in so doing they subvert the rhetoric of seduction or the language of evasion. Violated women speak in and through pictures of violation. Philomela's depiction of what Tereus did radically contradicts his story of her would-be death. The painting of Troy invaded speaks for Lucrece even as she speaks for the painted figure of Hecuba, and the graphic spectacle of her bloody corpse publishes the crime that Tarquin committed under the "color" of her lily-rose complexion: a color which, he thought, would "plead for [him] and tell [his] loving tale" (*Rape* 480). Pictures of rape tell a very different kind of tale. Even when they stand apart from a particular heroine, like the painting described at the beginning of *Daphnis and Chloe,* they alert us to the violence latent in the heroine's sexual initiation, the pain she is made to suffer in silence.

Pictures of rape, then, furnish a radical alternative to the pictures of still unravished beauty that typically activate a romantic quest. "Painting," Wendy Steiner notes, "has long stood as a symbol of the transcendent object—beautiful, outside of time's depredations, complete in itself" (*Pictures* 1). But in literature, verbalized depictions of beauty exposed to the male gaze typically generate a narrative of desire. In Sidney's *New Arcadia,* Pyrocles first conceives a passion for Philoclea when he sees a picture of a beautiful young maid, and it is the living picture of the veiled Hero standing at the altar of the temple of Venus that first excites Leander's desire for her. The potential for violence in this desire is all too plainly signified by the unlovely pictures that surround Hero: by the pavement mosaic of gods committing "ryots, incest, rapes." Unlike a verbalized picture of timeless beauty, which may indeed *initiate* a temporal unfolding of events, a verbalized picture of rape *is* a narrative, and the story it tells or foretells—often both—is precisely the story of how beauty is violated, coerced, or painfully initiated into sexual experience. The picture described at the beginning of *Daphnis and Chloe*—a picture of childbearing and infants exposed—is anything but transcendent. It presupposes a sequence of events leading to and from rape, and it prefigures the painful process by which Chloe's virginity is first threatened and then taken.

In the works we have considered here, therefore, verbalized depictions of rape enact—so far as language can—a revolution of the image against the word. Refusing to cooperate with the rhetoric of seduction, refusing to take its place in a narrative of male gratification, the picture of beauty becomes a picture of beauty violated, a picture drawn to expose and publish the violence men do under the "color" of their words.

Chapter Three

ROMANTIC EKPHRASIS
Iconophobia, Iconophilia, and the
Ideology of Transcendence

> Thou, with ambition modest yet sublime,
> Here, for the sight of mortal man, hast given
> To one brief moment caught from fleeting time
> The appropriate calm of blest eternity.
>   Wordsworth, "Upon the Sight of a Beautiful Picture,
>   Painted by Sir G.H. Beaumont" (1811)
>
> I say, a thing of beauty is a joy for a limited time only.
>   Josephine Humphreys

The concept of transcendence is anything but transcendent. The idea that a work of visual art perpetuates a fleeting appearance is so deeply embedded in the ideology we inherit from the romantic period that we may be startled to learn just how recently this idea has emerged in the history of discourse about art. It is nowhere to be found in the ekphrastic literature we have examined so far.[1] From Homer to Shakespeare, ekphrasis is driven by the pressure of narrative, which not only makes the verbalized work of art recall or prefigure what happens in the story that surrounds it but also turns graphic or sculptural stasis into process, arrested gesture into movement. This refusal to venerate the would-be timelessness of visual art is buttressed by the fact that up through the Renaissance, nearly all literary ekphrasis outside of Italy is notional. Since notional ekphrasis does not even presuppose the existence of the works of art it describes, it need hardly treat them as exempt from the ravages of time and historical contingency, and in this respect it reflects a conception that prevailed well beyond the Renaissance: the idea that visual art was perishable.

This idea rests firmly on a basis of demonstrable fact about all kinds of visual art, including sculpture. The picture of "blest eternity" that Wordsworth salutes in the lines of my epigraph has, so far as I can tell, disappeared. In *The Rape of Lucrece,* the heroine tears out the painted eyes of Sinon; in Browning's "Fra Lippo Lippi," the painter learns that the slaves shown manning the grille in his fresco of the fiery martyrdom of St. Laurence have been so fiercely "scratched and prodded" by pious viewers in just six months that the bricks behind the plaster will soon be showing through ("Fra Lippo Lippi" 327–32). And as I write these words in September 1991, restorers at the Florentine Aca-

91

demia are reassembling fragments of a toe that was smashed off the foot of Michelangelo's *David* by a deranged man.[2] Though the *David* will probably stay more or less well preserved for hundreds (perhaps thousands!) of years, anyone who has ever visited a museum of classical antiquities or an ancient site knows how little of classic sculpture survives intact, or survives at all. Ancient painting has fared even worse. Except for the anonymous frescoes excavated from the volcanic ash that buried (and thus preserved) such ancient sites as Pompeii, Herculaneum, and Akrotiri, no classical paintings remain. When Leon Battista Alberti writes of Timanthes' *Immolation of Iphigenia* in his treatise *On Painting* (1435–36), or when Franciscus Junius treats the works of Apelles and Parrhasius in his *Painting of the Ancients* (1638), they are both writing of pictures they never saw except in words—in ancient descriptions of them.

At least one critic in eighteenth-century England found these ekphrastic re-productions "so just, so lively, so distinguishing, that we may look upon them as copies of those divine originals. The moderns have not this advantage; all ideas of their works will vanish with their colours" (Webb 166). So says Daniel Webb in 1761. Using words to appropriate fully the representational power of paint, he not only asserts that language alone is capable of preserving the "idea" of this perishable medium but goes on to argue that paintings of the "modern" era— by which he chiefly means the Italian Renaissance—cannot match the emotive impact of what words alone tell us about ancient art.[3] Besides ensuring that the real winner in this would-be contest between modern paintings and verbalized ancient ones can only be language, Webb does not even consider the possibility that a painting might transcend time.

To be sure, this possibility had already become a certainty for a number of seventeenth-century poets. Edmund Waller salutes the "immortal colours" in a "deathless" portrait by Van Dyck ("To Van Dyck," 46–47); Andrew Marvell tells a painter to depict Lady Castlemaine "in colours that will hold" ("Last Instructions to a Painter," 79–81); John Donne predicts that when he comes back weather-beaten and careworn from his travels, the picture of his youthful face "shall say what I was" ("Elegie V: His Picture," 4–13). But tributes to the immortality of actual works of art—as distinct from notional or purely figura-tive portraits—are relatively scarce in England before the latter part of the eigh-teenth century.[4] The most notable seventeenth-century poems we have on actual portraits praise the artist's ability to make a face and figure express the mind—not to perpetuate a particular appearance.[5] Even in the earlier eigh-teenth century, when James Thomson describes in his blank-verse *Liberty* the resurrection of ancient sculptures discovered amid the ruins of Rome, he cele-brates not the timeless perfection of their arrested gestures but rather their ca-pacity to express vitality, breathing passion, and movement.[6] So far as I know, the first notable figure to speak of visual art as a medium that perpetuates a pose is Lessing, who writes in *Laocoon* (1766) that the single moment selected for sculpting or depiction may not be transitory if it is to receive "immutable per-manence from art."[7]

The romantic poets and painters radically revised Lessing's formulation. As the lines of my epigraph to this chapter indicate, Wordsworth admired Beaumont's painting precisely because it captured a fleeting moment, and the idea that visual art could make such a moment transcend time became an article of romantic faith. When in 1833 John Constable published a collection of mezzotints made from his paintings, he quoted one of Wordsworth's lines to help explain his transcendent aims:

> to arrest the more abrupt and transient appearances of the CHIAR'OSCURO IN NATURE; . . . to give "to one brief moment caught from fleeting time" a lasting and sober existence, and to render permanent many of those splendid but evanescent Exhibitions, which are ever occurring in the changes of external Nature. (Constable 9–10)

Constable stops short of Wordsworth's celestial heights; the poet's "calm of blest eternity" becomes in the painter's redaction "a lasting and sober existence." But poet and painter clearly share the belief that visual art has the power to perpetuate a moment, to raise it above time, change, and contingency.

This belief is itself a child of history. It originates chiefly with the birth of the public museum, which aims at once to preserve the history embedded in works of art and to protect those works *from* history, from the ravages of time.[8] The most famous of all poetic meditations on the timeless serenity of visual art—"Ode on a Grecian Urn"—was made possible by the collections of classical vases and marbles Keats saw at the British Museum, founded in 1753, which acquired the vases in 1772 and the marbles (from Lord Elgin) in 1816, just three years before Keats wrote his ode.[9] Yet if Keats could imagine a classical urn unravished by history, he also felt moved to acknowledge what "the rude / Wasting of old Time" had done to the Elgin marbles, and he must have known something of the questionable dealing by which they were acquired from an occupied country.[10] Not even Keats—the least political of all the major romantic poets—could wholly ignore the political circumstances under which a classical work of art might present itself to the modern eye.

To understand the distinctively romantic belief in the timelessness of visual art, then, we must consider all that threatens to undermine it: the perishable materiality of painting and sculpture and the pressures of historical contingency. We must also consider again, in terms of the ideology of transcendence, the paragonal struggle for power between image and word: the struggle that invariably complicates the verbal representation of visual representation. If Horace claimed to have built with his poetry a *monumentum aere perennius*—a monument more lasting than bronze—what does it mean for any poet to represent visual art as the very embodiment of perpetuity? And how can this iconophilic faith in the perpetuity of visual art be reconciled with the notes of iconoclasm and iconophobia that romantic poetry repeatedly sounds? To answer questions like these, I will consider how the romantic ideology of transcendence is at once articulated and challenged by the ekphrastic works of four major poets.

I
WORDSWORTH'S "PEELE CASTLE"

Written in the late spring or early summer of 1806, "Elegiac Stanzas, Suggested by a Picture of Peele Castle, in a Storm, Painted by Sir George Beaumont" (figure 2) comes at the end of what is generally considered Wordsworth's major phase—the period stretching from the first edition of *Lyrical Ballads* in 1798 to the completion of the first full-length version of *The Prelude* in 1806. Prolonged focus on this period can sometimes cast a blur on the forty-four years of continuous production that followed it. "Peele Castle," writes Karl Kroeber, "is unusual in Wordsworth's canon in being a poem about a painting" (45). Yet unless the canon excludes what he wrote after 1806, it includes no less than twenty-four ekphrastic poems in all, several of them considerably longer than "Peele Castle" and many of them worth more than a cursory glance.[11] Though I will not try to survey all of them here, they do furnish a generally neglected context for the study of Wordsworth's best-known poem about a painting.

Equally illuminating as an avenue of approach to this poem is what may seem at first a detour from it: Wordsworth's iconoclasm. To see how militant this can be, consider "Illustrated Books and Newspapers," a sonnet he wrote in 1846:

> Discourse was deemed Man's noblest attribute
> And written words the glory of his hand;
> Then followed Printing with enlarged command
> For thought—dominion vast and absolute
> For spreading truth, and making love expand.
> Now prose and verse sunk into disrepute
> Must lacquey a dumb Art that best can suit
> The taste of this once-intellectual Land.
> A backward movement surely have we here,
> From manhood—back to childhood; for the age—
> Back towards caverned life's first rude career.
> Avaunt this vile abuse of pictured page!
> Must eyes be all in all, the tongue and ear
> Nothing? Heaven keep us from a lower stage!
> (*PW* 3:75)

It would be hard to imagine anything more logocentric, anything more fervently devoted to the intellectual superiority of words over pictures, anything more steeped in iconophobic assumptions about the childishness and primitivism of visual art.[12] We may wonder just how well this sonnet represents the poet's lifelong views. Written just a few years after Dickens's *Pickwick Papers*

(1836–37) initiated the illustrated serial novel and in the very year that begot *The Illustrated London News* (first published 14 May 1842), Wordsworth's sonnet may be no more than a septuagenarian's bray at mass-produced images. But Wordsworth could be just as logocentric about fine art. According to Henry Crabb Robinson, who toured the sculpture museums and picture galleries of Italy with Wordsworth in 1837, the poet "in general . . . [would] not allow the plastic artist of any kind to place himself by the side of the poet as his equal."[13] Furthermore, much of the sonnet echoes Wordsworth's earlier poetry. The old poet who fears that the eyes will have it over the tongue and ear evokes the much younger poet who rejoiced—in the 1805 *Prelude*—at his liberation from the once-fashionable habit of looking for pictures in natural scenery: who proudly recalled that in so doing he broke the "despotic" power of the eye (11.173), and who also remembered the "sense / Of possible sublimity" he drew from

> whate'er there is of power in sound
> To breathe an elevated mood, by form
> Or image unprofaned.
>
> (2.324–26)

But if Wordsworth's late sonnet echoes the iconoclastic notes of his earlier poetry, it also casts a startling light on "Peele Castle"—especially since an engraving of Beaumont's picture served as a frontispiece for volume 2 of the 1815 edition of Wordsworth's poems. Frontispieces illustrating the poems of the man who would eventually condemn illustrated books, in fact, appeared in both volumes of the 1815 edition, in *The White Doe* volume of 1815, in the *Peter Bell* volume of 1819, and in all four volumes of the edition of 1820. What distinguishes the *Peele Castle* frontispiece is that each of the others was based on a picture painted to illustrate a Wordsworth poem.[14] Only *Peele Castle* suggested a poem, reversing the direction of stimulus from poet to painter.

How then does Wordsworth's "Peele Castle" reflect the iconoclasm evident in the poetry he wrote before and after it? And what has this iconoclasm to do with the ideology of transcendence that he projects onto painting elsewhere, as in the lines of my first epigraph? To answer these questions we must consider the variety of pictures Wordsworth represents in his poem before describing the one painted by Beaumont:

> I was thy neighbour once, thou rugged Pile!
> Four summer weeks I dwelt in sight of thee:
> I saw thee every day; and all the while
> Thy Form was sleeping on a glassy sea.
>
> So pure the sky, so quiet was the air!
> So like, so very like, was day to day!
> Whene'er I looked, thy Image still was there;
> It trembled, but it never passed away.

How perfect was the calm! it seemed no sleep;
No mood, which season takes away, or brings:
I could have fancied that the mighty Deep
Was even then the gentlest of all gentle Things.

Ah! THEN, if mine had been the Painter's hand,
To express what then I saw; and add the gleam,
The light that never was, on sea or land,
The consecration, and the Poet's dream;

I would have planted thee, thou hoary Pile
Amid a world how different from this!
Beside a sea that could not cease to smile;
On tranquil land, beneath a sky of bliss.

Thou shouldst have seemed a treasure-house divine
Of peaceful years; a chronicle of heaven;—
Of all the sunbeams that did ever shine
The very sweetest had to thee been given.

A Picture had it been of lasting ease,
Elysian quiet, without toil or strife;
No motion but the moving tide, a breeze,
Or merely silent Nature's breathing life.

Such, in the fond illusion of my heart,
Such picture would I at that time have made:
And seen the soul of truth in every part,
A steadfast peace that might not be betrayed.

(1–32)

Wordsworth begins with a typically ekphrastic gesture toward prosopopeia: he apostrophizes what we might at first take to be the picture designated by his title, or the rugged pile *in* the picture.[15] But the object of his apostrophe turns out to be singularly elusive. Since the picture stirs a memory of a real object that Wordsworth once saw, we might infer that he is actually speaking through rather than to the picture, apostrophizing the object it signifies.[16] Yet even this inference crumbles when we learn that the object apostrophized—a castle moated by a glassy sea—is not the same as the object depicted, a castle in a storm.

Of course the pictured castle must resemble the remembered castle well enough to evoke it, and thus to show that the identity of the "rugged Pile" can survive a change in the weather. But Wordsworth clearly separates the apostrophized castle from the pictured one, which is never apostrophized. Not until the thirteenth stanza of the poem is it mentioned at all, and then only in the third person as "this huge Castle" (49).

What Wordsworth apostrophizes, then, is neither the castle of Beaumont's picture nor the castle it signifies (the *idea* of a castle in a storm) but rather a castle depicted in his memory—what he calls in "Tintern Abbey" a "picture of the mind" (60). Such a picture is at once the mind's possession and the mind's construction. When Wordsworth returns to the Abbey and the river Wye in 1798, the "beauteous forms" of landscape that his memory preserves from his first visit in 1793 constitute, as Marjorie Levinson has shown, not an accurate record of what he must have found there but an idealized version of it, purged of any reference to what other visitors reported: the pollution of the river, the charcoal-burning furnaces along its banks, and the profusion of "vile hovels" (Levinson 24–32). Wordsworth constructs the pictures he stores in his memory, where they become objects of intense contemplation. What he says of the boyhood of the Wanderer in the first version of *The Ruined Cottage* (completed 1798) can surely be applied to himself:

> deep feelings had impressed
> Great objects on his mind, with portraiture
> And color so distinct [that on his mind]
> They lay like substances, and almost seemed
> To haunt the bodily sense. He had received
> A precious gift, for as he grew in years
> With these impressions would he still compare
> All his ideal stores, his shapes and forms,
> And being still unsatisfied with aught
> Of dimmer character, he thence attained
> An *active* power to fasten images
> Upon his brain, and on their pictured lines
> Intensely brooded, even till they acquired
> The liveliness of dreams.
> (81–94; in *PW* 5:381)

Here the process of remembering is plainly figured as idealizing depiction: objects become "pictured lines," which in turn acquire the dreamlike vividness of "ideal stores." Years after writing these lines, Wordsworth told Aubrey de Vere that Scott erred in making notes on landscape for use in writing his poems. Instead, said Wordsworth, he should simply have fixed his eye reverently on his surroundings, taken them into his heart, and then—after a lapse of several days—"interrogated his memory as to the scene. He would have discovered that while much of what he had admired was preserved to him, much was also wisely obliterated. That which remained—the picture surviving in his mind—would have presented the ideal and essential truth of the scene, and done so, in a large part, by discarding much which, though in itself striking, was not characteristic" (Grosart 3:487).

Like the memory-picture thus described, the picture Wordsworth preserves from his four-week sojourn within sight of Peele Castle in the late summer of 1794 is unmistakably idealized.[17] The castle in the center of this picture is not just a remembered image but a symbolic one—a sign of memory itself at its most idealizing. Speaking to his sister Dorothy near the end of "Tintern Abbey," Wordsworth looks forward to a time

> when thy mind
> Shall be a mansion for all lovely forms,
> Thy memory be as a dwelling-place
> For all sweet sounds and harmonies.
> (139–42)

As Frances Yates has shown, the concept of memory as a place—more precisely a building in which we may store images—has an ancient history that begins with the very man who first compared poetry to painting.[18] Without reviewing that history here or even trying to learn how much Wordsworth knew of it, we can see that the rugged pile of the opening stanza of "Peele Castle" is a site of memory-pictures, a place at which—if not in which—the poet has stored idealized images of sea and sky.[19]

The remembered picture is doubly pictorial, for it includes what might be called a natural picture: a reflection of the castle "sleeping on a glassy sea," where its Form or Image—the terms are almost Platonic—could be seen whenever Wordsworth looked: "It trembled, but it never passed away." The mere existence of the reflection certifies the perfection of the calm, for without such calm there would be no reflected picture at all. Wordsworth thus recomposes an image he may well have drawn from William Lisle Bowles's *The Picture* (1803), a long blank-verse response to Rubens's *Château de Steen* (1636).[20] In Bowles's poem, the image of a barely ruffled sea serves as a simile for the "quiet gladness" (41) of Rubens's sunlit chateau and wooded plain:

> All is quiet here,
> Yet cheerful as the green sea, when it shines
> In some still bay, shines in its loneliness
> Beneath the breeze, that moves, and hardly moves,
> The placid surface.
> (156–60)

In "Peele Castle," the placid surface of Bowles's figurative sea is doubly pictorialized. Besides acquiring a reflection, it becomes a literal part of the memory-picture Wordsworth preserves from his sojourn near the castle. The whole picture re-created in words exemplifies the ideal serenity that he typically imputes to works of visual art. In "Upon the Sight of a Beautiful Picture" (*PW* 3:6), a sonnet composed in 1811 about another painting by Beaumont, he praises the art that could arrest the movement of such shifting elements as clouds, smoke, and sunbeams, could show "the Bark upon the glassy flood / For ever anchored in her sheltering bay," and could by this means give "to one brief moment caught from fleeting time / The appropriate calm of blest eternity."

Strikingly enough, this tribute to the transcendent serenity of a picture comes after—not before—"Peele Castle." Five years after rejecting the memory-picture of a castle mirrored in a "glassy" sea as a "fond illusion," Wordsworth reads an actual picture complete with "glassy flood" as an icon of eternal calm. This almost worshipful reversion to the kind of picture he rejects in "Peele Castle" becomes even more startling when we realize that the "glassy flood" did not appear in Beaumont's picture; along with various other details it was added by the poet, who thereby composed in words yet another picture of ideal tranquillity.[21] Imperturbable calm remained for Wordsworth a specifically pictorial ideal. In a sonnet he wrote on Da Vinci's *Last Supper* in 1820 (*PW* 3:183–84), he notes the deterioration of the fresco—the damage done by "searching damps and many an envious flaw"—but insists that the love, mercy, goodness, and "calm ethereal grace" emanating from the painted figure of Christ "have not failed to awe / The Elements," that his expression and gesture "still bespeak / A labour worthy of eternal youth!"[22]

Clearly then, the memory-picture re-created in the opening stanzas of "Peele Castle" exemplifies the ideal calm Wordsworth typically saw in actual paintings. And here this ideal calm is implicitly gendered. When we are told that the reflected "Form" or "Image" of the castle was "sleeping on a glassy sea," we are reminded of Milton's Eve, whose first act was to become entranced with "vain desire" for her own image reflected in the "wat'ry gleam" of a lake (*Paradise Lost* 4.460–66).[23] Since Eve is herself the image of Adam—he "whose image" she is (472)—her reflection is the image of an image, like the entrancing reflection of the castle depicted in Wordsworth's memory. But in Wordsworth's poem, the "sleeping" reflection also evokes the sleeping beauty, the figure lustfully watched by a figure who is usually male.[24] We have seen Tarquin gazing on the sleeping figure of Shakespeare's Lucrece; in Keats's *Eve of St. Agnes*, Porphyro gazes on the sleeping Madeline. In each case, the gazer's admiration for beauty in repose is precisely what ignites the desire to violate or penetrate that repose, as Wordsworth himself suggests in a sonnet of 1846 on a painting by Lucca Giordano (1632–1705) brought back to him from Italy by his son John:

> Giordano, verily thy Pencil's skill
> Hath here portrayed with Nature's happiest grace
> The fair Endymion couched on Latmos-hill;
> And Dian gazing on the Shepherd's face
> In rapture,—yet suspending her embrace,
> As not unconscious with what power the thrill
> Of her most timid touch his sleep would chase,
> And, with his sleep, that beauty calm and still.
>
> (*PW* 4:18)

Here a female gazes on a sleeping male. But since she is a goddess and he is not, the gazer's place remains—in spite of the gender reversal—the site of power. Suspending her embrace, she knows only too well that she holds the power to banish his sleep and thus violate the still perfection of his beauty.

We are now, I hope, in a better position to understand the opening stanzas of "Peele Castle." Beginning with an apostrophe to the image of a castle placed within a memory-picture, Wordsworth represents both the image and its watery reflection as components of a picture that radiates transcendent calm—precisely the calm he typically imputes to paintings. Yet his language subtly converts the image of the castle to that of a sleeping beauty. Such a picture is bound to excite profound ambivalence, to provoke in the male viewer the iconophilic desire to gaze and the iconoclastic urge to violate. It is precisely the movement from one response to the other that the rest of the poem enacts.

The first response—the desire to gaze—takes the form of a desire to depict. The desire is deeply qualified, for it is based on a condition contrary to past fact ("if mine *had been* the Painter's hand"), and what the poet "would have" done under this condition has no necessary connection to his present feelings. Wordsworth offers us here a quite possibly unique variation on a peculiar kind of ekphrasis: the advice-to-a-painter poem.

In the earliest examples, which first appear among the odes of the sixth-century B.C. Greek poet Anacreon, the poet typically exhorts a painter to depict his mistress *as he describes her,* to represent his words about her.[25] When the advice-to-a-painter poem resurfaced in seventeenth-century England, it was made to serve various other purposes: Edmund Waller's *Instructions to a Painter* (1665) is a panegyric to the Duke of York, who commanded the British fleet in the war between England and Holland, and Andrew Marvell's *Last Instructions to a Painter* (1667) is an Opposition satire leveled at the court and government of Charles II.[26] But the Anacreontic note is plainly echoed in poems such as Ben Jonson's *The Picture of the Body* (first published 1640), which tells a painter how to represent the beauty of Lady Venetia Digby, and in 1800, just a few years before Wordsworth wrote "Peele Castle," Thomas Moore published his translation of Anacreon's Odes, including one that gives directions for the portrayal of a handsome young man: "And now, with all thy pencil's truth / Portray Bathyllus, lovely youth."[27]

Wordsworth's debt to the kind of poem that imagines or commissions the painting of a beautiful object is plain enough. Whether Anacreontic or not, however, the distinguishing thing about advice-to-a-painter poems is their self-sufficiency. While every other kind of ekphrasis—even notional ekphrasis—posits the existence of the work it represents, the advice-to-a-painter poem is wholly logocentric. As Mary Osborne notes, "the device of directing an artist was purely rhetorical. . . . No picture was expected to result from the directions. The 'advice' motif was only an enveloping design, or framework—a structural pattern" (Osborne 9). In the perennial war between word and image, the poet advising the painter assumes a double superiority, giving orders that language alone can fill by verbal specification and rhetorical framing, using description to preempt depiction even while seeming to authorize it.

Wordsworth exploits and accentuates this verbal self-sufficiency. In stanzas

4–8 of "Peele Castle" he constructs a verbal "Picture" (25) that isolates itself from all paintings, both actual and possible. The painting he "would have" produced differs radically from "this" (18)—Beaumont's painting, first mentioned only now, which has thus far been utterly occluded by his own memory-picture. Furthermore, the verbal picture cannot exist in paint because such an existence rests on a condition contrary to past fact. He could not have obeyed his own instructions without becoming a painter and thus forsaking the metaphors that make this "poet's dream" impossible to visualize, let alone depict: the smiling sea, the treasure-house of peaceful years, the sky of bliss, the chronicle of heaven. The consecrating "gleam, / The light that never was, on sea or land" is not a description of what pigment might offer to the eye but a figure *for* these figures. The picture that the poet "would have" commissioned from himself is a metaphorical re-vision of a picture that has been represented in terms chiefly literal—the memory-picture.[28] Ironically enough, as Wordsworth moves from remembering what he saw to imagining what he would have painted, his language grows less visual, more figurative, and yet also more abstract, until at last his hypothetical picture becomes a painting of "steadfast peace that might not be betrayed."

In the first half of the poem, then, the poet is fixated by a picture that he sees only in memory and can reproduce only in words. The fixity of his enraptured gaze is signified by a series of repetitions: the memory of seeing "every day" the castle and its reflected double, the virtual identity of one day to the next ("So like, so very like, was day to day"), the reiteration of the memory-picture in the hypothetical painting. In place of change, there is mere pulsation (the image "trembled") and intensification: days so *very* like, the gleam superimposed on a glassy sea. Since the repetition is just superficially incremental, the first half of the poem forestalls narrative. Rather than moving from a memory picture to an actual painting, or inferring (as ekphrasis traditionally does) any kind of story from the moment depicted, it can only envision a hypothetical painting of time suspended: a painting in which the castle would have seemed "a chronicle of heaven." The trembling image that "never passed away" in the memory picture is repeated by the hypothetical picture of steadfast, indestructible peace.

Beneath or behind these purely verbal pictures of transcendence lies Beaumont's painting of Peele Castle in a storm. The presence and pressure of this painting can be felt in the very first stanza, where the sleeping beauty of the castle's reflected image subtly foretells the inevitability of a violent awakening, of something like rape. If Wordsworth often treats painting as an art of transcendence, of images lifted from the stream of time to the plateau of eternity, he could also see that a picture of perfect calm might be nothing more than an illusion, or at best a temporary refuge from temporal experience.

This point had already emerged in a poem by Robert Southey that Wordsworth knew and admired. Written in 1795, the poem salutes a landscape by Gaspar Poussin in suggestively equivocal terms:

Gaspar! how pleasantly thy pictured scenes
Beguile the lonely hour! I sit and gaze
With lingering eye, till dreaming Fancy makes
The lovely landscape live, and the rapt soul
From the foul haunts of herded human-kind
Flies far away with spirit speed, and tastes
Th' untainted air, that with the lively hues
Of health and happiness illumes the cheek
Of mountain Liberty. . . .

. . . .
Friend of my lonely hours! thou leadst me
To such calm joys as Nature, wise and good,
Proffers in vain to all her wretched sons,—
Her wretched sons who pine with want amid
The abundant earth, and blindly bow them down
Before the Moloch shrines of Wealth and Power,
Authors of Evil. Well it is sometimes
That thy delusions should beguile the heart,
Sick of reality.[29]

The painting Southey represents in these lines offers much of what Wordsworth sees in his memory-picture: "untainted air" (compare Wordsworth's
"pure . . . sky"), blissful isolation "from the foul haunts of herded human-
kind" (Wordsworth's seascape is utterly unpopulated), "lingering" gratification
for the enraptured gaze, and gentle stimulus for "dreaming Fancy"—the sort of
stimulus that made Wordsworth think he "could have fancied that the mighty
Deep / Was even then the gentlest of all gentle Things." The painting leads the
viewer beyond society and its evils—beyond the wealth and power blindly wor-
shiped by earth's "wretched sons"—to the "calm joys" offered by Nature. But
possibly because the cold, wet summer of 1795 made the food from Nature's
"abundant earth" both scarce and costly in the year this poem was written
(Butler 191), Southey frankly admits the picture is a beguiling delusion, a pla-
cebo for those who are "sick of reality."

In *The Picture* of 1803, Bowles uses a different strategy to accommodate the
conflict between tranquillity and violence that he finds *within* Rubens's landscape. He begins with something like the euphoric mood of Southey's opening
lines. Gazing on a "rich creation" that surpasses the beauty of anything wrought
by Fancy (lines 2–6), he finds in Rubens's rural summer morning a "sweet . . .
sense of quiet gladness," balm for those "sick / Of vanities" and "the toiling
crowd" (35–41). But in the foreground he catches the disturbing sight of a
creeping hunter with phallic rifle in hand—"the deadly tube" (88)—who has
already frightened the birds. The hunter exemplifies the way Death can invade
"the sweetest scenes / of human loveliness":

with his unheard step,
In darkness shrouded, yet approaching fast,
Death, from amidst the sunny flowers, lifts up
His giant dread anatomy, and smites,
Smites the fair prospect once, whilst every bloom
Hangs shrivelled, and a sound of mourning fills
The lone and blasted valley. . . .

(100–112)[30]

Besides personifying the generalized threat of Death, the hunter prefigures a more particular menace in 1803, when the peace of Amiens broke down and left England once again facing the prospect of a French attack. Though Bowles draws no explicit connection between the hunter and war, the painting reminds him that the "rural peace" of England is threatened with invasion (197–205). But he is confident that the invaders will be repelled, leaving the English, "when peace illumes once more" their nooks and vales, to "think upon the distant storm / That howled, but injured not!" (216–20).[31] Thus, in spite of the menacing hunter, in spite of the political storm that a painting of rural peace brings to an English mind in 1803, Bowles sees transcendent serenity in Rubens's landscape. "*All* is quiet here / Yet cheerful as the green sea" shining under a breeze that barely ruffles its surface (156–60).

"Peele Castle" reveals traces of each strategy used in the poems by Southey and Bowles. Southey's account of Gaspar's landscape as a beguiling refuge from reality is explicitly recalled by what Wordsworth finally says about his hypothetical picture of the castle—the product of a "fond illusion"—and implicitly recalled by the language of suspension and negation he applies to both of his pictures: the "sleeping" image that "never passed away," the calm that "*seemed* no sleep" which could be interrupted, "the light that never was," and "no motion but the moving tide." All these negatives imply a tide of positives that will overwhelm them. The memory of the reflected image that "never passed away" from the surface of a "mighty Deep" that seemed "the gentlest of all gentle Things" must be overwhelmed by the memory of the brother who *did* pass away in the Deep when he was shipwrecked and drowned in February 1805 (Pinion 61), a little over a year before this poem was written. Thus, just as Bowles acknowledges the specter of Death invading Rubens's landscape of bright serenity, Wordsworth gazes at his hypothetical painting of Peele Castle with a consciousness of "deep distress" (36).

But several things distinguish what Wordsworth does in "Peele Castle" from what is done in either of the poems by Southey and Bowles. First, the pictures he describes in the first half of the poem—the memory-picture and the hypothetical picture—are firmly placed within the framework of a narrative about his own life. Though both of these placid pictures seem to foreclose the possibility of narrative, as I have argued, the very fact that they represent a state of

2. George Beaumont. *Peele Castle.* Ca. May 1806. Private collection.

"sleeping" calm portends a violent awakening, and the inevitability of this consequence is signaled by the temporal markers so conspicuously used to designate the poet's *experience* of the pictures: once, THEN (uppercased), at that
time, the simple past (was) and the past conditional (would have). In the middle of the poem, it is precisely the shift from past tense to present ("so once it
would have been—'tis so no more") that initiates the shift from the recollection
of enraptured gazing to the acknowledgment of pain.

Secondly, besides treating calm and disruption as stages of a personal narrative rather than spatially juxtaposed elements of a single picture, Wordsworth
moves from one picture to another, more precisely from a set of mental pictures
to an actual painting: Beaumont's picture of Peele Castle in a storm (figure 2).
This move is generally read as the sign of a mature awakening. Discarding the
dreamy pictures of sleeping beauty, the poet finds in Beaumont's picture of the
castle a sublime manifestation of how he might endure the storms that have
assailed him:

> Not for a moment could I now behold
> A smiling sea, and be what I have been:
> The feeling of my loss will ne'er be old;
> This, which I know, I speak with mind serene.

> Then, Beaumont, Friend! who would have been the Friend,
> If he had lived, of Him whom I deplore [i.e., lament],

This work of thine I blame not, but commend;
This sea in anger, and that dismal shore.

O 'tis a passionate Work!—yet wise and well,
Well chosen is the spirit that is here;
That Hulk which labours in the deadly swell,
This rueful sky, this pageantry of fear!

And this huge Castle, standing here sublime,
I love to see the look with which it braves,
Couched in the unfeeling armour of old time,
The lightning, the fierce wind, and trampling waves.
                                                  (37–52)

Set beside the stanzas on Wordsworth's own pictures of the castle, these stanzas establish a whole set of antithetical terms. Calm gives way to storm, joy to anger, love to fear, and beauty to sublimity. Pursuing the sexual meanings that Edmund Burke attached to the last pair of terms, we can also see that an essentially feminine vision has given way to an essentially masculine one.[32] The castle that appeared a sleeping beauty in the memory-picture is now represented as militantly erect in Beaumont's painting, "standing here sublime" in its ancient armor.

Since Wordsworth has already called his own hypothetical picture of the castle a "Poet's dream," and since he goes on to dismiss the "blind" happiness of the heart that is "housed in a dream" (54), it is tempting to subsume all of the foregoing antitheses under the opposition between dream and reality. It is likewise tempting to believe that in discarding his dream pictures, Wordsworth jettisons the ideology of transcendence they enshrine. He would have us believe that he is now ready to face death, violence, passion, contingency, and all the thousand natural shocks that flesh is heir to. Yet the would-be awakened Wordsworth bears a startling resemblance to the dreamer. As Marjorie Levinson has noted, the "mind serene" with which he contemplates his present state mirrors the "glassy sea" of the memory-picture (Levinson 111). When he tells us that the feeling of his loss "will ne'er be old," he forgets the simple truth Shelley would later enunciate in *Adonais:* that "grief itself [is] mortal" (line 183). From one of Wordsworth's own letters we know that during the visit to London which led him to Beaumont's picture—a visit he made more than a year after his brother's death—he "enjoyed himself highly" (*Letters* 2:31). When he represents his mind as serenely impervious to any feeling other than loss, when he says in effect that he is now housed in grief, has he awakened from the stasis of the dream world into the unpredictable flux of reality, or has he simply placed himself in another dream house?

A further problem with the inference that Wordsworth has turned from dream pictures to reality is that reality, as Levinson observes, is signified in this poem by a painting (112). What looks like an iconoclastic attack on the ideology of transcendence, on pictures of a timeless beauty, becomes an iconophilic tribute to yet another kind of picture—this one a painting of timeless sublimity. Or so Wordsworth tells us. To measure the truth of what he says about the painting, we should first examine the painting itself—or at least a suitable reproduction of it.[33]

Beaumont's *Peele Castle* shows lightly agitated waves foaming up over the rocks in the center; in the middle distance at right, a hull leans into the crest of a gentle swell as a canopy of dark clouds opens up behind it to reveal a golden sky above a reassuringly level horizon. The mildness of the storm represented in this picture becomes all too clear when we consider what J. M. W. Turner does with the sea in a work painted just about a year before Beaumont's: *The Shipwreck*, first exhibited in 1805 (Butlin and Joll #54). In Turner's picture, lifeboats packed with men and women pitch and wallow in a swirling trough of foam amid fragments of wreckage; the shattered hull of the ship founders behind them, and the horizon is a mountain range of waves spread out against a solid mass of leaden clouds. No such turbulence marks Beaumont's picture. Though a jagged needle of lightning points toward the ship, neither ship nor castle seem seriously threatened by wind or waves.

What happens to Beaumont's painting in Wordsworth's poem can be understood with a little help from Jacques Derrida. In *The Truth in Painting,* Derrida faults Martin Heidegger and Meyer Schapiro for their overdetermined interpretations of Van Gogh's *Old Shoes with Laces* (1886). In the eyes of Heidegger, Van Gogh depicts "a pair of peasant shoes" expressing the whole life of the woman who wore them (Heidegger 162–63); in Schapiro's opinion, the shoes belong to Van Gogh himself, "by that time a man of the city" (Schapiro 205). Derrida finds both readings of the picture vitiated by a naive referentialism, by the assumption that the painting must refer to a determinable set of shoes. They may not even be a pair, Derrida insists (*Truth* 264), let alone a pair owned by someone we can identify. For Derrida, the impossibility of tying the shoes to a particular owner or even to each other casts serious doubt on Heidegger's claim that Van Gogh's painting exemplifies the "unconcealing of being" by revealing "what the product, the pair of peasants' shoes, *is* in truth" (quoted *Truth* 324).

Wordsworth's account of Beaumont's painting provokes comparable objections. Describing the hypothetical painting in which he "would have" represented Peele Castle surrounded by ideal calm, he tells us that he would have "seen the soul of truth in every part" (31). Though he now sees this earlier impulse as the product of illusion, he implicitly claims that he *has* found the truth in Beaumont's picture—more precisely in what he takes to be its staging of the conflict between the raging elements and the persevering castle. But the almost level sea in Beaumont's picture is hardly a "deadly swell" evincing the "anger" Wordsworth anthropomorphically attributes to it; the foam from the "trampling waves" barely touches the base of the castle; and as I have noted already, the clouds in what Wordsworth calls a "rueful sky" are open to a light surrounding the ship.

A still more striking disparity emerges when we consider Wordsworth's lines on Beaumont's depiction of the castle itself. When Wordsworth says that the castle stands "sublime," he treats it as a site of power rivaling that of the elements.[34] For him its power lies in its resistance: in the "unfeeling armour" in which it is "cased," in the dauntless "look" with which it "braves" the lightning, wind, and waves. Yet except for its elevation, which gives it some dignity (it's the highest earthbound object in the picture), the castle is picturesque rather than sublime, and its shattered walls show plainly that it is anything but impervious to assault. Wordsworth's metaphors of protective enclosure give no hint of whatever "truth" the painting itself reveals about this ruin.

Instead of representing Beaumont's painting, then, Wordsworth constructs in words yet another imaginary picture of his own. To make this picture, he projects all of the feelings arising from the memory of his brother's death—anger, sorrow, and fear—onto the elements. At the same time, he identifies himself with a castle remade in the image and likeness of his newfound impassivity. Cased in this psychic armor even as he bids farewell to the heart that lives blindly "alone, / Housed in a dream," he can once again transcend contingency. Though he considers himself "humanized" by his brother's death and separates himself from those who live "at distance from the Kind [humankind]," he has learned how to resist further claims on his sympathy, further shocks to his self-possession.

This power of resistance, which is also the power to imagine pictures of resistance, supplants the "power [that] is gone," the power to imagine pictures of transcendently beautiful calm. In identifying himself with an impregnable fortress of his own verbal making, Wordsworth resolves the paragonal conflict between word and image that has driven this poem from the beginning. In the first half of the poem, Beaumont's painting of Peele Castle is occluded by two pictures of it drawn in words: the memory picture and the hypothetical picture. Ostensibly the poet tells us how these verbal pictures of ideal calm gave way to an actual painting of stormy violence, and thus of how he progressed from illusion to a reality signified by the truth of a painted image. But the simple arc of this narrative twists when the poet's words reconstruct the painting rather than revealing its truth. Only after he remakes the painting verbally can it represent his new vision of the world, which embodies a new, stoic version of transcendence.

II
"ALL BREATHING HUMAN PASSION FAR ABOVE": KEATS AND THE URN

In turning from "Peele Castle" to "Ode on a Grecian Urn," we turn from autobiography to impersonal meditation, and also from the sunset of Wordsworth's

major phase to the blazing noon of Keats's whole poetic life. The beauty of this
noon has not lacked admirers. While "Peele Castle" has been relatively neglected, the ode has generated so much commentary that we may well wonder
whether there is anything left in it for criticism to ravish. I believe there is—for
the simple reason that scarcely any published work of criticism has examined
the ode in light of the ekphrastic tradition that stands behind it.

I must hasten to say, however, that this is precisely the light in which the
poem has been extensively scrutinized in a recent dissertation by Grant Scott.
Together with several other poems generated at least in part by Keats's experience of the visual arts, Scott sets the "Urn" not just against the ancient history of
ekphrasis but also against the new vogue of ekphrastic poetry that emerged in
eighteenth-century England and was reenergized in the early nineteenth century by the importation of the Elgin marbles. Reading the "Urn" in light of
these traditions, Scott argues that it reflects the "inherent tendency" of
ekphrasis "to conceive aesthetic relations between poet and *objet d'art* in terms
of gender and sex role" ("Seduced" viii). For Scott as for W. J. T. Mitchell,
whose theory of ekphrasis he adopts, ekphrasis is a mode of writing in which
the male poet ambivalently responds to an image typically viewed as female: an
image that excites both "ekphrastic hope"—the desire for union—and the
"ekphrastic fear" of being silenced, petrified, and thus unmanned by the Medusan "other" (Mitchell, "Ekphrasis"). "The urn," Scott writes, "shares a number
of attributes with Medusa, a figure whose gaze, according to Freud, at once
promises to stiffen and threatens to castrate the enthralled male." In Keats's
poem, he adds, the fear of castration reveals itself "in terms of silence, and as an
imminent and terrifying loss of voice" ("Seduced" 154–55).

This Medusa model of ekphrasis can be plausibly invoked wherever the conflict between word and image demonstrably becomes a conflict between male
authority and the female power to enchant, subvert, or threaten it. Thus we
may think of Medusa's power when we see that the frescoes represented in the
first book of the *Aeneid* have been commissioned by Dido, that Aeneas is stupefied and fixated by these enchanting images, and that in this silent and vulnerable mood he first sees the living beauty of the woman who threatens to fix him
forever in Carthage, aborting his mission to found Rome. We may likewise
note that the frenzied Cleopatra depicted on the shield of Aeneas with the twin
snakes of death behind her—the woman who has seduced Antony and now
dares to challenge Augustus—not only recalls Dido at her most furious but also
plainly evokes Medusa. Furthermore, as these two examples together suggest,
the power to petrify a male viewer lurks quite as much in the beauty of an image
as in the ghastliness of it. Medusa herself, as Shelley reminds us in a poem I will
discuss below, personifies the combination of the two, and the fixating effect of
a beautiful picture is evident in Wordsworth's "Peele Castle." As for Keats, "The
Eve of St. Agnes" seems to offer a perfect instance of beauty petrifying the male
viewer: when Porphryo sees that the tender notes of his lute have fluttered the

eyelids of Madeline, the sleeping beauty he has come to regard as a sacred icon, he sinks to his knees, "pale as smooth-sculptured stone" (297).

Nevertheless, if the Medusa model can open our own eyes to the sexual antagonism that so often charges the ekphrastic encounter between word and image, it can also blind us to other things. It has blinded several very good critics, as I will shortly demonstrate, to the true meaning of the word "gazer" in what might seem to be the paradigmatic instance of Medusan ekphrasis—Shelley's "On the Medusa of Leonardo da Vinci." But for the present I will merely note some of the things the model cannot explain about the examples I have just cited.

It will not explain how the male viewer is threatened by a work in which the fixating or menacing effect of one image is vanquished by another: more specifically, how Aeneas is threatened by a shield that represents Augustus's defeat of Cleopatra, or how such a shield could be construed as Medusan in its total effect. It will not explain why Wordsworth feels fortified rather than petrified by the "sublime" seascape that displaces his memory picture of tranquil beauty. And it will not explain why Porphyro is petrified by the *wakening* of Madeline—by the very move that takes her out of passivity and iconic stasis into active desire.[35]

In short, the Medusa model simply will not work as a master theory of ekphrasis. It cannot even adequately explain how depictions of rape affect the meaning and movement of narratives in which they appear. Such depictions do indeed threaten male authority by exposing its barbarity, as we have seen, and threaten too the order and legitimacy of the married state by implicitly exposing the violence endemic to sexual initiation. But these pictures of violated women—pictures of *women* silenced—do not silence or petrify the viewer, who in any case is just as likely to be female as male. Philomela's weaving stirs Procne to rescue her and plot their revenge against Tereus; the painted rape of Troy moves Lucrece to rage at Sinon's perfidy, even as the living picture of Lucrece's bloody corpse later moves her husband and his comrades to take revenge against Tarquin.

To serve adequately as an instrument of explication, then, the Medusa model should be reconceived as a *strand* in the fabric of ekphrasis, one of several ways in which ekphrasis manifests the antagonism of word and image. When the conflict between the two becomes a conflict between narrative and stasis, when ekphrasis converts the picture of an arrested action into a story, as it typically does, we can read this conversion in terms of gender: the male as agent of narrative overcoming the female as image, as fixed and fixating object of desire. But in Keats's "Urn," as we will shortly see, a poet who *resists* the traditionally ekphrastic impulse to narrate also reveals—by his very act of resistance—his detachment from the figures, his distance from their transcendent stasis, his capacity to articulate what this transcendence costs. Thus, even in a poem that explicitly feminizes the work of art, that figures it as a still unravished bride, the Medusa model cannot adequately explain what the poet does with the sculpted figures on the urn. Here the alternative to ekphrastic narrative—to the masculine conversion of image into story—is something quite different from the silent stupefaction with which Aeneas beholds the Carthaginian frescoes.

Keats's response to the urn likewise differs sharply from Wordsworth's response to Beaumont's *Peele Castle*.[36] For while Wordsworth elicits or constructs from the painting an image of transcendent endurance, Keats does the converse with the urn. Viewing an object that represents a state of bliss raised "far above" all breathing human passion, he forges a mordant critique of transcendence, and more especially of the notion that any work of visual art can satisfactorily represent it.

Because this critique is paradoxically embedded in a language of iconophilic homage, it can be easily overlooked. But we can begin to appreciate the complexity of what Keats does with the figures on the urn when we consider what he had already done in "On Seeing the Elgin Marbles," written in March 1817, a little over two years before the ode. In this sonnet, as Scott has demonstrated, Keats reflects both of the two conflicting reactions provoked by the fragments of Parthenon sculptures ever since Lord Elgin brought them to London in the years just after 1800. In the eyes of admirers like Benjamin Robert Haydon, the painter who introduced them to Keats, the marbles were grand, elegant, perfect works of genius: artifacts—as Scott acutely says—that their admirers "had already restored in their minds" ("Seduced" 60). In the eyes of detractors like Byron, they were no more than "Phidian freaks / Misshapen monuments and maimed antiques" (*English Bards and Scotch Reviewers* 1029–30, Page and Jump 126). But Keats's sonnet, as Scott says, "entertains both positions simultaneously" (61). Seeing both glory and ruin, the speaker of Keats's sonnet feels in their presence "a most dizzy pain / That mingles Grecian grandeur with the rude / Wasting of old time," and the conspicuously paratactic structure of the ending ("a billowy main, / A sun, a shadow of a magnitude") reflects the fragmentary condition of the marbles.[37]

In turning from the Elgin Marbles sonnet to the "Ode on a Grecian Urn," we are turning from a poem about fragments of actual sculptures to a poem about an imaginary artifact in perfect condition. In his own way, Keats now performs the act of restoration that he refused to undertake with the Elgin marbles. The urn, as Ian Jack has demonstrated (to my satisfaction at least), is an ideal object verbally *composed* from various actual sources: neo-Attic vases, the paintings of Claude Lorraine, and the Elgin marbles (Jack 217–19). Such a construct neatly suited *Annals of the Fine Arts,* the periodical where Keats's ode first appeared in January 1820, for this, as Jerome McGann observes, was "one of the age's chief ideological organs for disseminating" the idea that the best of Greek art "actually [embodied] . . . a perfect and complete idea of The Beautiful" (*Beauty of Inflections* 44). But what does it mean for an imaginary urn—no matter how tangible its proposed sources—exemplify the actual achievement of ancient Greek sculptors? To ask this question is to see that Keats's very conception of the urn—an object as elusive as the little town emptied by the figures represented on it—subtly subverts the ideology of transcendence that his poem purports to serve.

Its subversiveness, however, springs only in part from its imaginary condition, which must be distinguished from the purely figurative condition of the sculpted figures who appear in the "Ode on Indolence," written about the same time as the "Urn." The sculpted figures in "Indolence" enter the poem as the vehicle of a simile describing phantoms seen by the speaker in a summer's day reverie ("They passed, like figures on a marble urn"), and they fade out of sight for good by the end of the poem. By contrast, the urn of the "Urn" is consistently *represented* as an actual object facing the speaker throughout the poem. The question implicitly asked by the ode, then, is this: supposing that a sculpted Greek urn has survived in perfect condition, what sort of transcendence does it possess?

Initially, the urn answers this question by silence. Like unheard melodies, the "still unravished bride of quietness" is said to be transcendently eloquent, for by stillness and silence alone it expresses "a flowery tale more sweetly than our rhyme." Yet as soon as he apostrophizes this silent figure, the speaker of the "Ode" begins to violate its silence.[38] To address and still more to interrogate a womblike vessel as a still unravished bride of quietness is to threaten her with rape, which bears a profoundly paradoxical relation to speech. For all its silencing brutality, rape can empower a woman's voice. In the *Metamorphoses,* Philomela is a silent beauty until Tereus takes her. Only then does she speak for the first time, denouncing him for his barbarity and threatening to tell the whole universe what he has done.[39] When this threat prompts Tereus to cut off her tongue, she then demonstrates by her weaving that nothing can silence her, that she has learned how to speak through her art.[40]

The speaker of Keats's ode hardly seems another Tereus. Rather than silencing the virgin artifact, he longs to hear it speak, or more precisely to understand what its silence is saying. Yet the opening stanza plainly expresses an almost violent urge to *make* it speak. Traditionally, we have seen, ekphrasis is prosopopeial; like the sepulchral epigrams from which it partly derives, it aspires to give the work of art a voice. But unlike Dante, who readily identifies the sculpted figures on the wall of purgatory and who knows exactly what they are saying to each other, Keats knows nothing of the figures on the urn, nothing of the "leaf-fring'd legend" that "haunts about [its] shape." He must therefore interrogate the urn, and the very word *legend* underscores his desire to hear it speak and know its story.

Since *legend* originally meant "to be read," ancient travelers could make a sepulchral inscription speak by reading it aloud. But whether or not we imagine the design on the urn as fringed or bordered with a band of ornamental leaves, as Jack suggests (283 n13), the speaker finds no inscription on the urn, or at least none that he can read. Without an inscription, he cannot make the urn speak, and without its voice in the opening stanza he has no story—no legend in the sense of narrative, which is what ekphrasis traditionally tries to construct from a work of art.[41] Like the urge to make the urn speak, the urge to make a story from an image is subtly gendered. As a still unravished bride, the urn appears to the male storyteller the way Philomela first appeared to Tereus: beautiful, silent, and fixed, waiting for a man to initiate the story of her life. From Tereus to Tarquin, as we have seen, the mere sight or *description* of a beautiful woman goads the man to act out the story of desire that he first writes in his own mind. But the urn checks this desire. It refuses to play a part in any story, to signify a narrative, or to answer the kinds of questions typically anticipated and answered by inscribed monuments. "What men or gods are these?" the speaker asks. Instead of saying something like, "I am the tomb of famous Glauca" or "My name is Ozymandias," the urn speaks only silence, voicing neither story nor circumstantial facts until it finally produces a conundrum that seems to transcend narrative and circumstance alike: "Beauty is truth, truth beauty."[42]

But to think of the poem in terms of timeless transcendence is to miss the insistent pressure of narrative that it reveals and the strength of poetic will required to resist that pressure. We can judge the strength of Keats's resistance by contrasting the ode with a sonnet he wrote about two years earlier, "On a Leander [Gem] Which Miss Reynolds, My Kind Friend Gave Me." In this little poem about an engraved gem representing Leander's ill-fated swim across the Hellespont, Keats turns the engraved figure of Leander into the complete story of his drowning, concluding with his death in the very last line: "He's gone— up bubbles all his amorous breath." By contrast, the ode checks the narrative impulse by restricting it to the world outside the urn. Keats can tell the story of actual passion because it changes, moving from desire to consummation and satiety—"a heart high sorrowful and cloy'd / A burning forehead, and a parching tongue." But since the feelings of the lovers sculpted on the urn are said to hover "far above" all human passion, the lovers themselves stand above change, so that their loves—or rather their mode of existence—cannot be narrated.

Yet part of what teases us out of thought in this poem is precisely its narrativity. Even though Keats suppresses the narrative impulse that ekphrasis typically releases, he does not simply exchange the language of temporality for the language of spatiality, as William Carlos Williams does with Breughel's *Return of the Hunters* in "Hunters in the Snow." He does not simply represent the lovers as figures deployed in space. Instead he calls them into life as his auditors, and to these imagined auditors he speaks a language of temporality that is paradoxically and repeatedly affirmed by denial. If the pregnant moment of visual representation enables us to see readily what precedes and what will follow it, we can only conclude that Keats perversely chose to misread the figures on the urn. For the moment we identify them with the living figures they represent, we must also imagine them *completing* the action signified by the pregnant moment of pursuit, and thus providing a narratable answer to the question that any picture of an arrested act provokes: "What will happen next?" To this question, which is conspicuously missing from the series of questions in the first stanza, the only possible answer allowed by Keats's negation of narrative would seem to be: "nothing." Yet that is not the answer Keats gives. On the contrary, he uses the language of narration—more precisely of prediction—to say what *will* happen in the absence of change. In other words, he tells a *story* of changelessness. In place of the actual moment-to-be so strongly implied by the pregnant moment represented, he tells us what will happen to figures simultaneously quickened by desire and arrested by art. What will and must happen—the ugly truth devouring the sculpted beauty—is that the lovers will become unbearably frustrated:

> Bold lover, never, never canst thou kiss,
> Though winning near the goal—yet, do not grieve:
> She cannot fade, though thou hast not thy bliss,
> For ever wilt thou love, and she be fair!

These lines are profoundly self-contradictory. To imagine a figure on the urn as a lover caught in a state of permanently arrested desire is to expose him to the strain of time even as we profess to exempt him from it. Forever denied the bliss of consummation, the sculpted lover transcends pain no more than do the sculpted effigies of dead knights and ladies praying and "seem[ing] to freeze" in the chapel of "The Eve of St. Agnes," where the beadsman's "weak spirit fails / To think how they may ache in icy hoods and mails" (14–18).[43] What are we to make of the prohibition against grief? To tell the sculpted lover not to grieve is to endow him with the *capacity* to do so, and thus to imply that he will do so forever, for the fixity of sculpture makes him powerless—both physically and psychologically—to do anything other than what he is now doing. If by chance he *is* grieving in the eternal now of the moment represented, he can never obey the speaker's command. He can never stop grieving.

The prohibition of grief is just one illustration of the way Keats's language excites the expectation of change even while ostensibly celebrating the beauty and joy of changelessness. If the songs of the melodist are "for ever new," each song would have to be different, or at least played differently, from the one before; if the lovers face the prospect of "more happy love! more happy, happy love!" they are simultaneously offered an increase in their happiness and reminded that changelessness means no increase at all—simply more of what they now possess, which is forever less than what they do not now and therefore never can possess: the happiness "still to be enjoyed."

Traditionally, as we have seen, ekphrasis is dynamic and obstetric, delivering from the pregnant moment of visual art the extended narrative which it embryonically signifies. Keats's poem simultaneously excites and frustrates the narrative urge, fully exploiting all the expectations that the sculpting of a fervent lover provokes, yet building up against any advance to gratification an impregnable wall of negatives: "Bold lover, never, never, canst thou kiss, / Though winning near the goal." Keats's poem thus makes explicit what all ekphrasis implicitly reveals: the inseparability of representation and misrepresentation. On the one hand, the ekphrastic conversion of visual art into narrative seems to restore the totality that is just fractionally represented—hence misrepresented—

by graphic art; on the other, the Heraclitan flow of narrative overrides, rapes, and thus misrepresents the beauty of what can be experienced in a single instant, or what might be experienced forever if, as Kenneth Burke suggests, we could move beyond the process of becoming into the eternal present of pure being (449). But Keats's own language defines the being of the figures on the urn as process. Though "far above" all breathing human passion, they are also said to be "For ever panting," forever breathing in and out—the essential act of life as we know it.

The moment sculpture pants, it loses its transcendent superiority to the narratable contingencies of breathing human life. These include not just the cloying of erotic bliss but the extinguishing of passion and finally of life itself, for the urn is a charnel as well as a virgin bride, made to hold the ashes of the dead. By thus subjecting the transcendent beauty of the sculpted image to the temporalizing pressures of verbal art, Keats makes us see that neither verbal nor visual art can ever fully represent "being"—no matter how near the goal they come.

The conflict between verbal and visual representation in this poem offers us a generally neglected way of interpreting the urn's gnomic utterance. In treating the ode as a poem of symbolic action, Burke equates "beauty" with "act" and "truth" with "scene," the world in which action occurs (460). But since the poem repeatedly threatens to rape the fixed beauty of visual art with the language of narrative, the urn's statement can be read as a final commentary on the *paragone* between the two. Up to the very moment when the urn finally speaks, the poem seems to tell us that we cannot have both at once, that we must choose between the narratable truth of a passionately mutable life and immutable beauty of graphic art.[44] We must sacrifice one to the other just as the lives of the lovers must be sacrificed to the beauty of the poses they hold forever in marble, and just as the life of the little town must be sacrificed to a ritual from which none of its inhabitants will ever return. Consider the opening lines of the last stanza: "O Attic shape! Fair attitude! With brede / Of marble men and maidens overwrought." The brilliant puns here work like the rabbit-duck drawing that Wittgenstein used to show how a single image can offer the eye two competing aspects (194e–197e). Because each aspect of the drawing negates the other, we can see the drawing as either a duck *or* a rabbit but not both at the same time. Likewise, the words "brede" and "overwrought" can signify (to the reader's ear at least) either a living breed of men and maidens overwrought with unbearably prolonged desire, *or* a decorative braid of unbreeding marble figures done in bas-relief on an urn that is embroidered or "overwrought" with them. Instead of fusing truth and beauty, the puns ask us to choose between them: between the narratable truth of living desire, which may in time become overwrought, and the timeless beauty of visual art, which turns human figures into well-wrought formal patterns.[45]

In equating truth with beauty, then, the urn affirms what the poem has so far denied. By the very act of speaking, the urn crosses the line between visual and verbal representation, between the fixed, silent beauty of graphic stillness and the audible movement of speech. This transgressive act can be read in two ways. If the still unravished bride is now speaking, she has in some sense been ravished, and her speech is at once the sign and child of this violation. But what she says is very far from the outcry of a victim, whether of rape or interrogation. Her voice preempts the interrogating, narrating voice of the male speaker.[46] She not only declares that visual art *can* speak, but also that visual and verbal representation are one, that language achieves its greatest beauty and highest truth when it transcends narrative, when it represents not what has been or will be but *is*. "Beauty is truth, truth beauty." In the second half of this chiastic utterance, the verb drops away, so that language assumes the juxtapositional effect of sculpture. Entering and envoicing the mute still object, language abandons its narrative impulse and gives itself up to the lasting suspension of visual art.

It would thus seem that Keats's critique of visual representation—more precisely of the idea that visual art can be transcendently beautiful—finally becomes a work of iconophilic homage. Having repeatedly demonstrated the conflict between the beauty of sculptural stasis and the narratable truth of action, he apparently dissolves the conflict by taking visual art as the model for a language of transcendence that aspires to represent being rather than becoming. But verbal representation does not thereby dissolve into visual representation, for the work of visual art on which Keats finally models his language is itself mediated by language. The urn is as imaginary as the little town emptied by the religious ritual sculpted on it, and while we may recognize allusions to actual vases or other works of ancient art in Keats's account of the urn, we cannot know it except through Keats's words. Keats pays his tribute, therefore, to an object created by language, or more precisely to the *idea* of visual representation, which language alone expresses here.

The result is an object quite different from the mental pictures that Wordsworth constructs with words in the first half of "Peele Castle." Wordsworth replaces two mental pictures of transcendent beauty with a "real"—actually reconstructed—picture of transcendent endurance. Keats keeps his eye on a single work of art throughout his ode, but his tribute to the timelessness of its beauty cannot finally be separated from his critique of the transcendence exemplified by its sculpted figures. His poem actualizes the potential that ekphrasis has always possessed—the capacity to question and challenge the art it ostensibly salutes. Thus he makes the act of iconophilic homage a work of critique, a verbal demonstration of all that must be sacrificed to make the idea of visual representation at once beautiful and true.

III

DISINTEGRATING SUBLIMITY, PETRIFIED BEAUTY:
SHELLEY'S "OZYMANDIAS" AND "MEDUSA"

The critical strain underlying the ostensible iconophilia of Keats's ode subtly connects it with another conspicuous example of romantic ekphrasis: Shelley's

"Ozymandias." This brief meditation on the monumentalizing of political power is at once ironic, iconoclastic, and revisionary. It radically revises the image of power constructed in Virgil's description of the shield of Aeneas, where the triumphant Augustus, fresh from his victory at Actium, appears seated in majesty at the snowy threshold of the brand-new shining temple of Apollo—the very spot that would later be occupied by a statue of the god himself (*Aeneid* 8.720). But Shelley was doubtless thinking less of ancient Roman than of modern British politics when he first published his sonnet in Leigh Hunt's liberal *Examiner* in January 1818. The year before, Hyde Park's Apsley House had been bought by the Duke of Wellington, fresh from victory at Waterloo, who would soon be honored by a triple-arched screen and triumphal arch at the south end of the park: the screen adorned with a sculptured frieze, the arch surmounted by a huge equestrian statue of the duke.[47] However much Shelley may have foreseen this monumentalizing of Wellington, it is surely significant that his sonnet first appeared in the *Examiner,* whose editors (John and Robert Hunt) had already spent two years in jail for attacking the Prince of Wales, who regularly attacked the European despotisms that Wellington helped to restore, and who in the very month they published Shelley's poem were denouncing British poets for their political spinelessness—for "a sort of shuffling on the side of principle, and tenaciousness on the side of power" (quoted Butler 144). Shelley challenges the tenacity of power itself by attacking an icon made to represent and perpetuate it. While Keats exposes the contradictions inherent in the marble perpetuation of an erotic moment, Shelley goes one step further, undermining the assumption that visual art *can* perpetuate—or even unequivocally honor—what it represents:

> I met a traveller from an antique land,
> Who said—"Two vast and trunkless legs of stone
> Stand in the desert. . . . Near them, on the sand,
> Half sunk a shattered visage lies, whose frown,
> And wrinkled lip, and sneer of cold command,
> Tell that its sculptor well those passions read
> Which yet survive, stamped on these lifeless things,
> The hand that mocked them, and the heart that fed;
> And on the pedestal, these words appear:
> My name is Ozymandias, King of Kings,
> Look on my Works, ye Mighty, and despair!
> Nothing beside remains. Round the decay
> Of that colossal Wreck, boundless and bare
> The lone and level sands stretch far away."

Shelley's sonnet questions what Keats's ode takes wholly for granted: the imperishability of visual art. While Keats confidently predicts that the urn will survive the wasting of the present generation as of so many others that came before it, Shelley foresees the ultimate dissolution of the statue. And to signify the imminence of this dissolution, Shelley complicates the opposition between sculptured fixity and narrative movement in an extraordinary way: he verbally perpetuates a moment in the history of a statue. The statue was designed to represent political power at its most intimidating, most enduring, and therefore most sublime.[48] Yet this would-be embodiment of transcendent power is gradually disintegrating, and Shelley catches it at a pregnant moment of transition between erectness and prostration: the standing legs recall the self-assertive majesty of the original monument while the shattered, half-sunk visage looks ahead to its final oblivion—its ultimate leveling—in "the lone and level sands."

In the sestet of this sonnet, Shelley evokes the inscriptive origins of ekphrastic prosopopeia when his unnamed traveler quotes the daunting words carved on the pedestal. He thus envoices the statue, which resoundingly declares, "Look on my works, ye Mighty, and despair." But these words simply accentuate the transitional status of the monument. The single meaning they originally conveyed has disintegrated into a double meaning that looks backward and forward in time. Like the statue on which they are inscribed, the words at once recall the invincible assurance of Ozymandias and foretell the coming dissolution of his works.

The expression fixed on the shattered, half-sunk face, therefore, cannot serve as the pregnant moment of a narrative to be ekphrastically inferred or furnished about the life of Ozymandias himself. Instead, the fixity of the expression signifies the rigidity of Ozymandias's despotic arrogance, which has petrified his face in a "sneer of cold command" that the sculptor has at once imitated and obeyed, since he undoubtedly worked under orders from the ruler himself. Ozymandias sought to perpetuate his power through the medium of sculpture, through "lifeless things" that would permanently represent his personality. But the sculptor's hand—or the statue's sculpted hand—mocks the passions that it represents, and time in turn mocks any aspirations that the sculptor might have had for the immortality of his art. Forever committed to one unchanging expression, neither Ozymandias nor the sculptor can command or control the leveling effects of time, which convert the face of power into an object of ridicule or—as with the grandiloquent inscription—impose upon its twisted features a meaning radically different from the one originally intended, so that what were once the frown and wrinkle and sneer of absolute authority become at last the marks and signs of desperation.

Shelley thus reveals that in spite of its claims to permanence, both the matter and the meaning of visual art can be fundamentally changed by time, reconstituted by successive interpretations. As William Freedman has shown, the whole poem is a study in mediation. After the opening words it is spoken not by the poet himself but by a "traveller" he has met, which is of course Shelley's way of personifying or envoicing a text—his not yet definitely identified literary source.[49] The poet draws the voice of the traveler from the text just as the traveler himself draws the voice of Ozymandias from the inscription on the pedestal. And in each case the relation is mediated. Shelley reads a text in which the traveler reports his reading of an inscription.

Before quoting the inscription and thus envoicing the statue as a whole, however, the traveler reads and envoices the sculpted visage. Its "frown, / And wrinkled lip, and sneer of cold command," he says, "*Tell* that its sculptor well those passions read, / Which yet survive, stamped on these lifeless things, / The hand that mocked them, and the heart that fed." The sculpted face visually represents the expression of the living ruler, which originally signified passions that the sculptor has inferred or "read" from it. Between the sculpted face and the actual one, therefore, stands the interpretive act of the sculptor, who knows how to read faces well and to represent them in stone so that their expressions can *be* read—can tell us what they signify. Yet the sculpted face tells us as much about the sculptor's ability to read Ozymandias as about Ozymandias himself. As a result, we are led to compare the sculptor's reading of the ruler with the inscription—with the ruler's own reading of himself and his works.

To compare the sculptor's representation of the ruler with the words of his own self-representation is to see that each corroborates the other. Ozymandias's statement can be read as a comment on the statue—clearly one of his most stupendous works—and the statue can be read as a sculpted response to the statement, a way of interpreting it in stone. Neither statue nor statement, however, communicates what Ozymandias presumably intended by them both: an immutable assertion of his power. The meaning of both changes radically as the all-too-perishable medium in which they are wrought disintegrates.

It would seem, then, that this Goliath of a statue has been felled by the Davidian slingshot of words, by the ironies and ambiguities that language is uniquely equipped to deploy. In the process, a verbal construct takes the place of a sculptured one. Paraphrasing what Horace said of his odes, Shelley might have said of this sonnet, "Exegi monumentum petra perennius"—I have built a monument more lasting than stone. Raising up his own little tower of words to mark the inexorable leveling of the ancient statue, this sonnet manifests what virtually all ekphrasis latently expresses: the poet's ambition to make his words outlast their ostensible subject, to displace visual representation with verbal representation. The words ostensibly addressed by Ozymandias to his "mighty" adversaries may also be construed as covertly addressed by the poet himself to all mighty rulers who would seek to consolidate their power in works of stone.

But why should we grant to any work of language the transcendence here denied to a work of sculpture? If the stone of the statue can disintegrate, the inscription will perish with it, for the inscription is a material object made with letters carved in perishable stone. The fate of everything wrought and inscribed by order of Ozymandias should prompt us to ask how long any work of representation, whether verbal or visual, can endure. If words cut in stone cannot last, what will happen to words written on paper or printed in a book? From time to time, as we learn in *The Prelude,* Wordsworth so vividly envisioned the apocalyptic destruction of everything wrought by humankind that he felt half-inclined to bury books of poetry in order to preserve them. "Oftentimes at least," he writes,

> Me hath such deep entrancement half-possessed
> When I have held a volume in my hand—
> Poor earthly casket of immortal verse—
> Shakespeare or Milton, labourers divine.
>   (1805 5.161–65)

If it is fantasy to believe that the immortal words of Shakespeare or Milton can die, Wordsworth reminds us that even those words are buried in the material caskets we call volumes, that they can never escape material form. Likewise, Shelley's sonnet asks us to envision the materiality of the letters used to make words. Beneath the iconoclastic skepticism of the sonnet, therefore, beneath its challenge to the transcendent durability of sculpture, lurks an unstated question about the durability of the poet's own language. The struggle for power between word and image in ekphrastic representation has never before been quite so annihilating in its implications.

Some two years after composing this profoundly skeptical sonnet on the disintegration of the material sublime, Shelley produced its complement: a poem on the petrifaction of beauty in a painting of Medusa once attributed to Leonardo da Vinci.[50] "On the Medusa of Leonardo da Vinci" is an uncompleted poem of five ottava rima stanzas first printed from Mary Shelley's transcript by Thomas Hutchinson in 1904, with a sixth stanza from Mary's transcript first printed by Neville Rogers in 1961 (Rogers 9–12). Since the poem is not widely known and since the meaning of a key word in it depends on the full surrounding context, I quote all six stanzas from Rogers's text, reproducing his spaces for missing words:

I

> It lieth, gazing on the midnight sky,
>   Upon the cloudy mountain-peak supine;
> Below, far lands are seen tremblingly;
>   Its horror and its beauty are divine.
> Upon its lips and eyelids seems to lie
>   Loveliness like a shadow, from which shine,
> Fiery and lurid, struggling underneath,
> The agonies of anguish and of death.

II

> Yet it is less the horror than the grace
>   Which turns the gazer's spirit into stone.
> Whereon the lineaments of that dead face
>   Are graven, till the characters be grown
> Into itself, and thought no more can trace;

'Tis the melodious hue of beauty thrown
Athwart the darkness and the glare of pain,
Which humanize and harmonize the strain.

III

And from its head as from one body grow,
    As   grass out of a watery rock,
Hairs which are vipers, and they curl and flow
    And their long tangles in each other lock,
And with unending involutions show
    Their mailed radiance, as it were to mock
The torture and the death within, and saw
The solid air with many a ragged jaw.

IV

And, from a stone beside, a poisonous eft
    Peeps idly into those Gorgonian eyes;
Whilst in the air a ghastly bat, bereft
    Of sense, has flitted with a mad surprise
Out of the cave this hideous light had cleft,
    And he comes hastening like a moth that hies
After a taper; and the midnight sky
Flares, a light more dread than obscurity.

V

'Tis the tempestuous loveliness of terror;
    For from the serpents gleams a brazen glare
Kindled by that inextricable error,
    Which makes a thrilling vapour of the air
Become a   and ever-shifting mirror
    Of all the beauty and the terror there—
A woman's countenance, with serpent locks,
Gazing in death on Heaven from those wet rocks.

ADDITIONAL STANZA

It is a woman's countenance divine
    With everlasting beauty breathing there
Which from a stormy mountain's peak, supine
    Gazes into the   night's trembling air.
It is a trunkless head, and on its feature
    Death has met life, but there is life in death,
The blood is frozen—but unconquered Nature
    Seems struggling to the last—without a breath
The fragment of an uncreated creature.

In her searching commentary on this difficult poem, Carol Jacobs asks a crucial question about the second line of stanza 2: "Who is the gazer—Perseus, his predecessor, the painter, the poet, the reader?" (167). Though she goes on to say that "there are no clear-cut answers to these questions," she soon enough furnishes one: the gazer is the spectator of the painting, and it is the *spectator's* spirit that is turned to stone (168–69). This reading of "gazer" has been adopted by two other distinguished critics. John Hollander asserts that in the second stanza "the viewer of the painting [becomes] *its* victim" ("Poetics," 211), and W. J. T. Mitchell treats the supposed petrification of the viewer in Shelley's poem as the paradigmatic example of what happens to the poet who confronts a work of visual art. "Medusa," he writes, "is the perfect prototype for the image as a dangerous female Other who threatens to silence the male voice and fixate his observing eye. . . . Medusa fully epitomizes the ambivalence that Keats hints at [in the "Urn"]: instead of 'teasing us out of thought' with a paralyzing eternity of perfect desolation, she paralyzes thought itself, first by turning 'the gazer's spirit into stone,' and then by engraving the lineaments of the Gorgon onto the beholder's petrified spirit . . ." ("Ekphrasis" 709).

There are two attractive reasons for taking the spiritually petrified gazer as the spectator. One is that the living Medusa had the power to petrify anyone who looked at her, and that even after her death her apotropaic image was used on a shield to "frighten [the] fear-numbed foes" of Athena (*Metamorphoses* 4.779–803). The other reason is that in contemporary critical theorizing about the visual arts, the gazer is almost always treated as the (male) spectator whose control of the viewing process is questioned, challenged, or in some way subverted by a threatening alien image that dares to look back.[51] It is not surprising, then, that the word "gazer" in a poem about Medusa has led three critics to gloss it as "spectator." But it *is* surprising that not one of these critics has considered a far more obvious candidate for the role of the gazer: the head of Medusa.

The case for this candidate is formidable. In the very first line of stanza I, the head lies "gazing on the midnight sky"; in the last line of stanza V, it is "gazing in death on Heaven"; in the fourth line of the additional stanza, it "gazes into the night's trembling air." If the gazer is *not* the head that is repeatedly and explicitly said to be gazing, where are we told or even led to infer that it is the spectator? How are we signaled that in stanza II, and only stanza II, the poem turns away from the head and the objects that surround it, which are otherwise the only things described? The more we study the poem, the more the questions multiply. If the "gazer" is the speaker, how are the lineaments of Medusa's face graven on the speaker's petrified spirit? Where does the speaker sound spiritually petrified? How is the speaker silenced? If the speaker's observing eye is fixated on the face, how does it manage to take in the eft and the bat? If the gazer isn't the speaker or the head, who is it? And finally, if the head retains its power to petrify the spirit of anyone who gazes on it, how does the eft manage to peep right into "those Gorgonian eyes" without in any way stiffening?

I raise all these questions because to my knowledge no one else has. Every recent piece of criticism I have read on this poem simply assumes that the gazer is the viewer of the picture. If instead we take the gazer as the head, the poem becomes a study in the petrifaction of beauty, in what happens when the petrifying impact of Medusa's gaze is turned inward on her own spirit.[52] Traditionally, painted faces and figures were supposed to express the vitality of the human spirit, release it to the eye. Alberti wrote that painting moves the beholder "when each man painted there clearly shows the movement of his own soul" (77), and in Shakespeare's *Rape of Lucrece,* as we have seen, the painted faces of Ajax and Ulysses "most expressly told" their feelings and temperament (1394–1400). Leonardo himself declared: "The motions and postures of [painted] figures should display the true mental state of the originator of these motions, in such a way that they could not signify anything else" (145–46). What Shelley sees in this would-be Leonardo painting of a severed head is precisely the reverse of such expression. Instead of exhibiting or signifying a human spirit to the viewer, the grace that lies on the dead countenance of Medusa "like a shadow" turns back upon her spirit, converting it to stone and then engraving the features of the face upon the petrified spirit in such a way as to make it inscrutable: a blank where "thought no more can trace."

In stanza II, then, the painted face becomes a sculpted soul, a face "graven" upon Medusa's spirit. The allusion to sculpture—more precisely to the carving or incising of features in stone—commands special attention because, except in its title, the poem makes no reference to the pictorial status of the head. In turning from paint to the art of sculpture, the poem recalls "Ozymandias," but with a crucial difference: while "Ozymandias" represents the disintegration of a monument that expresses—as visual art traditionally should—the passions of the man sculpted, this poem treats stone as the means by which beauty obliterates a woman's spirit. Paradoxically, her spirit is petrified not so much by horror or by anything like the ruler's rigidity of purpose as it is by "grace"—by the beauty and loveliness spread over her face. Insofar as the painting expresses any inner vitality at all, it is the vitality of horror: "the glare of pain," the "agonies of anguish and of death" signified by the tangled mass of serpents. "Struggling underneath" the upturned face, as the painting itself independently shows, the fiery vipers shining out from the shadow of loveliness twist and turn not just like hair or underwater grass but also like thoughts. As the sculptor's hand (or sculpted hand) mocked the inner life of Ozymandias, the endless involutions of the radiantly writhing vipers seem to mock—at once to imitate and ridicule— "the torture and the death within" the head, the mental anguish of a dying soul.

In exhibiting both beauty and horror, the painted head combines the features that Edmund Burke so carefully distinguished and that Wordsworth's "Peele Castle" assigns to sharply contrasting pictures of serenity and violence, the beautiful and the sublime. While the loveliness of Medusa's countenance epitomizes beauty, which Burke specifically identified with "the *beauty* of the *sex*" (42), the snakes and the "poisonous eft" peeping into her eyes recall his observation that "ideas of the sublime" could be raised by "objects of terror" such as "serpents and poisonous animals of all kinds" (57). But Shelley's account of the painting sharply alters the meaning and effect of Burke's key terms. Burke demands "clear and bright" colors in objects he considers beautiful (117) and "obscurity" in those he considers sublime (58). In Shelley's poem, loveliness lies "like a shadow" on the painted face of Medusa, and the sublime serpents radiate light—"the glare of pain."[53] More importantly, the beauty portrayed in the painting excites none of the love that Burke said beauty caused (91) but rather petrifies and obliterates the spirit beneath it. Insofar as there is life in this head, it expresses itself as the pain of a final struggle against a petrifying death, for ironically enough, it is darkness and pain "which humanize and harmonize the strain" of beauty's "melodious hue."

In radiating horror and "the glare of pain," the writhing serpents signify life itself, more precisely a living resistance to petrifaction. Keats explained a similar conception of pain in a well-known letter of 21 April 1819, just a few months before Shelley wrote this poem. The world, writes Keats, is "a vale of soul-Making," a place in which a "World of Pains and troubles" is required to form a soul (*Letters* 2:102–03). The "easeful Death" that Keats erotically solicits in "Ode to a Nightingale," written soon after the letter (in May 1819), would mean ceasing "with no pain," but he knows only too well that such a death—at once beautiful and painless—would make of him an insensate "sod." Two years later, when fatally wracked with tuberculosis, Keats clung to his pain as to life itself: "I wish for death every day and night to deliver me from these pains," he writes, "and then I wish death away, for death would destroy even those pains which are better than nothing" (*Letters* 2:345).

In the "Medusa" likewise, the contrast between pain and beauty becomes a contest between life and death, persevering vitality and numbing petrifaction. Yet in the second half of the poem, beauty and terror mingle so intimately that even Shelley's own way of polarizing the two cannot keep them fully distinct. The flaring of the midnight sky displays not only a "light more dread than obscurity"—an explicit revision of Burke—but also "the tempestuous loveliness of terror." The beauty of terror itself is a "brazen glare" kindled by the writhing of the gleaming serpents, here called "inextricable error."[54] With its Latinate use of "error" for wandering, this striking phrase derives, as Rogers notes (16), from Virgil's name for the Cretan labyrinth represented in the Cumaean temple of Apollo: he calls it "inextricabilis error" (*Aeneid* 6.27). Shelley's allusion to the labyrinth conjures up its Minotaur, the monstrous product of another commingling of beauty and terror, the queen and the bull. But while Virgil's beast is wholly monstrous, the rank perversion of beauty, Shelley's Medusa defies categorization. The light radiated by the serpents makes the air a "thrilling vapour" that reflects the inextricable complexity of her head: the petrifying beauty of her face, the lovely terror of her serpent-locks.

Like the vaporous mirror described here, the aesthetic categories used to define the head are "ever-shifting," detached from any consistent set of oppositions and from any reference to pictorial composition. But the Additional

Stanza clearly represents the picture of a transitional moment. It is the moment of dying, the moment at which "unconquered Nature / Seems struggling to the last" before surrendering "without a breath." The painting depicts what is quite literally Medusa's last gasp: a spiral plume of vapor rising from her lips to join the "thrilling vapour of the air." By perpetuating this moment of "life in death," the painting makes the face transcendent: "a woman's countenance divine / With everlasting beauty breathing there." But the beauty is everlasting only because, as we have already learned, it petrifies the spirit of the gazer, freezing her blood and turning her breath (*spiritus*) to stone. "Gazing in death on Heaven," the face of beauty is becoming a mask of death.

In contrasting ways, then, each of Shelley's two ekphrastic poems contests the claims of transcendence made by and for visual art. Neatly divided between a statue and a painting, the works represented by these two poems also exemplify contrasting archetypes of gender: the sublimity of masculine power standing up and voicing its authority, and the beauty of a woman's supine face reduced to the silence of final expiration. But Shelley reconstitutes both of these archetypes. While "Ozymandias" registers the gradual disintegration of a statue made to signify enduring power, "Medusa" discerns in the painting of the head the petrifying impact of beauty on life itself, which is here signified by the serpentine writhing of its final resistance to death. We shall now see how the vision of sculpture as an essentially petrifying art gradually comes to eclipse its claims to transcendent beauty and energy in the poetry of Byron.

IV

IDEALITY AND FIXITY: BYRON ON SCULPTURE

It is not surprising that Byron's interest in the fine arts has provoked so little interest from students of his poetry. Aside from a short poem on a bust by Canova and the stanzas on ancient sculpture in the Fourth Canto of *Childe Harold's Pilgrimage*, Byron has left us no ekphrastic poetry: no verses representing a work of graphic art, and certainly nothing comparable to Keats's "Ode on a Grecian Urn." Yet there is ample evidence that Byron could appreciate both painting and sculpture. Though he repeatedly declared his ignorance of painting, he was dazzled by the works he saw in Florence and Venice, and Stendhal tells us that he was moved to astonishing eloquence by his visit to the Brera Gallery in Milan. "I admired," Stendhal writes, "the depth of sentiment with which the great poet comprehended the most opposite painters: Raphael, Guernico, Luini, Titian etc. *Hagar Dismissed by Abraham* electrified him; from that moment admiration made us quite speechless; he improvised for an hour, and better, in my opinion, than Madame de Stael."[55]

While Byron's poetry largely suppresses this remarkable sensitivity to painting, it plainly expresses his admiration for sculpture. Calling sculptors "a race of mere imposters," the narrator of *Don Juan* says at one point, "I've seen much finer women, ripe and real / Than all the nonsense of their stone ideal"

(2.118).[56] But if the iconoclastic narrator speaks for Byron at all here, then Byron can only be playfully denying one of his own habitual tendencies, which—as Larrabee notes (168)—was precisely to measure the beauty of actual women against the ideal standard furnished by ancient sculptures such as the Venus de Medici. In canto 4 of *Childe Harold's Pilgrimage,* finished several months before *Don Juan* was begun, the narrator rapturously salutes the Medician Venus as the embodiment of "what mind can make, when Nature's self would fail" (4.49), and later on he rhetorically asks: "Where are the forms the sculptor's soul hath seized? / In him alone. Can Nature show so fair?" (4.122). Byron's own answer is clearly "no." Speaking unequivocally for himself in 1821, he declared that "sculpture in general . . . is more poetical than nature itself, inasmuch as it represents and bodies forth that ideal beauty and sublimity which is never to be found in actual nature" (Prothero 5:549).

There is nothing distinctively Byronic about this formulation, which closely resembles the view that Joshua Reynolds had some years before attributed to the "poets, orators, and rhetoricians of antiquity." In this ancient view, the ideal beauty represented in the arts descends to earth from heaven by means of "poetical" inspiration, which is why "Phidias, when he formed his Jupiter, did not copy any object ever presented to his sight; but contemplated only that image which he had conceived in his mind from Homer's description" (Reynolds 42). Reynolds himself departs from this ancient view by defining ideal beauty as an abstract idea or "central form" drawn from the comparative study of various objects (44–45). For him as for Byron, sculpture embodies an ideal form superior to any actual one. But while Reynolds derives the ideal form from particulars by a kind of aesthetic induction, Byron traces works of sculpture to the soul of the sculptor alone, a soul possessed of ideal forms that are "never to be found in actual nature."

Byron's conception of sculpture, therefore, reflects an academic neoclassicism lightly inflected by the kind of Platonism he had acquired from Shelley. His taste in sculpture was fundamentally conservative, and as Larrabee observes, it was this that led him to reject the Elgin marbles as "Phidian freaks / Misshapen monuments and maimed antiques" (see above, p. 110). Beyond what they had suffered from the rude wasting of old time, Byron found the Elgin figures graceless and brutal, too close to nature and too far from the ideal elegance prescribed by neoclassical standards and enshrined in statues such as the Medician Venus. In *English Bards,* then, and much more extensively in *The Curse of Minerva,* written two years later (in 1811), Byron endorsed the position that Payne Knight and the academic critics had taken against the value and Phidian authenticity of Elgin's remarkable imports.

In view of Byron's contempt for these "Phidian freaks," we may wonder why he lacerated Elgin for taking them out of Greece instead of congratulating him for removing a blight upon the Acropolis. The answer seems to be that Byron saw Greece as the beautiful but supremely vulnerable victim of successive invaders—first the Goths, then the Turks, and now the "Pictish peer" (*Curse*

97–110, Page and Jump 143). Whatever the value of the marbles Elgin took, the fact that he took them made him—for Byron—one more barbarian, one more despoiler of Greece and its marble poetry. Some years after writing *The Curse of Minerva*, in fact, Byron implicitly acknowledged the value of the Elgin marbles when he explained why he had so vigorously opposed their removal to England. "The ruins," he wrote, "are as poetical in Picadilly as they were in the Parthenon; but the Parthenon and its rock are less so without them. Such is the Poetry of art" (Prothero 5:549).

"Poetry of art" is a suggestively polysemous phrase. It can signify either the poetic effect that works of marble have upon the viewer or the verbal poetry that such works elicit from the viewer. Here I will focus on the poetry that sculpture elicited from Byron—on his own ekphrastic poetry of sculpture. And since Byron's concept of sculpture seems in many ways a mere reflection of academic doctrine and well-established assumptions, I will identify the points at which Byron's poetry transforms these assumptions—and even undermines them.

Consider first his little—and little noted—poem "On the Bust of Helen by Canova," written November 1816:

> In this beloved marble view,
> Above the works and thoughts of man,
> What Nature *could*, but *would not* do,
> And Beauty and Canova *can!*
> Beyond imagination's power,
> Beyond the Bard's defeated art,
> With immortality her dower,
> Behold the *Helen* of the *heart.*
>
> (Page and Jump 101)

This brief and yet also extravagant tribute to the work of a contemporary Italian sculptor is noteworthy for one thing: it places sculpture not only above nature (as Byron does elsewhere) but even above poetry: "beyond imagination's power, / Beyond the Bard's defeated art." It is startling to set this praise for a sculpted Helen beside what Lessing says in *Laocoon* about Homer's verbal account of her. By eschewing description, by merely intimating the beauty of Helen in the speech of the old man who says that she was worth the war which cost so much (*Iliad* 3.156–58), Homer conveys—says Lessing—"an idea of her beauty which far surpasses anything art [i.e., visual art] is able to accomplish toward that end" (Lessing 111). Whether or not Byron knew the *Laocoon*, which was not Englished until 1826, he clearly inverts the values of Lessing's comparison. In the process he also sets aside one of the most fundamental doctrines in the long history of theorizing about the sister arts, which is that painting and sculpture take their inspiration from poetry.

Byron's poetry takes much of *its* inspiration from sculpture. In the Fourth Canto of *Childe Harold's Pilgrimage*, a canto he started just seven months after the Canova poem, he successively salutes—though in discontinuous stanzas— the Venus de Medici, the Dying Gaul (the work he called the Gladiator), the Laocoon, and the Apollo Belvedere. Two things about these ekphrastic passages clearly reflect prevailing assumptions and tastes. First, all of the works they describe were well known to Byron's readers and had already been described in poems such as Thomson's *Liberty* (1736), which—as Jerome McGann notes (*Fiery Dust* 105)—Byron had used in writing the first two cantos of *Childe Harold*. Secondly, Byron repeatedly acclaims the vitality embodied in these celebrated works of sculpture, and in so doing reflects what Larrabee calls a long-standing literary convention: the practice of discovering life and breath in statuary (Larrabee 278). In Byron's poem, the Venus de Medici "loves in stone" (4.433); the Apollo Belvedere "breathes the flame with which 'twas wrought" (4.1467); the tortured Laocoon emits "gasp on gasp" (4.1440); and even the dying Gladiator "expire[s]" (4.1268)—literally breathes out the last of his life.

In thus imputing life to sculpture as well as in choosing to celebrate such works as the Laocoon, Byron follows well-established precedents. But the sheer number of variations that he works upon the theme of breathing statuary distinguishes his ekphrastic passages from those we find in poems such as Thomson's *Liberty*. For one example, compare Thomson's lines on the Dying Gladiator with Byron's stanzas on the same figure:

Thomson:

Of raging aspect rushed impetuous forth
The Gladiator: pitiless his look,
And each keen sinew braced, the storm of war,
Ruffling, o'er all his nervous body frowns.
The dying other from the gloom she drew.
Supported on his shortened arm he leans,
Prone, agonizing; with incumbent fate
Heavy declines his head; yet dark beneath
The suffering feature sullen vengeance lours,
Shame, indignation, unaccomplished rage;
And still the cheated eye expects his fall.
                              (*Liberty* 4.152–62)

Byron:

I see before me the Gladiator lie:
He leans upon his hand—his manly brow
Consents to death, but conquers agony,
And his drooped head sinks gradually low—
And through his side the last drops, ebbing slow
From the red gash, fall heavy, one by one,
Like the first of a thunder-shower; and now

The arena swims around him—he is gone,
Ere ceased the inhuman shout which hail'd the wretch who won.

He heard it, but he heeded not—his eyes
Were with his heart, and that was far away;
He reck'd not of the life he lost nor prize,
But where his rude hut by the Danube lay
There were his young barbarians all at play,
There was their Dacian mother—he, their sire,
Butcher'd to make a Roman holiday—
All this rush'd with his blood—Shall he expire
And unavenged?—Arise! ye Goths, and glut your ire!
                    (*Childe Harold* 4.1252–69)

In Thomson's poem, the Dying Gladiator is just one of several celebrated figures unearthed at the dawn of the Renaissance by the Goddess of Sculpture, who first exhumes the victorious Gladiator in all his "pitiless" fury and then the Dying Gladiator ("the dying other") in his complex mood of agonized exhaustion and sullen vengefulness. The vengefulness reappears at the end of Byron's passage, but now it participates in a much more complicated series of reflections on the gladiator himself and the fate of Rome, so that Byron's ekphrasis is at once more intensive and more extensive than Thomson's: more personal, more penetrating, and far more fully narrated. While Thomson's Goddess unearths various works among unspecified "hoary ruins" (*Liberty* 4.134), Byron locates the Dying Gladiator within the Coliseum. Placing it directly before him, he represents it as a man actually dying, so that instead of simply recording the arrested moment in Thomson's manner ("And still the cheated eye expects his fall"), Byron tells the full story of the man's end: the last drops of blood fall one by one, the arena swims around him, and then he dies—with the crowd still shouting.

But Byron does not stop there. After giving us an external narrative of the gladiator's death, he tells the story again—from inside the man's head. In the first stanza, he represents the final moments of the physical man, with just a hint of what his facial expression signifies about his feelings: "his manly brow / Consents to death, but conquers agony." In the next stanza, he imagines what the gladiator saw in his heart: a picture of the family he left behind. The stark contrast between that tender domestic scene and the brutality of gladiatorial slaughter is what begets the cry for Gothic vengeance at the end.

This cry complicates the meaning of the gladiator's death. For as we move from the passionately charged moment of that death to the echoing silence of the ruined Coliseum in the ensuing lines (4.1270–1287), we can see what Gothic vengeance has done. We can see that the call for vengeance at the end of the second stanza is just as inhuman as the shout at the end of the first that helped to provoke it. Hence the story of the gladiator's death and the vengeance that follows it must give way finally to a meditation on what McGann calls "the ultimate human horror" (*Fiery Dust* 42), the cycle of historical vengeance that turns the Roman empire into a "Ruin past Redemption's skill" (4.1303).

Byron's stanzas on the Dying Gladiator show how he can make a work of sculpture not just come alive as a "breathing" figure in the traditional way but also *participate* in the ever-changing life of his own narrative, in the restless movement of his meditations. But the practice of drawing sculpture into the stream of his own narrative does not prevent Byron from stopping to admire works of sculpture as such. Though he treats the Dying Gladiator as if it were real, not sculpted at all, his lines on the Belvedere Apollo pay explicit tribute to a work of art as such. In the shining delicacy of this statue, he says,

> are exprest
> All that ideal beauty ever bless'd
> The mind within its most unearthly mood,
> When each conception was a heavenly guest—
> A ray of immortality—
>
> (4.1453–1457)

In celebrating the "ideal beauty" that he finds in the statue, Byron echoes Reynolds, who spoke of "Ideal Beauty" as a "divine" principle of creation and as the sign of genius in works of art (45). Byron reaffirms this principle in terms that seem to proclaim the ultimate supremacy of the artist. The immortality he finds in works of ancient sculpture comes not just from the divinity of the figure represented—whether Venus or Apollo—but from the power of mind which at once generates the work and is in turn signified by it. Just as Canova's Helen shows that sculpture can surpass nature, the Venus de Medici demonstrates "what mind can make, when Nature's self would fail" (4.439). Hence Bruce Haley argues that the sculpted forms of *Childe Harold* IV "symbolize the creative mind's godlike triumph over man's weaknesses and illustrate . . . that the poem's central subject is the autonomous or 'independent' mind" (Haley 264).

If Haley is right, Byron's response to ancient sculpture constitutes not so much a radical revision of academic neoclassicism as a translation of its major premises into the language of romantic transcendence and autonomy. Yet such a language cannot adequately explain what Byron has done. To understand his poetry of sculpture, we must see how he uses sculpture to reveal something latent in *Childe Harold* and then manifest in *Don Juan:* the insidious connection between love and death.

Byron actually began to explore the erotic effect of sculpture well before he started writing *Childe Harold.* In *The Curse of Minerva* (1811), he slyly notes the impact of Elgin's giant statues on many a languid maid, who yearningly sighs at the long limbs and mighty backs of men far more "proper"—which is to say far more desirable—than her modern-day suitors (lines 185–94, Page and Jump 144). There is nothing quite like the playfully lubricious tone of this passage in the Fourth Canto of *Childe Harold's Pilgrimage,* written some six years afterwards, but in the later work Byron explicitly eroticizes both the

Apollo Belvedere and the Medici Venus. He treats the Apollo as "a dream of Love, / Shaped by some solitary nymph, whose breast / Longed for a death-less lover from above" (4.1450–52), and he imagines the Venus glowing with desire for Mars "while [her] lips are / With lava kisses melting while they burn, / Shower'd on his eyelids, brow, and mouth, as from an urn!" (4.456–58).

It is precisely in the rhyming of "burn" with "urn" that Byron links the eroti-cism of sculpture to the idea of death. Though urns can sometimes signify life,[57] Byron has already referred to them as cineraria, urging "those who find contemplation in the urn / To look on One [Rousseau] whose dust was once all fire" (3.718–19). Since cantos 3 and 4 repeatedly connect fire with dust and ashes, the rhyming of "burn" with "urn" in the stanzas on the Medici Venus clearly invites us to construe the urn as a repository of ashes, and also reminds us that Florence—where he sees the Venus—is a city of the dead. Just three stanzas after the passage on Venus, Byron tells us that Santa Croce's holy pre-cincts hold the ashes of four great men (4.477–86), and later on he speaks of Rome as "the Niobe of nations" holding "an empty urn within her wither'd hands, / Whose dust was scatter'd long ago" (4.703–6). The showered kisses of Venus have turned to scattered dust even as Rome herself has become a Niobe petrified in lifeless monuments and statuary.

Significantly, two of the four sculptures described in *Childe Harold* IV—the Laocoon and the Dying Gladiator—represent the very moment of dying, and Byron's account of the gladiator vividly turns the vocabulary of eroticism into a language of death. In the passage on Venus, her kisses are "showered" on Mars's eyelids, brow, and mouth; in the stanzas on the dying gladiator, the last drops of the gladiator's blood, "ebbing slow / From the red gash, fall heavy, one by one, / Like the first of a thunder-shower" (1256–58). Equally telling is the order of the ekphrastic passages, which begin with Venus (433–68), proceed to the dying Gladiator (1252–69) and the doomed Laocoon (1432–40), and end with Apollo (1441–67). Thus two erotic figures frame two dying ones, and even the immortal beauty of the triumphant Apollo is subtly infected by inti-mations of mortality. Fresh from shooting the python with his "unerring bow," he seems to reverse the fate of the serpent-bound figure described just before his own, and to defy erosion as well: the final lines on the sculpted Apollo say that "Time itself hath hallowed it, nor laid / One ringlet in the dust—not hath it caught / A tinge of years, but breathes the flame with which 'twas wrought" (1456–68). Yet the ominous conjunction of flame and dust belies the claim these very terms are used to make. Insofar as the sculpted figure of Apollo breathes erotic fire, it inevitably leads to dust, to ashes, and to death. Like the "bold lover" whose passion is timelessly frozen on Keats's urn, this marble "dream of Love" becomes at last a funerary figure.

The movement from eroticism to death that subtly permeates the poetry of sculpture in *Childe Harold* becomes an essential part of Byron's narrative in *Don Juan*, specifically in the Haidee episode of cantos 2–4. *Don Juan* does not offer the prolonged descriptions of sculpture that *Childe Harold* gives us; instead it makes passing references. But in these references, Byron uses sculpture to signify at once the suspensive force of erotic attraction and the way this suspension prefigures the cessation of life.

Critics agree that *Don Juan* is a poem of perpetual motion. Its essential reality, says Alvin Kernan, "is the constant flow of life leading on from change to change" (Kernan 350), and Jerome McGann finds it "always in transition" (*"Don Juan" in Context* 95). Yet in fact the flow of change can sometimes freeze. Consider what happens from the first part of canto 3, when Lambro returns to find his house usurped by revelers, to the first part of canto 4, when he menacingly confronts his daughter and her lover. During this segment the narrator's *mind* is continuously in motion, ranging with typical restlessness from the pleasures of the feast to the banalities of Southey and Wordsworth, but the relationship between Juan and Haidee remains unchanged, indefinitely suspended, immutably sculpted—so to speak—by their desire to perpetuate it. On the night they pledge their love to one another, Haidee sits on Juan's knee, and "thus they form a group that's quite antique, / Half naked, loving, natural, and Greek" (2.1551–52). Whether or not Byron is thinking of a Cupid and Psyche that he may have seen at the Uffizi, as Larrabee suggests (123), this is the first of many references that define the love between Juan and Haidee in sculpturesque terms, and thus tempt us to believe—or wish—that it may last indefinitely. In any case, it *does* last all the way through canto 3, which is an extraordinary length of time for anything to remain unchanged in this poem. In canto 2, where Juan and Haidee fall in love, the narrator introduces the theme of inconstancy at the very moment when they pledge their hearts to each other. Just after they do so, he mischievously reminds us of the woman that Juan has left behind and mock-solemnly denounces inconstancy (1657–68), thus implying that Juan will prove inconstant again. But Juan and Haidee do keep faith with each other for two full cantos, and in canto 4, the narrator himself contemplates their constancy with amazement. "Moons changing had roll'd on," he says, "and changeless found / Those their bright rise had lighted to such joys / As rarely they beheld throughout their round" (4.121–23).

Yet even as this spectacle of constancy seems to enchant the narrator, the poem compels us to see that changelessness negates life, and the desire for changelessness can lead only to death. This point first emerges plainly near the end of canto 2, where we learn that one of Haidee's greatest pleasures is to watch over Juan while he sleeps, perfectly tranquilized and immobilized in her arms—"like death without its terrors" (2.1575–76). The simile here is extraordinarily suggestive. In the usual kind of "sleepwatching," as in Shakespeare's *Lucrece* and Keats's "Eve of St. Agnes," the watcher is a male and the sleeper a female whose beauty at once transfixes him and excites him to wake her up, to move from passive voyeur to active lover, and thus to convert a static picture into a passionate process.[58] But Haidee does not wish to awaken Juan. She is simply transfixed by the sight of his "stirless, helpless, and unmoved" form (1571). This enchanting and enchanted state of suspended animation—

death's second self—resembles death itself all too closely, and the sole alternative to the changes that life would inevitably bring is precisely death. Shortly after expressing his admiration for the changelessness of the lovers' mutual devotion, the narrator says: "Mix'd in each other's arms, and heart in heart, / Why did they not then die?" (4.209–11).

This question leads to the actual story of Haidee's death, or rather of her dying, which is significantly represented as a process of gradual petrifaction. Instead of eliciting life from sculpted figures, as he did in *Childe Harold,* Byron shows the living, breathing form of Haidee turned into the rigidity of sculpted marble, which now comes to signify death. As she and Juan sleep, she dreams first of being chained to a rock on the seashore (4.241–48)—an Andromedan image of fixity—and then of finding herself in a cave hung with marble icicles where her teardrops freeze to marble as they fall (4.257–64). When she awakens to the horrifying presence of her father and he threatens to shoot Juan, she thrusts herself between them and stands "pale, statue-like, and stern" (4.340). When he seizes her, she implicitly becomes a Laocoon in his arms, which grasp her "like a serpent's coil" (4.381). Finally, to describe the coma that she falls into after Juan is wounded and taken away, the narrator explicitly evokes three of the four sculptures described in *Childe Harold,* including the Laocoon:

> The ruling passion, such as marble shows
>   When exquisitely chisell'd, still lay there,
> But fix'd as marble's unchanged aspect throws
>   O'er the fair Venus, but for ever fair;
> O'er the Laocoon's all eternal throes,
>   And ever-dying Gladiator's air,
> Their energy like life forms all their fame,
> Yet looks not life, for they are still the same.
>   (4.481–88)

Paradoxical to the point of self-contradiction, the final couplet of this stanza radically revises the traditional conception of sculpture as the embodiment of life. The prolonged tributes to the vitality of marble figures that Byron offered in *Childe Harold* have now contracted to just three lines, one each for the Medici Venus, the Laocoon, and the Gladiator. Each of these statues eternally radiates a lifelike energy and thus recalls what Byron had said about them in the earlier poem. But from the ever-fair Venus to the ever-dying Gladiator, they are perpetually fixed, and therefore perpetually lifeless. Their life*like* energy "looks not life, for they are still the same." Insofar as Haidee's long sleep makes her resemble a work of sculpture, then, it also gives her the face of fixation—the face of death. And if sculpture symbolizes the lover's desire to perpetuate the beauty of the beloved, it also reveals the price to be paid for the realization of that desire.

In *Childe Harold* Byron eloquently articulates his admiration for the energy, the erotic power, and the ideality of sculpture. But the restlessness of his imagination compelled him to see the link between the fire of erotic statuary and the ashes of death. In *Don Juan* he tightens the bond between sculpture and death by treating statuary as one more example of the fixity which he found fundamentally incompatible with life. In using sculptural terms to define at first the beauty of an indefinitely protracted love affair, then states of mortal terror, and finally the stasis of a coma, Byron undermines the traditional conception of sculpture as an art of lifelike energy and the romantic conception of it as an art of transcendent beauty. For him it signifies the kind of beauty that may be admired but nonetheless must be finally relinquished by anyone truly committed to a quest for life.

⅋

Romantic ekphrasis is the expression of a profound ambivalence toward the timelessness of visual art. All four of the major romantic poets we have considered—Wordsworth, Keats, Shelley, and Byron—could be entranced with the kind of beauty they saw in painting and sculpture. Wordsworth salutes the "calm of blest eternity" in Beaumont's "Beautiful Picture"; Shelley finds "everlasting beauty" in the painted face of Medusa; Keats sees the lover's quarry on the urn as eternally beautiful ("she cannot fade"); and for Byron, the Belvedere Apollo embodies "ideal beauty." But in romantic ekphrasis, the beauty of a transcendent calm—of "the one brief moment caught from fleeting time"—cannot long withstand the pressures of narrative, the disruptive energies of the sublime, the shocks of historical contingency, and the rude wasting of old time as it erodes the perishable stuff of which visual art is made. "Peele Castle" shows one strategy for accommodating all these threats to the ideology of transcendence. Constructing a narrative in which youthful illusion seems to become mature perception, Wordsworth actually substitutes one form of transcendence for another. He forsakes the beautiful, maternal, amniotic calm of the remembered sea for what he takes to be a picture of lasting endurance: the sublime, phallic, paternal authority of the castle standing up against the ferocity of a storm. But if Wordsworth trades one picture of transcendence for another, Keats, Shelley, and Byron all in different ways challenge the notion that visual art can give us any images of timeless perfection. "Ozymandias" represents the mock sublimity of a statue in the process of disintegrating; "Medusa" reveals the petrifying effect of precisely the kind of beauty that a painted face offers us; the "Urn" shows how sculpted beauty sacrifices life itself in order to transcend change; and in *Don Juan* works of sculpture come to signify something like rigor mortis.

The great paradox of romantic ekphrasis, then, is that it simultaneously constructs and deconstructs the concept of visual art as a medium of transcendence. Until the founding of institutions like the Royal Academy of Art (begun 1768) and museums like England's National Gallery (opened 1824), the idea that works of painting and sculpture might last forever—might indefinitely survive the shocks of historical change—could scarcely be entertained. In the romantic era, the recovery of the Elgin marbles and the renewed impact of all the ancient statuary on display in Rome made it possible for poets to *imagine* works of visual art unravished by change. But everything they saw—most especially the Elgin fragments—bore evidence of what time had done to them. So while Keats's sonnet on the fragments represents their ruined state, his ode on the urn provides a vision of ancient sculpture perfectly restored. At the same time, the very idea of timeless perfection in visual art threatened the verbal authority of the romantic poets, whose great ambitions sometimes produced no more than fragments of the epic tradition such as Keats's Hyperion poems or Byron's unfinished *Don Juan*.[59] The self-sufficient ekphrastic *poem*—first fully established in the romantic period—is itself a fragment of this tradition, since ekphrasis began as epic digression, a descriptive detour from the great narrative road.[60] When the representation of a work of art is no longer surrounded by a larger narrative that subsumes it, when the work of art becomes the poet's chief or only subject, the struggle for mastery between word and image intensifies. In romantic poetry, therefore, the iconophilic impulse to revere the timeless beauty or sublimity of the icon is checked by all that words can do to undermine its authority, to reveal its material impermanence, or to expose its petrifying impact on the narratable flow of life.

Chapter Four

MODERN AND POSTMODERN EKPHRASIS

ENTERING THE MUSEUM OF ART

In the past forty years, the production of ekphrastic poetry has become nothing less than a boom. A complete collection of later twentieth-century poems about paintings would fill at least several volumes, but a passing glance at recent anthologies—and published lists—helps to show why the compiler of one such list should use the word "explosion" to denote the multiplicity of contemporary poems about works of visual art (see Janik 140). In 1973, Gisbert Kranz published *Das Bildegedicht in Europa,* which includes an eighty-page list (121–200) of European ekphrastic poems ranging from ancient times to our own, but chiefly the latter.[1] In 1978, Eugene Huddleston and Douglas Noverr published a list of over eight hundred American poems that could be linked in some way to visual art, including more than a hundred poems about specific paintings written within the past forty years. Six years later came *The Poet Dreaming in the Artist's House,* a collection of eighty contemporary poems in English about the visual arts (Buchwald and Roston). In 1986, three collections of contemporary British poems on visual art surfaced in England—two from the Tate Gallery (Abse, Adams) and a third in a special issue of *Word & Image* (2:1) that included thirty-one ekphrastic poems—almost all published for the first time—by poets such as Seamus Heaney, John Hollander, and W. D. Snodgrass. Two years later, in 1988, J. D. McClatchy published something very much akin to these collections: a book of essays on visual art by twentieth-century poets. And the following year, Beverly Long and Timothy Cage published a bibliography of more than a hundred contemporary American poems that represent identifiable paintings.

The salience of ekphrasis in modern and contemporary poetry becomes still more striking when we consider that at least one poem about a work of visual art has come from almost every major poet of our time. And the best-known ekphrastic poems of the twentieth century are like so many peaks rising from surrounding foothills. W. H. Auden's "Musee des Beaux Arts" and William

135

Carlos Williams's "Landscape with the Fall of Icarus" are just two of the eighteen poems written about Breughel's well-known painting of Icarus in the years from 1923 to 1974 (Clements 254). Likewise, Williams's "The Hunters in the Snow" is merely the best known of four American poems on Breughel's *Hunters*, which has also been verbally represented by John Berryman, Norbert Krapf, and Joseph Langland. Even Williams's whole ekphrastic volume—his *Pictures from Breughel and Other Poems* (1962)—has led the way to successors such as Robert Fagles's *I, Vincent: Poems from the Pictures of Van Gogh* (1978). And Fagles holds no ekphrastic monopoly on Van Gogh, whose *Starry Night* (1889) has prompted poems by Anne Sexton and W. D. Snodgrass as well as by Fagles himself.[2]

Wherever we turn in contemporary poetry, we find poems incited by works of visual art. Wallace Stevens's *Man with the Blue Guitar* (1937) is generally read as a poetic commentary on *The Old Guitarist* (1903) of Picasso, whose *Night Fishing at Antibes* (1939) occasioned a later poem by Nancy Sullivan.[3] James Merrill's "The Charioteer of Delphi" is at once a poetic response to the ancient bronze figure now standing in the Delphi Museum and a companion to Rainer Maria Rilke's "Archaic Torso of Apollo," on the headless figure of a Miletan youth in the Louvre. To this already formidable body of ekphrastic work by greater and lesser poets of our time could be added Yeats's well-known words on the sculpted Chinamen in "Lapis Lazuli"; Adrienne Rich's "Mourning Picture" (1965), which envoices the dead girl depicted in a memorial painting by her father, Edwin Romanzo Elmer; and Robert Lowell's "For the Union Dead," with its lines on Augustus St. Gaudens's high-relief bronze memorial to Colonel Robert Shaw and the black soldiers who bravely followed him into a devastating hailstorm of Confederate artillery. Given all this ekphrastic activity among the poets of our time, it seems hardly surprising that one of the most remarkable and certainly one of the most celebrated of all contemporary poems should be a supreme example of ekphrastic art: John Ashbery's 552-line meditation on a self-portrait by Parmigianino.

What can be said about this embarrassment of riches? What generalizations are possible or plausible in the face of such poetic abundance? Without pretending to have assimilated more than a modest fraction of all twentieth-century poems about visual art, I could begin by suggesting that they repeatedly display the basic features we have found permeating ekphrasis from Homer onwards: the conversion of fixed pose and gesture into narrative, the prosopopeial envoicing of the silent image, the sense of representational friction between signifying medium and subject signified, and overall the struggle for power—the *paragone*—between the image and the word. Among the poems just cited, for instance, Rich's "Mourning Picture" is throughout an exercise in paragonal prosopopeia, spoken posthumously by a girl whose language strives to outdo the painting of her black-clad parents sitting with the remembered image of their child outside their clapboard house on a hill overlooking western Massachusetts. Her language strives to recreate "each shaft of grass" in words that make us feel "its rasp on her fingers" and see "the map of every lilac leaf / or the net of veins on my father's / grief-tranced hand." The child's words also tell a story that looks beyond the painting, predicting that her parents "will move from the house" and give away the toys and pets depicted with them. Likewise, Lowell's lines on St. Gaudens's relief of Shaw and his men marching off to war place this sculpted moment in the stream of history: "Two months after marching through Boston, / The regiment was dead." And when we turn from Lowell's account of St. Gaudens's bronze regiment to Merrill's account of the bronze charioteer, we find once more the language of representational friction: a "green bronze hand" that "seems less to call / His horses back than to wait out their run"; "flutings" not of a marble column but of a tunic draped "from the brave patina of breast"; and "gentle eyes glass brown" that "look shining and nowhere / Unless indeed into our own."

Such familiar features as these give fresh evidence that ekphrasis is an enduring as well as ancient poetic mode, that much of what Homer did in representing the shield of Achilles can be recognized—can be known again—in the work of contemporary poets. But if contemporary ekphrasis offered us nothing more than the pleasure of recognizing an ancient literary mode, it would not engage us for long. We need to know, as we consider the ekphrastic poetry of our own time, just what *makes* it modern or postmodern, just what distinguishes a poem such as "Musée des Beaux Arts" from Homer's account of a shield or Shakespeare's description of a painting or Keats's meditation on a Grecian urn.

These questions might be answered in two stages. First of all, the ekphrastic poetry of our time completes the transformation of ekphrasis from incidental adjunct to self-sufficient whole, from epic ornament to free-standing literary work. In classical literature, the work of art is itself an adjunct or ornament, something made to decorate a shield, a cup, a robe, or a swordbelt. Correspondingly, ekphrasis originates as a seemingly ornamental adjunct to a larger text, a descriptive digression from the main line of epic narrative. But Jacques Derrida has cogently challenged the very notion of subordination presupposed by this concept of ekphrasis, more precisely the Kantian notion that a painting or sculpted figure can be subdivided into *ergon* and *parerga,* the centralized *work* and the marginalized adornments of framing, drapery, and colonnades— whatever borders or apparels the work. "A parergon," Derrida contends, "comes against, beside, and in addition to the *ergon,* the work done [*fait*], the fact, the work, but it does not fall to one side, it touches and cooperates within the operation, from a certain outside."[4] What Derrida says of the parergon in visual art can be said of the ekphrastic passage, which is commonly regarded as mere adornment of the epic text but which—as we have seen—is quite capable of revealing or prefiguring its most central themes.[5] Such revelatory power helps to explain why the ekphrastic passage eventually became the self-sufficient entity we know as the ekphrastic poem.

In England this development comes remarkably late. While Giambattista

Marino's *Galeria* gave Italian readers a whole gallery of ekphrastic poems in 1620, English poetry offers nothing comparable until much later. Aside from a few poems on portraits in the seventeenth century, the first truly distinguished specimens of self-sufficient ekphrastic poetry emerge in the romantic period, when—as we have seen with Keats's "Urn"—the establishment of the museum began to make individual works available for detailed scrutiny. Essentially, the poem focusing on a single work of art—on the single moment captured by a single painting—is a late product of the long process by which serialized depiction and narrative painting gave way to the unitemporal record of a momentary perception.[6] When Aeneas entered the new Carthaginian temple of Juno, he found a series of pictures telling a story of the Trojan War. Likewise, when a fourteenth-century Christian entered the Upper Church of Saint Francis at Assisi, he found the life of the saint narrated in frescoes (whether by Giotto or not makes no difference here). But as a general rule, the only tale told by the pictures in a modern temple of art is the curatorial story of how an artist developed, how a national culture was formed, or how the style of a "period" evolved.[7] Since museums can seldom display any more than a small fraction of the works required to tell such stories in full, the stories are typically signified by individual works: by the masterpieces that mark a transition, epitomize a period, or encapsulate a style. While the art historian may elaborately contextualize a work of art, the museum individuates it *for the eye,* sets it off for contemplation or veneration in its own framed and labeled space, presents it to us as a self-sufficient icon. And the individuated work of art begets the individual ekphrastic poem.

At the same time, the place where the poet must go to see this individuated work of art furnishes the second part of the answer to the question of what distinguishes the ekphrastic poetry of this century from its predecessors. Twentieth-century ekphrasis springs from the museum, the shrine where all poets worship in a secular age. *Voices in the Gallery* is the title of a recent collection of ekphrastic poems (Abse), and it is still more significant that the first major specimen of ekphrastic poetry written in this century should be explicitly titled "Musée des Beaux Arts." Only in a museum would Auden encounter a painting of Icarus incongruously juxtaposed with paintings of martyrdom and Christ's nativity: paintings put together not because they successively tell anything like a coherent story but because they all come from the same hand. Auden's own generalization about these paintings—that they all show how well the Old Masters understood suffering—has become so familiar that we generally fail to see how different the paintings are, how strange it is to link a picture of comically splashing legs with pictures of torture and miraculous birth.

I shall have more to say about Auden's poem in particular, but what I chiefly aim to do in this final chapter is to show how the experience of the museum and all the apparatus of institutionalized art in our time—especially reproductions and art-historical commentary—has informed the writing of ekphrastic poetry. In the very title of his "Musée," Auden tells us exactly where he saw

Breughel's *Landscape with the Fall of Icarus;* in *Pictures from Breughel,* we can see what Williams took from the commentaries of Gustave Gluck in the book of reproductions he consulted in the late 1950s to refresh his memory of the Breughels he saw some thirty years earlier at Vienna's Kunsthistorische Museum; in "Self-Portrait" Ashbery not only refers to that museum (indirectly) but also quotes the sources he has read on Parmigianino's painting and openly writes about the reproduction of it that appears in Sydney Freedberg's book on the painter. These poetic moves are all unmistakably of our time. If any modern poet ever did, no postmodern poet ever would deplore—with Walter Benjamin—what an age of mechanical reproduction has done to the unique "aura" of a work of art. Reproduction is too deeply embedded in our experience of art, too much a part of the world that ekphrasis now represents. To stop seeing reproductions we would have to give up our eyes.

The ekphrastic poetry of our time, then, represents individual works of art within the context of the museum, which of course includes the words that surround the pictures we see, beginning with picture titles. Without a title, could Auden or anyone else know that the splashing legs in Breughel's painting belong to Icarus, or even to a drowning man? Picture titles are merely the first of the words we encounter along with the pictures we see in museums. From titles we move to the curatorial notes on the museum wall, to catalogue entries, to exhibition reviews, to the explanatory notes that invariably accompany reproductions, and to the pages of art history. Synecdochically, the museum signifies all the institutions that select, circulate, reproduce, display, and explain works of visual art, all the institutions that inform and regulate our experience of it—largely by putting it into words.

The story of what poets make from this museum of words in the twentieth century begins, as I have already suggested, with Auden's "Musee." But the story has a prelude of sorts in a poem composed sixty years before our century began. Written about an imaginary picture displayed in a private house, this poem nevertheless prefigures much of what twentieth-century poets must grapple with as they encounter actual works of art in a museum. For the entire poem is spoken by a connoisseur exhibiting a picture of his own, a picture he alone controls the viewing of and—he believes—has the authority to explain.

I

GAZE AND GLANCE IN BROWNING'S "MY LAST DUCHESS"

It may seem strange that the considerable body of Victorian poetry about the visual arts should be represented in this book by the work of Browning rather than of Dante Gabriel Rossetti, the poet and painter who not only helped to found the Pre-Raphaelite Brotherhood but also composed a conspicuously ekphrastic set of *Sonnets for Pictures.*[8] Unlike Rossetti, Browning seldom writes at length about a particular work of art. He is far more interested in dramatizing the life of the painter who produced it, the painter who typically speaks for himself in Browning's dramatic monologues. In the opening section of "Fra Lippo Lippi," for instance, the painter has much less to say about the visual art he is creating—"saints and saints / And saints again" (47–48) than about what Michael Leslie calls "the cheap but powerful music of the invisible life beneath the window through which he escapes." Even at the end, when the Fra tells of his plans for what would become his *Coronation of the Virgin* (Saint Ambrogio, Florence), he gives little more than a cast of its characters—"God in the midst, Madonna and her babe, / Ringed by a bowery flowery angel brood" plus "i' the front, of course a saint or two" (348–52)—before imagining himself rescued from yet another adulterous scrape by the hand of an angel: an episode scarcely suggested by the painting itself, which merely shows the painter labeled "Iste perfecit opus" [This man made the work] kneeling piously in the lower right corner. For Browning, the individual painting is typically not so much an object of scrutiny as a point of departure for dramatization or speculation. In "The Guardian Angel," as Leslie notes, he gives just a few lines to what Guercino's *Guardian Angel* actually shows—an angel teaching a child to pray by "holding the little hands up, each to each / Pressed gently." The rest of the poem is largely an apostrophic appeal for angelic protection modulating into a vision of what such protection might do for the speaker (now the poet himself), who ends by saying that he has "translat[ed] . . . to song" the "one thought" which the picture stirred in him.

But pictures actually lead Browning to many thoughts. If he paragonally turns them into imaginary episodes, prayers, and the language of "song," his poems about works of visual art nonetheless reveal an acute awareness of the circumstances under which they are produced and received. Unlike Rossetti, who writes only about what he sees within a painting, Browning treats it in terms of the artist standing behind it and the viewer standing (or sitting) before it. In "Fra Lippo Lippi," he evokes not only the life of the painter but the response of those who first saw his paintings, including those who—as already mentioned—clawed to bits the torturers depicted in his painting of St. Laurence's martyrdom. In "The Guardian Angel" likewise, we learn not only of "dear Guercino's fame" and sufferings but also of the place where Browning saw his painting: in the chapel at Fano, where he went three times to view it "and drink [the angel's] beauty to our soul's content." Browning's poems about painting are steeped—or at least dyed—in the lore of art history. To the best of my knowledge, he is the first English poet to use the writer that would later be so conspicuously quoted in the opening lines of Ashbery's "Self-Portrait": Giorgio Vasari. Though Browning nowhere cites Vasari by name, he plundered Vasari's biography of Andrea del Sarto (his teacher) for his own "Andrea del Sarto," just as he raided Vasari's *Lives of the Painters* for "Fra Lippo Lippi."

Written in 1842, four years before he eloped to Italy with Elizabeth Barrett and about ten years before he wrote "Andrea del Sarto" and "Fra Lippo Lippi" (both ca. 1853), "My Last Duchess" bears no visible trace of Vasari, for it concerns an imaginary painting by an imaginary painter. But this curiously belated specimen of notional ekphrasis is partly based on historical facts about an actual Duke of Ferrara, and it bears all the essential traces of art-historical structure—of genesis and reception—that we find in the later poems. We learn who painted the picture, how and why it captures a particular expression, and—just as importantly—how it is exhibited, how it may be viewed. What makes this poem truly remarkable in the history of ekphrasis is its speaker. He is neither the painter nor the poet nor the painted duchess herself, who might have been envoiced like Dante's sculpted Virgin or Adrienne Rich's painted child. Instead, Browning's poem is spoken by the man who *owns* the painting and who completely controls the conditions under which it may be seen.

Since the Duke draws a curtain to display the painting to his auditor, critics such as W. David Shaw have compared him to a theatrical producer. But as the patron and connoisseur of art, as the supreme collector of beautifully wrought paintings and sculptures, he is the prototype of the modern museum director. In the museum of his own *palazzo* he knows the history of every work: whom or what it represents, who created it, how it was made, and whom it was made for. Furthermore, like the director of any museum, he decides just how each work of art will be exhibited, when it can be seen, where the viewer will sit to look at it, and what the viewer will be told about it. A modern museum director may have trouble seeing the Duke as a kindred spirit, but museumgoers know very well that watercolors and other light-sensitive pictures are often kept under curtains, that viewing hours are always limited and often inconvenient (the locked door and the closing bell are the art-lover's twin nemeses), and that pictures are always displayed with explanatory words of some kind, whether printed, tape-recorded on portable audio cassettes, or delivered *viva voce* by museum guides. Short of being an artist himself, the Duke combines all of the functions presupposed or exercised by the modern museum. He commissions art, collects it, guards it, carefully regulates its exhibition, provides a seat from which it can be viewed (admittedly not always available in modern museums), and—above all—explains it to the viewer:

> That's my last Duchess painted on the wall,
> Looking as if she were alive. I call
> That piece a wonder, now: Fra Pandolf's hands
> Worked busily a day, and there she stands.
> Will't please you sit and look at her? I said
> "Fra Pandolf " by design, for never read
> Strangers like you that pictured countenance,
> The depth and passion of its earnest glance,
> But to myself they turned (since none puts by
> The curtain I have drawn for you, but I)

And seemed as they would ask me, if they durst
How such a glance came there; so, not the first
Are you to turn and ask thus.

(1–13)

The opening words of this monologue radiate the sense of power that comes with absolute possession. The second word out of the speaker's mouth is the possessive pronoun *my,* which he applies both to the Duchess and the painting of her, and the whole of his discourse about her is calculated to make the viewer's experience of the picture utterly dependent on the Duke: on the Duke's management of the curtain, on the Duke's capacity to anticipate as well as answer any questions the painting might provoke in the viewer. On the surface at least, this master of rhetorical manipulation sounds supremely in control.

What he actually expresses, however, is the *will* to sound controlling, to dominate the picture with his words. His failure to dominate it—more precisely to dominate the person it represents—emerges plainly in the middle of the poem, where he repeatedly interrupts himself with commonplace interjections about his own incapacity to explain or regulate the duchess's character: "She had / A heart—how shall I say?—too soon made glad" (21–22); "She thanked men,—good! but thanked / Somehow—I know not how—" (31–32); "Even had you skill / In speech—(which I have not)—to make your will / Quite clear . . ." (35–37). Though the last of these interjections is patently disingenuous, they cannot all be explained as rhetorical ploys, as so many artful gestures of self-deprecation calculated to disarm his auditor. On the contrary, they express what Herbert Tucker calls "a private struggle" (178).

Signs of this struggle actually begin to appear in the very opening line of the Duke's monologue, where the word "painted" radically destabilizes the meaning of "Duchess." With a little help from Stanley Fish and his theory of reader response, we can see that a slow reading of the first line provokes two successive responses, two quite different ways of construing "Duchess." By themselves, the first four words might plausibly refer to a living woman pointed out to the auditor, just as one might *sotto voce* identify a former spouse at a cocktail party ("That's my ex-husband over there at the bar"). But the word "painted" instantly subverts this meaning of "Duchess," turning it into a signifier just as difficult to grasp and construe as the meaning of her painted glance. Does the phrase "my last Duchess" now denote a painting, or the person signified by that painting? Here is a variant of the ambiguity we met in the opening lines of Wordsworth's "Peele Castle," where the "Pile" apostrophized by the poet ("I was thy neighbour once, thou rugged Pile") seems at first to denote the castle of Beaumont's painting, then the actual castle, and finally the castle of the poet's own mental picture. In Browning's poem, the meaning of the key term "Duchess" remains ambiguous. The Duke cannot resolve the ambiguity because the painted image of his former spouse disturbs him quite as much as her actual face did—which is why he keeps the painting covered. For all his mastery of rhetoric, the Duke simply does not know how to master her image with words. If we suppress for a moment the phrase "painted on the wall," his opening sentence could all too easily refer to a skillfully embalmed corpse: "That's my last Duchess . . . / Looking as if she were alive." But with or without the "painted" phrase, the ending of the sentence merely accentuates its ambiguity. While the antecedent of "she" must be "Duchess," is it the painted duchess or the real one? What would it mean to speak of a painted duchess as alive?

We could say, of course, that "alive" here means lifelike. But the subjunctive "were" signals a condition contrary to fact and gives us the first hint that the woman represented by the painting is dead. What we begin to see through the words of the Duke is something like the picture described in Edgar Allen Poe's "The Oval Portrait," a short story first published—by an astonishing coincidence—in the very same year (1842) that "My Last Duchess" first appeared. In Poe's story, the narrator is spellbound by the "absolute *life-likeness* of expression" he finds in the portrait of a young girl who turns out to have been the painter's wife. But he also learns that to create this lifelike expression in paint, the painter drained the very life it represents, letting the ghastly light of his studio wither the health and gleeful spirit of his beautiful bride, drawing "the tints which he spread upon the canvas . . . from the cheeks of her who sate beside him" as he worked (Poe 483). When he at last achieves "*Life* itself" on the canvas, he finds that his wife is dead (Poe 482–84).

Unlike the husband of Poe's story, Browning's Duke is not a painter. But the Duke clearly sees in the "earnest glance" captured by the painter the hint of an adulterous desire for the painter himself, and his suspicions could only be strengthened by what he repeatedly calls a "spot of joy" (14–15, 21) in the cheek of the painted Duchess: a spot called up, the Duke suggests, by some chance remark of the painter. To the Duke's suspicious eye, the spot of joy is a stain of guilt. Yet it is also essential to the verisimilitude of the painting, to the lifelikeness which is repeatedly said to stand for—and thus displace or even preempt—the life itself. Like the story of the portrait in Poe's tale, the Duke's account of the painting begins and ends with a wondering tribute to its verisimilitude: "Looking as if she were alive" is echoed by his final words on the portrait, "There she stands / As if alive" (46–47). The sinister meaning subtly implied by the first statement has become all too plain by the time we hear its echo, which immediately follows the Duke's report on what he did about the Duchess's indiscriminately bestowed smiles: "I gave commands; / Then all smiles stopped together" (45–46).

One of her smiles, of course, survives in the portrait itself, which preserves the joyous appearance of the Duchess's face while ensuring that it can henceforth be seen only under the Duke's supervision. Like the sea horse tamed by Neptune in the bronze sculpture wrought for the Duke by Claus of Innsbruck, the very last thing he commends to his auditor's notice, the Duchess's uncontrollable delight in everyone and everything she sees has been tamed by art, metastasized by paint. She has been made to take her place among the *objets d'art* of a connoisseur's exquisite collection.[9] Yet he does not and cannot describe her painted image with a connoisseur's detachment, or with a purely aesthetic admiration for its beauty. The instability of his language, beginning with the ambiguous syntax of his opening sentence, shows only too clearly that he has not destroyed the power of her glance. Far more subtly and powerfully than Shelley's "Medusa," this poem exemplifies the Medusa theory of ekphrasis. In spite of himself, the Duke's monologue shows that the painted image of his former wife leaves him powerless to explain her glance, or even to gaze at it for more than a few seconds at a time.

I wrote "gaze" by design, for in this most dramatically paragonal of all ekphrastic poems, the Duke's rhetorical struggle with the Duchess's painted face can be usefully defined in terms of Norman Bryson's distinction between the glance and the gaze. The gaze is timeless, magisterially synoptic, and rational; the glance is time-bound, fragmentary, and restless.[10] While Bryson uses both terms to designate ways of looking *at* a painting, they inevitably refer to qualities *in* a painting, most importantly to the contrast between its geometric structure, which can be synoptically absorbed in a timeless gaze, and the texture of its details (like a spot on a cheek), which must be picked up individually— glanced at—as the viewer's eye travels through time across the field of the painting. The glance, Byrson argues, relentlessly subverts the magisterial authority of the gaze:

> The flickering, ungovernable mobility of the Glance strikes at the very roots of rationalism, for what it can never apprehend is the geometric order which is rationalism's true ensign. . . . Before the geometric order of pictorial composition, the Glance finds itself marginalised and declared legally absent, for this celebration of a faculty of mind to step outside the flux of sensations and to call into being a realm of transcendent forms . . . is beyond the scope of its comprehension: all it knows is dispersal—the disjointed rhythm of the retinal field; yet it is rhythm which painting of the Gaze seeks to bracket out. Against the Gaze, the Glance proposes desire, proposes the body, in the *durée* of its practical activity: in the freezing of syntagmatic motion, desire, and the body, the desire of the body, are exactly the terms which the tradition seeks to suppress. (*Vision* 121–22)

"Glance" is Bryson's metonymy for whatever in a painting provokes the *viewer* to glance, to catch at a sidelong angle its sensory textures, to see what the magisterial gaze overlooks and suppresses. But in the portrait of the Duchess, the glance literally emanates from a painted face. What Bryson says of the contest between glance and gaze within the viewer (or of the difference between paintings that gratify the gaze and those that excite a glance) applies with very little adjustment to the contest between the painted glance of the Duchess and the Duke's habit of gazing at works of art. The Duke keeps the portrait curtained because, as I have already noted, he finds looking at it profoundly disturbing. He no sooner invites his guest to sit and look at it than he expects the guest to turn away and ask about the origin of its profoundly passionate glance. Does this tell us that the Duke can read the mind of his guest, as he himself would clearly like to believe, or that he is simply projecting onto the guest his own anxiety about the painted glance: his own instinct to turn from it, his own incapacity to make rational order from the lability of its "faint / Half-flush" (18–19), or from what Bryson would call its "flickering, ungovernable mobility"? Either way, the painted glance "proposes desire, proposes the body" and raises a question he can never satisfactorily answer in words.

The deepest irony of the poem is that for all its silence, the painted face speaks far more eloquently than the Duke does. Like Philomela, the Duchess has been denied the use of her tongue, and her portrait is nowhere prosopopeially granted a voice; just once we are told that the living Duchess "thanked men," and even that may have been with a blush rather than words (31). Thus the Duke's monologue displaces the story she might have told about herself. Yet in presuming to speak for her, to tell the story of why she was silenced, the Duke is compelled to acknowledge the indefinable, inarticulable expressiveness of her painted glance. As Tucker suggests, the Duke's question about the origin of the glance—more precisely, the Duke's supposition that anyone who looked at the painting would want to ask *him* "how such a glance came there"—sounds at first art-historical: how did the painter learn to represent such a glance? But the question points beyond the origins of artistic technique to the genesis of passion itself (Tucker 178–79). It points to the unpredictable spontaneity of joy, to the indeterminacy of what can neither be put into words nor comprehended by the orderly and ordering gaze but can only be expressed by and caught with a glance. Though the Duke owns the painting and rigorously controls its exhibition, its painted glance expresses all he can never possess or regulate: the Duchess's irrepressible readiness to be delighted by "anybody's gift" (34).

The real object of the Duke's ekphrastic monologue emerges only at the end of the poem, where we learn that his auditor is an emissary from the family of the woman he plans to marry next. Like the museum director cultivating a potential benefactor, he plainly wants the auditor to see that he is a man of consummate good taste and venerable lineage, possessor of beautiful objects and "a nine-hundred-years-old name" (33). Just as clearly, he wants the auditor to know what sort of fealty he expects from his future wife, and what penalty she will pay if he fails to get it. But the painted glance subverts the lesson that Duke tries to draw from it. In spite of his command to stop all of the Duchess's smiles, the portrait preserves her glance of inscrutable joy, her challenge to his possessive authority, her refusal to accept his demand that she smile only for him. Even after her death, her image stubbornly declines to obey his word.

II

THE MUSEUM IN AUDEN'S "MUSÉE"

To turn from "My Last Duchess" to Auden's "Musée des Beaux Arts" (*CP* 146–47), written—in late 1938—nearly a hundred years after Browning's poem, is to move from the private museum of a Renaissance Duke to the kind of public museum in which great works of art are now commonly displayed. It is also to move from notional ekphrasis to actual ekphrasis, from an imaginary painting wrought wholly of words to the verbal representation of a painting that can be positively identified and independently seen.[11] Taking full critical advantage of this independent availability, I will shortly examine Auden's poem in light of the painting. For the moment, however, I wish to consider what the public museum of Auden's poem shares with the private, imaginary museum of Browning's duke. Just as Fra Pandolf's portrait of the duchess in Browning's poem is juxtaposed with the bronze by Claus of Innsbruck, a work of art displayed in a public museum is almost always juxtaposed with other works. Consequently, Auden acknowledges the institutional *site* of his encounter with a painting not only in his title but also in his opening reference to the Old Masters, whose works can be directly known only in museums, and in his brief allusions to paintings that swam into his ken as he made his way to or from the one that struck him most. In fact it is these other paintings that first illustrate his generalization about the wisdom of the old masters:

> About suffering they were never wrong,
> The Old Masters: how well they understood
> Its human position; how it takes place
> While someone else is eating or opening a window or just
>   walking dully along;
> How, when the aged are reverently, passionately waiting
> For the miraculous birth, there always must be
> Children who did not specially want it to happen, skating
> On a pond at the edge of the wood:
> They never forgot
> That even the dreadful martyrdom must run its course
> Anyhow in a corner, some untidy spot
> Where the dogs go on with their doggy life and the torturer's horse
> Scratches its innocent behind on a tree.

Curiously enough, this passage on the other paintings is slightly longer than the one devoted to the only painting Auden names—Breughel's *Icarus,* as he calls it (for reasons I will discuss below). The other paintings, to which Auden merely alludes, have been identified by Long and Cage (287) as two other Breughels: *The Census at Bethlehem* (1566) at the Brussels Musée and *The Slaughter of the Innocents* (ca. 1564) at Vienna's Kunsthistorische Museum. Neither one of them exactly fits Auden's description. In *The Census,* which represents Bethlehem as a snow-covered Flemish village, children are shown skating (among other things) on the ice around a cluster of trees at right, but the crowd of mostly older people massed around the building at left have gathered to be counted and taxed, not to wait passionately and reverently for the miraculous birth, and they appear to be suffering—if at all—no more than taxpayers usually do at the approach of April 15. There is real anguish in *The Slaughter*, where mothers are shown weeping for their slain or doomed infants while dogs indifferently leap about in the snow, but I cannot quite detect any torturer's horse scratching its ass on a tree in this picture, and strictly speaking, the slaughter of those who cannot deliberately choose to accept death cannot be called a "martyrdom."

Since Auden does not mention either *The Census* or *The Slaughter* by name, it may be captious to complain that he has reconstructed them, or that he has tacitly moved *The Slaughter* from Vienna to Brussels to join the other Breughels there in an imaginary exhibition hung for him alone. But what he does with Breughel's paintings as well as with their location should prompt us to wonder—more than critics usually do—about what he says of the Old Masters. If they were "never wrong" about the juxtaposition of suffering with signs of indifference to it, what would Auden say of Breughel's *Parable of the Blind* (figure 10), which he could certainly have seen in Naples and which depicts a row of blind men tumbling miserably into a ditch while not a single animate creature—neither man nor beast—is shown anywhere else in the picture, let alone shown displaying indifference to their plight? Viewed in light of the museum where this poem is nominally set, and more specifically of the paintings to which it alludes, Auden's grand generalization about the Old Masters is at best idiosyncratic.[12] We should read it not as a universal truth—which it certainly is not—but as a clue to the state of mind that Auden's *speaker* brings to the viewing of Breughel's *Landsape with the Fall of Icarus* (figure 3).

To grasp this state of mind, we must understand what is signified by the museum constructed in the poem—the museum surrounding the speaker. According to Michael Riffaterre, the "musée" of the title prefigures the aesthetic detachment epitomized by the "expensive delicate ship that must have seen / Something amazing, a boy falling out of the sky." Riffaterre writes:

> What "expensive," "delicate," "museum," and "beaux arts" have in common . . . is that from the viewpoint of representation they are all askew, irrelevant on the plane of factual, discrete bits of information, and that is what now makes them relevant on the higher plane of united, unified textuality. For as a paradigm, they all refer to a detached aesthetic distance, to a preference for form, to an ideal of beauty, that presupposes elitism and the trappings of social privilege, collecting fine arts, taste, and money lavished on artifacts. They all function as variants of *academic*. (8)

Given the sort of funds that most academics have to lavish on artifacts, I should rather say that all these aesthetic elements in the poem function as variants of *connoisseurship,* or curatorship. But the state of aesthetic detachment—even numbness—induced by the sheer multiplicity of pictures in a museum might indeed help to explain the startling juxtaposition of desperation and indifference that the poem finds in the painting. Here, we are told,

> everything turns away
> Quite leisurely from the disaster; the ploughman may
> Have heard the splash, the forsaken cry,
> But for him it was not an important failure; the sun shone
> As it had to on the white legs disappearing into the green
> Water; and the expensive delicate ship that must have seen
> Something amazing, a boy falling out of the sky,
> Had somewhere to get to and sailed calmly on.

The point of view implicitly imputed to the painting as a whole might be that of the sun, mirror of the viewer's eye: the sun resting on the horizon at the vanishing point and gazing dispassionately—like an appreciative connoisseur—at the vivid flash of white legs against green water. Moreover, as Riffaterre observes, the ship is "the most exemplary passerby in the indifference sequence" (8), for in abandoning the drowning man to his fate, it breaks one of the most fundamental laws of the sea. But how far does the indifference to Icarus's plight extend? If the splash and forsaken cry that the ploughman may have heard did not signify "an important failure" for him, is this also the attitude implied by the painting as a whole, or by the poem? Mary Ann Caws answers both questions with a yes. The poem, she writes, subordinates the disaster to "the aesthetic stress of the picture: ship and sea in their splendor, dwarfing the human fate" ("Double Reading" 328). Riffaterre demurs, arguing that the poem assumes a moral authority which preempts the aesthetic standards of the painting. "Auden's words," he says, "focus on the disaster by stressing that [the painting] pretends to ignore it" (12–13). More precisely, we could say that the poem leads us to see how the painting pretends to *subordinate* the disaster to other sights, or actually does subordinate it by making it far less conspicuous than the ship and the ploughman. But above all, Auden's poem makes us see how the moral meaning of the painting—the meaning it is said to illustrate—is largely constructed by the words of the title with which the museum has labeled it.

Consider for a moment what we could make of this painting without its title. Even if its three standing figures should remind us of book 8 of *The Metamorphoses,* where the flight of Daedalus and his son is said to have been witnessed with stupefaction by "some fisherman, . . . or a shepherd, leaning upon his crook, or a ploughman, on his plow-handles" (217–19), could we recognize the splashing legs as those of Icarus? Could we do so without any sign of Daedalus in the picture to guide us, with a setting sun scarcely high enough to melt the wax of high-flying wings, and with a flagrantly non-Ovidian ship to lead us off the scent? Would we even know that the splashing legs belong to a

3. Pieter Breughel. *Landscape with the Fall of Icarus.* Ca. 1558. Musées Royaux des Beaux-Arts, Brussels.

drowning man and not to a swimmer happily disporting while the ploughman toils? And would we sympathize more readily with the swimmer than with the laboring man of the soil?[13]

The honest answer to all of these questions is no. Neither we nor Auden himself could see a drowning Icarus in this painting without the words of its title, *Landscape with the Fall of Icarus,* which in the poem becomes simply "Breughel's *Icarus.*" Auden's compression of the long title sharpens the point of what the curator's label leads us to see in the painting: a meaning borrowed from another Breughel painting which hangs in Brussels's Van Buuren Museum and which is almost identical to the Beaux Arts *Icarus* except—a crucial except—for the presence of a winged man flying through the sky at the very top (figure 4). In the Beaux Arts picture, this unmistakable sign of Daedalus—the sign that would lead us to identify the splashing legs as those of his fallen son— is missing. Its place is taken by the key word in the title, the only word Auden cites.[14]

The Van Buuren Museum version makes it clear that the shepherd leaning on his crook and looking skywards in both pictures is not just heartlessly turning away from the drowning man but looking up at the winged Daedalus: precisely what Ovid says all three men were doing as he flew overhead. Auden alludes to Daedalus, perhaps unwittingly, when he says that the ship "must have seen / Something amazing." What it saw, of course, was not just the falling boy but the flying father who wrought the Cretan *maze* in which both were imprisoned until Daedalus fashioned the wings that let them escape.[15] But the poem itself turns away from the suddenly bereaved Daedalus, who must surely be suffering just as much as his son is, and likewise from the mysterious corpse lying in the shadowy woods at left.[16] The sole beneficiary of the poem's sympathy is Icarus.

The exclusiveness of this sympathy is strange enough in light of what the picture shows us of him: a comically upended pair of legs. It is stranger still in light of the paintings allusively described in the first half of the poem, especially *The Slaughter of the Innocents,* where the juxtaposition of visibly anguished mothers with frisking dogs and stolid horses leading their horsy lives illustrates far more vividly than *Icarus* the originating premise of the poem. Even with its title, nothing in the painting itself compels us to think about the suffering of Icarus, and there is good reason to believe that Breughel painted his vainly kicking legs simply to signify his folly. In a 1553 etching made by George Hoefnagel after Breughel (figure 5), an upended Icarus kicks his way down from the clouds into a winding river dotted with sailboats, and the legend reads: "INTER UTRUMQUE VOLA, MEDIO TUTISSIMUS IBIS" [fly between the extremes, in the middle is the safest way].[17]

Spurning or turning away from this simply prescriptive moral, the poem gives Breughel's *Icarus* a quite different meaning. Focusing on the figure designated by the key word in its title, the poem works from suggestions made by other Breughel pictures that Auden linked to this one, even though he saw them in different museums. Each of those other pictures portrays a momentous event in the life of a family. In the figure of a heavily cloaked woman riding a mule across the center foreground, *The Census at Bethlehem* signifies the imminence of Christ's nativity, and *The Slaughter of Innocents,* as already noted, openly depicts the killing of infants before the eyes of their mothers. In addition, both paintings include figures indifferent to the momentous event, and both require knowledge of a text in order to be fully understood. We must know the New Testament to recognize the mule-riding woman as the Virgin Mary and to know why the infants were slaughtered.

As exemplified by these pictures, then, three things characterize the suffering portrayed by the Old Masters: it is juxtaposed with signs of indifference, its meaning depends on the viewer's knowledge of a text, and it is emphatically *familial.* We can now see how Auden would be led to make the neglected suffering of Icarus the moral center of Breughel's picture. Like the paintings of scriptural events, *Landscape with a Fall of Icarus*—the only painting Breughel did of a mythological subject (Stechow 50)—depends on a text. Furthermore, the Ovidian text on which it depends makes this subject poignantly familial: the son calling the father's name up to the very moment when the sea catches his lips ("oraque caerulea patrium clamantia nomen / excipiuntur aqua"), the "pater infelix" calling in vain on the son until he sees the wings floating on the waves (*Met.* 8.229–33). Isolated from the father's anguish, the suffering of

4. Pieter Breughel. *The Fall of Icarus.* David and Alice Van Buuren Museum, Brussels.

the son becomes in Auden's poem the sole center of feeling in a seascape of cool indifference, and though it was Icarus who recklessly flew up and away from his father, his own "forsaken cry" here—the sole note of prosopopeia in the entire poem—calls to mind what another dying son famously cried to his father: "My God, my God, why have you forsaken me?" (Mark 15:34).

Viewing Breughel through the words of Ovid and turning them into an echo of the last words of Christ, Auden's speaker turns the painting itself into a verbal narrative of suffering wilfully ignored. The assertive power of the word over the image in this narrative becomes all too clear as inferential subjunctives— mere conjectures about the story told by the picture—turn into unequivocal indicatives: the ploughman *may* have heard the splash and the cry, but for him it *was* unimportant; the ship *must have seen* an amazing sight but *sailed* calmly on. Consider the question begged by this final would-be statement of fact. Since the ship is something Breughel added to Ovid's story of Icarus, we have no textual guidance on its movements; how then do we know it *will* ignore a splash just now occurring, that it will not even try to come about and rescue the boy? Its Falstaffian sails (oddly incongruent with its level hull, the calm sea, and the droop of the horse's tail and ploughman's tunic) tell us only that the wind at sail level is strong. Even if the ship did sail on, it could not have sailed calmly.

Auden's "Musée des Beaux Arts" is anything but a "straightforward reading of an art work," as one critic recently called it (Suzanne Ferguson 31). It is the verbal reconstruction of a painting whose meaning is initially determined—for

5. Georg Hoefnagel. *River Landscape with the Fall of Icarus.* 1553. Etching after Pieter Breughel. Bibliothèque Royale Albert Iᵉʳ, Cabinet des Estampes, Brussels.

all who see it in the Brussels museum—by the words of the title affixed to it there. Viewing Breughel's picture in light of these words, in light of Ovid's words, in light reflected from Breughel's paintings of biblical subjects, and in light of the texts that stand behind those paintings, Auden remakes the picture in words as a museum-class specimen of how the Old Masters could represent suffering, as a story of private anguish publically ignored. If Browning's "My Last Duchess" points the way to the modern museum of art, Auden's "Musée" takes us into it.

III

THE BREUGHEL MUSEUM OF WILLIAM CARLOS WILLIAMS

William Carlos Williams wrote a dozen poems about pictures by Breughel: "The Dance" in 1942, the long passage (which may count as a poem) on *Adoration of the Magi* in part 3 of *Paterson* V (1958), and a group of ten poems that first appeared in the *Hudson Review* (Spring 1960) and then in a volume titled *Pictures from Breughel* (1962). These poems do not conspicuously evoke the world of the museum or deploy the language of connoisseurship. There is noth-

6. Pieter Breughel. *The Peasant Dance* (*The Kermesse*). Ca. 1558. Kunsthistorisches
Museum, Vienna.

ing in them quite like Auden's knowing reference to the wisdom of the Old
Masters, with its suggestion of long and meditative hours periodically spent in
major galleries. Yet the Breughel poems evoke the world of the museum every
time they mention Breughel's name. Apart from the artist's signature, which
may be missing or difficult to read, it is typically the authority of the museum
that establishes and certifies the authorship of a painting. When Williams
writes of "Breughel's great picture, The Kermess" in the first and last lines of
"The Dance," his first Breughel poem, he salutes an authorship that is at once
artistic and museological, an authorship proclaimed by the museum that
houses the painting and reinforced by all the art historical commentary on
Breughel's mastery. The very title of Williams's ekphrastic volume—*Pictures
from Breughel*—affirms the primacy of the artist and his authorship, and tributes to Breughel's mastery of pictorial organization permeate the poems themselves, where the *Adoration of the Magi,* for instance, is said to reflect "the
resourceful mind / that governed the whole" and the figures in *The Wedding
Dance* come through as "Disciplined by the artist / to go round / & round."[18]

    The homage to Breughel's organizational power is in part self-referential.
The words on Breughel's *Wedding Dance* also describe "The Dance," where—
as Sayre notes—Williams creates "a circular poetic structure to rival the structure of both dance and painting" (138). In this earlier poem on *The Peasant
Dance / Kermesse* (figure 6), Williams shapes and disciplines the words them-

selves to go round, using repetition and internal rhyme to re-create in language the effect of repeated circling: "the dancers go round, they go round and / around" in "rollicking measures" mimicked by Williams's own rollicking dactyls; their bellies are "round as the thick- / sided glasses whose wash they impound"; they "prance as they dance / in Breughel's great picture" and in Williams's poem, whose last line (as just noted) echoes and thus rounds back to its first one.

Yet Williams's poem is anything but an iconic sign of Breughel's painting. It is a work of language remaking visual art. Besides adding "a bugle and fiddles" which are nonexistent in the painting, it also speaks of round bellies that have evidently been transplanted from *The Wedding Dance,* since the only clearly visible waist in *The Peasant Dance / Kermesse* is that of the rather trim woman at right.[19] Williams had his own way of driving words around. When he returned to Breughel in *Pictures,* he did not revive the blank verse dactyls of "The Dance," not even to represent another painting of circling dancers. Instead he devised what is sometimes called—with unwitting irony—"the Breughel stanza" (which is a little like calling the style of Tom Stoppard's *Rosencrantz and Guildenstern Are Dead* Shakespearean). With its three short free verse lines of variable feet, the "Breughel" tercet bears a wholly arbitrary relation to the structure of Breughel's paintings. "In fact," as Sayre notes, "the blocklike shape of the tercets seems dramatically opposed to the 'roundness' of the poem's subject matter" (138). What the poems share with the paintings they represent is not a particular shape but simply evidence of shap*ing,* signs of an organizing hand. When the final stanza of "Hunters in the Snow" says that Breughel has chosen a winter-struck bush "for his foreground to / complete the picture" of returning hunters, we are not asked to see the bush as in any sense the "end" of the picture; we are invited rather to see the principle of organization that links poetic closure with pictorial enclosure. Beyond all its ostensible subjects, in fact, beyond "the basic rhythms of man's life" (Conarroe, "Measured Dance" 569) and the seasonal cycle suggested by poems about pictures of winter hunting, summer haymaking, autumn harvesting, and the springtime fall of Icarus, *Pictures from Breughel* thematizes the shaping of a work of art.[20]

The thematizing of artistic organization goes hand in hand with Williams's museological—and distinctively modern—focus on the artist. But in focusing on the artist, the Breughel poems also show us how modern ekphrasis revives its ancient ancestor. In *The Iliad,* the shield of Achilles is represented as the handiwork of Hephaestus, whose act of making ("he made the earth upon it") is repeatedly affirmed; in the *Aeneid,* Daedalus gets full credit for the bas-reliefs in the Cumaean temple of Apollo, and Vulcan for the shield of Aeneas. After Virgil, ekphrasis largely excludes the names of makers. The masterpieces so conspicuously wrought by mythical artisans give way to anonymous works of art.[21] We learn nothing, for instance, of who created the paintings described in *Daphnis and Chloe* or *Leucippe and Clitiphon* or Chaucer's *Knight's Tale* or Shakespeare's *Rape of Lucrece.* Not until the seventeenth century do the names of artists begin to reappear in ekphrastic poetry, and not until the twentieth century does ekphrastic poetry represent a work of art in such a way as to foreground an authorship reliably established by curatorial authority.[22]

With Auden and still more with Williams, who—as Sayre says—"consistently turns his description of the work to a consideration of the work's making" (135), we return to what might be called the ekphrasis of artistic creation— with a difference. The artists saluted in twentieth-century ekphrasis are historic rather than legendary or mythical figures, and their work is represented as in part a representation *of the artist himself:* of his insight into suffering, of "the living quality of / the man's mind" with "its covert assertions / for art, art, art!" and even of the artist's own face.[23] It does not matter that the painting represented in "Self-Portrait," the first of the *Pictures from Breughel,* depicts an old shepherd rather than Breughel himself; Williams firmly believed that *all* painting is self-portraiture.[24] From this point of view, Ashbery's "Self-Portrait" is—as we will shortly see—the supreme example of what happens to ekphrasis in the twentieth century.

But just as Ashbery's treatment of Parmigianino's self-portrait will differ radically from Williams's account of Breughel's self-revealing landscapes, Williams's response to Breughel's art differs sharply from Auden's. While Auden sounds like a man long familiar with museums and the masterworks they exhibit, Williams often sounds like an amateur seeing a picture for the first time. Consider for instance what he does with Breughel's *Icarus* in the second poem of the series, "Landscape with the Fall of Icarus":

> According to Breughel
> when Icarus fell
> it was spring
>
> a farmer was ploughing
> his field
> the whole pageantry
>
> of the year was
> awake tingling
> near
>
> the edge of the sea
> concerned
> with itself
>
> sweating in the sun
> that melted
> the wing's wax
>
> unsignificantly
> off the coast
> there was

7. Pieter Breughel. *The Harvesters.* 1565. Metropolitan Museum of Art, New York, Rogers Fund, 1919 (19.164). All rights reserved, The Metropolitan Museum of Art.

> a splash quite unnoticed
> this was
> Icarus drowning[25]

Citing Breughel as if he were a storyteller, the poem recapitulates his version of the ancient myth: Icarus fell in the spring when a farmer was ploughing a field near the seacoast and sweating in the sun that melted the wax of the boy's wings, and he drowned in an inconspicuous splash. Williams's version of Breughel's version of the myth includes a place and a time but no specifically pictorial detail, nothing like the flash of white-on-green that Auden's poem delivers in its final lines.

In fact Williams has been faulted for slighting most of the details in the pictures that his poems purport to represent. "The Corn Harvest," for instance, written about the painting now generally known as *The Harvesters* (figure 7), concentrates on the ellipse of figures resting around the base of the tree at lower right and therefore ignores—according to one meticulously calibrated estimate— about 92 percent of the picture (Lawson-Peebles 18). Besides such large-scale sins of omission, Williams's poems about Breughel's pictures also include sins of commission. In "The Dance" (1942), as we have seen, Williams adds "a bugle and fiddles" to *The Peasant Dance / Kermesse,* and in "The Hunters in the Snow," on the painting of the same name (figure 11), he turns the haloed figure on the inn-sign into a crucifix. Finally, Williams has been faulted for distorting the Breughel canon in "Self-Portrait," the first of the *Pictures from Breughel.* The picture represented in this poem is not a painting of Breughel and, though once attributed to him, has been generally considered the work of another since the middle 1920s.[26]

But ekphrastic poetry is not art history, even though modern ekphrasis—as we have seen—approaches the border between the two, and postmodern ekphrasis—as we will shortly see—crosses it. Ekphrasis never aims simply to reproduce a work of visual art in words, so there is no point in judging ekphrastic poetry by a criterion of fidelity to the work it represents. We can much better judge it by asking what it enables us to see in the work of art, or even just to see, period.[27] By this criterion, Williams often does surprisingly well. The critic who faults "The Corn Harvest" for ignoring 92 percent of the picture identifies many of the details that Williams misses (Lawson-Peebles 18), but the poet's concentration on the ellipse of resting figures allows him to see certain things the critic overlooks, such as the fact that the sleeping reaper "carelessly / . . . does not share" the shade of the tree with the gossiping women. Ironically, the sleeping reaper thus becomes in Williams's poem the hub around which all the busy harvesters visually turn. He is

> the resting
> center of
> their workaday world

Williams chooses what he wants us to see in Breughel's picture, but he also takes and adapts interpretive points from the commentaries of Gustave Gluck in *Peter Breughel the Elder* and Thomas Craven in *Treasury of Art Masterpieces,* both of which books he consulted while writing his poems (*CP* 2:504). He certainly drew on them for "The Adoration of the Kings," where he describes Breughel's *Adoration* (figure 8) as

> a scene copied we'll say
>
> from the Italian masters
> but with a difference
> the mastery
>
> of the painting
> and the mind the resourceful mind
> that governed the whole
>
> the alert mind dissatisfied with
> what it is asked to
> and cannot do

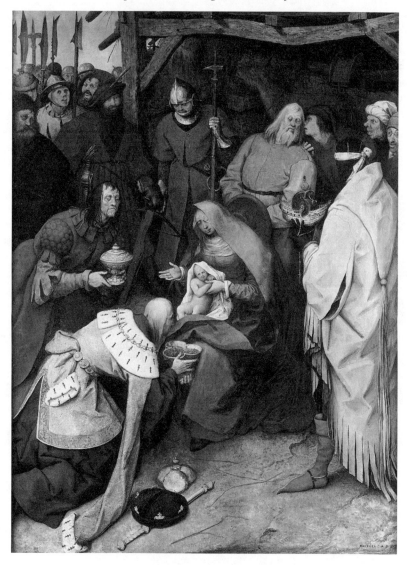

8. Pieter Breughel. *Adoration of the Magi.* 1564. National Gallery, London.

accepted the story and painted
it in the brilliant
colors of the chronicler

At least three texts stand behind this poem. Besides Matthew 2:1–12, the scriptural source of the painting itself, Williams here conflates what he learned

from Gluck and Craven about Breughel's transformation of the Italian mannerism that his Flemish contemporaries thoughtlessly adopted and that his own
"un-Italian" painting reflects with a radical difference.[28] From Craven also
Williams picked up hints about Breughel's capacity to organize his compositions and make their colors glow.[29] Yet the only text that Williams explicitly
cites as a source or precursor for this poem is his own previous treatment of *The
Adoration* in part 3 of *Paterson,* book 5, written two years before the Breughel
poems first appeared.

The Breughel passage in *Paterson* begins by saluting the painting of a baby
"new born! / among the words" (226). The arresting phrase evokes not only
the mystery of Christ as the word incarnate but also all of the scriptural words
and iconographic traditions—part verbal, part iconic—on which Breughel
draws, as well as the considerable body of art historical commentary on his
painting.[30] Yet the words the poet sees surrounding the image of the baby are
simply those he prosopopeially elicits from the soldiers in the painting, words
spoken by the "whispering men with averted faces / . . . / as they talked to
the potbellied / greybeard" who turns out to be Joseph (226). Williams's own
words secularize the painting. He does something like what he earlier did in
"The Dance," which overlooks all iconographic signs of a collision between the
sacred and the profane in Breughel's *Kermesse* to focus simply on the rollicking
gyration of dancers going "round and / around."[31] In the *Paterson* passage
Williams can hardly ignore the scriptural source for what he explicitly calls the
painting of "a Nativity": of a scene "authentic / enough, to be witnessed frequently / among the poor" and actually witnessed here by kings who "had eyes
for visions / in those days—and saw, / saw with their proper eyes" (*Paterson*
226–27). But the secularism of the poet's own vision is evident in what he says
about the Christ child's purely human parentage—"born to an old man / out
of a girl and a pretty girl / at that"—and about the gifts that Breughel shows in
the kings' hands:

> (works of art,
> where could they have picked
> them up or more properly
> have stolen them?)[32]

The very aura of Breughel's painting as a work of art draws special attention
to the works of art depicted in it. But in our age, the age of the museum, works
of art have become commodities bought, traded, stolen, or acquired under conditions not always wholly distinguishable from robbery or fraud. The questionable dealing that brought the Elgin marbles to the British Museum has since
been reenacted many times in the annals of acquisition. And if the work of art
has become a commodity, it can never be wholly detached from the reproductions through which we so often experience it. Hence, even while celebrating
the authenticity of Breughel's work, Williams parenthetically evokes Gluck's
reproduction of it:

                    —but the Baby (as from an
                    illustrated catalogue
                    in colors) lies naked on his Mother's
                    knees
                                      (*Paterson* 226)

Williams's Breughel, then, is not the painter of sacred texts or iconograph-
ically readable meanings—of verbal messages conveyed in visual form. What
does Williams mean when he says that Breughel simply "painted / what he
saw" (*Paterson* 226)? Seductive in its simplicity, this formulation recalls—from
eighteenth-century England—the Earl of Shaftesbury's impatience with the
enigmas of visual emblem and iconic allegory, with anything "*fantastick, miraculous,* or *hyperbolical*" that might distort "the compleatly imitative and illusive
Art of PAINTING."[33] For Williams, however, painting was not illusion but
representation. Declaring that "even the most abstract, the most subjective, the
most distorted art" was representational, he wrote: "The only question that can
present itself is: What do you choose to represent?"[34] Here all questions about
verisimilitude seem usurped by a single question about signification. If the
painter can represent anything at all by any means, the Gombrichian notion of
art as an illusionistic record of perception—the record of what the painter
saw—gives way to the Brysonian concept of art as a site of sign-production.[35]
But Williams never goes this far in the Breughel poems. On the contrary, he
represents Breughel's paintings as representation*al* in the ordinary mimetic
sense of the term.

At the same time, Williams's poems on these paintings inevitably reflect the
ways in which he experiences them: through reproductions that transmit them
to his eye or revive them in his memory, through commentaries that purport to
explain them. "The basic note" of the *Adoration,* says a Max Dvorak quoted by
Gluck, "is a clumsy, stupidly rigid astonishment" (Gluck 42). In the *Paterson*
passage Williams describes the soldiers in the painting as "savagely armed men"
who are

                              showing their
                    amazement at the scene,
                    features like the more stupid
                    German soldiers of the late
                    war

At first glance, Williams seems to have twisted Dvorak's comment into a
gratuitously jingoistic slur against the losers of World War II. But later in the
passage on the *Adoration,* this growl of insult modulates into a curious note of
sympathy. The soldiers in the painting, Williams writes, are depicted not only
as stupid savages but also as long-suffering veterans:

                    —the soldiers' ragged clothes,
                    mouths open,

> their knees and feet
> broken from 30 years of
> war, hard campaigns, their mouths
> watering for the feast which
> had been provided
>
> (*Paterson* 228)

The soldiers of these lines bear curiously little resemblance to those in the painting, whose clothes are tidy enough to be new, whose knees and feet are scarcely visible (whatever their condition), and whose mouths are watering—if at all—for a feast that is nowhere in sight.[36] Williams evidently aimed to construct in words a painting that would exemplify the "two sides" of Breughel's vision: his unflinching perception of brutishness and his sympathy for what even brutes feel.

Pictures from Breughel repeatedly shows not just how Williams verbally transforms the works of Breughel but also how he reconstructs the words of art historians. Apropos *The Wedding Banquet* (figure 9), he evidently learned from Gluck (quoting Dvorak again) that the bearded man in black at the end of the table is "perhaps" a landowner or judge or "mayor of the village" (Gluck 49). Williams calls him simply "the bearded Mayor" in "Peasant Wedding," where the pouring figure on the extreme left is likewise unequivocally identified as the "bridegroom" even though that is just one of several possibilities proposed by Gluck (49). Still more revealing is Williams's reworking of Gluck's remark that "The dishes are being brought in by two peasant youths on an unhinged stable door" (Gluck 49). In the poem this becomes:

> dishes are being served
> clabber and what not
> from a trestle made of an
>
> unhinged barn door by
> two helpers one in a red
> coat a spoon in his hatband

To compare Williams with Gluck here is first of all to see that Williams has noticed something the art historian has overlooked: the spoon in the hatband of the red-coated server.[37] But Williams amplifies Gluck's comment even more suggestively at the very point where he seems most indebted to it. While Gluck simply identifies what the servers are using to carry the dishes—"an unhinged stable door"—Williams highlights the metamorphosis of one object into another: the dishes rest on a trestle *made* of an unhinged door. Furthermore, because the participle *made* comes between the passive verb *are being served* and its agent, *by / two helpers,* the syntax suggests that the door was transformed—made into a trestle—by the same two men who are carrying it. Thus Williams's lines turn the painted object into a compressed narrative of its genesis, and at the same time situate it in a network of visual metonymy that makes every object human because it has been touched or turned by human hands, like the dishes *being* handed from the trestle to the table by the man in the red hat.

What is not human by metonymy becomes so by metaphor, as in the first two stanzas:

> Pour the wine bridegroom
> where before you the
> bride is enthroned her hair
>
> loose at her temples a head
> of ripe wheat is on
> the wall beside her the
>
> guests seated at long tables

The "head / of ripe wheat"—an unremarkable metaphor by itself—captures what the picture shows us: the visual rhyme between the loose, uncovered tresses of the bride and the crossed sheaves of wheat hung on the wall beside her like a long straight headdress. Here as later in the poem, Williams's nonstop syntax is relentlessly synaptic. At the ends of lines ("on / the wall") and even of stanzas ("an / / unhinged barn door") he breaks up phrases precisely to bring out the connective force of enjambment; within lines he suppresses breaks to accentuate continuity. Moving uninterruptedly from *temples* to *a head,* for instance, he prompts us to link the two, reading *a head / of ripe wheat* as an appositional metaphor for *her hair / loose at her temples.* That the *head* metaphor can also be applied to the wheat alone (wheat *as* head) exemplifies the fluidity of Williams's syntax, which aims to give the reader something like the freedom of movement offered to a viewer.[38] As a viewer's eye darts from the temples of the bride to the sheaves of wheat, or from the red coat of the server to the spoon in his hatband, so move the lines of the poem.

Yet for all its fluidity—its back-and-forth indeterminacy of reference—Williams's syntax is directive. It masters the endlessly diverting multiplicity of images in the painting by mapping an itinerary for the eye: a narrative of the viewing process itself. This kind of narrative differs as much from the art historian's analysis of geometrical form—the fixed, abstract object of the synoptic gaze—as it does from stories about the *action* represented by the painting, stories about what preceded and followed the moment depicted. We have already seen examples of each in the Breughel poems. "Icarus" tersely recapitulates the Icarus myth, and "The Corn Harvest" synoptically defines *The Harvesters* as "organized" about a young reaper who constitutes the "resting / center" of the workaday scene. But "Peasant Wedding" plots the journey of the eye, tracing a rough ellipse from the pouring figure at bottom left to the bagpipers at upper left, to the bearded Mayor at upper right, and finally to the serving men at lower right. There are two detours from this elliptical movement: (1) starting from the pourer, the eye of the poem darts to the bride and the head of wheat before tracking up the table of guests to the bagpipers; (2) from the Mayor, the eye

9. Pieter Breughel. *The Wedding Banquet.* Ca. 1558. Kunsthistorisches
Museum, Vienna.

returns to the bride and the gabbing women next to her before proceeding to
the servers. Thus the poem represents the painted bride as a figure who repeatedly draws and deflects the eye of the viewer but neither fixes nor determines its
movements, which follow a peripheral itinerary.

Two other poems show Williams in the act of reading aloud, so to speak, the
compositional structure of a Breughel painting. Both poems focus on spatial
patterns and thus accentuate the organizational mastery of the artist. But while
"The Parable of the Blind" turns Breughel's linear design into a compressed
narrative that makes the moral meaning of his composition explicit, "The
Hunters in the Snow" tells a suspended story of figures caught in wintry space.
Instead of following the course of their lives, the poet tracks the movement of
his own eye as it seeks to know a pattern that it verbalizes but will not gloss.

Like *The Adoration of the Kings,* Breughel's *Parable of the Blind* (figure 10) is
based on a scriptural text that largely determines—one might say overdeter-
mines—its meaning. When the disciples of Christ told him that the Pharisees
were shocked by his teachings, he said: "Leave them alone. They are blind
guides! But if one blind man leads another, they will both fall into the ditch!"
(Matthew 15:14). The passage is quoted by Gluck, who also notes that
Breughel represents six men "forming a diagonal across the picture surface"
with the first already fallen into the ditch (at lower right), the second about to
fall, and the others—linked to the first two by extended sticks and hands—

10. Pieter Breughel. *The Parable of the Blind.* 1568. Museo e Gallerie Nazionale di Capodimonte, Naples. Photo: Alinari/Art Resource, New York.

bound to share their fate (Gluck 48). Guided, no doubt, by Christ's use of blindness to signify Pharisaical teaching, Gluck reads the picture allegorically: "probably," he says, Breughel was thinking of wandering preachers who lead vast crowds into "blind delusion" (48).

Comparison of Williams's "Parable" with Gluck's commentary on Breughel's *Parable* shows that Williams follows Gluck only to the edge of allegory. Ignoring the meaning of the parable, refusing to read Breughel's figures as allegorical signs, the poem concentrates on the meaning of his composition, on the horribly ironic story told by a line

> of beggars leading
> each other diagonally downward
>
> across the canvas
> from one side
> to stumble finally into a bog
>
> where the picture
> and the composition ends back
> of which no seeing man
>
> is represented

The explicit reference to *composition*—a word used three times in the eight short tercets of the poem—once again prompts us to see the link between pictorial and poetic structure. As Breughel's diagonal of figures draws the viewer's eye down to the bog in the lower right corner of his painting, Williams's tercets significantly end with phrases denoting decline and fall: "diagonally down-ward" and "into a bog."[39] But Williams's verbal composition moves beyond the point where the pictorial composition "ends." Besides noting the presence of blind men, he registers the startling absence of any seeing man, of a viewer *in* the painting, or even—at the risk of being "wrong" by Auden's standards—of any sighted figure ignoring what the blind men suffer. The blind men are seen only by the viewer *of* the painting, which shows us inanimate structures stand-ing up while men and their sticks—their worse than useless props—rise only to collapse:

> a peasant
> cottage is seen and a church spire
>
> the faces are raised
> as toward the light
> there is no detail extraneous
>
> to the composition one
> follows the other stick in
> hand triumphant to disaster

The final tercet encapsulates the meaning of Breughel's composition. Reconstructed in words, the diagonal of figures stumbling downward with faces expectantly raised becomes a narrative of delusion, the short story of a tragic fall.

No such cautionary narrative emerges from Williams's verbal reconstruction of *The Hunters in the Snow* (figure 11). Wendy Steiner has explained at length how Williams's "The Hunters in the Snow" exploits the ambiguities of Breughel's picture: its division of stress between the foreground figures, who recall the medieval practice of using human activities to signify the season, and the disproportionately large snow-covered precipices in the background, which mark a shift to landscape painting as an independent genre and to a Renais-sance focus on natural signs of winter.[40] The ambiguity here is spatial as well as thematic. Though the spear-bearing hunters trudging down the snowy hill cu-riously anticipate the stick-bearing blind men of *Parable* (painted three years later), the poem makes no explicit reference to the hunters' descent, and scarcely any to the meaning of their movement:

> The over-all picture is winter
> icy mountains
> in the background the return
>
> from the hunt it is toward evening
> from the left
> sturdy hunters lead in
>
> their pack

11. Pieter Breughel. *Hunters in the Snow.* 1565. Kunsthistorisches Museum, Vienna.

Steiner aptly notes the ambiguity of the third line. While "in the back-ground" belongs syntactically to "icy mountains" and "the return" to "from the hunt," the string of phrases in the third line suggests that the hunters' return may be figuratively backgrounded by the prominence and thematic importance of the mountains in "the over-all picture" (*Colors* 80). "The return" also sug-gests the return of the viewer's eye from background to foreground, from mountains to figures. What the poem makes truly indeterminate, however, is the destination of the returning hunters.

The absence of any specified destination is one of several things that distin-guish Williams's poem from what John Berryman does with Breughel's *Hunters* in "Winter Landscape," written in 1938–39, some twenty years before "Hunters in the Snow." Berryman's poem plainly tells us that the hunters are returning "to their town" with all its light and companionship, and the final stanza accentuates the line of their movement as they "ankle-deep in snow down the winter hill / Descend." The prospect of homecoming suggested by these passages is undermined by the dark prospect of a devastating war in which "all their company / Will [be] . . . irrecoverably lost"; then "their configura-tion with the trees" will show "what place, what time, what morning occasion" sent them out with their "tall poles" to hunt and return, and thus heedlessly to signify a calamitous plunge into war.[41]

Nothing of this dark allegory informs Williams's "The Hunters in the

Snow." His poem represents the painted hunters moving at once through time and space—"it is toward evening" when they "lead in / their pack"—but the single preposition "in" is the only word that signifies where they are headed. "From the left" they move "in," presumably toward the center of the picture, but in doing so they pass "the inn-sign" and the huge bonfire flaring beneath it. What we begin to see in this curious configuration of words—this verbal composition wrought to represent and rival a painted one—is a determination to suspend meaning, to withhold signification, to suppress both destination and denotation. Paradoxically, the suspension of meaning is most evident at precisely the point where the poem seems to invoke a higher meaning, when we are told that

> the inn-sign
>
> hanging from a
> broken hinge is a stag a crucifix
>
> between his antlers

Since the inn-sign in the painting shows no crucifix, only a stag and a haloed praying figure, these lines often puzzle commentators on the poem. But they can be readily glossed by anyone who follows—as Williams obviously did—the hint furnished by Gluck. Gluck says that the inn sign, which reads "In den Hert" [Inn to the Stag] bears "the painted legend of St. Hubert or St. Eustace" (44). Both these men were hunters converted by seeing a crucifix between the antlers of a stag while hunting, and the vision of St. Eustace was the subject of a painting by Pisanello in which the crucifix is clearly shown.[42] The question, then, is why Williams drags this bit of iconographic lore into a poem that is otherwise innocent of it, why he who ignores virtually all signs of Christianity in Breughel's other paintings should tease an invisible crucifix out of this one.

A partial answer is that the reference to the crucifix illustrates once more how much these poems depend on the curatorial and art historical commentary that surrounds Breughel's paintings and thus informs Williams's experience of them. Typically Williams secularizes Breughel and celebrates him for representing life *tout court,* for paintings unburdened by period styles or iconographic messages: in "Haymaking" he salutes

> painting
>
> that the Renaissance
> tried to absorb
> but
>
> it remained a wheat field
> over which the
> wind played

Yet not even these lines simply express a naive admiration for recognizable form. They could be written only by someone who knew something, as

Williams clearly did, about the place of the Renaissance in the history of art, and who could also generalize about the *kind* of landscapes Breughel produced, since the poem is a verbal composite of two paintings.[43] Williams brings to these poems a knowledge of art history, however fragmentary, and his debts to specific commentaries—as we have seen—are plain enough to anyone who knows what he read.

But why does he advertise his debt in "The Hunters" by referring to a crucifix that cannot be seen in the painting? The answer, I believe, is that he wants his verbal reconstruction of the painting to include an *unregarded* sign of Christianity. As Christ hung on the cross, the sign hangs "from a / broken hinge"; more precisely it hangs askew from one good hinge because the other one is broken and no one has bothered to fix it. Though the sign signifies both the warm hospitality of the inn and the redemptive power of Christ, it draws the attention of no one: neither the women tending the fire right under it in "the cold / inn yard" nor the hunters, even though the kneeling figure painted on the sign is a patron saint of hunters.

Very well: does the neglected sign of Christ thereby signify that all these unregarding figures have forsaken his teachings? I think not. Whether or not the painting suggests this, which seems to me unlikely, the poem represents the sign of the crucifix-bearing stag as merely one of many patterns to be seen in the painting. If we want to look for patterns, we can that the bird in flight at upper right forms a cross on its side, and we can also see that the spear borne by the hunter nearest the fire crosses behind a tree at precisely the angle that would be made by the cross beam of the crucifix on the tilted inn-sign—if we could see that crucifix. If the painting as a whole hovers, as Steiner suggests, between medieval iconography and Renaissance naturalism, its patterns also hover between higher meaning and plain geometry: the sort of patterns we fail to see not because we are irredeemably blind or irreligious but simply because we pass them every day, and the eye readily passes from one to another.

In "The Hunters in the Snow" Williams constructs a verbal picture of Breughel's patterns that is also a narrative of the viewer's eye in motion. From the icy mountains in the right background the poem shifts diagonally back to the hunters at lower left, crossing the diagonal edge of the hill. Then (following the point of the tree-crossing spear) it moves to the inn sign at upper left, down to the women under the sign, and recrosses "to the right beyond / the hill" where we find "a pattern of skaters." Finally the poem returns to the foreground where, in the center, Breughel "has chosen / / a winter-struck bush . . . / . . . to / complete the picture . . . "

When printed on a single page (it straddles two pages in the *Collected Poems*), the poem can be viewed iconically, with the icy mountains of the top (first) stanza and the winter-struck bush of the bottom (last) one framing what comes between, just as they do in Breughel's painting. But the poem is less a verbal icon than a narrative of the viewing process, the story of how an eye educated by viewing itself as well as by art historical reading discovers—finds and reveals—compositional structure by traveling back and forth across a painting. Unlike Berryman, Williams does not press the patterns of the painting into meaning; he declines to make them speak. On the whole, in fact, though the early "Dance" resounds with prosopopeial music ("the squeal and the blare and the / tweedle of bagpipes") and though *Pictures from Breughel* evokes a few sounds (the gabbing of the women in "Peasant Wedding" and the gaping-mouthed "Oya!" in "The Wedding Dance"), the Breughel poems represent silent compositions not by envoicing them but rather by telling how the poet's eye—the eye of the art-book-reading museum-goer—wanders through them.

IV

THE MUSEUM-GOER IN THE MIRROR:
ASHBERY'S "SELF-PORTRAIT"

. . . if,
Without pathos, he feels what he hears
And sees, being nothing otherwise,
Having nothing otherwise, he has not
To go to the Louvre to behold himself.
Granted each picture is a glass,
That the walls are mirrors multiplied,
That the marbles are gluey pastiches, the stairs
The sweep of an impossible elegance,
And the notorious views from the windows
Wax wasted, monarchies beyond
The S.S. *Normandie,* granted
One is always seeing and feeling oneself,
That's not by chance.
Wallace Stevens, "Prelude to Objects"

"Self-Portrait in a Convex Mirror," a long poetic meditation on a painting of that name by Francesco Parmigianino (figure 12), is the work of a poet steeped in visual art. William Carlos Williams has left enough commentary on painting and painters to fill a volume, but John Ashbery's collected writings on visual art could fill several of them. With the exception of Frank O'Hara, who—besides writing poetry—went to work for the Museum of Modern Art in 1951 and became its curator before he died in 1966, Ashbery is surely the premier combination of art critic and poet in our time. He has probably written more about art—especially twentieth-century art—than any other American poet ever has. During the years from 1955 to 1965, when he lived in Paris, he wrote regular columns on art for the *Herald Tribune* and frequent essays for *Art International;* he also served on the editorial board of *Art and Literature: An International Review* for its three-year lifetime (1964–67) and was executive editor of *Art News*

12. Francesco Parmigianino. *Self-Portrait in a Convex Mirror* (1524).
Kunsthistorisches Museum, Vienna.

from 1965 to 1972. He has been nothing if not prolific. By the time he became art critic for *New York Magazine* in 1978, he had already published more than five hundred reviews, articles, and catalogue notes about artists and their works.[44]

The full story of what Ashbery's poetry owes to his experience of visual art would probably require careful scrutiny of all these items—however ephemeral some of them may be—as well as of the volumes of poetry he has published under titles drawn from paintings, such as *The Tennis Court Oath* (1962). It would surely require close analysis of poems such as the early sestina called "The Painter," first published in *Some Trees* (1956), of the much later "And *Ut Pictura Poesis* Is Her Name," and of all the other allusions to painters and painting that ripple through Ashbery's poems. But none of this discussion could pretend to be anything more than a prelude to the main event: an explication of "Self-Portrait in a Convex Mirror."

Probably the most resoundingly ekphrastic poem ever written and certainly one of the longest, "Self-Portrait" was an instant success. When its appearance in *Poetry* was shortly followed by a volume named for it, *Self-Portrait in a Convex Mirror* (1975), the volume won the Pulitzer Prize, the National Book Award, and the National Book Critics Circle Award. The poem itself, besides generating an ever-growing hum of critical commentary, was further enshrined in the Arion edition of 1984. Limited to 175 copies, this edition prints the 552 lines of the poem radially on 27 large paper disks which must be rotated to be read and which are interleaved with circular prints by Willem de Kooning and various other modern masters and by a Richard Avedon photograph that catches a slightly startled, bare-faced Ashbery reaching into the breast pocket of his seersucker jacket, evidently tucking his glasses away so that he will look better for the camera. The whole set of disks is accompanied by a record of Ashbery reading the poem and is encased in a stainless steel cannister cut into concentric rings with a bright little convex mirror as its shining hub: a design that uncannily evokes the shield of Achilles even as it suggests a secular monstrance, a high-kitsch host raised up for our cultural genuflection and worship, the supreme icon of our self-obsessed and self-referential postmodernity. In her notes on the record sleeve, Helen Vendler writes that modern secular art has turned "from the hidden world of religious mystery, and [lost] its iconic function." Yet nothing could be more iconic or more hieratic than this way of publishing Ashbery's poem.

To find the Arion edition a more than faintly ludicrous enterprise is not to say that Ashbery's poem deserves such a designation: merely that it deserves to be read and studied as he himself first published it, unencumbered by the apparatus of idolatry. Likewise it deserves to take its rightful place in the long history of ekphrasis. When Helen Vendler writes that its apostrophe to a long-gone Parmigianino "makes it an elegiac ode" (Arion record sleeve notes), she erases its true ancestry. If, as Eliot says, the historical sense is precisely what makes a writer "most acutely conscious of his place in time, of his own contemporaneity" (Eliot 1502), then we cannot fully understand what "Self-Portrait" means for our time until we can see its relation to the long ekphrastic tradition that stands behind it.

The first thing that links and yet also distinguishes "Self-Portrait" from its ekphrastic predecessors is the salience of its references to art history and the curatorial world of the museum. We have seen that the museum begins to play a part in ekphrastic poetry at least as early as Keats's sonnet on the Elgin marbles in 1817, but its part remains silent until Auden's "Musée des Beaux Arts" of 1938. And likewise silent—up to "Self-Portrait"—is the role played in ekphrasis by art-historical commentary and reproductions. We need a footnote to know what Vasari contributed to Browning's "Fra Lippo Lippi," just as we need footnotes to know what Craven and Gluck and their reproductions contributed to *Pictures from Breughel*. But in "Self-Portrait" Ashbery advertises his sources. More than once he quotes and explicitly cites not only Vasari but also Sydney Freedberg's *Parmigianino* (1950), a modern scholarly monograph. As a professional art critic who knows something of art history, Ashbery thus aligns his poem with the long river of ekphrastic prose that flows beside ekphrastic poetry from at least the time of Philostratus's *Imagines* in the third century A.D. Moreover, he draws into the poem his experience of both museums and reproductions. Though he does not say that what he first saw of Parmigianino's *Self-Portrait* was a reproduction accompanying a *New York Times Book Review* essay on Freedberg's book, he does tell us that he saw the original in the summer of 1959 in Vienna (lines 256–57)—an obvious allusion to the Kunsthistorisches Museum there.[45] Museums and reproductions also furnish him with the figures he uses to represent a past that is forever overtaking the present and devouring its uniqueness. Writing of "the long corridor that leads back to the painting" (387), he locates it in a present already institutionalized by uneventfulness:

> I think it is trying to say it is today
> And we must get out of it even as the public
> Is pushing through the museum now so as to
> Be out by closing time. You can't live there.
> The gray glaze of the past attacks all know-how:
> Secrets of wash and finish that took a lifetime
> To learn and are reduced to the status of
> Black-and-white illustrations in a book where colorplates
> Are rare. That is, all time
> Reduces to no special time. No one
> Alludes to the change; to do so might
> Involve calling attention to oneself
> Which would augment the dread of not getting out
> Before having seen the whole collection
> (Except for the sculptures in the basement:
> They are where they belong).
>
> (395–410)

The tenor of the tropes here is a little elusive; I must confess that I don't know why modern reproductions of Renaissance paintings such as the *Self-Portrait* should exemplify "the gray glaze of the *past*." On a literal level, however, the passage clearly captures the condition of the modern museum-goer: impelled now and then to go back to a particular painting, inexorably expelled by the imminence of closing time, dreading to miss any of the collection, and forced to rely on reproductions at least part of the time because "you can't live" in a museum. This, I take it, is Ashbery's way of saying that his poem derives as much from his study of Freedberg's reproduction of the *Self-Portrait* as from his memory of the original in Vienna.

What he says about reproductions, however, is curiously and even disingenuously dismissive—with something of Benjamin's nostalgia for the "aura" of uniqueness that mechanical reproduction supposedly dissolves. The phrasing here is at once overwrought and banal: "the secrets of wash and finish" that a twenty-year-old Parmigianino deployed in his *Self-Portrait* (painted in 1524, as Ashbery surely knew from reading Freedberg) took considerably less than his thirty-six-year lifetime to learn, and modern technology has made good color-plates anything but rare: a color reproduction of the *Self-Portrait* adorns the album cover in the Arion edition of Ashbery's poem. So what is Ashbery formulating here? Perhaps a covert analogy: the gray glaze of a black-and-white reproduction stands about as far from the golden glow of the original as the original does from the self or soul it purports to represent. We have already learned that the painted eyes through which the soul "swim[s] out" belong to a face englobed, recessed from the convex picture plane, "unable to advance much farther / Than your look as it intercepts the picture" (25–31). Moreover, in the poet's apostrophe to the painter,

> your eyes proclaim,
> That everything is surface. The surface is what's there
> And nothing can exist except what's there.
>
> (79–81)

In passages like these, the gap between the original painting and the reproduction of it gives way to the far greater gap between the painter's inaccessible soul and the face of it superficially reproduced on the convex surface. To the poet's eye this painted face is not a key to the "movements of the soul," as painted bodies were for Alberti and Leonardo, but rather an inscrutable object of contemplation. The contemplation begins in the opening lines of the poem, which precisely describe the painting's appearance and then offer a narrative of its making that is at once Homeric and Vasarian:

> As Parmigianino did it, the right hand
> Bigger than the head, thrust at the viewer
> And swerving easily away, as though to protect
> What it advertises. A few leaded panes, old beams,
> Fur, pleated muslin, a coral ring run together
> In a movement supporting the face, which swims
> Toward and away like the hand
> Except that it is in repose. It is what it is
> Sequestered. Vasari says, "Francesco one day set himself
> To take his own portrait, looking at himself for that purpose
> In a convex mirror, such as is used by barbers . . .
> He accordingly caused a ball of wood to be made
> By a turner, and having divided it in half and
> Brought it to the size of the mirror, he set himself
> With great art to copy all that he saw in the glass,"
> Chiefly his reflection, of which the portrait
> Is the reflection once removed.
>
> (1–17)

The opening three and a half lines—a sentence fragment—sound as if they came from the middle of a conversation, which is what Ashbery later said we are constantly in.[46] This description of a painting seems dependent on something conceptually prior, some unnamed act to which the act of depiction is compared: X did it—or now does it—"as Parmigianino did it." The logical candidate for this unnamed act is Ashbery's own act of composition. To write a poem about a self-portrait in a convex mirror is inevitably to find oneself—or imagine oneself—mirrored by it, as the poet later suggests when he says that the painting of the rounded reflecting surface is so carefully rendered

> that you could be fooled for a moment
> Before you realize the reflection
> Isn't yours.
>
> (233–35)

As he begins a poem that will freely alternate its focus between himself and his nominal subject—"the strict / Otherness of the painter in his / Other room" (238–40)—the poet contemplates the self-portrait of a fellow artist who is also an alter ego: a man whose virtuosity in representing himself "naturally" distorted by a convex mirror could well serve as a model for any postmodern poet seeking to represent a self that he or she knows can only be misrepresented or refracted by the very words that purport to advertise it.

But within the characteristically postmodern self-referentiality of the opening passage lies a richly Homeric core. The first four words—"as Parmigianino did it"—prefigure the passage quoted from Vasari, whose story of the shaping and the painting of the convex ball recalls Homer's narrative about Hephaestus's making of Achilles' shield. Not only does a halved ball resemble a shield; the right hand of the painted figure is "thrust at the viewer" along the picture plane "as though to protect / What it advertises": the "sequestered" face recessed above it. The metaphor implied here displaces the quite different trope that Ashbery could easily have taken from Freedberg, who says that "the hand serves as a *bridge* into the depth of the picture where the head is placed" (105, emphasis added). For Ashbery the hand is what Desmond Morris would call a barrier signal: something "to fence in and shore up the face" (65), or a shield, as the poet explicitly says in his final apostrophe to a painter whose uncanny verisimilitude ("aping naturalness") remains in the end "a frozen gesture of welcome"—"a convention":

> Therefore I beseech you, withdraw that hand,
> Offer it no longer as shield or greeting,
> The shield of a greeting, Francesco.
>
> (525–27)

Ekphrasis originates in the Homeric story of a shield designed precisely "to protect / What it advertises": the Greek way of life.[47] Just as metaphor itself is a "figured curtain," in Shelley's phrase, which both hides and reveals what it represents, the hand of a painter—or of a writer—may be aptly figured as a shield, instrument at once of self-revelation and self-defense. Rembrandt's self-portraits are studies in the shadowy enclosure of radiant self-disclosure, and as Rousseau brilliantly demonstrates in the opening paragraphs of the *Confessions,* a truly masterful autobiographer knows how to construct a rhetorically shielded self, how to greet the reader with a hand that protects the writer.

There is something wilfully hypocritical, then, in the poet's importuning of the painter to withdraw his hand, to withdraw the painted counterpart of all the conventions and rhetorical devices used by the poet himself to expose and shield his own life in this "Self-Portrait" that is both ekphrastic and self-reflective. In the opening lines of the second section of the poem he briefly interrupts his commentary on the painting to say, "I think of the friends / Who came to see me, of what yesterday / Was like" (103–5). Who are the friends? What did he think of them? What was yesterday like? We never learn, because the formulas of personal reminiscence are abruptly broken off by the poet's return to the painting, to the world of the painter and the people who came to see *him* (109–10).

I will return to the passages of self-reflection because as much as anything else, they distinguish this poem from its ekphrastic precursors. But consider first how this postmodern meditation on the self-portrait of an Italian mannerist recalls certain specimens of ekphrasis: the classic narratives of shield-making, Dante's prosopopeial envoicing of the sculpted angel greeting the virgin, and Keats's apostrophe to the sculpted urn, which is repeatedly echoed by Ashbery's apostrophes to a painted face whose lips are "moistened as though about to part / Releasing speech" (510–11) and to a portrait that "says" the soul is a captive, bound to "stay / Posing in this place" (34–39).[48] There is even something like the representational friction we have seen (in Homer, Dante, and Shakespeare) between signifying and signified, medium and referent. But instead of exploiting the difference between the ball of wood and the mirror it is made to signify, Ashbery treats the painted face as something that breaks the illusion of the painted mirror. The mirror, he says, is so carefully depicted that you could be led to think the reflection your own until you realize it isn't:

> You feel then like one of those
> Hoffman characters who have been deprived
> Of a reflection, except that the whole of me
> Is seen to be supplanted by the strict
> Otherness of the painter in his
> Other room.
>
>   (235–40)

The startling shift in pronouns—from the universalized "you" to the particular "me"—underlines the sense of instability that this painted reflection provokes.[49] We have here an inversion of what Lacan calls the mirror stage (*stade du miroir*), where the child takes the image of the other as an anticipatory reflection of him or herself—an image of the corporeal unity the child expects to achieve (Lacan 160). Here the momentary sense that "you" have no reflection at all—no tangible, external confirmation of the coherence of your body— gives way to a sense of otherness, usurpation, displacement. The painted mirror reflects not the "me" I expected to find there but "the painter," a third person radically distinct from both "you" and "me."

The poet thus exposes the heart of a problem we can begin to discern in one of the first commentaries on Parmigianino's self-portrait—the passage from Vasari that is partially quoted at the beginning of the poem:

> One day he began to paint himself with the help of a concave barber's mirror. Noticing the curious distortions of the buildings and doors caused by the mirror he conceived the idea of reproducing it all. Accordingly he had a ball of wood made, and cutting it out to make it of the same size and shape as the mirror he set to work to copy everything that he saw there, including his own likeness, in the most natural manner imaginable. As things near the mirror appear large while they diminish as they recede he made a hand with wonderful realism, somewhat large, as the mirror showed it. (Vasari 3:8)

What we begin to see in this passage—though Vasari himself seems not fully aware of it—is the paradox inherent in representing a convex reflection "in the most natural manner imaginable," in producing the "wonderful realism" of a disproportionately large hand. We grasp the force of this paradox when we recall that the mirror is the most powerful and enduring of all figures for both verbal and visual representation. Alberti liked to think that Narcissus invented painting by the very act of falling in love with his own reflection. "What else can you call painting," Alberti asked, "but a similar embracing with art of what is presented on the surface of the water in the fountain?" (64). In literary theory likewise, as M. H. Abrams showed some forty years ago, the mirror is the traditional king of metaphors for verisimilitude: Hamlet tells the players that drama should aim "to hold, as 'twere, the mirror up to nature" (3.2.19), and Samuel Johnson wrote that Shakespeare's own greatest achievement lay in offering us "a faithful mirrour of manners and of life."[50] What then happens when the metaphor is turned inside out, when a work of art faithfully mirrors a mirror that distorts what it reflects? We get a startling critique of the notion that any kind of mirror—whether literal or metaphorical, pictorial or verbal—can represent the world as it is.

This critique originates with Plato, the first western theorist to use the mirror as a metaphor for artistic representation. When Plato compares the painter to a person holding a mirror up to the universe, he does so precisely to argue that painting appeals to our basest impulses: manipulating appearances, it represents not the true dimensions and proportions of things but only their appearances, so that "the body which is large when seen near, appears small when seen at a distance" (*Republic* 10.602). The trick of thus manipulating appearances was fundamentally transvalued in the Renaissance, when it became known as the science of perspective. Since the artists of the Renaissance essentially adopted the Protagorean principle that man is the measure of all things, the capacity to represent what we *see* became virtually identical with the capacity to represent what *is;* to capture the way things "really" looked was to capture the way they really were. But when Parmigianino captures the way his upper body really looks in a convex mirror, he is actually inviting us to consider the elegance and style with which he has mirrored an appearance made by artifice. Thus Parmigianino's "wonderful realism," as Vasari calls it, merges with Mannerism, a term derived from Vasari's own use of *maniera* to describe the distinctive manner—grace, sophistication, "the stylish style" (Shearman 64)—of painters like Parmigianino.

To see how Vasari describes what Parmigianino stylishly wrought "in the most natural manner imaginable" is to see the complexity of the already verbalized portrait that Ashbery contemplates in this poem. It is also to see that the mannerist painter and the postmodern poet cannot be simply polarized in terms of totalizing idealism and deconstructive skepticism. Richard Stamelman calls Ashbery's poem "a radical criticism of the illusions and deceptions inherent in traditional forms of representation that insist on the ideal, essential, and totalized nature of the copied images they portray" (608). But how does Parmigianino's self-portrait make such a claim? Aside from the face, which Vasari himself calls "divine," how are the images idealized or totalized? The proportional relation between face and hand is anything but ideal, and several other images are fractional: a slim crescent of window at left, a "Sliver of window or mirror" ("Self-Portrait" 84) at right. In addition, the absence of the left hand (which was no doubt occupied in painting the picture) openly violates the rule of completeness that Joshua Reynolds thought indispensable in the portrayal of a principal figure and exemplarily observed by Raphael's cartoon of Paul preaching at Athens: the rule that both hands must be shown lest the viewer wonder—as Reynolds charmingly puts it—"what is become of the other hand" (216).

The idealism of the portrait, then, is confined to the image of a face which Vasari called that "of an angel rather than a man" (8). The phrase is quoted by Freedberg, who finds "no trace of the bizarre in the expression of the sitter's face" but rather "a gentleness and an unaffected grace which makes Vasari's judgment of *piu tosto d'angelo che d'uomo* seem not far exaggerated" (Freedberg 106). Yet the paradoxical implications of Vasari's commentary on the "realism" of the portrait become unmistakably explicit in Freedberg's discussion of it, which can also be read as a critique of Vasari:

> It is true that Francesco has counterfeited a real image on his panel, and that he has done so with remarkable scientific truth. But though the counterfeit is visually exact as a rendering of a thing seen, the thing seen is not in itself an ordinary image, but a singular distortion of objective nor-

malcy. " . . . seeing these eccentricities . . . the wish came to him to imitate [all this] for his caprice . . ." says Vasari: Francesco's realism has been employed to create an effect which is capricious and bizarre. Realism in this portrait no longer produces an objective truth, but a *bizarria.*

The character of this *bizarria* is important, for it is symptomatic of Francesco's attitude toward an important aspect of High Renaissance style. He has chosen to paint a capricious and psychologically piquant image, which is to a considerable extent distorted. It violates the fundamental High Renaissance principle of representation of an idealized norm; however, its distortion does not create a feeling of disharmony. Further, again despite their degree of distortion, the forms retain a strong measure of ideal beauty. . . . Francesco here admits elements which are visually abnormal, and which are, because of this visual abnormality, also in part of abnormal psychological effect. Nevertheless, this early portrait preserves much of the High Renaissance qualities of harmony and ideality which (though they diminish in his succeeding work) Francesco will never entirely discard. (106)

In striving to explain how (or simply to assert that) Parmigianino's portrait melds the ideal and the bizarre, harmony and distortion, the normal and the abnormal, Freedberg openly admits the contradictions that Vasari merely hints at. To preserve Parmigianino's place in the period model constructed by art history and the museum, Freedberg must affirm that his early portrait "preserves much of the High Renaissance qualities of harmony and ideality."[51] Yet Freedberg can hardly help noticing how the portrait threatens to subvert these qualities and violate High Renaissance norms. His equivocation prompts Ashbery to meditate on the symbiosis of beauty and distortion in "our dreams." Just as Freedberg weaves the words of Vasari into an argument about Parmigianino's idiosyncratic way of conforming to period norms, Ashbery weaves the art historical words of Freedberg into a meditation on our psychic needs:

> Sydney Freedberg in his
> *Parmigianino* says of it: "Realism in this portrait
> No longer produces an objective truth, but a *bizarria.* . . .
> However its distortion does not create
> A feeling of disharmony. . . . The forms retain
> A strong measure of ideal beauty," because
> Fed by our dreams, so inconsequential until one day
> We notice the hole they left. Now their importance
> If not their meaning is plain.
> They were to nourish
> A dream which includes them all, as they are
> Finally reversed in the accumulating mirror.
> They seemed strange because we couldn't actually see them.
> And we realize this only at a point where they lapse

Like a wave breaking on a rock, giving up
Its shape in a gesture which expresses that shape.
The forms retain a strong measure of ideal beauty
As they forage in secret on our idea of distortion.
(186–202)

Fed by our dreams and secretly fed by our idea of distortion, ideal beauty now becomes something momentary and even violent, like a breaking wave whose shape emerges only at the instant of its disintegration.[52] The breaking wave is just one of the many oceanic and natatorial metaphors that Ashbery uses to represent the portrait and the face within it, which—as the opening lines tell us—"swims / Toward and away like the hand / Except that it is in repose" (6–7) and is kept "lively and intact in a recurring wave / Of arrival" (23–24). In place of the narrative that ekphrasis traditionally generates from a work of visual art, Ashbery writes of cyclic movement by a face that signifies a captive soul, "life englobed" (55) in the rounded portrait like a fish in a bowl:

The soul establishes itself.
But how far can it swim out through the eyes
And still return safely to its nest?
(24–26)

The mixed metaphor underlines the irony of the painted soul's condition. Superficially free as a fish *or* a bird, officially (as it were) licensed to roam the ocean or the air, it is perpetually balked, like the figures on Keats's urn:

it must stay
Posing in this place. It must move
As little as possible.
(37–39)

Not even the hand, which underlies the face as "a dozing whale on the sea bottom" underlies "the tiny, self-important ship / On the surface" (77–79) can liberate the soul. Though "big enough / To wreck the sphere" (72–73), it cannot even be made to "stick . . . / Out of the globe" because it forms a segment of the very circle that entraps the soul (56–65).

The figure of the englobed and captive soul is richly evocative. The captive soul recalls the ancient Orphic doctrine—better known as the adopted child of Plato—that the soul is a prisoner of the body. The englobed soul evokes Shakespeare's sonnet 146, where the speaker apostrophizes his own soul as "the center of my sinful earth" and asks: "Why dost thou pine within and suffer dearth, / Painting thy outward walls so costly gay?" But to set either of these earlier figures beside the one Ashbery constructs from Parmigianino's portrait is to see at once what makes the later figure so different. Though a soul afloat within a watery globe is more visible than a soul caught in earth, or even within the body's clay, a *painted* soul cannot readily be liberated from—or even

sharply distinguished from—a painted enclosure. Instead it assumes the insub-
stantiality of the painted outer walls, or—in Ashbery's figure—of a breaking
wave. Just as the ideal beauty of the portrait secretly feeds on distortion, the
would-be solid core of the fluid sphere occupies a hollow:

> The pity of it smarts,
> Makes hot tears spurt: that the soul is not a soul,
> Has no secret, is small, and it fits
> Its hollow perfectly: its room, our moment of attention.
>   (43–46)

The hollow occupied by the soul is its double, its after-image, its empty reflection. In the later recasting of Freedberg's assertion about Parmigianino's forms,
"hole" is the verbal reflection of soul, its empty echo: the forms retain their ideal
beauty "because / Fed by our dreams, so inconsequential until one day / We
notice the hole they left" (191–93).

   In this passage and throughout the poem, Ashbery is reflecting on reflection
itself, for the mirrored image is the middle term that mediates between ideal
beauty and emptiness, the soul and the hole. If the mirror traditionally exemplifies perfect representation, as I have noted above, it can also signify the very
opposite of substance. In Plato's analysis of what we can see when newly re-
leased from the cave of shadowy appearances, the reflection of an object is little
better than its shadow, an empty substitute from which we should turn to the
thing itself, and thence to the source of all reflected light. We should turn from
the sun reflected in the moon, in water, or in "any alien medium" to the sun "as
it is itself" (*Republic* 7.516B). Mirrors feed us vacancy. If painting was invented by Narcissus, as Alberti liked to think, then a painter who takes the mirrored image of himself as his model would seem to be implicitly revealing the
narcissistic origin of his enterprise and the vanity—in every sense—of the image he constructs.

   This Platonic line of thought about the vanity of the mirrored image leads
almost inevitably to its gender. Father of vanity (as well as of painting),
Narcissus is a sterile progenitor, a eunuch who begets no more than his own
image.[53] In western literature and iconography this narcissistic eunuchry is typically imaged as female, as a woman so entranced with her own reflection that
she cannot think of men without fear and loathing. I have already noted that
before Milton's Eve became the mother of us all, she fell in love with her own
reflection in a lake and would indefinitely have "pin'd with vain desire" for it
had she not been prised away and led to Adam, who strikes her first as "less
fair, / Less winning soft, less amiably mild, / Than that smooth watery image"
(*Paradise Lost* 4.465–80). The point of this story, which Eve tells on herself, is
that she must learn to forsake the empty charms of her own mirrored image for
the substantial wisdom of Adam, "he / Whose image thou art," as a voice presumably divine informs her (4.471–72). In Pope's *Rape of the Lock*, Belinda is
similarly admonished. Enraptured by her own mirrored face as she cosmetically

arms herself to meet the man she both desires and fears, she is cut down by a pair of scissors and lectured on the superiority of "merit" to purely visible charms. (Here, significantly, the centerpiece in the program of instruction designed to cure the woman of her speculophilia is a kind of rape.)

To depict one's own reflection, then, is seemingly to align oneself with the stereotypically female image of vanity, with all that is empty and useless without a male to invade, impregnate, and fill it up. Vasari does not fully grasp what he implies when he represents Parmigianino's painted face as essentially, even transcendently female: "di bellissima aria . . . e piu tosto d'angelo che d'uomo" ("of most beautiful aspect . . . and rather more of angel than of man").[54] Nor does Freedberg think of vanity when he quotes these words, or when the angelic beauty of the painted face, together with what he calls "the exceptional sensitiveness and grace" of the painted hand, leads him to insist that Parmigianino's "forms retain a strong measure of ideal beauty" (Freedberg 106). Yet Ashbery, who—as noted before—twice quotes these words (190–91, 201), empties them of cogency even as he does so. In Ashbery's redaction of Freedberg's redaction of Vasari, ideal beauty collapses into the "hole" of female inner space, the wavy fluid of the painted womb that englobes the painted face.[55]

Thus, it would seem, Ashbery uses the poetic word to subdue and even negate the power of the image. He makes it female by castrating it, representing the pseudo-phallic hand that "One would like to stick . . . / Out of the globe" as something fragmentarily uterine, joined to "the segment of a circle" (56–57, 63). But Parmigianino's self-portrait cannot be vanquished so easily, nor would it have occupied Ashbery for so many lines if it could be. In the poet's eyes, this apparently effeminate portrait of a painter narcissistically entranced with his own reflection effects something boldly original in the history of art:

> The consonance of the High Renaissance
> Is present, though distorted by the mirror.
> What is novel is the extreme care in rendering
> The velleities of the rounded reflecting surface
> (It is the first mirror portrait),
> So that you could be fooled for a moment
> Before you realize the reflection
> Isn't yours.
>
> (228–35)

To grasp this passage fully, we must unpack the crucial phrase so innocuously wrapped in parentheses. Parmigianino's painting was actually not the first mirror portrait. The self-portraits painted before it, such as Dürer's *Portrait of the Artist as a Young Man,* required the use of mirrors, and in the background of the Arnolfini portrait of 1434, long before Parmiginino's birth, Jan van Eyck depicted a convex mirror reflecting two figures from the rear.[56] But in this painting and others like it, as Freedberg notes, the mirror is shown *within* the picture (Freedberg 146, note 4). Parmigianino was the first to make a mirrored image fill a whole painting and, more importantly, to represent it *as* mirrored. Here is Freedberg again, fully explaining what Ashbery squeezes into a single parenthesized line: "The mechanical agency through which a self-portrait is achieved, the mirror, had never before been openly confessed, nor indeed exploited as it is here, nor had it been used as the vehicle for the formal structure of a portrait" (105). In other words, Parmigianino's *Self-Portrait* is not the first mirror portrait of any kind but the first mirror portrait that *openly reveals itself as such.* This is at once the source of its distinction in the history of portraiture and the source of its power over the imagination of a postmodern poet.

Significantly, Ashbery's parenthetical allusion to the self-conscious artificiality of this portrait—to the painter's deliberate displaying of the "mechanical agency" by which he represents himself—is immediately followed by the first passage in which the poet tries to read the painting as a mirror of himself. Strictly speaking, this reading is of course mistaken, as we have already seen. Yet just as the explicit depiction of the mirror separates Parmigianino's self-portrait from its predecessors, the poet's repeated references to himself make this poem virtually unprecedented in the history of ekphrasis:

> We have surprised him [the painter]
> At work, but no, he has surprised us
> As he works. The picture is almost finished,
> The surprise almost over, as when one looks out,
> Startled by a snowfall which even now is
> Ending in specks and sparkles of snow.
>
> (240–45)

Contesting Murray Krieger's argument that ekphrasis superimposes "the frozen, stilled world of plastic relationships . . . upon literature's turning world to 'still' it " (*Ekphrasis* 265–66), Richard Stamelman argues that the ekphrastic object in this poem "is perpetually in movement, swerving in and out of the poet's consciousness; it never has time to lie still, to settle or harden into a solid object" (615). This time Stamelman is right. From the opening lines, the painted face and hand swim toward and away because the poet never objectifies the painting, never pretends to hold it still for a detached, impersonal analysis such as the art historian typically provides. Instead he repeatedly presents himself as a viewer in psychic motion, subject to fits of boredom and distraction ("The balloon pops, the attention / Turns dully away" [100–101]), openly disclosing the states of mind with which he reflects—and reflects upon—this portrait of a mirrored face. Here the traditionally ekphrastic impulse to deliver in words the story signified by the pregnant moment of graphic art gives way to the desultory, inconclusive story of what the poet thinks and feels as he contemplates the painting.

This is something new in ekphrasis. With the notable exception of "Peele Castle," where commentary on a painting turns into autobiographical reflection, earlier ekphrastic poetry represents the poet's state of mind chiefly by indirection, if at all. Only rarely does the poet say explicitly what he or she feels about a work of art, as when a death-obsessed Anne Sexton tells us of Van Gogh's *Starry Night:*

> This is how
> I want to die:
>
> into that rushing beast of the night,
> sucked up by that great dragon, to split
> from my life with no flag,
> no belly,
> no cry.
>
> *(Complete Poems* 54)

In place of this stark, single response, Ashbery traces the undulations of his meditation on a painting, blending art history with personal history, including the record of his encounter with the painting at Vienna's Kunsthistorische Museum, "where / I saw it with Pierre in the summer of 1959" (256–57). For all the novelty of his approach to this novel painting, however, Ashbery's poem simply makes explicit what all ekphrasis entails and implies: the experience of the viewer, and the pressure of that experience on his or her interpretation of the work of art.

No account of what a painting or a piece of sculpture *is* or represents can ever be wholly objective. As Paul and Svetlana Alpers showed some years ago, interpretive judgments shape even the coolly analytic prose of the art historian furnishing a set of seemingly incontestable "facts" about a work of art (452–53). By training and habit, the art historian reads the individual work as a link in a developmental chain. The work must be made to play its part in what Preziosi calls "consistent and internally coherent narratives of development, filiation, evolution, descent, progress, regress" ("Question" 370). While ekphrasis traditionally turns the depicted moment into a story of what the painting represents, art history sets the work within a story of art itself. Both moves are fundamentally interpretive, which is why I cannot agree with David Carrier when he treats ekphrasis and interpretation as two contrasting modes of writing about art.[57]

When Ashbery quotes the words of Vasari and Freedberg in his poem, he is quoting interpretations of Parmigianino's *Self-Portrait:* interpretations that help each of these writers tell a particular kind of story. For Vasari, who believed that painters advance by perfecting the means of representing the natural world and who wanted to tell the story of how Italian artists did so, Parmigianino's painting was distinguished by its "wonderful realism." For Freedberg, who wants to fit the painting into a story about Parmigianino's gradual turning from High Renaissance norms to mannerist tension, the early *Self-Portrait* "retain[s] a strong measure of ideal beauty."[58] Each commentary reveals the mindset of the commentator—if not his state of mind.

It is the latter, of course, that Ashbery represents along with the painting: his state of mind as viewer of a painted reflection, reader of art historical commentary on it, one-way interviewer of Parmigianino, and skeptical observer of his own mobile self. He never fixes his relation to the painted figure. Throughout the poem, as David Kalstone observes, "the poet speaks to the portrait in easy consultation with a familiar, but with an ever changing sense of whether he is addressing the image, trapped on its wooden globe, or addressing the free painter standing outside his creation" (178). In fact the poet speaks at times to neither image nor painter, but to us *about* it and him, as in the opening lines on the making of the portrait, when—in the words quoted from Vasari— Parmigianino "set himself / With great art to copy all that he saw in the glass" (14–15). What Ashbery does with this Vasarian sentence later in the poem typifies the mobility of his perspective. Having already turned the painter from referent to addressee ("Francesco, your hand is big enough / To wreck the sphere" [72–73]), he speaks of the portrait as "the record of what you accomplished by sitting down / 'With great art to copy all that *you* saw in the glass'" (142–43, emphasis mine).

The shift from speaking *of* the painting to speaking *to* the painter—a shift made near the end of the first section of the poem—plainly signifies a quickening of the desire to penetrate the portrait, to reach the core of its meaning, to disclose the self it represents. But the poet cannot extract from the portrait— still less verbalize—an inner meaning. "Your eyes proclaim," he says to the painted face, "That everything is surface" (79–80). In place of the soul that Alberti thought every well-painted figure should express (77), Ashbery finds only a rounded emptiness that he defines in a succession of diminishing tropes: the whole world of the portrait is "a globe like ours, resting / On a pedestal of vacuum, a ping-pong ball / Secure on its jet of water" (89–91).[59] Even after writing nearly a hundred lines about the portrait, the poet insists "there are no words for the surface, that is, / No words to say what it really is, that it is not / Superficial but a visible core" (92–94).

In frustrating the poet's quest for a core, the painting not only stifles his capacity to speak about it but also disperses his concentration and turns his field of vision into a centrifugal whirl. The "balloon pops, the attention / Turns dully away" (100), like that of Auden's non-witnesses "walking dully along" past suffering or "turn[ing] away / Quite leisurely from the disaster." Seasons and thoughts that defy the control of a curved hand "peel off and fly away at breathless speeds" (117–18); the little world around him—"desk, papers, books, / Photographs of friends, the window and the trees"—becomes a "carousel starting slowly / And going faster and faster" (124–26). As a stay against such dispersal, the poet has

> only the chaos
> Of your round mirror which organizes everything

Around the polestar of your eyes which are empty,
Know nothing, dream but reveal nothing.
(120–23)

Yet for all the emptiness he ascribes to the core of the painting, the poet insists on positing a presence within it: the presence of a would-be auditor, or of what he later calls—after reverting to the third person—"the strict / Otherness of the painter in his / Other room" (239–40). Viewed as other but also as a refuge from centrifugal dispersion, the painted face becomes something like a Virgil to the poet's Dante:

My guide in these matters is your self,
Firm, oblique, accepting everything with the same
Wraith of a smile, and as time speeds up so that it is soon
Much later, I can know only the straight way out,
The distance between us.
(132–36)

The poem has begun by suggesting that Parmigianino's way of representing himself ("As Parmigianino did it") might serve as a model for the poet's own project in self-representation. Here the poet takes the painter as his guide across the very distance that divides them, the only "straight way"—*diretta via*—out of the whirling path of time, dispersal, and contingency.

The conflict between the poet's longing to find a self in this painting and his repeated insistence on the absence of a self within it—on the emptiness of its core—has been suggestively read as evidence that Ashbery plays Whitman against Stevens: that he poignantly recalls the transcendent self celebrated in "Song of Myself" ("And nothing, not God, is greater than one's self is" [1271]) even as he echoes the deconstructive notes of "The Man with the Blue Guitar" (itself a meditation on Picasso's *The Old Guitarist*), where Stevens posits "an absence in reality" (XXII.5) and questions the very possibility of defining the self: "Where / Do I begin and end?" (XII.7).[60] Certainly "Self-Portrait" speaks with more than one voice. It vacillates between affirming a self—or the poet's desire for one—and exposing its absence, denying its wholeness or presence in any form of representation, and thereby stripping self-portraiture "of authority and authenticity," as Stamelman says (611). In the very face of such denial and disrobing, the poem sustains the possibility of a self. Even as the poet hollows out the portrait with metaphors of emptiness—ping-pong ball, popping balloon, "bubble-chamber" (170), hourglass (176)—he speaks to the painter within it. In the very act of discovering that the painted mirror fails to reflect the viewer and thus seems to deny his existence, the poet sees "the whole of me / . . . supplanted by the strict / Otherness of the painter," implicitly affirming the identity of each.

The contradiction between affirming and denying the presence of a self within the painting is reinforced by complementary polarities. Against the frame-encircled "enchantment of self with self"—which could be either the painter's self-enchantment or the poet's fascination with him—press "the extraneous" and contingent forces that the painting forever rules out (144–46): the city (Rome or New York) lurking behind the mirrored studio and seeking to "siphon off" its life (264–65); the wind of entropy that "saps all activity, secret or public" (274); the sands of time "hissing / As they approach the beginning of the big slide / Into what happened" (492–94) while the mirrored room of the painting "contains this flow like an hourglass / Without varying in climate or quality" (176–77). "Stable within / Instability" (88–89), the portrait disturbs us precisely because it resolutely excludes the flow of change that engulfs individual identities. Its "will to endure" reminds us of "Our own, which we were hoping to keep hidden" (412–13).

More potent than the conflict between perpetuation and contingency, however, is the quintessentially ekphrastic struggle for mastery between image and word. From his very first words, the poet sets out to rival as well as represent Parmigianino's self-portrait, to portray himself "as Parmigianino did" by incorporating all the elements of a poet's studio—"desk, papers, books / Photographs of friends" (125–26) along with Parmigianino's painting and all the furniture of his mind—in the convex mirror of the poem. The painting itself, of course, does not live in his studio; it hangs in Vienna's Kunsthistorische Museum, where he saw it with Pierre in the summer of 1959. Since there is no mention of its colors, the picture described in this poem is evidently the black-and-white reproduction numbered plate 122 in Freedberg's *Parmigianino,* where "colorplates / Are rare" (402–3) and where it is surrounded by the words of commentary that play such a conspicuous part in the poem. In all but the Arion edition, the poem is unaccompanied by reproductions of any kind. Having entered a studio of words through a book of reproductions (a portable museum of words), the painting is at once represented and displaced by language.

But the poet's words cannot deconstruct it. It has already deconstructed itself. By faithfully representing the way a convex mirror distorts what it reflects, the portrait subverts the assumption that the world can be undistortedly mirrored by any medium of representation. At the same time, the angelically serene face of the painter fixed in the center of the aqueous globe fixes the viewer with a gaze of overpowering poignancy. In painting what the mirror reflects, Parmigianino depicts himself *as viewer,* which is why the painted face usurps not only the reflection of ourselves that we momentarily expect to see in the painting but also our vantage point. We are not so much gazing as gazed *at,* and

> there is in that gaze a combination
> Of tenderness, amusement and regret, so powerful

In its restraint that one cannot look for long.
The secret is too plain. The pity of it smarts,
Makes hot tears spurt: that the soul is not a soul,
Has no secret, is small, and it fits
Its hollow perfectly: its room, our moment of attention.
That is the tune but there are no words.
The words are only speculation
(From the Latin *speculum,* mirror):
They seek and cannot find the meaning of the music.

(39–50)

If we calculate what this passage takes away, we must also measure what it leaves. While it clearly diminishes and demystifies the soul, which "has no secret," it implicitly affirms the soulfulness of the painting, which could hardly bring tears to the eyes if it expressed nothing at all. Significantly, what it expresses defeats the power of words, for they are only speculation, verbal mirrors of the mirror-image. For all its doubling and distortion, what the painting expresses cannot be nullified by rhetorical flourishes, by a verbal sleight of hand:

and those assholes
Who would confuse everything with their mirror games
Which seem to multiply stakes and possibilities, or
At least confuse issues by means of an investing
Aura that would corrode the architecture
Of the whole in a haze of suppressed mockery,
Are beside the point.

(426–32)

The painted face haunts the poet, who "cannot look [at it] for long" yet cannot long think of anything else. Even the entropic wind that "saps all activity" becomes in the opening lines of the final section a source of revival: "A breeze like the turning of a page / Brings back your face" (311–12). The page on which words are printed is here displaced by a plate—a page from a book of reproductions. In the end the painted face reproduced on this page becomes something like a belle dame sans merci, by turns erotic and chilling. With "gloss on the fine / Freckled skin, lips moistened as though about to part / Releasing speech" (509–11), it seductively straddles the border between image and word, luring the viewer behind or beyond language to "what could have been our paradise: exotic / Refuge within an exhausted world" (513–14). But the hand that offers "the shield of a greeting" makes only "a frozen gesture of welcome" (519), and the convex image—dismissed by the poet—retreats

at a speed
Faster than that of light to flatten ultimately
Among the features of the room, an invitation

Never mailed, the "it was all a dream"
Syndrome, though the "all" tells tersely
Enough how it wasn't. Its existence
Was real, though troubled, and the ache
Of this waking dream can never drown out
The diagram still sketched on the wind,
Chosen, meant for me and materialized
In the disguising radiance of my room.
(530–40)

If "Self-Portrait" recalls both Whitman and Stevens, its debts to Keats—
and specifically to the ekphrastic Keats—are nowhere more evident than in this
nearly final passage of the poem. Like the passionate figures of the urn who
finally retreat into the "overwrought" pattern of a "cold Pastoral," the erotic
image freezes and flattens out, taking with it the dream of iconic realization, of
the two-dimensional figure three-dimensionally materialized. Yet the disen-
chanted poet, who resembles both the painfully awakened knight of "La Belle
Dame" and the inescapably self-conscious dreamer of "Ode to a Nightingale,"
cannot simply relinquish the image he has dreamed about, and certainly cannot
reduce it "all" to the words of a dismissive cliche. In the opening stanza of the
nightingale ode, the speaker's heart "aches" with a drowsy numbness that
makes him feel he is sinking to Lethe—drowning in a river of forgetfulness—
and in the final words of the poem, when the vision of an ecstatic union with
the immortality of the bird's song has fled, he asks himself, "Do I wake or
sleep?" Ashbery turns Keats's provocative question into a troubled statement.
"The ache / Of this waking dream" is, I gather, the ache of a conventionally
awake self-conciousness dreaming of "reality": the ache of a mind awakened
from entrancement by a picture into what Shelley called—in his elegy for
Keats—"the dream of life" (*Adonais* 343). The aching dream we typically regard as wakefulness will never drown out—will never sink to Lethean
forgetfulness—the image of the painter's reflected gaze. "Its existence / Was
real, though troubled."

The past tense here is extraordinarily revealing. As the poet experiences it, the
image is both real and temporal, even ephemeral. Though preserved in a museum, the painting represented by this poem cannot be seen continuously—
precisely because it is *in* a museum, which the public must leave each day "so as
to / Be out by closing time. You can't live there" (396–98). In the museum of
words constructed by curators and art historians, the painting is equally time-
bound: bound to the historical moment of its making, to its place in the narrative of the artist's life or in the story of art itself. Acutely conscious of his own
time and place, of when and where he saw the painting and now writes his
poem, Ashbery turns the art historian's "period" into a moment of his own his-

tory: into the record of his struggle to articulate the meaning of a gaze at which he "cannot look for long" (42) and for which "there are no words" (47). In the unending struggle for power between the image and the word, in the long history of ekphrasis stretching from Homer to the present, John Ashbery's "Self-Portrait in a Convex Mirror" will remain, I suspect, an enduring reflection on where we are now.[61]

Notes

INTRODUCTION

1. On the Renaissance tradition of *paragone,* a contest or dispute about the relative merits of different arts, ideas, or philosophies, see Hagstrum 66–70.

2. Composed from the Greek words *ek* (out) and *phrazein* (tell, declare, pronounce), *ekphrasis* originally meant "telling in full." It has been variously used and variously defined. First employed as a rhetorical term in the second century A.D. to denote simply a vivid description, it was then (in the third century) made to designate the description of visual art (Bartsch 9, 32n). But it has not been confined to that meaning. In its first recorded appearance in English (1715), it was defined as "a plain declaration or interpretation of a thing" (cited *OED*), and in a recent handbook of rhetorical terms it is called simply "a self-contained description, often on a commonplace subject, which can be inserted at a fitting place in a discourse" (Lanham 39). My own definition of ekphrasis follows the lead of the *Oxford Classical Dictionary* (*OCD*), which defines it as "the rhetorical description of a work of art."

3. First published in 1967, this essay has reappeared as an appendix to Krieger's *Ekphrasis: The Illusion of the Natural Sign* (1991), from which I now cite it. Krieger's new book reaffirms his original conception of ekphrasis while constructing a semiotic argument about its claim to be a natural sign. As before, he applies the term to all description of visual objects, all "word-painting," not just to the representation of visual art (9). But now ekphrasis becomes an exercise in illusion. It includes "every attempt, within an art of words, to work toward the illusion that it is performing a task we usually associate with an art of natural signs" (9). While admitting that this formulation presupposes a "naively 'realistic'" notion of pictorial mimesis (12n), Krieger contrasts the supposed "immediacy of the picture" with "the mediation of the code," and argues that the ekphrastic impulse originates from a longing for the former (11–12). Despite periodic critiques of pictorialism by theorists such as Ficino and Burke, Krieger finds this "lingering semiotic desire for the natural sign" (22) permeating the history of critical theory and of literature itself.

My own approach to ekphrasis differs sharply from this. Where Krieger defines ekphrasis as an impulse toward illusionistic word-painting, I treat it as a kind of poetry that deliberately foregrounds the *difference* between verbal and visual representation—and in so doing forestalls or at the very least complicates any illusionistic effect. Also, while Krieger concentrates "on critical and theoretical discourse . . . rather than on the practice of the arts themselves" (5), I use the practice of the arts—more precisely the history of ekphrastic poetry—to construct a theory of ekphrasis.

For a fuller account of Krieger's *Ekphrasis,* see Heffernan, "Lusting for the Natural Sign," *Semiotica* 98 (1994): 219–28.

4. While acknowledging Frank's 1945 essay "Spatial Form," Krieger notes that Frank is more interested in the modernity of spatial metaphors "than in the generic spatiality of literary form and—even more to *my* point—in the inevitability of spatial language by the critic or by the poem as its own aesthetician" (Krieger 264n). It is precisely these latter points that Mitchell pursues in his own "Spatial Form" essay of 1980.

5. Krieger repeatedly denies that he is subjecting poetry to a *static* formalism. "In resistance to the ekphrastic impulse," he writes, "it cannot be too often urged that the aesthetic desire for pure and eternal form must not be allowed merely to freeze the entity-denying chronological flow of experience in its unrepeatable variety" (285–86). But if the "ekprastic impulse" is a formalizing tendency that must be *resisted,* can the "ekphrastic principle" embrace both movement and stable form, "the empirically progressive" as well as "the circular" (287)? In his *Theory of Criticism,* Krieger writes that "the critic's descriptions of the object in formal and spatial terms . . . are *his* weak metaphors, which, if he takes them too seriously, will distort—by freezing—the object" (39). If ekphrasis is simply a weak metaphor for poetic integrity and a continuing threat to poetic vitality, its critical value is minimal. To maximize its critical value, we must identify the distinguishing features of ekphrasis as a literary mode.

6. In a paper on "Postmodern Ekphrasis" delivered at the Tenth International Colloquium on Poetics at Columbia University in 1986, Linda Hutcheon applied the term *ekphrasis* to such postmodern phenomena as the incorporation of newspaper articles in the novels of Julio Cortazar and John Fowles. Likewise, in a dissertation titled *Figures in the Carpet: The Ekphrastic Tradition in the Realistic Novel* (Rice University 1981), Mack L. Smith defines *ekphrasis* as the introduction of any work of art—whether verbal or literary—into another work of art, so that his examples range from the description of portraits in *Anna Karenina* to the debate about *Hamlet* in Joyce's *Ulysses.* My own definition of *ekphrasis* rests on what I believe to be a fundamental distinction between writing about pictures and writing about texts.

7. A similar distinction is made by Lessing, who says that a poet may imitate an artist in one of two ways: taking the work of art as his model, or borrowing the artist's "manner of presentation." Though some commentators (including this one) have suggested that Lessing denigrates ekphrasis, he actually finds originality in the first kind of imitation, which is plainly ekphrastic even though Lessing does not use the word: "The first [kind of imitation]," Lessing writes, "is part of that general imitation which is the essence of [the poet's] art, and whether his subject is a work of other arts or a work of nature, he creates as a genius." By contrast, Lessing condemns as servile the poetic imitation of an artist's style (45). In other words, while he might have approved a poem *about* a photograph by Stieglitz, he would have faulted "The Red Wheelbarrow" for its photographic *manner* of representation.

8. Iconicity has come to mean any "natural" or "motivated" similarity between words and what they signify, so that it includes not only onomatapoeia and texts with visually significant shapes (concrete poetry) but also certain kinds of syntax. Roman Jakobson, for instance, sees iconicity in Caesar's "I came, I saw, I conquered" because the order of the clauses corresponds to the chronological order of the events they signify (Jakobson 345–59). For extensive discussion of iconicity in literature, see the entire issue of *Word & Image* 2 (1986), especially the introduction by Max Nanny (197–208).

9. I am thinking here specifically of Ian Hamilton Finlay's "XM poem" (1963) in Emmet Williams, *Anthology of Concrete Poetry* (n.p., poems printed in alphabetical or-

der of authors' names). On the general topic of pattern poetry—another name for iconic poetry—see Dick Higgins, "Pattern Poetry as Paradigm."

10. Crane himself tried (unsuccessfully) to use one of Joseph Stella's paintings of the Brooklyn Bridge as a frontispiece to *The Bridge,* and he described the poem in explicitly pictorial terms, speaking of its "architectural method" and comparing the interdependence of its sections to the interdependence of the frescoes in the Sistine Chapel (Irwin 288–89). But however much Crane's poem may resemble or evoke a painting by Stella or any other work of art, the bridge represented in the poem is not itself representational; it is an object made to serve a practical, physical purpose. I should add that I recognize the considerable differences between the panoramic scope of *The Bridge* and the minimalist focus of "The Red Wheelbarrow." The only point I wish to make here is that while each poem may remind us of pictures, neither one is ekphrastic in the strict sense I have proposed.

11. All translations from the *Iliad* are by Richmond Lattimore. I will return to the lines on the ploughed earth in chapter 1. For further analysis of their representational complexity, see Becker, "Shield," to which my own analysis is partly indebted.

12. The term comes from Lessing, who asserts that painting can represent only a single moment of an action "and must therefore choose the one which is most suggestive [*pragnantesten,* most pregnant with meaning] and from which the preceding and succeeding actions are most easily comprehensible" (78).

13. I do not mean here that a picture *cannot* tell a story, or that it cannot tell a story without the aid of a text, or that pictures differ essentially from texts because texts tell self-sufficient stories while pictures do not. Since a poem such as Yeats's "Leda and the Swan" does *not* tell a self-sufficient story while a painting such as Gainsborough's *Two Shepherd Boys Fighting* does, I am not speaking categorically about what pictures can or cannot do. I merely describe what ekphrasis typically does with visual art.

14. Genette's rigorous ranking of narration and description recalls the ideology of Renaissance art critics, who, Svetlana Alpers writes, treated imitation or pictorial "description" as "the handmaiden of narrative concerns," as a "means . . . to narrative ends" ("Describe or Narrate?" 17–18). See also Alpers's *The Art of Describing.*

15. "L'ekphrasis est un fragment anthologique, transferable d'un discours a un autre" (Barthes 183).

16. On the traditional association of pictures with female beauty, a recurrent theme of this book, see Simone de Beauvoir: "While the boy seeks himself in the penis as an autonomous subject, the little girl coddles her doll and dresses her up as she dreams of being coddled and dressed up herself; inversely, she thinks of herself as a marvelous doll. By means of compliments and scoldings, through images and words, she learns the meaning of the terms *pretty* and *homely;* she soon learns that in order to be pleasing she must be "pretty as a picture"; she tries to make herself look like a picture, she puts on fancy clothes, she studies herself in a mirror, she compares herself with princesses and fairies" (279). And again: "It is not only that girdle, brassiere, hair-dye, make-up, disguise body and face; but that the least sophisticated of women, once she is 'dressed,' does not present *herself* to observation; she is, like the picture or statue, or the actor on the stage, an agent through whom is suggested someone not there—that is, the character she represents, but is not. It is this identification with something unreal, fixed, perfect as the hero of a novel, as a portrait or bust, that gratifies her; she strives to identify herself with this figure and thus to seem to herself to be stabilized, justified in her splendor" (533). My thanks to Virginia Heffernan for drawing these passages to my attention.

17. Unlike Jean Hagstrum, who makes this envoicing a necessary condition for ekphrasis (18n), I treat it as one of several features that may not all be present in any one ekphrastic poem or passage.

18. Since beauty is for Lessing "the supreme law of the visual arts," everything—including expression—must "give way completely if not compatible with beauty" (15).

19. Beth Newman has shown how the power of the male narrator's gaze in *Wuthering Heights* is defied and finally defeated by a young woman who silently stares back at him when he first sees her, and whose portrait hangs before him as he hears the story that he has transcribed for us. On this contest of gazes, in which a "fascinating" woman assumes the Medusan power to transfix the male viewer, see Newman 1029–34.

20. I call it a mode rather than a genre (as Krieger does) because it lacks the distinguishing formal features we find in such traditional genres as epic, dramatic, and lyric. Some of the participants in the 1986 Columbia colloqium on ekphrasis claimed that ekphrasis deserves no special literary status at all because it can appear within works of various genres (such as epic) and because no formal or syntactic features distinguish it from any other kind of literature. But the same objections could be made about elegy. Though commonly regarded as a distinctive genre, it also turns up in epics and novels: book 6 of the *Aeneid* opens with a brief elegy to Caieta, the hero's nurse, and Pushkin's *Eugene Onegin* includes Lensky's proleptic elegy on himself (6.22). As to the second objection, what are the formal or syntactic features common to Milton's "Lycidas," Gray's "Elegy in a Country Churchyard," Auden's "In Memory of W. B. Yeats," Wordsworth's "Elegiac Stanzas Suggested by a Picture of Peele Castle, in a Storm," and Robert Lowell's "For the Union Dead"—all of them elegies and the last two ekphrastic as well?

21. It is sometimes difficult to say precisely when ekphrasis is notional and when it is not. Giambattista Marino's *Galeria* (1620), for instance, is a collection of poems representing both actual and imaginary paintings in ways that blur the distinction between the two. But since we can usually tell the difference, the concept of notional ekphrasis remains a useful one.

22. For part of the Continental story, see Bergmann. Notable recent studies of ekphrasis in fiction include Gysin, Mandelker, and Witemeyer.

23. Michael Baxendall suggestively explores the relation between ancient ekphrasis and modern art criticism in the introduction to *Patterns of Intention,* and Svetlana Alpers has examined Vasari's use of ekphrasis ("*Ekphrasis* and Aesthetic Attitudes"). Though David Carrier has argued that ekphrasis and interpretation are contrasting modes of writing about works of art, he ignores the interpretive aim that permeates the theory and practice of ekphrastic rhetoric from its very beginnings. Philostratus, for instance, wrote his commentaries on paintings precisely in order to teach the young how to interpret them (*Imagines* 5). See also Conan, Becker ("Reading" 11–14), and page 223, note 57 of the present book.

Sharpening a point made in my essay, "Ekphrasis and Representation," I must add here that I now consider picture titles ekphrastic only when applied to the work by someone other than the artist. When applied by the artist, a title is—as Hazard Adams argues—"integral to the work" and therefore part of what is to *be* described, interpreted, or both (Adams 10).

CHAPTER ONE

1. "Structurally," writes Mark Edwards, "the description of the shield can be considered part of a hugely expanded arming scene, glorifying Achilles before he begins his

mighty deeds of battle . . ." (278). And again: "Just as the massive catalogues of Greeks and Trojans in the second book appropriately introduced the conflict that fills the poem, so this mighty *ecphrasis* fittingly proclaims the entry into battle of the mightiest hero of all" (284).

2. Lines 823–24. Finding "many parallels" between the scenes on the shield and the rest of the poem, Atchity says (241) that "Hephaistos clearly intends his pictures to be imitations of Iliadic reality; he speaks of the Ocean to Thetis (18.399) in exactly the same terms as he will depict it on the shield (18.607)"—i.e., as a circling stream. Oliver Taplin (6–7) aptly links the spectacle of wives and children and old men on the walls of the besieged city (18.514–15) with the speech in which Hector urges the boys and elders of Troy to take up a stand on its encircling bastions (8.518–19). "The city on the shield," writes Taplin, "stands for every threatened homeland; within the *Iliad* Troy is such a city" (7). Taplin also connects (7) the murderous ambush of the shepherds and herdsmen on the shield (18. 520–29) with Achilles' slaughtering of the seven brothers of Andromache when they were tending sheep and oxen (6.421–24).

3. Michael Lynn-George notes: "Thetis dives back to earth with the shield as the sun rises [18.615–16; 19.1–2], marking yet another day of slaughter in which the shield is caught up in . . . complexity and fury. In the *Iliad* the immortal work of art on the shield does not simply transcend the narrative as a final vision: that which is constructed out of sequence in response to loss is plunged back within a sequence of loss and death" (197).

4. Atchity 179, 160. Cf. E. T. Owen, *The Story of the Iliad* (Ann Arbor: Univ. of Michigan Press, 1946), 187–88: The shield "is a breathing-space in the battle, in which we have time to look around us and remember that this is only an incident in the busy world of human activities." Taplin restates this point with specific reference to the besieged city: "The city on the shield puts the *Iliad* itself into perspective; it puts war and prowess into perspective within the world as a whole. On the shield the *Iliad* takes up, so to speak, one half of one of the five circles. It is as though Homer has allowed us temporarily to stand back from the poem and see it in its place—like a 'detail' from the reproduction of a painting—within a larger landscape, a landscape which is usually blotted from sight by the all-consuming narrative in the foreground" (Taplin 12).

5. When Odysseus meets the shade of Ajax in the *Odyssey*, he sees that Ajax is still angry with him for winning the arms of Achilles in their dispute, and he regrets that "so high a head has gone under the ground for the sake of that armor" (11. 543–49). From other sources we learn that Ajax apparently "went mad with anger and disappointment and finally killed himself" (*OCD*).

6. The danger they face is repeatedly dramatized in scenes that show what happens to those who come out of protective enclosures. The soldiers who set out from the walled city to stage an ambush are soon caught up in a bloody battle (18.530–40), and the cattle who trot out of the farmyard into an open pasture meet two lions who seize and devour one of the bulls (573–83). Also accentuating the vulnerability of the figures on the shield is the gold that most of them are made with. Though gold is later said to stop the spear of Aeneas (20.267–68), it seems hardly capable of doing so, as Edwards notes (279)—unless of course this gift of a god was supernaturally impenetrable.

7. In book 20, when Achilles' shield is pierced by the spear of Aeneas, we are told that the two outside plates are bronze, the two inside are tin, and the one in the middle gold (20.269–70)—with no reference to the silver mentioned in 18.475. And if each of the five plates represents a distinct theme, as Thibaud contends (301), how can gold and

silver both appear in the dancing scene (598), or gold appear in so many scenes (507, 517, 561–62, 577)? Strangely enough, nowhere in the long passage from book 18 are we told just which kind of metal is used for each plate—even though the material of each plate used in the shields of Ajax and Agamemnon has been precisely specified in the much shorter passages devoted to those shields earlier (7.222–23; 11.33–35).

8. Gerald Prince notes that "narrative prefers tensed statements (or their equivalent) to untensed ones" and adds: "The hallmark of narrativity is assurance. It lives in certainty. This happened, then that; this happened because of that; this happened and it was related to that" (Prince 74–75).

9. This is equally true of the spatial relations between one scene and another. As Michael Lynn-George observes, "the shield's structure combines a spatial indeterminacy with a fracturing of space into a multiplicity of different, separate sites—a plurality of places combined with a certain placelessness. . . . The shield's architecture is fissured by time, its fragmented space never simply framed as a totality which can be grasped all once. With the sole exception of the river Okeanos, situated on the rim of the shield, none of the shield's scenes is assigned a fixed, determinate place in relation to the other scenes; and not even when bounded by Okeanos does the shield present itself as an object which can be visualised in its entirety as the totality of a closed form. The shield is thus shaped by two processes: where the work of art tends to transform time into space, space is in turn traversed by time" (178).

10. Alberti's *Della Pictura* (1435–36) did not explicitly proscribe multitemporal paintings, but as Wendy Steiner shows (Steiner, *Pictures* 23–26), it led through Leonardo to the unitemporal standard that Lessing takes to be normative, and that has in fact powerfully influenced the theory and practice of painting for the past four hundred years.

11. "It is not even clear," writes Taplin (3), "that the shield is to be envisaged as decorated with five concentric circles." For a recent diagram, see Willcock 270.

12. Taplin rightly declares: "Nothing really like this shield has ever been found nor ever will be" (3).

13. William Kumbier kindly drew my attention to the importance of the Greek word for "elaborating" in this passage.

14. I render the active *poikille* as passive in order to preserve Homer's word order. Lattimore's rendering of *amphigueeis* as "smith of the strong arms" is curiously and uncharacteristically inaccurate.

15. Ingarden 222–24, 236–38. For a fuller discussion of these matters, see Heffernan, "Space and Time."

16. Lines 497–500. As Willcock notes (270), lines 499–500 may also mean that one man claims to have made a payment while the other denies receiving it. But given the theme of vengeance in the poem—Achilles would never take anything less than Hector's life for the killing of Patroclus—it seems equally plausible to suppose that the man who refused ransom wanted blood. See Hammond on this point.

17. As Lattimore says plainly, "The *Iliad* is not the story of Troy. Neither the beginning nor the end of the war is narrated in the [poem]. We begin in the tenth year of the siege (2.134) and we end, some weeks later, still in the twelfth year, with the city still untaken" (17).

18. The lines describing the allegorical figures of Hate, Confusion, and Death (535–38) also appear in the pseudo-Hesiodic *Shield of Hercules* (156–59) and may have been interpolated after Homer's time; see Willcock 271. But lines 539–40, which are not in

dispute, plainly refer to *nekrous . . . katatethnotas,* "the corpses of those who had fallen."

19. "In this configuration of image and narrative the possibility of the stationary, a fixity of position suggested by the Greek word *stasis,* is combined with the other sense of that word, 'discord, contest, division'" (Lynn-George 185). Lattimore renders line 533 as "These stood their ground and fought a battle," but according to Willcock, the verb for placing here is "always transitive" (271).

20. Some commentators believe the gold has been enameled (see Monro 352), but here as elsewhere in this passage on the work of a divine craftsman, Homer is significantly reticent about the details of the craftsman's technique.

21. I take this phrase from Bruce Kawin, who used it at a Faulkner symposium in 1978.

22. Byron echoes this turn in the Waterloo passage of *Childe Harold's Pilgrimage,* where his lament for the death of his cousin Frederick Howard in the recent slaughter there is accompanied by the recognition that the battlefield is reviving "With fruits and fertile promise, and the Spring" is once again contriving "her work of gladness" (*CHP* 3.267–68). But instead of simply turning from meditations on death to a celebration of renewal, Byron turns *back* to the ineradicable memory of loss.

23. The disputed line begins after the first part of line 604 of the received text and reads: "and a divine[ly inspired] minstrel, playing the lyre, was singing (*emelpeto*)." On the authenticity of this line see Taplin 20, note 27, and Willcock 272.

24. Though anciently attributed to Hesiod, which would date it about 700 B.C., this work has been disconnected from him by modern scholarship. Whoever wrote it, there are some striking similarities between the *Shield* and the Homer passage. Homer's account of the personified figures (Hate, Confusion, and Death) directing the slaughter in the passage on the city at war (18.535–38) closely resembles lines 153–58 of the *Shield;* the *Shield's* description of Lapiths and Centaurs fighting "even as if they were alive" (Hesiod line 59) echoes Homer's account of sculpted armies battling "like living men" (539); and on the shield of Hercules as on the shield of Achilles, the Ocean flows around the rim (Homer 18.607–8; *Shield* 315–16).

According to George Kurman, the *Shield of Hercules* displays three innovations that will later become widely adopted in ekphrastic poetry and that are only "hinted at" in Homer's epics: historicity, exemplified by "quasi-historical heroes such as Theseus and Perithous"; the "imminent quickening" of sculpted figures repeatedly said to appear "as though they were alive" (lines 189–90, 194–95, 242–43); and timelessness, manifested by chariot racers caught "in an unending toil, and the end with victory never came to them, and the contest was ever unwon" (lines 310–11) (Kurman 2–3). There is "no precedent" in Homer, says Kurman, for this "commentary on the power of art to illustrate history, create life, and frustrate time" (3). But Homer surely anticipates the comment on the life-creating power of art when he says that the fighting soldiers met "like living mortals" (quoted above), and as noted earlier, he does more than hint at the endlessness of sculpted combat when he writes of men "placing the battle" in language suggesting the erection of a statue. Significantly, Homer never tells us who won. As for historicity, it is admittedly missing from Homer's ekphrasis, but is no more than "hinted at" by the quasi-historical personages mentioned in the *Shield of Hercules.*

For an illuminating analysis of the *Shield* in light of ancient rhetorical theorizing about ekphrasis, see Becker, "Reading."

25. "The *idea* of the Shield of Aeneas," writes P. T. Eden, "unquestionably derives from Homer's Shield of Achilles" (163).

26. See Leach, *Virgil's Eclogues* 175 and Boyle 28.

27. See David Slavitt's very free translation of the third eclogue: "Every writer I know / hates other writers" (12).

28. On this point, writes Boyle, "the contrast with Theocritus's first idyll . . . is pointed and significant" (29).

29. Since we are told that in looking at the walls Aeneas fed his mind on an empty picture (*pictura . . . inani* [464]), the walls are evidently decorated with paintings rather than reliefs. Austin notes that Virgil would have known paintings such as those described here since "Trojan scenes (among them the dragging of Hector's body and Priam's ransoming) were found on the portico of Apollo's temple at Pompeii" (156).

30. In W. H. Auden's "The Shield of Achilles" (1952), we likewise see the handiwork of Hephaistos through the eyes of Thetis, who cries out in dismay at scenes of destitution, execution, and armies mindlessly massing on a barren plain. But Auden's poem is of course a drastic revision of Homer's passage on Achilles' shield.

31. Translations of Virgil are my own.

32. The bracketed "hic" can be understood as silently repeated from the previous line, "sunt hic etiam sua praemia laudi"—"here too are the rewards of fame."

33. The picture of Penthesilea clearly anticipates the description of Camilla entering battle with one side exposed for fighting ("unum exserta latus pugnae" [11.649]). "The Amazons," writes Austin, "traditionally kept the right breast uncovered, to leave the arm free" (165). Cf. Eugene Delacroix's *Liberty Leading the People* (1830), where Liberty appears as a woman holding up the tricolor in her right arm and fully exposing her right breast.

34. Priam is also a sorrowing figure, of course, and his outstretched hands supplicate Achilles just as the women supplicate Pallas. But the women are depicted as explicitly sorrowing—"tristes" (481). In the Homeric scene that stands behind this painting, Hecuba and a throng of noble women carry a robe to Athena and "with a wailing cry" lift up their hands to her (*Iliad* 6.301).

35. An oracle said that Troy could not be taken if Rhesus's horses cropped Trojan grass or drank from Trojan rivers, and legend testified that if Troilus lived to be twenty, Troy could not be taken (Austin 159–60).

36. "Solve metus; feret haec aliquam tibi fama salutem" (463). Literally, "Unbind your fear; this notoriety will bring you some security."

37. Lee Patterson observes that since the frescoes appear in Juno's temple to commemorate her triumph over her Trojan enemies, they promise no real *salus* to Aeneas, and they are empty—"inanes"—"because Aeneas empties them of their historical force by ignoring their commentary upon his own situation" (457). Yet if Aeneas fails to grasp what the pictures imply about the dangers that Carthage poses for him, he is nonetheless superbly qualified—as a key participant in the Trojan war—to turn the pictures into narrative. As Patterson himself notes, "his discourse . . . explicates the images on the temple walls by unfolding them into a narrative that makes available the meanings they encapsulate" (457).

38. The lines on Dido's entrance clearly imply that she has the power to deflect his fixated gaze:

> Haec dum Dardanio Aeneae miranda videntur,
> dum stupet obtutuque haeret defixus in uno,

regina ad templum, forma pulcherimma Dido,
incessit magna iuvenum stipante caterva.
(494–97)

While these [pictures] seem marvelous to the Trojan Aeneas,
while he is stunned and in one gaze clings fixed [to them],
the queen, the most beautifully formed Dido,
enters the temple with a great jostling mob of young people.

39. Virgil, says R. D. Williams, inherits a "strong Greek tradition that Troilus was ambushed when unarmed" (147).

40. Virgil's "inscribitur" is itself a word of borderline meaning. Though "inscribere" always meant "to write, "scribere" could mean either write *or* draw. (Horace, for instance, writes, "scribetur tibi forma et situs agri" [the form and site of the field will be drawn for you]). So Virgil's "inscribitur" might well be translated "is marked," which can mean written upon, drawn upon, or simply scored. To this extent the Latin lexicon supports Meltzer's suggestive argument that Virgil's epic and the frescoes represented in it both treat "'writing' as *the act of leaving a trace*" (54). But this does not mean that the difference between verbal and pictorial traces is "unessential," as Melzter says (54). Graphic as it is in evoking the picture of Troilus *in extremis,* Virgil's passage shows us how the *meaning* of Troilus's valedictory mark is constructed by words.

41. "The gaze," writes Patterson, "is one pole of a dialectic of which the other is some form of discursive exposition. The gaze implies a nostalgic evasion of understanding, a lowered state of consciousness that is figured by a trance-like stupor that must be broken, both to disarm its dangerous seductions and to unlock the riches its object contains" (458). But in light of this formula, what happens to Aeneas is singularly ironic: the gaze initiated by the seductive power of a painted image is broken by the still more seductive beauty of an actual woman who *prompts* the gazer to tell the story of what he has been gazing at.

42. W. J. T. Mitchell observes: "the treatment of the ekphrastic image as a female Other is a commonplace in the genre. One might argue, in fact, that female otherness is an overdetermined feature in a genre that tends to describe an object of visual pleasure and fascination from a masculine perspective. Since visual representations are generally marked as feminine (passive, silent, beautiful) in contrast to the masculine poetic voice, the metaphor goes both ways: the woman is 'pretty as a picture,' but the picture is also pretty as a woman" ("Ekphrasis" 701). Though there is not much pretty about the Carthaginian frescoes, it is clear that for Aeneas (until he meets Dido) they are at least as entrancing as a woman.

43. Since Daedalus is said to have worked in gold ("in auro" [32]), the scenes were presumably sculpted in relief on the walls.

44. After describing the sculptures, Virgil says that all the Trojans "would have read over them further with their eyes" ("protinus . . . / per*leg*erent oculis" [6.34]) if Achates had not returned with the Sybil.

45. Lines 29–30. Since Virgil uses the perfect tense for the main verb here ("resolvit"), these lines seem to comment on the history of the labyrinth rather than describing the painting of it (introduced in line 27).

46. In her appeal to Vulcan, Venus herself cites his response to this earlier request from "the daughter of Nereus" (8.383–84).

47. Venus's seduction of Vulcan recalls not only the Demodocan story of Ares and Aphrodite but also Hera's deception of Zeus, whom she seduces and overpowers with sleep so as to keep him from aiding the Greeks against the Trojans. To enlist the help of the god Sleep in this stratagem, she promises him that her son Hephaistos will make him a throne and a footstool (14.235–40). (My thanks to James Tatum for alerting me to Virgil's use of these Homeric episodes.)

48. The word "textum," which literally means something woven, was being figuratively used to denote verbal composition at least by the time of Quintilian in the first century A.D. It seems more than possible that Virgil was playing on the two meanings here.

49. Eden plausibly suggests that the scenes of battle and triumph are separated from all the preceding scenes by a broad band of ornamental sea like the Ocean River on the rim of Achilles' shield in the *Iliad* and of Hercules' shield in the *Shield of Hercules* (Eden 178). On the latter (though not on its rim) we also find dolphins swimming in a surging sea—two of them silver, like the "argenti claro delphines" circulating through Virgil's sea (Hesiod 209–12; *Aeneid* 8.673).

50. Eden notes that the actual ships at Actium could have had bronze only in their rams and prows (179).

51. Insofar as they recall the pair of serpents who kill Laocoon and his sons (2.203–27), the snakes signify the imminence of disaster, and they may specifically anticipate Cleopatra's suicide, though Eden notes that most other sources connect that with just one snake (186). But the combination of snakes, bellicosity, and femininity in the description of Cleopatra clearly ties her to Allecto—the Fury who, masquerading as a priestess of Juno, ignites Turnus's rage against the Trojans and thus sabotages their alliance with the Rutulians. Essentially, the whole of the Rutilian war against the Trojans is made to seem the product of female hysteria. Relentlessly hating the Trojans because of Paris's abduction of Helen, Juno cannot bear to see them prosper in Italy, or to see Aeneas marry Lavinia, daughter of the Rutulian king Latinus. So she summons Allecto to rouse Latinus's queen Amata against the marriage, and also to rouse Turnus against what is—in effect—a Trojan abduction of the woman previously promised to him. (Juno sees Aeneas as a second Paris—"alter Paris" [7.321]—whom she plans to destroy.) In making war on Rome, therefore, Cleopatra is reenacting the hysterical fury personified by Allecto.

52. Mars, shown raging in the middle of the fight ("medio in certamine" [700]), is clearly the *sculptor's* icon—a figure wrought in steel ("caelatus ferro" [701]) to embody allegorically the spirit of the battle. Likewise Actian Apollo, who is shown surveying the battle from above ("desuper") and pulling his bow to scatter Rome's enemies (704–5), is the sculptor's way of representing divine influence on the victory. But Neptune, Venus, and Minerva are icons brandished by the Roman navy, since the Egyptian gods are said to hold their weapons ("tela tenant") against ("contra") the Roman gods (699–700). Elsewhere on the shield, the scene depicting the procession of conquered races includes the rivers Euphrates, Rhine, and Araxes (726–28)—which must mean pictures or statues of personified river gods carried in the procession (Eden 191).

53. As Eden notes, the medieval use of adjacent panels to portray the life of a single person derives from Roman practice (179).

54. Since the new temple was actually dedicated on 9 October, 28 B.C., some fourteen months after Augustus's triumphal return (13–15 August, 29 B.C.), Virgil conflates two different events (Eden 190). At the same time, he strengthens the link between

Augustus and Aeneas, who vowed at Cumae that he would dedicate to Phoebus and Diana a temple of solid marble (6.69–70).

55. The snowy threshold ("niveo . . . limine") of the new temple depicted on the shield recalls the snowy tents ("niveis . . . velis") of Rhesus depicted at Carthage (1.469), but instead of signifying vulnerability, the whiteness now helps to create a picture of imperial magnificence.

56. According to Pliny the Elder, Augustus "surpassed all others" in the public display of pictures (327)—a gesture of already proven political impact. A century before Augustus's time, Lucius Hostilius Mancinus won a consulship by exhibiting and explaining in the Forum a picture of the storming of Carthage, in which he had played a leading part (Pliny 326).

57. See Shapiro 103. The daughter was Hypermestra, who spared her husband Lynceus and helped him to escape; on his return he killed Danaus and all the other daughters and with Hypermestra begot the royal line (*OCD*).

58. "If there be likeness to nature without any check of difference," writes Coleridge, "the result is disgusting, and the more complete the delusion, the more loathsome the effect. . . . You set out with a supposed reality and are disappointed and disgusted with the deception; whilst, in respect to a work of genuine imitation, you begin with an acknowledgement of total difference, and then every touch of nature gives you the pleasure of an approximation to truth" ("Poesy or Art" 256).

59. Teodolinda Barolini says that earlier in this canto, when Dante apostrophizes Rehoboam in response to "'l tuo segno" (12.47) ["your image" or "your sculpted sign"], he "establishes an identity between *res* and *signum* that reminds us that this is God's art, an art in which there is no gap between presentation and representation, is and as" (Barolini 47–48). But Dante's language makes the difference clear. However lifelike Rehoboam's *segno* might be, it is not the same as the man himself; if it were, all the figures said to be sculpted in the pavement here would have to be actually present in purgatory—which could hardly be true of such characters as Briareus (12.28–30) and Arachne (12.43–45).

60. Chaucer (who certainly knew the *Commedia*) may be suggesting this in the Prologue to the Wife of Bath's Tale, when the wife rhetorically asks, "Telle me also, to what conclusion / Were members maad of generacion, / And of so parfit wys a wight ywroght?" (115–17). If, as has been plausibly suggested, the word "wight" may be amended to "wright," the wife is asking why each human being was so perfectly made (or wrought) to be a maker.

61. Virgil may have picked up this sort of locution from Theocritus's first Idyll, where the goatherd describes a prize cup on which is carved—among other things—an old fisherman gathering up his net from a cast. "You would say," says the goatherd, "that he was fishing with all the strength of his limbs" (lines 37–38).

62. See also the *Argonautica* of Apollonius of Rhodes (also third century B.C.), where the designs said to be embroidered on Jason's cloak include Phrixus the Minyan conversing with his ram: "So vividly were they portrayed, the ram speaking and Phrixus listening, that as you looked you would have kept quiet in the fond hope of hearing some wise words from their lips" (Apollonius 56 [1.764–67]).

63. The prime source for this conception of Christ is of course the Gospel of John (1:1–15), but Chiampi aptly quotes Saint Ambrose's commentary on Luke: "And in the Gospel it is not voice which is seen; rather that which is superior to the voice, that is, the Word. . . . You realize therefore that the Word has been seen and together heard by

the Apostles. They have seen the Lord, not only in his body, but also in as much as Word; they have seen the Word, those who saw with Moses and Elijah, the glory of the Word. They have seen Jesus" (*Commentary on the Gospel according to Luke, Patrologia Latina,* ed. J. P. Migne [Paris, 1844–] 15:1535; trans. Chiampi 110).

64. It must be noted here that long before Dante, in the ekphrastic passages of his third-century A.D. *Imagines,* Philostratus the Elder elicits words from painted figures. Describing a painting of Hermes, Maia, and Apollo, he writes that Apollo "looks as though he were about to say to Maia: 'Your son whom you bore yesterday wrongs me; for the cattle in which I delight he has thrust into the earth, nor do I know where in the earth. Verily he shall be thrust down deeper than the cattle'" (Philostratus 103).

65. Barolini observes that this is the only use of "storiata" in the whole of the *Commedia* (47)—a fact which further underlines its significance. Dante's use of "istoria" here may have had some influence on Alberti, who makes it a key term in his *Della Pittura* of 1435–36, though Alberti's "istoria" means something closer to the expression of a theme than the telling of a story; see John R. Spencer's discussion in Alberti 23–28.

66. From an epigram of Theocritus in book 7 of the *Greek Anthology,* 262. See also Friedlander and Hoffleit, 9: "I am the column of Xenvares, son of Meixis, upon his grave" (600 B.C.).

67. "Seeing" 70–79. As Vickers notes, the base text for the story of Trajan and the widow—a *Vita Gregoria* by an anonymous monk of Whitby—indicates that Gregory learned of Trajan's action one day while examining the architecture of Trajan's forum, and on Trajan's column—the only significant part of his forum that remains—one relief shows a sitting Trajan looking down on a kneeling figure.

CHAPTER TWO

1. At the end of the story, the description of what Procne and Philomela finally become underscores the likelihood that Philomela's "purpureas . . . notas" are pictorial. Bloodstained from killing Tereus and metamorphosed into birds, they display on their breasts the marks of their brutal deed ("caedis / . . . notae" [669–70]), and their feathers are marked with blood ("signataque sanguine" [670]) in language recalling what Arachne delineated ("designat" [103]) to rival the pictures of Minerva. We shall see that Philomela's weaving is explicitly pictorial in Achilles Tatius's *Leucippe and Clitophon.*

2. On this point Joplin (58n) cites Page du Bois, *Centaurs and Amazons: Women and the Pre-History of the Great Chain of Being* (Ann Arbor: Univ. of Michigan Press, 1982) 78 and Herodotus's *History,* chapter 6.

3. See Frazer's note on Ovid's *Fasti* 2.629.

4. Joplin 49. This is actually true in only some versions of the story. Since Ovid clearly links the women's murder of the boy with degenerate Bacchanalian rites (6.587–600), the ending of the *Metamorphoses* version may well be misogynist, as Joplin argues (62n). But in the *Fasti,* which includes a different version, he treats the women no more censoriously than he treats Tereus, who was "duabus iniquus"—cruel to them both (2.629).

While writing this book, I recognized some essential features of the Philomela myth in *Thelma and Louise,* the 1991 movie written by Callie Khouri and directed by Ridley Scott. Louise's fatal shooting of the man who tries to rape her friend Thelma precipitates a long police hunt for them ending in a would-be perpetual flight: a final freeze-frame of the fleeing women in their car suspended in space over the Grand Canyon. Also, like

Philomela and Procne, Thelma and Louise are sometimes considered worse than the men who provoke them.

5. Aristotle quotes the phrase from *Tereus,* a lost play by Sophocles. See *Poetics* 1454a, line 36, in Aristotle 2:2328.

6. This sort of distinction is of course emphatically denied by Derrida, who takes all signifying activity as textual: "And thus we say 'writing' for all that gives rise to an inscription in general, whether it is literal or not and even if what it distributes in space is alien to the order of the voice: cinematography, choreography, of course, but also pictorial, musical, sculptural 'writing'" (*Grammatology* 9). Without some distinction between writing and depicting, however, we cannot understand or explain how the antagonism between them drives the *kind* of writing called ekphrasis.

7. This is not to say that literature typically gives women no voice at all. From the razor-tongued Wife of Bath to the irrepressibly garrulous Miss Bates (of Jane Austen's *Emma*), the female chatterbox is if anything a stock literary figure. But this figure is designed to provoke our censure and ridicule. In literature, a good woman is one who knows how to hold her tongue, as Penelope does in the *Odyssey* when Telemachus tells her not to complain about the songs she finds so painful to hear (1.325–64). In the first act of *King Lear,* two of the most vicious women ever put on a stage—Goneril and Regan—deliver speeches eloquent enough to win each of them a handsome portion of their father's kingdom, while (in our eyes, though not of course in Lear's) Cordelia demonstrates the sincerity of her love for him precisely by her incapacity to express it. At the end of the play, the sole point made by Lear's brief elegy for her is that she was a shining example of female reticence: "Her voice was ever soft, / Gentle, and low—an excellent thing in woman" (5.3.273–74). For an illuminating analysis of the various devices actually used in the England of Shakespeare's time to punish woman who talked too much, see Lynda E. Boose, "Scolding Brides and Bridling Scolds," *Shakespeare Quarterly* 42 (1991): 179–213.

8. Quoted from Plutarch's *Moralia* (346 f) by Jean Hagstrum (10), who also quotes Laurence Binyon as saying that "a precisely identical saying is proverbial among the Chinese" (Hagstrum 10n).

9. *Defense* 80. See also Sidney's passage on mimesis: "Poesy therefore is an art of imitation, for so Aristotle termeth it in the word *mimesis*—that is to say, a representing, counterfeiting, or figuring forth—to speak metaphorically, a speaking picture—with this end, to teach and delight" (79–80).

10. See Coolsen 2, citing Junius 237, 298, 262.

11. Coolsen 10 (note 23), citing Athenaeus, *Deiphnosophists* (circa A.D. 200), book 13, verse 590. Coolsen also cites John Lempriere's comment that this story concerned a different Phryne (*Classical Dictionary,* London 1809, under "Phryne"), but whether there were two Phrynes or one, the persuasive power of the accused Phryne would have depended on precisely the qualities that would make her pictorially appealing.

12. *Inst.* 6.1.32–33 in Quintilian 2:403. In light of this comment, it is striking to recall that prosecutors in the spring 1992 trial of four Los Angelos policemen charged in the beating of Rodney King relied so heavily on a videotape of the beating to speak for them that they lost their case.

13. In the typical European oil painting of the nude, writes John Berger, the principal protagonist is never painted. "He is the spectator in front of the picture and he is presumed to be a man. Everything is addressed to him. Everything must appear to be the result of his being there" (54). See also Michael Ann Holly, who defines gazing as "a

political issue. The person who does the looking is the person with the power" (395).

14. See Ovid, *Fasti* 2.41–43, and Livy, *Ab Urbe Condita* 1.57–60.

15. Even Helen has a distaff and a workbasket of yarn ready for spinning beside her when Telemachos finds her back in the house of Menelaos and chastising herself ("shameless me") for having provoked the Trojan war (4.131–34, 145–46). The figured weaving she did at Troy—a red robe depicting what Greeks and Trojans suffered there "for her sake" (3.128)—could be read as evidence of expiation or self-aggrandizement.

16. I owe these impressive statistics to William Anderson, quoted by Leach 102.

17. In the *Iliad* likewise, Athena's shield displays "the grim gigantic Gorgon, / A thing of fear and horror, portent of Zeus of the aegis" (5.741–42), and the same image is encircled in the very center of Agamemnon's shield (11.36–37). In his well-known essay on Medusa's head, Freud suggests that this horrifying image of serpentine locks projecting from an outraged face symbolizes the apotropaic effect of the exposed female genitals, exemplified by Rabelais's account of how the sight of a woman's vulva put the devil to flight (*Sexuality and the Psychology of Love* 212). This reading of the Medusa's head, of course, complements Freud's theory that the sight of a woman's genitals makes the male viewer fear castration—a fear accentuated by Medusa's flaunting of her phallic locks. But another reading emerges if we return to the moment at which Medusa was raped. Scandalized, no doubt, by the sight of Medusa's exposed genitals, "the daughter of Jove"—says Ovid—"turned away and covered her chaste face with her aegis" ("*aversa est et castos aegide vultus / nata Jovis texit*" [*Met.* 4.799–800]). Yet what she could not have failed to glimpse before doing so is the horrif*ied* face of a woman being raped. That is the expression shielded—but also covertly revealed—by the horrifying, petrifying face she has been made to assume.

18. Alfred Hoare's *Italian Dictionary* (Cambridge: Cambridge Univ. Press, 1915) defines "malefatta" as a "blunder made by an artisan in his work, *esp.* in weaving."

19. Matthew writes that Mary was to become a mother "through the influence of the Holy Spirit" (1:18–19), and according to John the Evangelist, John the Baptist testified that when he first saw Christ, he saw "the Spirit come down from heaven like a dove" (John 1:32). In a seventeenth-century *Annunciation* painted by the Master of the Barberini panels (National Gallery, Washington, repr. George Ferguson, plate 8), a dove directly hovering over the angel radiates threads of light to Mary's womb.

20. Catharine MacKinnon has argued that modern law on rape blurs this line by failing to make the woman's consent a necessary condition for legally permissible sexual intercourse. "The law of rape," she writes, "divides women into spheres of consent according to indices of relationship to men. Which category of presumed consent a woman is in depends upon who she is relative to a man who wants her, not what she says or does. These categories tell men whom they can legally fuck, who is open season and who is off limits, not how to listen to women. . . . Daughters may not consent; wives and prostitutes are assumed to, and cannot but. Actual consent or nonconsent, far less actual desire, is comparatively irrelevant" (175).

21. Joplin 44. She aptly cites Euripides' *Iphigenia in Aulis,* where the king's daughter is told that she will marry Achilles even as she is led to be literally sacrificed at the altar (lines 127–28, 134–35).

22. One of Chicago's anonymous readers rightly reminds me that *raptus* means both rape and abduction, and that rather than showing violent penetration, actual paintings usually signify rape by depicting abduction. Accepting these points, I will nonetheless

argue that in the novels of Longus and Achilles Tatius, descriptions of *imaginary* paintings representing rape combine with other verbal clues to expose the violence latent in sexual initiation.

23. Oothoon's conception of sexuality is so outrageously "open" that many critics have attacked it; for my own defense of it, see Heffernan, "Blake's Oothoon." A recent essay in *Lear's* likewise figures a woman's desire for intercourse as an expression of hospitality: "Inviting a man into your body," writes Mary Ellen Strote, "is a little like inviting a guest into your home" (36).

24. This second paragraph of this passage is from the translation of Thornley and Edmonds (Longus 7); the other paragraphs are from Winkler, "Education" 19–20 (first par.), 28 (third), 20 (fourth). Winkler's translation is very precise, but he translates only small portions of the text.

25. A further complication here is provided by the exegete mentioned at the end of the proem. As Winkler notes, the narrator "almost says that the following tale is a record of what the local tour guide told him" about the painting ("Education" 20). But since we hear no more of the exegete after the proem, his role is somewhat like that of the unnamed traveler in Shelley's "Ozymandias," who is represented only by his quoted description of the statue. Unlike Shelley's narrator, Longus's narrator sees the work of art for himself, but both need to see it also through the words of others—a fact which highlights the *mediated* quality of the reader's relation to both the statue and the painting.

26. Literature as well as visual art regularly requires inferences about both space and time. Though Lessing asserts that a poet "may, if he so chooses, take up each action at its origin and pursue it through all possible variations to its end" (23–24), Roman Ingarden aptly observes that "time-filling events are never represented in *all their phases*, regardless of whether it is a single event, consituting a whole, or a plurality of successive events." Represented time is therefore analogous to represented space, which can never be more than a segment—or set of segments—of real space. The gaps between the segments correspond to portions of space or time that are merely "corepresented," furnished or "taken as existing" by the reader's imagiantion (Ingarden 222–24, 237, 236–38).

27. See Bartsch 61. Among other things, the pomegranate is linked to the rape of Persephone, the virgin abducted by Pluto and returned to earth by Zeus, but compelled to spend part of each year in the underworld because she had eaten some pomegranate seeds while there.

28. Assuming that Achilles Tatius presupposes the reader's familiarity with Ovid's version of the Andromeda story (*Met.* 4.670–740), I use this version to help explain the context of the picture.

29. E. C. Harlan notes that "none of the known representations of Andromeda on the rock show her dressed as a bride." ("The Description of Paintings as a Literary Device and Its Application in Achilles Tatius," Ph.D. dissertation, Columbia University, 1965, quoted Bartsch 56–57). Bartsch suggests that Achilles Tatius adds this feature to connect the painting with the would-be sacrifice of Leucippe later, which Clitophon sees as a marriage to death (3.10.5; Bartsch 56–57). I agree, but I also believe—and argue—that the revival of Leucippe does not altogether break the links which this painting forges between marriage, sacrifice, and abduction.

30. Bartsch 69–70. The same is true of the sculpture group seen by Lucius in another well-known novel of the second century A.D.—Apuleius's *Golden Ass*. In Book the

Second, Lucius finds at Byrrhaena's house a marble statue of Diana rushing forward with her hunting dogs and backed by a grotto and stream where a horned Actaeon lurks, waiting for her to strip for her bath. In Book the Third, Lucius himself spies on Pamphile to see what magic she uses to change herself into a bird, takes some of her ointment in order to make himself a bird, and instead is turned into an ass. Thus, writes Page Dubois, "the elaborate statue, and the rhetorically devious description, provide a warning for Lucius and the reader about *curiositas*. . . . Apuleius's careful structuring of the *ekphrasis* presents, in an enclosed narrative, a predictive model for events that follow in the story" (Dubois 6–7). But the predictions made by the sculpture group of Diana and Actaeon are just partly fulfilled by what happens to Lucius, who is—among other things—eventually restored to his original shape.

31. From this point on in my own story of what happens to the myth of Philomela, I focus on England. For a recent study of what became of the myth in Renaissance Italy, see Jones, and for a broader treatment of Ovid's influence on European literature and art, see Martindale.

32. *Confessio Amantis* 7.5771–73 in Gower. In Chrétien de Troyes's twelfth-century version of the story, which was incorporated into the early fourteenth-century *Ovide Moralisé*, we are somewhat equivocally told that with variously colored threads Philomene portrayed ("portreite") what Tereus did to her and that all of it was written ("Tot ot escrit") on the cloth she sent to Progne (*Philomena* 1122–31).

33. I cite the text and line numbers of Chaucer's works from the edition of F. N. Robinson; see Works Cited, under Chaucer.

34. Caroline F. E. Spurgeon, *Five Hundred Years of Chaucer Criticism and Allusion, 1357–1900* (Cambridge, 1925) 1:146.

35. Part of the answer to this question could be that Diana is sometimes identified with Lucina, goddess of childbirth. Though she is represented in the temple as a huntress with bow and arrows seated on a hart, sculpted before her is the image of a women long in labor calling anxiously on Lucina for help (2075–86). But Emelye appeals to her strictly as the "goddesse of maydens" (2300).

36. Palamon has nothing to say either, but since he is finally getting the woman he wants, we know exactly what his silence means.

37. Hulse speaks of the picture as a mosaic (*Metamorphic Verse* 112), but since we are told that "underneath this radiant floure" was a statue of Danae—along with, presumably, statues of the other figures mentioned after her (141–56)—it is hard to tell for certain just what medium of depiction Marlowe is describing.

38. Iris was sometimes said to be the wife of Zephyrus, god of the West Wind (*OCD*); her affair with Zeus may have been Marlowe's invention.

39. This is only a guess. Since Silvanus was sometimes identified with Pan (*OCD*), Marlowe may have imagined the metamorphosis of Cyparissus (the lovely boy) as the syrinx-like consequence of Silvanus's pursuit of him. But in Ovid's version of the boy's story, he is beloved of Apollo, who turns him into a tree at his own request so that he can mourn the death of a stag he has accidentally killed (*Met.* 10.106–42).

40. Keach 93. He also points out that Hero's elaborate costume in the opening passage includes "a myrtle wreath" (1.17) and "sparrowes" (1.33), which specifically evoke Venus's erotic power (Keach 94).

41. "The cosmos these lovers uncover," writes Hulse, "is a purely physical and self-generative universe of Empedoclean strife." In Marlowe's poem, therefore, "the two

universal forces of Love and Strife, one creative and one destructive, are identical" (*Metamorphic Verse* 122).

42. Hero herself strives to preserve her virginity on her first night with Leander when he "clung" her body to his own: "She, fearing on the rushes to be flung, / Striv'd with redoubled strength: the more she strived, / The more a gentle pleasing heat revived," but she nonetheless "sav'de her maydenhead" (2.66–76). Since Leander's gripping of Hero also recalls Neptune's momentary seizing of *him* in his swim across the Hellespont (2.158–60), we could say that the passage just quoted completes his transformation from prey to predator.

43. Pyrocles disguises himself as the Amazon Zelmane, his former mistress, who resembles Philoclea (Sidney 78–80). In consequence, as Hulse observes, Pyrocles "becomes perfectly specular, utterly mimetic, projecting onto his beloved the image of his desires, and onto himself the image of his beloved. He embodies the artistic double gaze, for when he sees himself he sees his beloved, and when he sees her, he sees himself. This is the circularity of an aesthetic subjectivity with no bottom, no ground of resolution" (*Rule* 150).

44. Pyrocles' actions exemplify this formula even when—in his encounter with Zoilus—his female disguise makes him the *object* of male desire (459–60). The very fact that Zoilus's sexual overtures goad Pyrocles to kill him shows how fiercely unwilling he is to *be* sexually desired.

45. Britomart is passionately seeking the man represented by an image she has seen in a crystal mirror: an image of the "comely knight" Arthegall dressed in armor that is not only decorated with gold but inscribed "*Achilles armes, which Arthegall did win*" (3.2.25). Arthegall's capture of these arms presumably has something to do with the legend that the British race was founded by a Trojan named Brute (3.9.38–51), but in any case, the image of Arthegall is said to be dressed in arms that must include Achilles' shield, object of the first major exercise in ekphrastic representation. Could Britomart's quest for this man obliquely signify Spenser's own desire to revive and regenerate the ancient art of ekphrasis?

46. Paul Alpers suggests that the light wounding of Britomart is "in the mode of the Venus and Adonis tapestries," which are characterized by "pastoral prettiness" (377–78). But the further link with the would-be victim of the rapist—which Alpers does not note—gives the wound a deeper meaning and helps to explain, I believe, why Britomart reacts to her wound so fiercely, terrifying her attackers with her "flaming sword" (3.1.66).

47. See also the description of an arching vine in which grapes made of burnished gold are said to have been placed among real grapes that look like gems such as rubies and emeralds (2.12.54–55). "The artificial," writes Giamatti, "infects all around it with its artificiality. The real grapes, compared to gems, suddenly acquire an artificial quality which is increased when they are juxtaposed with the truly artificial gold grapes" (272). Likewise, the fountain in the midst of the bower is decorated with a trail of ivy made from colored gold as well as with statues or reliefs of "naked boyes" playing and bathing while two real damsels are bathing nude around the fountain (2.12.60–63).

The ivory of the gate, furthermore, recalls the ivory used for one of the two gates of the house of Morpheus (1.1.40), which in turn recalls the old Homeric legend that deceptive dreams emerge from an ivory gate while gates of horn disgorge dreams that come true (*Odyssey* 19.562–67; cf. *Aeneid* 6.893–96).

48. I recall an anecdote that Stanford White, the architect, once saw a workman fall off the stern of a tugboat right into the blades of the screw propeller. As blood and oil floated to the surface, White said, "Poor devil," and then "God, what color."

49. "The gods," writes Harry Berger, "are assaulted by their desire as if it were a hostile force over which they have no control" (175).

50. The only death of a male mentioned in the description of the tapestries is that of Hyacinth (3.11.37), killed—like Coronis—by Apollo's "haplesse hand." But unlike Coronis, Hyacinth was the victim of pure accident (he was struck in the face when Apollo's discus bounced up at him as he tried to retrieve it [*Met.* 10.178–85]).

51. Earlier in book 2, Arachne herself spreads her "subtile net" high over the Cave of Mammon (2.7.28).

52. In Ovid, the victory that Pallas represents herself as achieving in her dispute with Neptune is undercut by her loss to Arachne in the weaving context; Arachne also has the advantage of going second, and thus surpassing what's just been done. In Spenser, Pallas follows Arachne and outdoes *her* with the butterfly. So Spenser's Pallas enjoys a double victory: a victory over Neptune in the event she represents, and a victory over Arachne in the representational medium itself.

53. The Busirane episode concludes the first three books of *The Faerie Queene,* which were finished by December 1589 and published early in the next year; *Muiopotmos* was "probably composed in 1590" and published in 1591 ("Editor's Note[s]," Spenser 426, 484).

54. The question of whether or not Amoret's feelings on her wedding day can explain the tortures described in the final canto of book 3 is complicated by the fact that Spenser makes no reference to the wedding until the beginning of book 4. Since that appeared in 1596, six years after the publication of the first three books, Paul Alpers dismisses the notion that the wedding and tortures are causally linked: "Obviously," he writes, Spenser "thought Book III was intelligible by itself" and set out to explore "new, though related issues" in book 4 (110). But whatever Spenser intended in 1590, his later account of Amoret's abduction from the wedding feast, together with the new ending of book 3 (where the lovers' ecstatic reunion is replaced by their continued separation), surely invite us to reread his account of the tortures. Additionally, the sense of psychic invasion that Krier links with the public exposure of a wedding feast sheds further light on the intimations of rape that we have seen in descriptions of the wedding night in the ancient Greek novel. Krier aptly cites George Puttenham's observation that the music and uproar made by well-wishers outside the bedchamber of a newly married couple are commonly meant to overwhelm the "skreeking and outcry of the young damosell" (*The Arte of English Poesie* 1.26, cited Krier 190n).

55. Krier notes that Spenser's work in general makes the human body—not just the female body—vulnerable to invasion and wounding (Krier 124). But the female body is the chief object of invasion in book 3 of the *Faerie Queene.*

56. Berger says that Busirane "dips his pen . . . to inscribe the charms which bind Amoret," and thereby recalls "the influence of bards and rhymers in the masque" (184n; cf. 3.12.5). Since Spenser himself says of Busirane that "with living bloud he those characters wrate" (3.12.31), Berger's point is well taken. But just as Ovid's "notas" can mean either graphic signs or verbal ones, Spenser's use of both "figuring" and "wrate" to indicate what Busirane does with Amoret's blood suggests that the "straunge characters of his art" are at least in part pictorial, perhaps glyphic. The specimens of the art sponsored

NOTES TO PAGES 75–78

by Busirane that we have seen up this point—the tapestries and the mask—are highly pictorial.

57. My colleague Jonathan Crewe suggestively observes that in getting Lavinia to write, "Marcus and Titus . . . shift her into a 'medium' in which her plight will be reappropriated for their revenge, and ultimately for the restoration of (masculine) Roman order" (personal note to the author).

58. In George Pettie's "Tereus and Progne" (1576), Philomela herself becomes largely a writer: "she wrought and imbrodred cunningly in cloath the whole discourse of her course and carefull case" (50) and when she gave it to a passing gentleman for delivery to her sister, on it "was plainly written, to whom it should be delivered, and from whom" (51).

59. In *Titus,* Lavinia is briefly compared to Lucrece (4.1.61–64).

60. The painting, writes Maus, "seems to yearn for the missing dimension of temporality" (81).

61. The slightly ambiguous syntax probably results from the demands of meter and accentuation, which make "Helen's rape" fit Shakespeare's line better than "the rape of Helen." But given Lucrece's later denunciation of "the strumpet that began this stir" (1471), we might well construe Helen as in some sense a rapist herself: the person ultimately responsible for the Grecian rape of Troy.

62. Her impulse to tear Helen's beauty recalls her self-laceration just after the rape: "She desperate with her nails her flesh doth tear" (739). Later, tearing the painted image of Sinon, she compares him to the treacherous man "whose deed hath made herself herself detest" (1566).

63. Nancy Vickers argues that Collatine's praise of Lucrece is in the mode of "blazon," which was "first, a codified heraldic description of a shield, and, second, a codified description of an object praised or blamed by the rhetorician poet" ("This Heraldry" 213). Vickers aptly notes that while Ovid and Livy (Shakespeare's sources) both trace Tarquin's lust to the sight of Lucrece, Shakespeare's Tarquin is first goaded by Collatine's rhetoric ("This Heraldry" 213). But fine as it is, Vickers's argument fails to distinguish between what Collatine says about Lucrece (lines 11–21) and what the narrator says about the face actually seen by Tarquin (lines 50–70).

64. "The insistently visual coding of Lucrece in the first 575 lines as one who is seen but does not see, who is seen but not heard, can hardly be overemphasized" (Kahn, "*Lucrece*" 144–45). Commenting on what he calls the "sleepwatch" in art, Leo Steinberg notes that nearly all pictures showing a watcher observing a sleeper tip the balance firmly in favor of the watcher: "Whether the intrusion is tender or murderous, the one caught napping, victim or beneficiary, is the butt of the action. Sleep is the opportunity of the intruder" (99). See also Steiner, *Pictures* 47, 76–77.

65. On this point see Steiner, *Pictures,* chapter 2. The process by which gazing becomes a desire for sexual possession is wittily exemplified by a passage in Keats's *Eve of St. Agnes,* where the hero begs

> All saints to give him sight of Madeline
> But for one moment in the tedious hours,
> That he might gaze and worship all unseen;
> Perchance speak, kneel, touch, kiss—in sooth such things have been.
> (78–81)

66. We are later told that Sinon's treacherous words "like wildfire burnt the shining glory / Of rich-built Ilion" (1522–23). Lucrece herself, as she stands before the painting, yearns to quench with her tears "Troy that burns so long" (1468) and denounces Sinon for using false tears to burn it (1548–61).

67. The statue of Venus in *The Knight's Tale* (1955–66) is likewise described as a naked lady "fleytnge in the large see" and accompanied by the same iconographic signs—the doves, the garland of roses, and blind Cupid.

68. Since the narrator shortly tells us that he saw Aeneas's wife Creusa and his two sons fleeing Troy "with drery chere" (179), the word "chere" by itself tells very little.

69. See Kolve, "Chaucer" 304–6 and Bridges 155.

70. *Republic* 10.598–603 in Plato 1:855–601.

71. Philostratus 17, cited by Hulse (*Metamorphic Verse* 182); the parallel was first noted by Gombrich (*Art and Illusion* 211). A comparable passage appears in Richard Haydocke's translation of *A Tracte Containing the Artes of Curious Paintinge Carving & Building*, published in 1598 (four years after the publication of *Lucrece*), where Paolo Lomazzo notes with admiration "how on a flatte surface hee [the painter] can expresse three or fowre men one behinde another, yea a whole army, and a whole Province" (Lomazzo f. A ii verso).

72. In this instance Shakespeare's narrator fails to mention the sort of iconographic signs that Chaucer's narrator enumerates in describing the portrait of Venus. On the mechanism of projection, which Gombrich finds exemplified by Shakespeare's passage, see Gombrich 211–222.

73. Pliny 35.40.129, quoted by Alberti (73).

74. Her conclusion, as Katherine Eisaman Maus notes, is "patently false but entirely characteristic. . . . What she cannot tolerate is the possibility that there are no constants, that the relationship between body and soul is simply arbitrary" (72).

75. Quoted by Farmer (24), who also cites Castiglione's remark that cosmetic artifice is used by "the most wanton and dishonest women in the world" (*The Book of the Courtier*, trans. Thomas Hoby [London: J. M. Dent, 1928] 39). In his *Painting of the Ancients* (1637), Franciscus Junius quotes from Agellius's critique of the sophists: "Adorne any thing purely and soberly and it shall grow better and better; daube it over on the contrary with the painting colour of women, and it shall resemble a jugglers delusion" (Junius 117).

76. When Hamlet finds Ophelia reading a book of devotions while also (he may suspect) throwing herself in his way, he says: "I have heard of your paintings well enough. God hath given you one face, and you make yourselves another" (3.2.139–40). Cf. also Hamlet on Yorick's skull: "Where be your gibes now, your gambols, your songs, your flashes of merriment that were wont to set the table on a roar? Not one now to mock your own grinning? Quite chap-fall'n? Now get you to my lady's chamber, and tell her, let her paint an inch thick, to this favor she must come" (5.1.167–72).

77. Quintilian likewise argues that "the picture of a captured town" may be more moving than "the mere statement," but the context makes it clear that he means a *verbalized* picture designed to move "hearers" (Quintilian 8.3.67–68). Tarquin himself seems to regard both words *and* images equally powerless against the force of desire. Dismissing his own scruples about the rape before committing it, he says to himself, "Who fears a sentence or an old man's saw / Shall by a painted cloth be kept in awe" (244–45). The painted cloth, says Charlton Hinman in a note to this passage, is "a hanging painted with biblical or moral texts and illustrations" (Shakespeare 1422).

78. First printed in quarto in 1603, *Hamlet* was evidently written some years after *Lucrece,* but as early as 1601 Gabriel Harvey linked the two when he opined that both works "have it in them, to please the wiser sort" (*The Reader's Encyclopedia of Shakespeare,* ed. O. J. Campbell [New York: Crowell, 1966], quoted Maus 66).

79. I am considerably condensing the fine and complex argument made in Levin 141–62.

80. A few other examples: Looking through the curtains of Lucrece's bed, Tarquin is like a "grim lion fawn[ing] o'er his prey" (421); brandished over her, his blade is "like a falcon tow'ring in the skies" that with the mere shade of his wings terrifies the fowl below (506–7); at the moment of the rape he becomes a "wolf [seizing] . . . his prey" while "the poor lamb cries" until silenced by the "white fleece" of her own nightgown (677–79); and after the rape he is like a "full-fed hound or gorged hawk" (694).

81. This reverse metaphor, however, is nowhere made explicit in Shakespeare's text. The closest we come to it is in the description of Tarquin making his way to Lucrece: "the locks between her chamber and his will, / Each one by him enforced retires his ward" and "each unwilling portal yields him way" (302–3, 309). As Fineman suggests, this overcoming of resistance to penetration can certainly be read as an image of rape (40–41). It can also be linked to what Kahn sees as an equally clear image of rape in book 2 of the *Aeneid:* Virgil's account of the Greeks invading the inmost chambers of Priam's palace, forcing apart hinges, chopping through panels, and making huge openings (Virgil 2.479–82; Kahn, "*Lucrece,*" 156). But while Virgil's account of the fall of Troy is generally considered Shakespeare's source for his description of the painting, the latter makes no reference to specifically penetrative violence.

82. Shortly afterwards she tells her father and Collatine: "Mine enemy was strong, my poor self weak" (1646).

83. Kahn 146–47. Though Vesta is a virgin goddess, she is—as Kahn observes— "identified with the hearth fire, prime symbol of family life" (146). But it must be noted that neither Ovid nor Shakespeare explicitly mentions the hearth; they tell us simply that Lucrece was found spinning with her maids (*Fasti* 2.741–43; Argument of *The Rape of Lucrece* [Shakespeare 1419]).

84. What Fineman calls "the smirky collation of Lucrece's mouth with her vagina" (43) makes raping and silencing here virtually identical. See also Kahn 149.

CHAPTER THREE

1. A possible exception is the ancient Greek *Shield of Hercules,* where—as noted earlier—the chariot racers sculpted on the shield are said to be "engaged in unending toil, and the end with victory never came to them, and the contest was ever unwon" (lines 310–11). But the frustration of this "timeless striving," as Kurman calls it (3) is quite different from the timelessness of an arrested pose or the transcendent "calm" of a moment "caught from fleeting time." I must add, however, that the immortalizing power of painting *is* recognized in the poetry of the Italian Renaissance, as Anne Palladino has shown.

2. On the continuing relation between violence and art, specifically public art, see W. J. T. Mitchell, "The Violence of Public Art: *Do the Right Thing*" (*Critical Inquiry* 16 [1990]: 880–99).

3. "Had the painters of [Renaissance] Italy produced such expressions as those of the Ajax and Medea," writes Webb, "the wits of that country, would not have been wanting in doing them justice. I may perhaps, appear too general, when I include even Raphael

in this observation; but if you reflect, you will find, that his expressions are more ad-dressed to the understanding than the passions: They are more to be admired for their variety than force; they have little, either of the pathetic or sublime; and the images which they leave in the mind, slip from it, almost as hastily, as the picture from the eye. It is not so with the paintings of Timomachus and Aristides; the impressions we receive from them strike full upon the soul; they dilate it, like the bursts in the musick of Boranello; they agitate, they rouze it, like the symphonies of Yeomelli: Such expressions, (as was observed of the eloquence of Pericles) leave stings behind them" (Webb 167–68).

4. In 1592, Samuel Daniel assures Delia that "this picture" will "remaine thy lasting monument" (sonnet 34 of *Delia* in Lucy Gent, *Picture and Poetry, 1560–1620* [Leamington: James Hall, 1981] 141), but he refers to the verbal picture he himself is composing in his sonnets. The portrait Marvell commissions in his "Last Instructions" (1667) is likewise a purely rhetorical construct.

5. In Lovelace's poem on Peter Lely's *Charles I and the Duke of York* (1647), Lely is said to have represented the men's thoughts and feelings so well "that th'amazed world shall henceforth find / None but my *Lilly* ever drew a *Minde*" (quoted Farmer 57). Dryden uses similar terms to praise portraits by Anne Killigrew and Sir Godfrey Kneller. In painting James II, he writes, Killigrew's "hand call'd out the Image of his Heart / His Warlike Mind, his Soul devoid of Fear" ("To Anne Killigrew" 130–31); and of Kneller's portraits in general Dryden says: "Thy Pictures think, and we Divine their Thought" ("To Sir Godfrey Kneller" 72).

6. *Liberty* 4.141–206. Below I compare Thomson's account of the ancient sculp-tures with Byron's treatment of them in *Childe Harold's Pilgrimage*.

7. Lessing 20. Lessing was hardly the first to say that visual art could represent just one moment, for as shown by the record of a discussion at the French Academy in 1667, this point had been made long before *Laocoon* appeared (see Lee 62). But the idea that art *perpetuates* a moment of time in spatial form is essential to Lessing's distinction be-tween literature and the visual arts, and he is the first, I believe, to give it leading importance.

8. Essentially, the public museum was born in the eighteenth century. "In 1723, 1749, and 1772," writes Philip Fisher, "the Vatican collections were opened. The Sloane Collection, later called the British Museum, opened in London in 1759. In 1781 in Vienna all court-owned pictures were opened to the public three days a week, and, as a climactic act, the founding of the Louvre was decreed July 27, 1793" (Fisher 7). Fisher's new book is a comprehensive study of a topic that I merely consider in this chapter and the next: the cultural impact of the museum. I regret that Fisher's book came to my attention only after I had written nearly all of this one.

9. I accept Ian Jack's argument that Keats composed his urn from a variety of sources: neo-Attic vases, the Elgin Marbles, and the paintings of Claude Lorraine; see Jack 217–19.

10. Lord Elgin bought the marbles—fragments of Parthenon sculptures already damaged by the Turkish attack on Greece—in 1801–3, when the Turks occupied Greece. The question of whether he thus preserved the fragments from further deterio-ration or took unfair advantage of an occupied country is still debated. Byron called the marbles "the last poor plunder from a bleeding land" (*Childe Harold's Pilgrimage* 2.114).

11. Fifteen are sonnets appearing in *PW* 3:6, 36–37, 40, 50, 51, 53–55, 183–84, 225, 275, and 4:18. For the others see *PW* 3:176, 198–200, 229–31, and *PW* 4:120–25, 126, 159–60, 229–31, 320.

12. To some extent, however, Wordsworth's sonnet echoes Rousseau's *Essay on the Origin of Languages*, where the historical movement from pictures to languages is defined as a process of cultural ascent. "The depicting of objects," says Rousseau, "is appropriate to a savage people; signs of words and of propositions, to a barbaric people; and the alphabet to civilized peoples" (quoted Derrida, *Grammatology* 294).

13. "And in this," Robinson adds, "he is, beyond all doubt, right" (letter to Barron Field in W. Knight, *Life of William Wordsworth* [Edinburgh, 1839] 2:296, quoted Shackford 72).

14. Besides "Peele Castle," the poems illustrated were "Lucy Gray" in 1815, *The White Doe* in 1815, and *Peter Bell* in 1819. The four frontispieces then reappeared in the four volumes of 1820.

15. It may be theoretically possible to distinguish between the speaker of this poem and the poet himself, but since I know no way of defining the space between the two in this instance, I treat them as one.

16. This is precisely what Wordsworth does in the first of three sonnets he composed in 1818 that were—as the title plainly announces—"suggested" by William Westall's watercolors of Yorkshire caves (*PW* 3:36–37). With no reference to any picture, he apostrophizes the "pure element of waters" that Westall depicted.

17. Levinson argues that Wordsworth's idealized memory of Peele Castle represents the "golden days" of the French Revolution while Beaumont's stormy picture represents its destructiveness (120). This is plausible enough provided we bear in mind that Wordsworth's sojourn near the Castle came *after*, not before, the Terror had run its course. Since he learned of Robespierre's death in the early days of his visit (Pinion 18), and since we know from the *Prelude* that this news led him to believe in the imminence of "golden times" (1805 10.541), his idealized memory of the Castle might well be read as a picture of his temporarily revived faith in the beauty of the Revolution.

18. See Yates 28. According to legend, the locational system of memory was discovered by Simonides, whose famous dictum on painting and poetry I have already discussed.

19. In the painting he would have made, the castle would "have seemed a treasure-house divine / Of peaceful years." For more on Wordsworth's habit of associating memory with places and buildings, see Kerrigan.

20. Now in the National Gallery, the picture belonged to George Beaumont in Bowles's time and was well known to Wordsworth, who comments on it at length in a letter to Beaumont of 28 August 1811 (*Letters* 2:506). Given Wordsworth's friendship with Beaumont, his knowledge of the Rubens landscape, and his admiration for Bowles's sonnets, which are said to have "delighted" him when he read them in 1789 even as they deeply impressed Coleridge (see Greever 21, Pinion 8, and Coleridge, *BL* 1:13–17), it seems more than likely that he knew Bowles's *The Picture*.

21. The picture Wordsworth writes about, which I have not seen and have so far been unable to identify, was given to Wordsworth by Beaumont himself sometime before 28 August 1811, when Wordsworth sent him the sonnet. Wordsworth's recorded comments on the poem, together with the letter to Beaumont that accompanied it, indicate that its details include smoke and a band of travelers (both mentioned in the

poem), but "the rest were added," Wordsworth wrote, "in order to place the thought in a clear point of view, and for the sake of variety" (*Letters* 2:506–7).

22. See also his "Lines Suggested by a Portrait from the Pencil of F. Stone," composed 1834 (*PW* 4:120–24), where he writes of "Art divine, / That both creates and fixes, in despite / Of Death and Time, the marvels it hath wrought" (76–78). Wordsworth's faith in the immortality of painting clearly withstood what Italian works showed him of its mortality. In a letter to Haydon of 8 April 1842 he observed: "As to the comparative durability of Fresco and oil one thing is clear that in some situations, Fresco seems very perishable in others almost immortal. The deservedly celebrated Auroras of Guido, at Rome, seemed to my eye as fresh as yesterday; while other things in the same City had faded almost to perishing" (*Letters: Later Years* 3:1123).

23. See also Alberti's comment on Narcissus as the inventor of painting, quoted in chapter 4, p. 176.

24. In the myth of Cupid and Psyche, which is perhaps the oldest story of sleep-watching we have, the gazer is female. But in gazing on the sleeping Cupid she violates his command, and when she accidentally awakens him, she is punished (see Apuleius 121–23). The myth suggests that gazing—specifically gazing on a sleeping man—is an activity denied to women, or at least to any mortal woman, which is what Psyche is when she does her gazing. (On Diana's viewing of the sleeping Endymion, see below.)

25. Here, for instance, are the opening lines of Anacreon's Ode 28:

> Painter, by unmatch'd desert
> Master of the Rhodian art,
> Come, my absent Mistress take
> As I shall describe her.

Quoted from *Anacreon: With Thomas Stanley's Translation,* ed. A. H. Bullen (London: E. Bullen, 1893) in Osborne 79. There is a delicious pun on "take" in this translation which evokes—no doubt unwittingly—the story of what happened when Alexander asked Apelles to paint one of his most beautiful concubines in the nude: the painter fell in love with her, and Alexander gave her to him (Pliny the Elder, *Natural History*, book 25, chapter 10; p. 332 of John F. Healey's trans.). Significantly, the painter addressed in Anacreon's ode is allowed to see and "take" the poet's "absent Mistress" only through the medium of the poet's words.

26. As Osborne shows, advice-to-a-painter poems could be anacreontic, lyrical, historical, political, panegyric, satiric, or parodic (9–11). From 1640 to 1846 at least ninety advice-to-a-painter poems were written by poets including—besides Waller and Marvell—Ben Jonson, Swift, Cowper, Elizabeth Barret Browning, and Dickens (Osborne 36–77).

27. Ode 17 in Thomas Moore, *Odes of Anacreon. Translated into English Verse. With Notes* (London: John Stockdale, 1800), quoted Osborne 80.

28. Here I differ from Marjorie Levinson, who argues that Wordsworth's account of what he would have painted simply repeats his description of what he claims to remember seeing (107). What he remembers seeing is already idealized, as she suggests. But with the important exception of the line that eroticizes the memory-picture—the line about the castle's form sleeping on the glassy sea—the opening description is chiefly couched in terms used literally, such as "pure," "quiet," and "trembled."

29. "On a Landscape of Gaspar Poussin" in *The Complete Poetical Works of Robert Southey* (New York: Appleton, 1846) 146. In a note on "So fair, so sweet, withal so

sensitive," Wordsworth writes of this poem and one other as "beautiful effusions of poetic sentiment" (*PW* 4:125).

30. Bowles's language here strongly suggests another painting, Joseph Wright's *The Old Man and Death* (first exhibited 1774), where Death appears to the astonished man as a tall skeleton against a background formed by an overgrown ruin and a blasted tree. First exhibited in London in 1774, the painting was also on display there in 1801, when it was put up for sale (*Romantic Art* 70–71).

31. Bowles here echoes a passage from Coleridge's "Fears in Solitude, Written in April 1798, During the Alarm of an Invasion" (published 1798):

> may the vaunts
> And menace of the vengeful enemy
> Pass like the gust, that roared and died away
> In the distant tree: which heard, and only heard
> In this low dell, bowed not the delicate grass.
>
> (198–202)

Though Coleridge himself conspicuously acknowledged his debt to Bowles, as I have already noted, it is not generally recognized that Bowles may have owed something to him.

32. Burke treats the soft, smooth, undulating figure of a woman as a prime example of beauty (115), and to help illustrate the difference between the beautiful and the sublime he contrasts the lovable submissiveness of an indulgent mother with the fearful authority of a father (111–13).

33. Besides the small oil that I have reproduced as figure 2, Beaumont painted a larger oil of Peele Castle that is now in the Leicester Museum and Art Gallery. According to Jonathan Wordsworth et al., the small version is "probably" the one behind Wordsworth's poem (231).

34. "I know of nothing sublime," wrote Burke, "which is not some modification of power" (64). Drawing on Burke in his own uncompleted essay on the sublime (written 1811 or later), Wordsworth wrote that in the presence of the sublime, the mind is "conscious of external Power at once awful & immeasurable" (*Prose* 2:354).

35. For a full treatment of how Madeline and Porphyro liberate each other from enthralled gazing in this poem, see Steiner's *Pictures of Romance* 56–90.

36. Some critics (e.g., Claude Lee Finney, *The Evolution of Keats's Poetry* [Cambridge: Harvard Univ. Press, 1936] 1:391) have found an echo of "Elegiac Stanzas" in Keats's "To J. H. Reynolds, Esq." (written 25 March 1818), where at one point the poet describes himself as reading one evening on the rocky shore of a quiet sea and yet seeing "into the core / Of an eternal fierce destruction" in its depths (87–105). This passage strikes me as anticipating Melville or Conrad rather than echoing Wordsworth, but in any case, the cruelty of nature—its theme—is at most a subordinate theme of Wordsworth's poem.

37. Scott, "Seduced" 86. Scott aptly suggests that critics' attempts to make the ending coherent by supplying connectives between its parts are so many efforts "to 'restore' the work, as if it were indeed one of the busts in Elgin's collection" (87).

38. Though the speaker's gender is nowhere explicitly signaled, I believe it may be taken as male in the absence of any clues that it differs from the poet's gender. But the question of how we construe and construct the gender of the speaker in *any* poem deserves further study.

39. *Metamorphoses* 6.533–48. Prior to this impassioned speech, Philomela puts her arms around her father's neck to gain his consent to Procne's request that Philomela visit her (475–77), but we learn nothing of what Philomela said at this point, if she spoke at all.

40. In Blake's *America* likewise, the virgin daughter of Urthona is "dumb" until Orc "assay[s] his fierce embrace" (1.10) and thus provokes her to cry out at this violent initiation into what she calls the "eternal death" of generative life (2.17).

41. As Helen Vendler observes, Keats first assumes that this work "tells us a story" (*Odes* 118).

42. It is difficult if not impossible to say who or what makes the final statement of the poem: "that is all / Ye know on earth, and all ye need to know." Though Stillinger follows the 1820 edition of Keats's poems in placing quotation marks around "Beauty . . . beauty," no quotation marks enclose these words in the first two extant texts of the poem—Charles Brown's transcript of it and the version published in *Annals* (Stillinger 470). Nevertheless, since all three versions of the last two lines punctuate "Beauty . . . beauty" and "that is all" as two separate *statements,* and since the urn is unequivocally the source of the first one, I focus on that.

43. This slightly ambiguous passage means either that the beadsman's spirit falters *when* he thinks of their pain or (more probably) that his spirit simply cannot imagine what they feel. Either way, the moment we imagine any sort of consciousness within the effigies we must also imagine them in pain.

44. As Kenneth Burke notes, the urn's statement contradicts the far more readily defensible assertion that beauty is *not* truth (447). This contrary point is explicitly made by the sixth stanza of "Ode to a Nightingale" (written about the same time as the "Urn"), where the seeming beauty of a death accompanied by the bird's orgasmic serenade ("pouring forth [her] soul abroad / In such an ecstasy") is brutally crushed by the final lines: "Still wouldst thou sing, and I have ears in vain—/ To thy high requiem become a sod."

45. Nancy Goslee argues that Keats uses the contrast between sculpturesque and picturesque to symbolize the opposition between the timeless, objective serenity of classic culture and the restless, time-bound subjectivity of modern or "romantic" culture (5). Keats's "Urn," which Goslee does not treat, aptly illustrates her central point. Though the urn is sculpted marble, as the final stanza plainly indicates, the restless probing for specific answers in the opening stanza suggests the picture of a specific time and leaf-fringed place, and the situation of the youth "beneath the trees" is likewise picturesque. But while these picturesque qualities of the urn provoke the speaker's curiosity and sympathy with the mood of an erotic moment, the sculpturesque qualities of the urn—the timeless serenity of its "cold marble"—leave the speaker cool and detached.

46. Grant Scott objects that she isn't actually speaking, but is rather ventriloquized by the male speaker (letter to the author). But the same objection could be made to *any* speech that a poet might impute to or elicit from a work of visual art, and by analogy to any meaning that a critic might impute to or elicit from a work of verbal art. A poet who claims to report what a work of visual art "says" is entitled to at least as much credence—or suspension of disbelief—as a critic who claims to articulate (in his or her own words) what a work of literature "says."

47. They were erected in the years from 1825 to 1828. In 1883 the arch was moved to its present position at Hyde Park Corner, where it is known as Marble Arch; in 1912

the statue was transferred to Aldershot and replaced with a quadriga (a two-wheeled chariot drawn by four horses all harnessed abreast).

48. For Edmund Burke, the essence of the sublime lay in the power to excite terror or admiration; "the sublime, which is the cause of [admiration]," he wrote, "always dwells on great objects, and terrible" (113). See also note 34, above.

49. The text that Shelley's traveler most likely personifies is Diodorus Siculus's first-century B.C. description of a statue of Ramses II, but various other sources have been proposed; see Freedman 63–64.

50. According to Hollander, the painting is "seventeenth century, possibly Flemish and after a lost original by Leonardo or at least Vasari's description of it" ("Poetics" 211). Mary Shelley ascribes the poem to 1819. Since the painting was then (as now) in the Uffizi Gallery of Florence, where Shelley spent the autumn of 1819, it seems likely that it was composed then. See Rogers 12.

51. See for instance Michael Holly: "The concentration on the gaze as an interpretive principle cuts across a wide sampling of recent theoretical perspectives. Paintings are, after all, meant to be looked at, so it should come as no surprise that the investigation of who or what is presumed to be doing the looking is now viewed as a critically unsettling issue in poststructuralist writings on art" (373). See also Norman Bryson's remark that sight is always "constructed in relation to power, and powerlessness" ("Gaze," 107).

52. Grant Scott demurs. "The more I read this poem," he writes, "the more convinced I am that for it to work, the gazer must be the viewer of the painting, the ekphrastic poet, Medusa, and Perseus—all at once. To posit any one of these as the real [presumably *only*] gazer limits the poem's power and meaning" (letter to the author). The last point may be right, but the first one is anything but self-evident; it remains to be shown just how the *poem* establishes that the gazer "must be" all the figures Scott enumerates.

53. In the Platonic "Hymn to Intellectual Beauty" written three years earlier than "Medusa," Shelley speaks of intellectual (i.e., immaterial) beauty as "the awful shadow of some unseen Power" that visits each of us "like hues and harmonies of evening" (stanza 1). He thus anticipates the shadowy version of beauty that emerges in the later poem along with the musical metaphor he applies to it in "the melodious hue of beauty." But the petrifying effect of beauty is something new.

54. Their "fiery and lurid" gleaming recalls the "golden fire" of the flashing water-snakes seen by Coleridge's ancient mariner in a poem Shelley certainly knew ("The Rime of the Ancient Mariner" 281). But while Coleridge's snakes are simply transformed by moonlight from "slimy things" to creatures of wholly lovable beauty (283–84) the snakes described here generate a light at once beautiful and terrifying.

55. See Prothero 3:332, 377, 387; 4:106–7, 113; Murray 2:46; and—for Stendahl's report—Lovell 198–99.

56. Unless otherwise indicated, I quote Byron's poetry from *Byron*.

57. Donald Reimann has kindly drawn my attention to the urns of honey that appear in Thomas Taylor's version (published 1788–89) of the passage describing the cave of nymphs in the *Odyssey* (13:103–9). According to Kathleen Raine, who quotes Taylor's version (Raine 8), these urns reappear in Blake's so-called Arlington Court picture of 1821, which shows a small nymph pouring water from an urn near a pair of lovers. Raine glosses this set of figures as "an emblem of the source of all life" (9).

58. I am drawing here on Steiner, who—as already noted—takes the word "sleep-watching" from Leo Steinberg. See *Pictures* 3, 81.

59. On the fragmentary character of romantic poetry see Thomas McFarland, *Romanticism and the Forms of Ruin* (Princeton: Princeton Univ. Press, 1981), especially the first chapter.

60. It remains part of a larger narrative in Byron's poetry, but clearly assumes its independence in the work of the other three.

CHAPTER FOUR

1. See also his three-volume *Das Bildgedicht: Theorie, Lexikon, Bibliographie* (1981, 1987) and *Deutsche Bildwerke im Deutsche Gedicht* (1975), his anthology of German poems about German works of art.

2. Snodgrass's *After Experience* (1968) includes "VAN GOGH: 'The Starry Night'" along with poems on paintings by Matisse, Manet, Monet, and Vuillard.

3. Stevens's poem, however, is just incidentally ekphrastic; it says so little about the specific features of Picasso's painting that a critic as meticulous as Helen Vendler can write twenty-five pages on the poem (*On Extended Wings* 119–43) without even mentioning the painter's name.

4. Derrida, *Truth* 54, commenting on Kant 68. Further on he adds: "Where does a *parergon* begin and end. Would any garment be a *parergon*. G-strings and the like. What to do with absolutely transparent veils. And how to transpose the statement to painting. For example, Cranach's Lucretia holds only a light band of transparent veil in front of her sex: where is the *parergon?* Should one regard as a *parergon* the dagger which is not part of her naked and natural body and whose point she holds turned toward herself, touching her skin . . . A *parergon,* the necklace she wears around her neck? . . . If any *parergon* is only added on by virtue of an internal lack in the system to which it is added (as was verified by *Religion*), what is it that is lacking in the representation of the body so that the garment should come and supplement it?" (*Truth* 57–58).

5. To illustrate the traditional conception of ekphrasis, Scott ("Seduced" 21) aptly cites C. S. Baldwin's *Medieval Rhetoric and Poetic* (New York: Macmillan, 1928), which links the mode with "adornment" (174), "diffuseness" (174), "indulgence" (19), and "deviation" (188).

6. For a detailed account of this process, see Steiner, *Pictures* 7–42.

7. "Along with the 'work of art,' writes Fisher, "the museum displays and stabilizes the idea of a national culture, an identifiable *Geist,* or spirit, that can be illustrated by objects and set in contrast other national cultures" (8). Likewise, explaining how the discipline of art history systematizes the study of individual works, Donald Preziosi writes: "The pedagogical requirements of the system involve accessing the archival mass in such a way as to fabricate consistent and internally coherent narratives of development, filiation, evolution, descent, progress, regress: in short, a particular 'history' of artistic practice *in the light of* that narrative's relationship to others potentially embedded in the archival system" ("The Question of Art History" 370).

8. In partial explanation for my slighting of Rossetti, I could first of all say (again) that this book does not claim to be a systematic or comprehensive survey of ekphrasis but a selective study of what a succession of poets have done with the mode. Also, while Rossetti epitomizes the pictorialism of Victorian poetry, his ekphrastic sonnets do not move significantly beyond the ideology of transcendence that he inherits from his romantic precursors. In "A Venetian Pastoral," for instance, he salutes *Le Concert Cham-*

pêtre in the Louvre (once ascribed to Giorgone, now to Titian) as a painting of movement slowed to eternal calm: well water "sigh[ing] in" over the lip of a pitcher dipped in
it, a hand trailing upon the viol-string, "brown faces ceas[ing] to sing," the slim pipes
slipped from the mouth of the woman playing them, and finally "Life touching lips
with immortality" (Rossetti 153–54). As Hollander suggests ("Poetics" 214), Pater was
doubtless thinking of this sonnet when he cited the painting to illustrate the transcendent beauty of "musical intervals" in Venetian landscape painting, of moments in which
"life is conceived as a sort of listening, listening to music . . . to the sound of water, to
time as it flies" (Pater 120). For more on Rossetti and painting, see Ainsworth.

9. Apropos the sculpture of Neptune taming the sea horse, Gail S. Weinberg has
kindly drawn my attention to the passage on Neptune's calming of the winds in the first
book of the *Aeneid* (142–56). Since Virgil compares Neptune's act to the pacifying effect of a respected, authoritative voice on an urban riot, the sculpture may well signify
the art of ruling wisely. If so, it makes a last ironic comment on the style of ruling prac-
ticed by the man who commissioned it.

10. Bryson also implies—quite rightly, I think—that the gaze is frontal and the
glance oblique. Donald Preziosi has recently suggested that art history organizes works
of art in "an *anamorphic* manner, such that relationships among units in the archive are
visible (that is, legible) only from certain prefabricated stances, positions, or attitudes
toward the system" ("The Question of Art History" 370). Preziosi's metaphor is apt, but
must be qualified by the observation that art historians typically *present* their point of
view as frontal, as omnisciently central, with the anamorphic angle of their viewpoint
ideologically suppressed.

11. In Auden's case the move was not irrevocable. "The Shield of Achilles," which he
published some years after "Musée," evokes both Homer and the long tradition of notional ekphrasis he initiated. Further on I connect this poem with the figure of the shield
in Ashbery's "Self-Portrait."

12. Anthony Hecht suggests that it may have come "from a book on art history
rather than from a personal inspection of [Breughel's] paintings" (100). If so, the book
remains to be identified.

13. Given Auden's political views at the time he wrote this poem (late 1938), it is
somewhat ironic that the ploughman gets none of his sympathy. As Coombes observes,
"Auden was *in theory*, in the 1930s, a clamorous sympathizer with the working masses:
in *art* however they are (however prominent in the artwork at stake) 'someone else' and
(therefore?) 'dull'" (25). But a further problem here is that Breughel's ploughman looks
anything but exhausted by his day of toil. With his dainty tiptoe step, his bright red
blouse, and his immaculate tunic falling in elegant folds about his knees, he seems ready
to take his place in the peasant chorus of *Don Giovanni*.

14. It is of course the only word in the title denoting a human figure. "To me," writes
Auden elsewhere, "Art's subject is the human clay / And landscape but a background to
a torso" ("Letter to Lord Byron," pt. 4).

15. I owe this very good point to Kenneth Mason (283).

16. The pale head of this supine figure is barely detectable just above the head of the
ploughman's horse. As Gluck suggests in the 1936 edition of his *Peter Breughel,* which
Auden could have known, the corpse placed so near the ploughman illustrates—more
vividly than the distant legs of Icarus—the German proverb that "No plough comes to
a standstill because a man dies" (Gluck 24). The proverb reappears in Blake's *Marriage*

of Heaven and Hell, a work Auden knew very well indeed, as "Drive your cart and your plow over the bones of the dead" (Blake 35).

As Auden also knew, Ovid is quite explicit on the suffering of Daedalus, the wretched father, no more a father ("pater infelix, nec jam pater"), who called to his son in vain, caught sight of Icarus's wings floating on the waves, and cursed his art (*Met.* 8.229–34).

17. In a sonnet on Breughel's painting written in 1923, some fifteen years before Auden's "Musée," George Santayana treats Icarus as the embodiment of hubris:

> You cried you were a god, or were to be;
> I heard with feeble moan your boastful breath
> Bubble from the depths of the Icarian sea.
>   (quoted Clements 255)

18. I quote from "The Adoration of the Kings" and "The Wedding Dance." The impulse to celebrate painters and to identify paintings with them—to read paintings as so many autographs—is equally evident in *Paterson,* book 5, which is dedicated "To the Memory of HENRI TOULOUSE LAUTREC, *Painter*" and which invokes a litany of great artists and their iconic signatures: Leonardo, Picasso, Juan Gris, "Pollock's blobs of paint squeezed out / with design," "the neat figures of / Paul Klee, "Durer / with his melancholy," "Bosch's / congeries of tortured souls and devils / who prey on them" (213, 222).

19. Also, the men are shown drinking from earthenware jugs rather than glasses. But "jugs" would not have fit Williams's dactylic meter.

20. As Conarroe notes, we are tempted to find a seasonal structure in the Breughel poems because Williams wrote them (except for "The Dance") just after completing *Paterson,* which moves through a full cycle of seasons from spring to spring, and because several of them represent paintings that belong to Breughel's uncompleted series of the "Months." But Conarroe also observes—quite rightly, I think—that "the patterning of the twelve 'Pictures' is actually subtler and more interesting than any mere seaasonal scheme would be" (568). On Breughel's "Months" see also Stechow 86 and Gluck 43–44.

21. It is startling to realize that even in the ekphrastic prose of the third-century A.D. Philostratus, sometimes called "the father of art history," not a single artist's name is mentioned.

22. The title of Shelley's "On the Medusa of Leonardo da Vinci in the Florentine Gallery" (ca. 1819) explicitly locates the painting in a museum (the Uffizi) and plainly depends on a curatorial authority which turns out to have been unreliable, since the painting is no longer attributed to Leonardo. But in any case the text of the poem makes no reference to any artist; it treats the painting as if it were anonymous. On the treatment of artists in the ekphrastic poetry of Rossetti and Browning, see above.

23. I quote from Williams, "Haymaking." Apropos "his insight," I can only say that I have not yet seen an ekphrastic poem written about a work of art created by a woman—though I have no doubt such poems exist.

24. Commenting in 1951 on a portrait of him by Emanuel Romano, he wrote: "What the artist will paint is his creation, the hidden work of his own imagination; what he is—painted in the subtly modified contours of the sitter's face. It is his own face in the terms of another face.

"The artist is always and forever painting only one thing: a self-portrait" (Dijkstra 198–99).

25. Here and hereafter I quote the Breughel poems (1962 text) from Williams's *Collected Poems* 2:385–94. For detailed commentary on "Landscape with the Fall of Icarus," which I treat here only briefly, see Fairley.

26. See Lawson-Peebles 21 and Christopher MacGowan's note on "Self-Portrait" in Williams, *CP* 504. In the *Hudson Review*, where it first appeared, the poem was titled "The Old Shepherd." The painting Williams treats as a self-portrait of Breughel depicts a court jester named Gonella who lived at Ferrara at the court of Nicolo III d'Este (1393–1444). I like to think that Nicolo was an ancestor of Alfonso II, the sixteenth-century Duke of Ferrara who stands behind Browning's "My Last Duchess."

27. "Williams's 'translation' from painting to poem," writes Henry Sayre, "is not an exercise in repetition but a project in re-vision; it is not description, but re-creation" (135).

28. Gluck passes on Max Dvorak's observation that while certain features of *The Adoration*—such as the close-knit arrangement—suggest Italian mannerism, the painting reveals an "entirely un-Italian conception of the events described" (quoted Gluck 42). Craven's chief aim in his general commentary on Brueghel is to show how the artist repudiated the "heroic style" of Italy that his contemporaries so avidly imported (101).

29. "His figures," Craven writes, "were not thrown together in the haphazard fashion of the illustrator, but conceived as parts of an elaborate design of black and white masses enlivened with color" (101).

30. Jerome Mazzaro suggests—not very convincingly, in my view—that the kings bring the infant the gift of speech: "The baby, through the kings' gifts, assumes the qualities of language rescued by art" (161).

31. "The poem," Mazzaro observes, "gives no evidence that Williams knows that a kermesse is a saint's day. He describes the arrangement of the panel with no mention of the peasant dressed in the traditional costume of a fool or the church in the background ignored by the figures or the Madonna which looks down on the revelers from the tree on the right" (158). Williams also ignores what Grossman sees as the signs of lust and gluttony displayed by the figures at the table and "the peacock feather of vain pride" (Grossman 200, 202).

32. Though more provocative at first glance, Williams's characterization of the Magi as highway robbers is distinctly less heretical than his description of the Christ child as the son of Joseph and Mary: a notion flatly contradicted by Matthew 1:18, which defines Christ as the child of the Holy Ghost in a passage that Williams himself shortly quotes (*Paterson* 228).

33. *Characteristics of Men, Manners, Opinions, Times* (1711), quoted Barrell 29.

34. Dijkstra 197. This statement of 1966 reaffirms what Williams had said in 1926: "All painting is representation and cannot be anything else" (Dijkstra 69).

35. See Bryson, *Vision and Painting*, esp. chapter 6 (133–62). Long before Bryson's book appeared, the case for a semiotic—or linguistic—theory of visual art was made by Nelson Goodman. "Almost any picture," he wrote, "may represent almost anything; that is, given picture and object there is usually a system of representation, a plan of correlation, under which the picture represents the object" (38). What Bryson adds to this nakedly semiotic theory of visual art is a theory of how painted images are socially, economically, and culturally formed.

36. Equally curious is the reference to "30 years of / war." The Thirty Years War began in 1618, years after Breughel died; perhaps, since Williams has already alluded to World War II, he is thinking of the period between the outbreak of the first war and the end of the second one (1914–1945).

37. In the third and fourth stanzas the poet has already mentioned something else Gluck fails to note: "a hound under / / the table."

38. Conarroe writes: "The lack of conventional emphasis, coupled with the complete absence of commas and periods, makes it possible to read the poems as one reads a painting—the eye, moving fluidly across the details, is not stopped or slowed except by the viewer's own volition" (568).

39. In the *Hudson Review* version of the poem (Williams 506), these phrases each appear in the middle of a tercet; when he revised the poem for the *Pictures* volume, he deliberately moved them to the end position.

40. *Colors* 73–80. Though Breughel's painting has been variously titled *The Return of the Hunters* and *The Hunters in the Snow*, it's not clear how much credit Williams deserves for choosing the latter as the title of his poem. By juxtaposing the (medieval) figures with nature's snow, this title does indeed set up "the thematic opposition" of the poem, as Steiner suggests (80). But *Hunters in the Snow* is the title given by both of Williams's only known sources: Gluck (plate 31) and Craven (plate 55).

41. Shamelessly risking the intentionalist fallacy here, I draw freely on Berryman's own interpretation of the poem, which he wrote on the eve of the World War II and later (1965) called "a war-poem, of an unusual negative kind. The common title of the picture is 'Hunters in the Snow' and of course the poet knows this. But he pretends not to, and calls their spears (twice) 'poles,' the governing resultant emotion being a certain stubborn incredulity—as the hunters are loosed while the peaceful nations plunge again into war" ("One Answer" 69–70). The "morning occasion" of the hunt is presumably also a "mourning occasion," and the "three birds watch[ing]" the hunters in the last line become something like vultures. Berryman admitted that war "is not the subject of Breughel's painting at all" ("One Answer" 70), but in his reading of it the hunters seem to be yet another set of blind men heading for disaster.

42. Probably from the Pelligrini Chapel of St. Anastasia, Verona, the painting is reproduced in *Nonesuch Great Museums Series: National Gallery, London* (New York, 1969). I have no idea whether or not Williams knew this picture, but in any case I thank John Peters-Campbell for bringing it to my attention.

43. They are *The Hay Harvest* (Prague National Gallery; Gluck no. 28) and *The Corn Harvest* (Metropolitan, New York; Gluck no. 29). The poem was originally titled "Composite" (Williams 2:505).

44. My sources for this information are Perloff 172 and Crase 57.

45. On the *Times* reproduction see his Foreword to the Arion edition of "Self-Portrait." The 552 lines of the poem are regrettably unnnumbered in all editions known to me, but I have numbered them in my own copy of *Selected Poems* (1985) and henceforth cite them that way. If you figure about 30 lines per page, the line numbers should lead you fairly soon to the passages I quote.

46. "I think we're constantly in the middle of a conversation where we never finish our thoughts or our sentences and that's the way we communicate and it's probably the best way for us, because it's the one we have arrived at" ("John Ashbery in Warsaw," *Quarto* [May 1981] 14, quoted Stamelman 629, note 4).

47. Ashbery's poem is in this sense much closer to the spirit of Homeric ekphrasis than is W. H. Auden's "The Shield of Achilles" (first published 1952), where Hephaistos constructs for his horrified mother a desolating picture of modern war.

48. Though Ashbery is, so far as I know, the first poet to write a poem on Parmigianino's *Self-Portrait*, let alone giving it a voice, the painting is indirectly linked to a notorious example of pictures made to speak in the Renaissance through a poet's words. Vasari tells us that Parmigianino's *Self-Portrait* passed via the pope to his attendant, Pietro Aretino (Vasari 8). It was probably in 1525—about the time he would have received the painting—that Pietro composed a set of *Sonnetti Lussuriosi* to accompany the sixteen engravings made by Marcantonio Raimondi from Julio Romano's drawings of a man and woman copulating in sixteen different positions (*I modi*). The sonnets consist entirely of dialogue between the two. See Lawner 2–19.

49. The allusion to E. T. A. Hoffman's "Geschichte von Verloren Spiegelbild" (Story of the Lost Reflection) is singularly apt, since "Speigelbild" literally means "mirror-picture." (My thanks to Margaret Robinson for the Hoffman reference.)

50. Preface to Shakespeare (1759), quoted Abrams 32. For discussion of how reflections in water led English romantic poets and painters to reconceive the meaning and value of reflection itself, see Heffernan, *Re-Creation of Landscape* 201–24.

51. "Art history and the museum," as Preziosi observes, "have worked to promote the idea of the historical period as itself unified and homogenous, or dominated by a singular family of values and attitudes" ("The Question of Art History" 383).

52. Ashbery's simile may owe something to the final stanza of Wordsworth's "A Poet's Epitaph," which includes the line, "Come, weak as is a breaking wave" (*PW* 4:67).

53. Cf. Donne on lovers not yet sexually joined but entranced with their own self-portraits in the convex mirrors of each other's eyes: "And pictures in our eyes to get / Was all our propagation" ("The Ecstasy," 11–12).

54. The translation of Vasari here is Freedberg's (106).

55. A few lines later, Ashbery suggests the fetal state when he writes that the angelic face of the portrait wears the unfamiliarity of things long forgotten, "lost beyond telling / Which were ours once" (215–16).

56. For a good reproduction of this detail, see Seidel 80.

57. "An ekphrasis," writes Carrier, "tells the story represented, only incidentally describing pictorial composition. An interpretation gives a systematic analysis of composition. Ekphrases are not concerned with visual precedents. Interpretations explain how inherited schema are modified" (21). By "interpretation" here Carrier means art historical analysis. But there is no reason why art historians should be given a monopoly on interpretation, especially since they are generally none too eager to admit they practice it. According to Leo Steinberg, whose work on Michelangelo exemplifies what Carrier calls "interpretation," the aim of art historical interpretation is to make "visible what had not previously been apparent" so "that the picture seems to confess itself and the interpreter disappears" (*Michelangelo's Last Paintings* [New York, 1975] 6, quoted Carrier 1). On the other hand, the interpretive thrust of Vasari's ekphrases, one of which Carrier cites to exemplify the mode, is anything but invisible. In a detailed and thorough study of Vasarian ekphrasis, Svetlana Alpers writes: "Looking at art and describing what he saw legitimately involved for Vasari what we today might think of as 'reading in.' He was offering a guide and commentary whose force was supposed to result precisely from selectivity and reading in" ("Ekphrasis" 194–95).

58. In lines 222–25, Ashbery paraphrases Freedberg's point about the shift to mannerist tensions in Parmigianino's later portraits.

59. In *The Trembling of the Veil* (1922), W. B. Yeats writes that his "Lake Isle of Innisfree" (1890) was prompted by the sight and sound of "a fountain in a [London] shop window which balanced a little ball upon its jet" and which stirred memories of his native Irish water (M. H. Abrams et al., *The Norton Anthology of English Literature*, 5th ed. [New York: Norton, 1986] 2:1974). If Ashbery was thinking at all of Yeats's fountain, his focus on the ball makes of the image something quite different from what we find in Yeats's poem.

60. I am summarizing the argument of Lee Edelman (99–113), who contends that Parmigianino's painting obliquely designates Stevens's poem. "Just as Ashbery's poem presents itself under the name of Parmigianino's painting, so Parmigianino himself serves here as an alias, a cover, for the true literary antecedents of Ashbery's speculations . . . on the enterprise of representing the self" (99). I find Edelman's argument plausible except for this point. If Parmigianino is simply an alias for Stevens, it is hard to explain why the poem surrounds his painting with such an elaborate web of art historical commentary, or why, insofar as the portrait speaks for itself in Ashbery's poem, it "says" that "the soul has to stay where it is" (39, 34). This does not sound quite like the deconstructive voice of Stevens.

Besides Whitman and Stevens, the American figures lurking behind this poem may include Emerson, whose faith in "the infinitude of the private man" is ironically recalled—and subverted—by the passage on the inadequacy of each person's "one big theory to explain the universe." What is outside the individual is what matters, "to him and especially to us / Who have been given no help whatever / In decoding our man-sized quotient" (500–505). For an apt decoding of the final man-diminishing phrase, see Crase 60–62.

61. After this chapter was set in type, Michael Fried's comments on the painting of reflected figures in a lecture on nineteenth-century French realism (School of Criticism and Theory, Dartmouth College, July 1993) made me realize something I had wholly overlooked: Parmigianino's scrupulously ocular depiction of his mirror image includes a reversed left hand, which appears as his right, since his actual right hand—not reflected—was occupied in painting the picture. Because of this reversal, *any* faithful depiction of a mirrored image—whether the mirror is convex or flat—is bound to misrepresent what the mirror reflects.

Works Cited

Abrams, M. H. *The Mirror and the Lamp: Romantic Theory and the Critical Tradition.* New York: Norton, 1953.

Abse, Dannie, and Joan Abse. *Voices in the Gallery.* London: Tate Gallery, 1986.

Achilles Tatius. *The Adventures of Leucippe and Clitophon.* Ed. and trans. S. Gaselee. Loeb Classical Library. London: Heinemann, 1917.

Adams, Hazard. "Titles, Titling, and Entitlement To." *Journal of Aesthetics and Art Criticism* 46 (1987): 7–21.

Adams, Pat, ed. *With a Poet's Eye: A Tate Gallery Anthology.* London: Tate Gallery, 1986.

Ainsworth, Maryan Wynn. *Rossetti and the Double Work of Art.* New Haven: Yale Univ. Press, 1976.

Alberti, Leon Battista. *On Painting* [1435–36]. Trans. John R. Spencer. Rev. ed. New Haven: Yale Univ. Press, 1966.

Alpers, Paul J. *The Poetry of The Faerie Queene.* Princeton: Princeton Univ. Press, 1967.

Alpers, Paul, and Svetlana Alpers. "*Ut Pictura Noesis?* Criticism in Literary Studies and Art History." *New Literary History* 3 (1972): 437–58.

Alpers, Svetlana Leontief. "Describe or Narrate? A Problem in Realistic Representation." *New Literary History* 8 (1976): 16–41.

———. "*Ekphrasis* and Aesthetic Attitudes in Vasari's *Lives.*" *Journal of the Warburg and Courtauld Institutes* 23 (1960): 190–215.

———. *The Art of Describing: Dutch Art in the Seventeenth Century.* Chicago: Univ. of Chicago Press, 1983.

Anacreonta. Trans. J.M. Edmonds. Cambridge, Mass.: Harvard Univ. Press, 1979.

Apollonius of Rhodes. *The Voyage of Argo: The Argonautica.* Trans. E.V. Rieu. Baltimore: Penguin, 1959.

Aristotle. *Complete Works.* Ed. Jonathan Barnes. 2 vols. Princeton: Princeton Univ. Press, 1984.

Arpin, Gary Q. *The Poetry of John Berryman.* Port Washington, N.Y.: Kennikat Press, 1978.

Ashbery, John. "Self-Portrait in a Convex Mirror." In *Selected Poems,* 188–204. New York: Viking Penguin, 1985.

———. *Self-Portrait in a Convex Mirror: The Poem with Original Prints by Richard Avedon et al. . . . with a Forword by the Poet, A Recording of His Reading of the Poem, & on the Album an Essay by Helen Vendler.* San Francisco: Arion, 1984. Limited edition (175 copies).

Atchity, Kenneth John. *Homer's Iliad: The Shield of Memory.* Carbondale: Southern Illinois Univ. Press, 1978.

Auden, W. H. *Collected Poems* [*CP*]. Ed. Edward Mendelson. New York: Random House, 1976.

Auerbach, Erich. *Mimesis: The Representation of Reality in Western Literature.* Garden City, N.Y.: Doubleday Anchor, 1957.

Augustine, Saint. *The Confessions.* Trans. John K. Ryan. Garden City, N.Y.: Anchor, 1960.

Austin, R. G. *P. Vergili Maronis Aeneidos Liber Primus, with a Commentary.* Oxford: Clarendon, 1971.

Baldwin, C. S. *Medieval Rhetoric and Poetic.* New York: Macmillan, 1928.

Barclay, Craig R. "Schematization of Autobiographical Memory." Rubin 82–99.

Barolini, Teodolinda. "Re-presenting What God Presented: The Arachnean Art of Dante's Terrace of Pride." *Dante Studies* 105 (1987): 43–62.

Barrell, John. *The Political Theory of Painting from Reynolds to Hazlitt.* New Haven: Yale Univ. Press, 1986.

Barthes, Roland. "L'ancienne rhetorique, Aide-memoire." *Communications* 16 (1970): 179–89.

Bartsch, Shadi. *Decoding the Ancient Novel: The Reader and the Role of Description in Heliodorus and Achilles Tatius.* Princeton: Princeton Univ. Press, 1989.

Baxendall, Michael. *Patterns of Intention: On the Historical Explanation of Pictures.* New Haven: Yale Univ. Press, 1985.

Beauvoir, Simone de. *The Second Sex* [1949]. Trans. and ed. H. M. Parshley. New York: Vintage, 1989.

Becker, Andrew Sprague. "Reading Poetry through a Distant Lens: Ecphrasis, Ancient Greek Rhetoricians, and the Pseudo-Hesiodic 'Shield of Herakles.'" *American Journal of Philology* 113 (1992): 5–24.

———. "The Shield of Achilles and the Poetics of Homeric Description." *American Journal of Philology* 111 (1990): 139–53.

Bender, John B. *Spenser and Literary Pictorialism.* Princeton: Princeton Univ. Press, 1972.

Benjamin, Walter. "The Work of Art in the Age of Mechanical Reproduction." In *Illuminations,* trans. Harry Zohn and ed. Hannah Arendt, 217–51. New York: Schocken Books, 1969.

Berger, Harry, Jr. *Revisionary Play: Studies in the Spenserian Dynamics.* Berkeley: Univ. of California Press, 1988.

Bergmann, Emilie L. *Art Inscribed: Essays on Ekphrasis in Spanish Golden Age Poetry.* Cambridge, Mass.: Harvard Univ. Press, 1979.

Berryman, John. "One Answer to a Question." *Shenandoah* 17 (1965): 67–76.

———. "Winter Landscape." In *Collected Poems 1937–1971,* ed. Charles Thornbury, 3. New York: Farrar Strauss Giroux, 1989.

Blake, William. *The Poetry and Prose of William Blake.* Ed. David Erdman with commentary by Harold Bloom. Garden City, N.Y.: Doubleday, 1965.

Blessington, Countess of. *Conversations of Lord Byron,* ed. Ernest J. Lovell. Princeton: Princeton Univ. Press, 1969.

Bloom, Harold. "The Breaking of Form." In *Deconstruction and Criticism,* 1–37. New York: Continuum, 1979.

Blount, Anthony. "An Echo of the 'Paragone' in Shakespeare." *Journal of the Warburg and Courtauld Institute* 2 (1938–39): 260–62.

Bowles, William Lisle. *The Picture; Verses Suggested by a Magnificent Landscape of Rubens, in Possession of Sir George Beaumont.* London: Cadell and Davies, 1803.

Boyle, A. J. *The Chaonian Dove: Studies in the Eclogues, Georgics, and Aeneid of Virgil.* Leiden, E. J. Brill, 1986.

Brewer, William F. "What Is Autobiographical Memory?" Rubin 25–49.

Bridges, Margaret. "The Picture in the Text: Ecphrasis as Self-reflexivity in Chaucer's Parliament of Fowles, Book of the Duchess and House of Fame." *Word & Image* 5 (1989): 151–58.

Browning, Robert. *The Poems and Plays of Robert Browning.* New York: The Modern Library, 1934.

Bryson, Norman. "The Gaze in the Expanded Field." In *Vision and Visuality,* ed. Hal Foster, 87–108. Dia Art Foundation Discussions in Contemporary Culture, No. 2. Seattle, 1988.

———. *Vision and Painting: The Logic of the Gaze.* New Haven: Yale Univ. Press, 1983.

———. *Word and Image: French Painting of the Ancien Regime.* Cambridge, Cambridge Univ. Press, 1981.

Buchwald, Emile, and Ruth Roston, eds. *The Poet Dreaming in the Artist's House.* Minneapolis: Milkweed Editions, 1984.

Burke, Edmund. *A Philosophical Enquiry into the Origin of Our Ideas of the Sublime and Beautiful.* Ed. J. T. Boulton. Notre Dame, Ind.: Univ. of Notre Dame Press, 1958.

Burke, Kenneth. "Symbolic Action in a Poem by Keats." In *A Grammar of Motives,* 447–63. Berkeley: Univ. of California Press, 1969.

Bush, Douglas. *Mythology and the Renaissance Tradition in English Poetry.* New York: Norton 1963.

Butler, Marilyn. *Romantics, Rebels, and Reactionaries: English Literature and Its Background 1760–1830.* New York: Oxford Univ. Press, 1982.

Byron. *Poetical Works.* Ed. Frederick Page and John Jump. 3d ed. London and New York: Oxford Univ. Press. 1970.

Byron. Ed. Jerome McGann. Oxford: Oxford Univ. Press, 1986. *See also* Lovell; Prothero. When cited by title and line number(s) alone, Byron's poems are quoted from McGann's edition.

Carrier, David. "Ekphrasis and Interpretation: Two Modes of Art History Writing." *British Journal of Aesthetics* 27, no. 1 (Winter 1987): 20–31.

Catullus. *The Student's Catullus,* by Daniel H. Garrison. Norman: Univ. of Oklahoma, 1989.

Caws, Mary Ann. "A Double Reading by Design." *Journal of Aesthetics and Art Criticism* 41 (1983): 323–30.

———. *Textual Analysis: Some Readers Reading.* New York: Modern Language Association, 1986.

Chaucer, Geoffrey. *Works,* ed. F. N. Robinson. 2d ed. Boston: Houghton Mifflin, 1957.

Chiampi, James Thomas. "From Unlikeness to Writing: Dante's 'Visible Speech' in Canto Ten *Purgatorio.*" *Mediaevalia* 8 (1982): 97–112.

Clements, Robert J. "Breughel's *Fall of Icarus:* Eighteen Modern Literary Readings." *Studies in Iconography* 7–8 (1981–82): 253–68.

Cluver, Claus. "Painting into Poetry." *Yearbook of Comparative and General Literature* 27 (1978): 19–34.

Coleridge, S. T. *Biographia Literaria.* Ed. James Engell and Walter Jackson Bate. 2 vols. Bollingen Series 75. Princeton: Princeton Univ. Press, 1983.

———. "On Poesy or Art." In *Biographia Literaria,* ed. J. T. Shawcross, 2 vols., 2:253–63. London, 1907.

Conan, Michel. "The *Imagines* of Philostratus." *Word & Image* 3 (April–June 1987): 162–71.

Conarroe, Joel. *John Berryman: An Introduction to the Poetry.* New York: Columbia Univ. Press, 1977.

———. "The Measured Dance: Williams' 'Pictures from Breughel.'" *Journal of Modern Literature* 1 (1971): 565–77.

Coolsen, Thomas H. "Phryne and the Orators: Decadence and Art in Ancient Greece and Modern Britain." *Turner Studies* 7 (1987): 2–10.

Coombes, John E. "Constructing the Icarus Myth: Breughel, Brecht, and Auden." *Word & Image* 2 (1986): 24–26.

Crase, Douglas. "The Prophetic Ashbery." Lehman 30–65.

Craven, Thomas, ed. *A Treasury of Art Masterpieces from the Renaissance to the Present Day.* New York: Simon and Schuster, 1939.

Curran, Stuart. *Poetic Form and British Romanticism.* New York: Oxford Univ. Press, 1986.

Da Vinci, Leonardo. *Leonardo on Painting.* Ed. Martin Kemp, trans. Kemp and Margaret Walker. New Haven: Yale Univ. Press, 1989.

Dante Alighieri. *The Divine Comedy, Purgatorio.* Trans. with commentary by Charles S. Singleton. 2 vols. (1. Text and Translation; 2. Commentary). Princeton: Princeton Univ. Press, 1973.

Davidson, Michael. "Ekphrasis and the Postmodern Painter Poem." *Journal of Aesthetics and Art Criiticism* 42 (1983): 69–89.

Derrida, Jacques. *Of Grammatology.* Trans. Gayatri Spivak. Baltimore and London: Johns Hopkins Univ. Press, 1976.

———. *The Truth in Painting.* Trans. Geoff Bennington and Ian McLeod. Chicago: Univ. of Chicago Press, 1987.

Dijkstra, Bram, ed. *A Recognizable Image: William Carlos Williams on Art and Artists.* New York: New Directions, 1978.

Donaldson, Ian. *The Rapes of Lucretia: A Myth and Its Transformations.* Oxford: Clarendon, 1982.

Dryden, John. *The Poems,* ed. James Kinsley. 4 vols. Oxford: Clarendon, 1958.

Dubois, Page. *History, Rhetorical Description and the Epic.* Cambridge: D. S. Brewer, 1982.

Edelman, Lee. "The Pose of Imposture: Ashbery's 'Self-Portrait in a Convex Mirror.'" *Twentieth-Century Literature* 32 (1986): 95–114.

Eden, P. T. *A Commentary on Virgil: Aeneid VIII.* Leiden: E. J. Brill, 1975.

Edwards, Mark W. *Homer: Poet of the Iliad.* Baltimore: Johns Hopkins Univ. Press, 1987.

Eliot, T. S. "Tradition and the Individual Talent." *The Norton Anthology of English Literature,* ed. M. H. Abrams et al., 2 vols., 2:1501–8. New York: Norton, 1962.

Euripides. *The Bacchae.* Trans. William Arrowsmith. In *Greek Tragedies,* ed. David Grene and Richard Lattimore, 2d ed., 3:192–260. Chicago: Univ. of Chicago Press, 1991.

Fagles, Robert. *I, Vincent. Poems from the Pictures of Van Gogh.* Princeton: Princeton Univ. Press, 1978.

Fairley, Irene. "On Reading Poems: Visual and Verbal Icons in William Carlos Williams' 'Landscape with the Fall of Icarus.'" *Studies in Twentieth Century Literature* 6 (1981–82): 67–97.

Farmer, Norman K. *Poets and the Visual Arts in Renaissance England.* Austin: Univ. of Texas Press, 1984.

Ferguson, George. *Signs and Symbols in Christian Art.* New York: Oxford Univ. Press, 1961.

Ferguson, Suzanne. "Crossing the Delaware with Larry Rivers and Frank O'Hara: The Post-Modern Hero at the Battle of the Signifiers." *Word & Image* 2 (1986): 27–32.

Fineman, Joel. "Shakespeare's *Will:* The Temporality of Rape." *Representations* 20 (Fall 1987): 25–76.

Fish, Stanley. "Literature in the Reader: Affective Stylistics." In *Reader-Response Criticism: From Formalism to Post-Structuralism,* ed. Jane P. Tompkins, 70–100. Baltimore: Johns Hopkins Univ. Press, 1980.

Fisher, Philip. *Making and Effacing Art: Modern Art in a Culture of Museums.* New York: Oxford, 1991.

Frank, Joseph. "Spatial Form in Modern Literature," *Sewanee Review* 53 (1945): 221–40, 433–56, 643–53.

Frazer, James. *See* Ovid.

Freedberg, Sydney J. *Parmigianino: His Works in Painting.* Cambridge: Harvard Univ. Press, 1950.

Freedman, William. "Postponement and Perspectives in Shelley's 'Ozymandias.'" *Studies in Romanticism* 25 (1986): 63–73.

Freud, Sigmund. "Medusa's Head." In *Sexuality and the Psychology of Love,* ed. Philip Rieff. New York: Collier Books, 1963.

———. *The Standard Edition of the Complete Psychological Works.* Trans. James Strachey et al. 24 vols. London: Hogarth Press, 1953.

Friedlander, Paul. *Johannes von Gaza und Paulus Silentarius: Kunstbeschreibungen Justinianischer Zeit.* Leipzig, 1912.

Friedlander, Paul, and Herbert Hoffleit. *Epigrammata: Greek Inscriptions in Verse.* Berkeley: Univ. of California Press, 1948.

Genette, Gerard. *Figures II: Essais.* Paris: Seuil, 1969.

———. *Figures of Literary Discourse.* Trans. Alan Sheridan. New York: Columbia Univ. Press, 1982.

———. *Narrative Discourse: An Essay in Method.* Trans. Jane E. Lewin. Ithaca: Cornell Univ. Press, 1980.

Giamatti, A. Bartlett. *The Earthly Paradise and the Renaissance Epic.* Princeton, 1966.

Gluck, Gustave. *Peter Breughel the Elder.* Trans. Eveline Byam Shaw. Paris: Hyperion Press, 1936.

Gombrich, E. H. *Art and Illusion: A Study in the Psychology of Pictorial Representation.* Princeton: Princeton Univ. Press, 1960.

Goodman, Nelson. *Languages of Art: An Approach to a Theory of Symbols.* Indianapolis: Hackett, 1976.

Goslee, Nancy. *Uriel's Eye: Miltonic Stationing and Statuary in Blake, Keats, and Shelley.* University, Ala.: Univ. of Alabama Press, 1985.

Gower, John. *Selections from John Gower.* Ed. J. A. Bennett. Oxford: Clarendon Press, 1968.

Greek Anthology. Trans. W. R. Paton. New York: Putnam, 1917.

The Greek Romances of Heliodorus, Longus, and Achilles Tatius. Trans. Rowland Smith. London: Bell, 1901.

Greever, Garland, ed. *A Wiltshire Parson and His Friends: The Correspondence of William Lisle Bowles.* Boston and New York: Houghton Mifflin, 1926.

Grosart, Alexander B. *Prose Works of William Wordsworth.* 3 vols. London, 1876. *See also* Wordsworth.

Grossman, F. *The Paintings of Breughel.* 2d ed. London: Phaidon Press, 1966.

Gysin, Fritz. "Paintings in the House of Fiction: The Example of Hawthorne." *Word & Image* 5 (1989): 159–72.

Hagstrum, Jean. *The Sister Arts: The Tradition of Literary Pictorialism and English Poetry from Dryden to Gray.* Chicago: Univ. of Chicago Press, 1958.

Hammond, N. G. L. "The Scene in *Iliad* 18.497–508 and the Albanian Blood Feud." *Bulletin of the American Society of Papyrologists* 22 (1985): 70–86.

Haley, Bruce. "The Sculptural Aesthetics of *CHP* IV." *Modern Language Quarterly* 44 (1983): 251–66.

Hecht, Anthony. *The Hidden Law: The Poetry of W. H. Auden.* Cambridge: Harvard Univ. Press, 1993.

Heffernan, James A.W. "Blake's Oothoon: The Dilemmas of Marginality." *Studies in Romanticism* 30 (1991): 3–18.

———. "Ekphrasis and Representation." *New Literary History* 22 (1991): 297–316.

———. *The Re-creation of Landscape: A Study of Wordsworth, Coleridge, Constable, and Turner.* Hanover, N.H.: Univ. of New England Press, 1985.

———. "Space and Time in Literature and the Visual Arts." *Soundings* 70 (1987): 95–119.

Heidegger, Martin. "The Origin of the Work of Art." In *Basic Writings,* ed. David Farrell Krell. New York: Harper and Row, 1977.

Hertz, Neil. "Medusa's Head: Male Hysteria under Political Pressure," *Representations* 4 (1983): 27–54.

Hesiod (attrib.). *The Shield of Hercules. A Fragment.* In *The Works of Hesiod, Callimachus, and Theognis,* trans. J. Banks. London: George Bell, 1889.

Higgins, Dick. "Pattern Poetry as Paradigm." *Poetics Today* 10 (1989): 401–28.

Higgins, Lynn A., and Brenda Silver, eds. *Rape and Representation.* New York: Columbia Univ. Press, 1991.

Hollander, John. "The Poetics of *Ekphrasis.*" *Word & Image* 4 (1988): 209–19.

———. "Words on Pictures: Ekphrasis." *Art and Antiques* March 1984: 80–91.

Hollander, Robert. *Allegory in Dante's "Commedia."* Princeton: Princeton Univ. Press, 1969.

Holly, Michael Ann. "Past Looking," *Critical Inquiry* 16 (Winter 1990): 371–96.

Homer. *The Iliad of Homer.* Trans., with introduction, Richmond Lattimore. Chicago: Univ. of Chicago Press, 1951.

———. *Iliad, Books XIII–XXIV.* Ed. and annotated D. B. Monro, 4th ed. rev. by R. W. Raper. 1897; repr. Oxford: Clarendon, 1960.

———. *The Iliad of Homer: Books XIII–XXIV.* Ed. M. M. Willcock. London: Macmillan, 1984.

Huddleston, Eugene L., and Douglas A. Noverr. *The Relationship of Painting and Literature: A Guide to Information Sources.* Detroit: Gale Research Company, 1978.

Hulse, Clark. *Metamorphic Verse: The Elizabethan Minor Epic.* Princeton: Princeton Univ. Press, 1981.

———. *The Rule of Art. Literature and Painting in the Renaissance.* Chicago and London: Univ. of Chicago Press, 1990.

Hunt, John Dixon. *Self-Portrait in a Convex Mirror on Poems on Paintings.* London: Bedford College, [1980].

Ingarden, Roman. *The Literary Work of Art: An Investigation on the Borderlines of Ontology, Logic, and Theory of Literature.* Trans. George G. Grabowicz. Evanston, Ill.: Northwestern Univ. Press, 1973.

Irwin, John T. "Foreshadowing and Foreshortening: The Prophetic Vision of Origins in Hart Crane's *The Bridge.*" *Word & Image* 1 (1985): 287–95.

Jacobs, Carol. "On Looking at Shelley's Medusa." *Yale French Studies* 69 (1985): 163–79.

Jack, Ian. *Keats and the Mirror of Art.* Oxford Univ. Press, 1967.

Jackson, Thomas H. "The Virtues of Attending: Williams's 'The Corn Harvest.'" Caws, *Textual Analysis* 54–63.

Jakobson, Roman. *Selected Writings* II: *Word and Language.* The Hague, 1971.

James, Henry. *The American.* Introduced by Joseph Warren Beach. New York: Rinehart, 1960.

Janik, Phyllis. "Additional Poems about the Visual Arts: A Selected Annotated Bibliography." Buchwald and Roston 138–41.

Jones, Ann Rosalind. "New Songs for the Swallow: Ovid's Philomela in Tullia d'Aragona and Gaspara Stampa." In *Refiguring Woman: Gender and the Italian Renaissance,* ed. Marilyn Migiel and Julia Schiesari, 263–77. Ithaca, N.Y.: Cornell Univ. Press, 1991.

Joplin, Patricia Kleindiest. "The Voice of the Shuttle Is Ours." Higgins and Silver 35–64.

Junius, Franciscus. *The Painting of the Ancients, in Three Books.* London: Daniel Frere, 1638.

Kahn, Coppelia. "*Lucrece:* The Sexual Politics of Subjectivity." Higgins and Silver 141–59.

———. "The Rape in Shakespeare's *Lucrece,*" *Shakespeare Studies* 9 (1976): 45–62.

Kalstone, David. *Five Temperaments.* New York: Oxford Univ. Press, 1977.

Kant, Immanuel. *The Critique of Judgement.* Trans. James Creed Meredith. Oxford: Clarendon Press, 1952.

Keach, William. *Elizabethan Erotic Narratives: Irony and Pathos in the Ovidian Poetry of Shakespeare, Marlowe, and Their Contemporaries.* New Brunswick, N.J.: Rutgers Univ. Press, 1977.

Keats, John. *Letters of John Keats, 1814–1821.* Ed. H. E. Rollins. 2 vols. Cambridge: Harvard Univ. Press, 1958.

———. *Complete Poems,* ed. Jack Stillinger. Cambridge: Harvard Univ. Press, 1978.

Kernan, Alvin. "*Don Juan:* The Perspective of Satire." In *Romanticism and Consciousness: Essays in Criticism,* ed. Harold Bloom, 343–74. New York: Norton, 1970.

Kerrigan, John. "Wordsworth and the Sonnet: Building, Dwelling, Thinking." *Essays in Criticism* 35 (1985): 45–75.

Kolve, V. A. *Chaucer and the Imagery of Narrative.* London: Edward Arnold, 1984.

———. "Chaucer and the Visual Arts." In *Writers and Their Background: Geoffrey Chaucer,* ed. D. S. Brewer, 290–320. London: G. Bell, 1974.

Kranz, Gisbert. *Das Bildgedicht: Theorie, Lexikon, Bibliographie.* Vols 1–2, Cologne: Bohlau, 1981. Vol. 3, Cologne: Bohlau, 1987.

———. *Das Bildgedicht in Europa: Zur Geschichte und Theorie einer Literarischen Gottung.* Paderborn: Ferdinand Schoningh, 1973.

————, ed. *Deutsche Bildwerke im Deutsche Gedicht.* Munich: M. Hueber, 1975.

Krapf, Norbert. "Rural Lines after Breughel: Returning from the Hunt." *Poetry* 124 (1974): 338–39.

Krieger, Murray. *Ekphrasis: The Illusion of the Natural Sign.* Baltimore: Johns Hopkins Univ. Press, 1991. Includes as an appendix (263–88) Krieger's "*Ekphrasis* and the Still Movement of Poetry; or, *Laokoon* Revisited" (1967).

————. *Theory of Criticism: A Tradition and Its System.* Baltimore: Johns Hopkins Univ. Press, 1976.

Krier, Theresa. *Gazing on Secret Sights: Spenser, Classical Imitation, and the Decorums of Vision.* Ithaca and London: Cornell Univ. Press, 1990.

Kroeber, Karl. *Romantic Landscape Vision: Constable and Wordsworth.* Madison, Wis.: Univ. of Wisconsin Press, 1975.

Kurman, George. "Ekphrasis in Epic Poetry." *Comparative Literature* 26 (1974): 1–13.

Kuspit, Donald. "Traditional Art History's Complaint against the Linguistic Analysis of Visual Art." *Journal of Aesthetics and Art Criticism* 46 (1987): 345–49.

Lacan, Jacques. *Speech and Language in Psychoanalysis.* Trans. with notes and commentary by Anthony Wilden. Baltimore: Johns Hopkins Univ. Press, 1968.

Langland, Joseph. "Hunters in the Snow: Breughel." In *The New Poets of England and America,* ed. Donald Hall, 159–60. New York: Meridian, 1957.

Lanham, Richard. *A Handlist of Rhetorical Terms.* Berkeley: Univ. of California Press, 1968.

Larrabee, Stephen A. *English Bards and Grecian Marbles.* New York: Columbia Univ. Press, 1943.

Lattimore, Richmond, trans. with introduction. *The Iliad of Homer.* Chicago: Univ. of Chicago Press, 1951.

Lawner, Lynn, ed. and trans. *I Modi. The Sixteen Pleasures. An Erotic Album of the Italian Renaissance.* Evanston, Ill.: Northwestern Univ. Press, 1988.

Lawson-Peebles, Robert. "William Carlos Williams' *Pictures from Breughel.*" *Word & Image* 2 (1986): 18–23.

Leach, Eleanor Winsor. "Ekphrasis and the Theme of Artistic Failure in Ovid's *Metamorphoses.*" *Ramus* 3 (1974): 102–42.

————. *Virgil's Eclogues: Landscapes of Experience.* Ithaca, N.Y.: Cornell Univ. Press, 1974.

Lee, Rensselaer W. *Ut Pictura Poesis: The Humanistic Theory of Painting.* 1942. Repr. New York: W. W. Norton, 1967.

Lehman, David, ed. *Beyond Amazement: New Essays on John Ashbery.* Ithaca, N.Y.: Cornell Univ. Press, 1980.

————. "The Shield of a Greeting: The Function of Irony in John Ashbery's Poetry." Lehman 101–27.

Leslie, Michael. "Browning's Competition with Renaissance Art." Paper delivered at the Second International Word and Image Conference in Zurich, 1 September 1990.

Lessing, G. E. *Laocoon: An Essay on the Limits of Painting and Poetry* [1766]. Trans. with introduction and notes by Edward Allen McCormick. Baltimore: Johns Hopkins Univ. Press, 1984.

Levin, Harry. *The Question of Hamlet.* New York: Oxford Univ. Press, 1959.

Levinson, Marjorie. *Wordsworth's Great Period Poems: Four Essays.* Cambridge: Cambridge Univ. Press, 1986.

Linebarger, J. M. *John Berryman*. New York: Twayne, 1974.

Lomazzo, Giovanni Paolo. *A Tracte Containing the Artes of Curious Paintinge Carvings & Buildinge*. Trans. Richard Haydocke. Oxford, 1598.

Long, Beverly Whitaker, and Timothy Scott Cage. "Contemporary American Poetry: A Selected Bibliography." *Text and Performance Quarterly* 9 (1989): 286–96.

Longus. *Daphnis and Chloe*. Ed. and trans. George Thornley and J. M. Edmonds. Loeb Classical Library. Cambridge: Harvard Univ. Press, 1928.

Lovell, Ernest J., ed. *His Very Self and Voice: Collected Conversations of Lord Byron*. New York: Macmillan, 1954.

Lowell, Robert. "For the Union Dead." In *Selected Poems*, rev. ed., 135–37. New York: Farrar, Strauss, and Giroux, 1977.

————. "The Poetry of John Berryman." *New York Review of Books* 2 (28 May 1964): 3–4.

Lynn-George, Michael. *Epos: Word, Narrative, and the Iliad*. Atlantic Highlands, N.J.: Humanities Press International, 1988.

MacKinnon, Catharine A. *Toward a Feminist Theory of the State*. Cambridge: Harvard Univ. Press, 1989.

Mandelker, Amy. "A Painted Lady: *Ekphrasis* in *Anna Karenina*." *Comparative Literature* 43 (1991): 1–19.

Marling, William. *William Carlos Williams and the Painters, 1909–1923*. Athens, Ohio: Ohio Univ. Press, 1982.

Marlowe, Christopher. *The Poems*. Ed. Millar Maclure. London: Methuen, 1968.

Martindale, Charles, ed. *Ovid Renewed: Ovidian Influences on Literature and Art from the Middle Ages to the Twentieth Century*. Cambridge: Cambridge Univ. Press, 1988.

Mason, Kenneth. "Auden's 'Musee des Beaux Arts.'" *Explicator* 48 (1990): 283–84.

Maus, Katherine Eisamen. "Taking Tropes Seriously: Language and Violence in Shakespeare's *Rape of Lucrece*." *Shakespeare Quarterly* 37 (1986): 66–82.

McClatchy, J. D., ed. *Poets on Painters: Essays on the Art of Painting by Twentieth-Century Poets*. Berkeley: Univ. of California Press, 1988.

McGann, Jerome. *The Beauty of Inflections: Literary Investigations in Historical Method and Theory*. Oxford: Clarendon, 1985.

————. *Fiery Dust: Byron's Poetic Development*. Chicago: Univ. of Chicago Press, 1968.

————. *"Don Juan" in Context*. Chicago: Univ. of Chicago Press, 1976.

————. *The Romantic Ideology: A Critical Investigation*. Chicago: Univ. of Chicago Press, 1983.

————, ed. *Byron*. Oxford: Oxford Univ. Press, 1986.

Mazzaro, Jerome. *William Carlos Williams: The Later Poems*. Ithaca: Cornell Univ. Press, 1973.

Meltzer, Françoise. *Salome and the Dance of Writing: Portraits of Mimesis in Literature*. Chicago and London: Univ. of Chicago Press, 1987.

Merrill, James. "The Charioteer of Delphi." In *The Country of a Thousand Years of Peace and Other Poems*, 23–24. New York: Knopf, 1959.

Miles, Margaret. "The Virgin's One Bare Breast: Female Nudity and Religious Meaning in Tuscan Early Renaissance Culture." Suleiman 193–208.

Miller, David Lee. "The Death of the Modern: Gender and Desire in Marlowe's 'Hero and Leander.'" *South Atlantic Quarterly* 88 (1989): 757–87.

Mirollo, James V. "Sibling Rivalry in the Arts Family: The Case of Poetry vs. Painting in the Italian Renaissance." Unpublished typescript.

Mitchell, W. J. T. "Ekphrasis and the Other." *South Atlantic Quarterly* 91 (1992): 695–719.

———. *Iconology: Image, Text, Ideology.* Chicago: Univ. of Chicago Press, 1986.

———. "Spatial Form in Literature: Toward a General Theory." In *The Language of Images,* ed. Mitchell, 271–99. Chicago: Univ. of Chicago Press, 1980.

Monro, D. B. *See* Homer.

Moramarco, Fred. "John Ashbery and Frank O'Hara: The Painterly Poets." *Journal of Modern Literature* 5 (1976): 436–62.

Morris, Desmond. *Manwatching: A Field Guide to Human Behavior.* New York: Harry N. Abrams, 1977.

Mosher, Harold F. "Toward a Poetics of 'Descriptized' Narration." *Poetics Today* 12 (1991): 425–45.

Murray, John, ed. *Lord Byron's Correspondence.* 2 vols. New York: Scribner, 1922.

Newman, Beth. "'The Situation of the Looker-On': Gender, Narration and Gaze in *Wuthering Heights.*" *PMLA* 105 (1990): 1029–41.

Osborne, Mary Tom. *Advice-to-a-Painter Poems 1653–1856: An Annotated Finding List.* [Austin]: Univ. of Texas, 1949.

Ovid. *Fasti.* Ed. and trans. James Frazer. Loeb Classical Library. London: Heinemann, 1931.

———. *Metamorphoses.* Ed. and trans. Frank Justus Miller. Loeb Classical Library. 2d ed. 2 vols. Cambridge: Harvard Univ. Press, 1966–68.

Page, Frederick, and John Jump, eds. *Poetical Works* of Byron. 3d ed. London and New York: Oxford Univ. Press, 1970.

Palladino, Lora Anne. "Pietro Aretino: Orator and Art Theorist." Dissertation, Yale Univ., 1981. Ann Arbor, Michigan: Univ. Microfilms International, 1983.

Parry, Adam. "The Two Voices of Virgil's *Aeneid.*" In *Virgil: A Collection of Critical Essays,* ed. Steele Commager. Englewood Cliffs, N.J.: Prentice Hall, 1966.

Pater, Walter. *The Renaissance.* Ed. Donald L. Hill. Berkeley and Los Angeles: Univ. of California Press, 1980.

Patterson, Lee. "'Rapt with Pleasaunce': Vision and Narration in the Epic," *ELH* 48 (1981): 455–75.

Perloff, Marjorie G. "'Transparent Selves': The Poetry of John Ashbery and Frank O'Hara." *Yearbook of English Studies* 8 (1978): 171–96.

Pettie, George. "Tereus and Progne." In *A Petite Pallace of Pettie his Pleasure* [1576], ed. Herbert Hartman, 40–55. London: Oxford Univ. Press, 1938.

Philostratus the Elder / the Younger, *Imagines;* Callistratus, *Descriptions.* Trans. Arthur Fairbanks. Loeb Classical Library. Cambridge: Harvard Univ. Press, 1931.

Pinion, F. B. *A Wordsworth Chronology.* Boston: G. K. Hall, 1988.

Plato. *Dialogues.* Trans. B. Jowett. 2 vols. New York: Random House, 1937.

Pliny the Elder. *Natural History: A Selection.* Trans. John F. Healy. New York: Viking Penguin, 1991.

Poe, Edgar Allen. *Poetry and Tales.* Ed. Patrick F. Quinn. New York: Literary Classics of the United States [Library of America], 1984.

Pollitt, J. J. *The Ancient View of Greek Art: Criticism, History, Terminology.* New Haven: Yale Univ. Press, 1974.

Preziosi, Donald. *Rethinking Art History: Meditations on a Coy Science.* New Haven: Yale Univ. Press, 1989.

———. "The Question of Art History." *Critical Inquiry* 18 (1992): 363–86.

Prince, Gerald. "Narrativity." In *Axia: Davis Symposium on Literary Evaluation,* ed. Karl Menges and Daniel Rancour-Laferriere. Stuttgart: Hans-Dieter Heinz, 1981.

Prothero, Rowland, ed. *The Works of Lord Byron.* 13 vols. London: John Murray, 1898–1904.

Putnam, Michael C. J. "Daedalus, Virgil, and the End of Art." *American Journal of Philology* 108 (1987): 173–98.

Quintilian. *Institutio Oratoria.* Trans. H. E. Butler. 4 vols. London: G.P. Putnam, 1921.

Raaberg, Gwen. "*Ekphrasis* and the Temporal / Spatial Metaphor in Murray Krieger's Aesthetic Theory." *New Orleans Review* 12, Winter (1985): 34–43.

Raine, Kathleen. *Blake and Antiquity.* Princeton: Princeton Univ. Press, 1977.

Rapaport, Herman. "The Phenomenology of Spenserian Ekphrasis." In *Murray Krieger and Contemporary Critical Theory,* ed. Bruce Henricksen, 157–75. New York: Columbia Univ. Press, 1986.

Reynolds, Joshua. *Discourses on Art.* Ed. R. R. Wark. New Haven: Yale Univ. Press, 1975.

Rich, Adrienne. "Mourning Picture." In *The Fact of a Doorframe: Poems Selected and New 1950–1984.* New York: Norton, 1984.

Riffaterre, Michael. "Textuality: W. H. Auden's 'Musée des Beaux Arts.'" Caws, *Textual Analysis* 1–13.

Rogers, Neville. "Shelley and the Visual Arts." *Keats-Shelley Memorial Bulletin* 12 (1961): 9–17.

Romantic Art in Britain: Paintings and Drawings 1760–1860. Philadelphia: Philadelphia Museum of Art, 1968.

Rossetti, Dante Gabriel. *The Complete Poetical Works,* with biographical sketch by William M. Rossetti. New York: Crowell [1886].

Rubin, David C., ed. *Autobiographical Memory.* Cambridge: Cambridge Univ. Press, 1986.

Sayre, Henry M. *The Visual Text of William Carlos Williams.* Urbana: Univ. of Illinois Press, 1983.

Scott, Grant Fraser. "The Rhetoric of Dilation: Ekphrasis and Ideology." *Word & Image* 7 (1991): 301–10.

———. "Seduced by Stone: Keats, Ekphrasis, and Gender." Dissertation, Univ. of California at Los Angeles, 1989.

Shapiro, Meyer. "The Still Life as a Personal Object—A Note on Heidegger and Van Gogh." In *The Reach of Mind: Essays in Memory of Kurt Goldstein,* 203–9. New York: Springer, 1968

Seidel, Linda. "'Jan Van Eyck's Arnolfini Portrait': Business as Usual?" *Critical Inquiry* 16 (1989): 54–86.

Senn, Werner. "Speaking the Silence: Contemporary Poems on Paintings." *Word & Image* 5 (1989): 181–97.

Sexton, Anne. "The Starry Night." In *The Complete Poems.* Boston: Houghton Mifflin, 1981.

Shackford, Martha Hale. *Wordsworth's Interest in Painters and Pictures.* Wellesley, Mass.: Wellesley Press, 1945.

Shakespeare, William. *The Complete Works.* Ed. Alfred Harbage. Baltimore: Penguin, 1969.

Shapiro, Marianne. "Ecphrasis in Virgil and Dante." *Comparative Literature* 42 (Spring 1990): 97–115.

Shaw, W. David. "Browning's Duke as Theatrical Producer." *Victorian Newsletter* 29 (Spring 1966): 21.

Shearman, John. *Mannerism.* Harmondsworth: Penguin, 1967.

Shelley, Percy Bysshe. *Shelley's Poetry and Prose.* Ed. Donald Reiman and Sharon Powers. New York: Norton, 1977.

Sidney, Philip. *The Countess of Pembroke's Arcadia* [*New Arcadia*]. Ed. Victor Skretkowicz. Oxford: Clarendon Press, 1987.

———. *A Defense of Poetry.* In *Miscellaneous Prose of Sir Philip Sidney,* ed. Katherine Duncan-Jones and Jan van Dorsten. Oxford: Clarendon Press, 1973.

Singleton, Charles S. *See* Dante.

Slavitt, David, trans. *Eclogues and Georgics of Virgil.* Baltimore: Johns Hopkins Univ. Press, 1990.

Snow, Edward. "Theorizing the Male Gaze: Some Problems." *Representations* 25 (Winter 1989): 30–41.

Southey, Robert, "On a Landscape of Gaspar Poussin." In *The Complete Poetical Works,* 146. New York: Appleton, 1846.

Spenser, Edmund. *Edmund Spenser's Poetry.* Ed. Hugh MacLean. 2d ed. New York: Norton, 1982.

Stamelman, Richard. "Critical Reflections: Poetry and Art Criticism in Ashbery's 'Self-Portrait in a Convex Mirror.'" *New Literary History* 15 (1984): 607–30.

Stechow, Wolfgang. *Peter Breughel the Elder.* New York: Abrams, 1990.

Steinberg, Leo. *Other Criteria.* London: Oxford Univ. Press, 1972.

Steiner, Wendy. *The Colors of Rhetoric: Problems in the Relation between Modern Literature and Painting.* Chicago: Univ. of Chicago Press, 1982.

———. *Pictures of Romance: Form against Context in Painting and Literature.* Chicago: Univ. of Chicago Press, 1988.

Stevens, Wallace. *The Collected Poems.* New York: Knopf, 1974.

Strote, Mary Ellen. "Mirror, Mirror, on the Wall." *Lear's* June 1991: 35–36.

Suleiman, Susan Rubin, ed. *The Female Body in Western Culture: Contemporary Perspectives.* Cambridge: Harvard Univ. Press, 1985.

Sullivan, Nancy. "*Night Fishing at Antibes* by Picasso." In *The History of the World as Pictures.* Columbia: Univ. of Missouri Press, 1965.

Summers, David. *The Judgment of Sense: Renaissance Naturalism and the Rise of Aesthetics.* Cambridge: Cambridge Univ. Press, 1987.

———. "The 'Visual Arts' and the Problem of Art Historical Description." *Art Journal* 42 (1982): 301–20.

Taplin, Oliver. "The Shield of Achilles within the *Iliad.*" *Greece and Rome* 27 (1980): 1–21.

Theocritus. *The Greek Bucolic Poets,* with English translation by J. M. Edmonds. London: Heinemann, 1923.

Thibaud, Roger. "Le Bouclier d'Achille." In *Hommages a Jozef Veremans,* ed. Freddy Decreus and Carl Deroux, 299–307. Brussells: Latomus / Revue d'Etudes Latines, 1986.

Thomson, James. *The Complete Poetical Works.* Ed. J. Logie Robertson. London: Oxford Univ. Press, 1908.

Tucker, Herbert. *Browning's Beginnings: The Art of Disclosure.* Minneapolis: Univ. of Minnesota Press, 1980.

Vasari, Giorgio. *The Lives of the Painters, Sculptors and Architects* [1550]. Trans. A. B. Hinds and ed. William Gaunt. 4 vols. New York: Dutton, 1963.

Vendler, Helen. *The Odes of John Keats.* Cambridge: Harvard Univ. Press, 1983.

————. *On Extended Wings: Wallace Stevens' Longer Poems.* Cambridge: Harvard Univ. Press, 1969.

Vickers, Nancy. "This Heraldry in Lucrece' Face." Sulieman 209–22.

————. "Seeing is Believing: Gregory, Trajan, and Dante's Art." *Dante Studies* 101 (1983): 67–85.

Virgil. *P. Vergili Maronis Opera.* Ed. Frederick Arthur Hertzel. Oxford: Clarendon, 1900. *See also* Austin; Slavitt.

Webb, Daniel. *An Inquiry into the Beauties of Painting; and into the Merits of the Most Celebrated Painters Ancient and Modern.* 2d ed. London: J. Dodsley, 1761. Repr. in *Asthetische Schriften,* ed. Ingrid Kerkoff. Munich: Wilhelm Fink, 1974.

Willcock, M. M. *See* Homer.

Williams, Gordon. *Techniques and Ideas in the "Aeneid."* New Haven: Yale Univ. Press, 1983.

Williams, Kathleen. "Venus and Diana: Some Uses of Myth in *The Faerie Queene.*" *ELH* 28 (1961): 101–20. Repr. in Spenser, 658–70.

Williams, R. D. "The Pictures on Dido's Temple," *Classical Quarterly,* n.s. 10 (1960): 145–51.

Williams, William Carlos. *The Collected Poems* [*CP*]. Ed. A. Walton Litz and Christopher MacGowan. 2 vols. New York: New Directions, 1988.

Winkler, John J. *The Constraints of Desire: The Anthropology of Sex and Gender in Ancient Greece.* New York: Routledge, 1990.

————. "The Education of Chloe: Erotic Protocols and Prior Violence." Higgins and Silver 15–34.

Witemeyer, Hugh. *George Eliot and the Visual Arts.* New Haven: Yale Univ. Press, 1979.

Wittgenstein, Ludwig. *Philosophical Investigations.* Trans. G. E. M. Auscomb. Oxford: Blackwell, 1967.

Wolf, Leslie. "The Brushstroke's Integrity: The Poetry of John Ashbery and the Art of Painting." Lehman 224–54.

Wordsworth, Jonathan, Michael Jaye, and Robert Woof. *William Wordsworth and the Age of English Romanticism.* New Brunswick: Rutgers Univ. Press, 1987.

Wordsworth, William. *The Letters of William and Dorothy Wordsworth.* Ed. Ernest de Selincourt. 2d ed. revised by Chester Shaver, Mary Moorman, and Alan Hill. 6 vols. to date. Oxford: Clarendon, 1967–82.

————. *The Letters of William and Dorothy Wordsworth: The Later Years.* Ed. Ernest de Selincourt. 3 vols. Oxford: Clarendon, 1939.

————. *The Poetical Works* [*PW*]. Ed. Ernest de Selincourt and Helen Darbishire. 5 vols. Oxford: Clarendon. 2d ed. of vol. 2 revised by Helen Darbishire, 1952.

————. *The Prelude 1799, 1805, 1850.* Ed. Jonathan Wordsworth, M. H. Abrams, and Stephen Gill. New York: Norton, 1979.

————. *Prose Works of William Wordsworth.* Ed. W. J. B. Owen and Jane Worthington Smyser. 3 vols. Oxford: Clarendon, 1974. *See also* Grosart.

Yates, Frances. *The Art of Memory.* Chicago: Univ. of Chicago Press, 1966.

Yeats, William Butler. "Lapis Lazuli." In *The Poems: A New Edition,* ed. Richard J. Finneran, 294–95. London, 1984.

Index

Page numbers in italics refer to illustrations.